EARTHLY TREASURES

PSRL volume 40

EARTHLY TREASURES

Material Culture and Metaphysics in the *Heptaméron* and Evangelical Narrative

Catharine Randall

Purdue University Press
West Lafayette, Indiana

∞ The paper used in this book meets the minimum requirements of American National Standard for Information Sciences—Permanence of Paper for Printed Library Materials, ANSI Z39.48-1992.

Printed in the United States of America
Design by Anita Noble

Library of Congress Cataloging-in-Publication Data
Randall, Catharine, 1957–
Earthly treasures: material culture and metaphysics in the Heptaméron and evangelical narrative / Catharine Randall.
p. cm. — (Purdue studies in Romance literatures ; v. 40)
Includes bibliographical references and index.
ISBN 978-1-55753-449-1 (alk. paper)
1. Marguerite, Queen, consort of Henry II, King of Navarre, 1492–1549. Heptaméron. I. Title. II. Series.
PQ1631.H4R36 2007
843'.3—dc22

2006032639

For J. C. and R. H. B.

NO GREATER LOVE

... on earth as it is in heaven.

Contents

viii **Abbreviations**

ix **Acknowledgments**

1 **Introduction**
Objects of Desire: Reading the Material World Metaphysically in Marguerite de Navarre's *Heptaméron*

23 **Chapter One**
Telling *Tableaux* and Textual Resurrections: Marguerite de Navarre and the Evangelical Narrative

47 **Chapter Two**
Evangelical Dimensions in Decorative Arts: Emblems, Earthly Objects, and the Economy of Transcendence

77 **Chapter Three**
A New Medium for a New Message: Evangelicals and Decorative Arts

111 **Chapter Four**
Of Tableware, Chalices, and Axeheads: The Evangelical Narrative and Transitory Treasures

148 **Chapter Five**
The Evangelical Narrative: Des Périers, Du Fail, and Yver

173 **Chapter Six**
Earthly Treasures: Marguerite's *Mondain* Monstrances

195 **Chapter Seven**
Costuming the Christiform Text; or, *L'habit ne fait pas le moine*

231 **Chapter Eight**
Interior Decoration and External Trappings: Space for the Spirit

276 **Conclusion**
From Self to Soul: Treasures of the Heart

291 **Notes**

333 **Bibliography**

345 **Index**

List of Abbreviations

Hept.
Heptaméron, by Marguerite de Navarre

Miroir
Le miroir de l'âme pécheresse, by Marguerite de Navarre (1st ed. and uniform title; 2nd ed. published as *Le miroir de treschrestienne Princesse Marguerite de France...*)

Nouvelles
Nouvelles récréations et joyeux devis, by Bonaventure Des Périers

Acknowledgments

First and foremost, I would like to thank the Reverend Joseph McShane, Society of Jesus, President of Fordham University. When he hired me years ago, Father McShane asked what I, as an Episcopal woman scholar of sixteenth-century French, was going to offer to the Jesuit culture at Fordham. I volunteered that I might like to write a book on the Catholic Church's "jewel in the Crown" (as he termed her), Marguerite de Navarre. I hope he is pleased with what he set in process. I am also so grateful to Father McShane for all his encouragement and support over the years, as well as the open arms he and Fordham University extended to my daughter Sara, currently a flourishing sophomore at Fordham.

Fordham friends and colleagues, among them Dr. Fred Harris, Dr. David Myers, and Deans Brennan O'Donnell and Carol Rizzuti, have been kind and stimulating interlocutors.

Colleagues such as the late Gérard Defaux, Cynthia Skenazi, François Rigolot, Daniel Russell, Tom Conley, and Mary McKinley all provided timely and helpful comment on various stages of this project.

I would like to thank my conscientious and gifted editor, Susan Clawson of Purdue Studies in Romance Literatures. She has been a constant source of support and guidance, and I am grateful!

I would also like to thank the Interlibrary Loan library staff at Fordham University, especially Ms. Charlotte Labbé, for all the help in tracking down texts.

I could do nothing (indeed, I would *be* nothing) without the love and encouragement of my husband, Dr. Randall Balmer of Barnard College, Columbia University.

Woodbury, Connecticut
November 2006

Introduction

Objects of Desire

Reading the Material World Metaphysically in Marguerite de Navarre's *Heptaméron*

> Do not store up for yourselves treasures on earth, where moth and rust destroy, and where thieves break in and steal. But store up for yourselves treasures in heaven, where moth and rust do not destroy, and where thieves do not break in and steal. For where your treasure is, there your heart will be also.
>
> Matt. 6.19–21

The early years of the sixteenth century were rich and complex, a time of extravagance, costuming, and courtly masques coupled with skepticism about worldliness due to theological reform movements.[1] Marguerite de Navarre's *Heptaméron* participates in this complexity:[2] a collection of tales about often bawdy daily life, it is also a coherent, proselytizing work. As such, the text is a transitional document, both a reflection of its evangelical and Lutheran socio-cultural context and a harbinger of the Calvinist movement as manifest in narrative, art, and artifacts. The *Heptaméron* makes innovative use of the material objects produced by the commodity culture of François Ier's court. Marguerite develops a materialistic as well as a metaphysical[3] discourse. Her arguments are usually secularly prompted but often spiritually animated, composing a guide along the evangelical pathway to salvation.

Marguerite represents herself to her time, and to us, as doubled. On the one hand, there is the devout poet, devoted sister, ardent member of the Cercle de Meaux.[4] On the other hand, the author of the *Heptaméron* pens ribald stories about quotidian existence. Are there two Marguerites, or is there one? Marguerite's self-depiction as two distinct manifestations epitomizes a technique that she frequently uses in textual characters' development. Façades, mirror images, pairings of apparently dissimilar attributes, redundancies, ornate surfaces, and rhetorical embellishments are tools that she uses to represent a disjunction between materiality and metaphysics. Her text strives to heal this schism by using, then surpassing, elements of the world to attain an other-worldly perspective.

Marguerite's work is still very much informed by medieval Catholic theology. Late medieval Catholicism read nature as God's book, in which things were unambiguous markers of divine intention, and a transparent continuous communication flowed between creation and Creator. "The investment of [aspects of] nature [and culture] with unprecedented spiritual [weight] … could be undertaken with piety … because God was understood to have accomplished his most intimate internalization of the spirit within these apparently profane realms of the phenomenal."[5] However, Marguerite differs from how Catholic writers discern the *impresa* of the divine in the natural world—thereby holding up materiality as reminiscent of the divine; her evangelical focus instead scrutinizes narrative flow as evidence for the dynamic of the Logos.

The Evangelical Dimension

The evangelical movement of which Marguerite was part was a reforming impulse within the Catholic Church prior to the divisions caused by Lutheranism. Marguerite considered herself a good Catholic. Like other evangelicals, she sought to restore Catholicism by stripping away medieval distortions and accretions. In this respect, her thought is increasingly infused with Reformed theology, especially that of Luther.[6] The method that Marguerite develops to handle the new emphases brought by such an evangelical perspective is innovative. Like Luther, Marguerite explores the dialectic between the world and God. While the late medieval notion of *Teatrum mundi*, for instance, dramatizes God's plan through the representation of order in the world, Marguerite's treatment of *teatrum* and text problematizes earthly existence. For Marguerite, translucency, rather than transparency, characterizes the relationship between materiality and metaphysics: divine light, when shone on earthly objects, will irradiate and shine through them. In and of themselves, however, they are opaque. In a very practical way, Marguerite requires her reader to penetrate beneath opacity so that things hidden may be revealed. While the *Heptaméron*'s themes, and Marguerite's choice of objects, remain medieval, and the tradition of seeing the divine through the material continues, Marguerite's style evolves toward a more pronounced narrative emphasis on the depiction of the material world. Marguerite reads and applies St. Paul, as does Luther, but she also refers extensively to the Gospel of Matthew. St. Matthew's message cautions that things of the earth are over-valued, as well as apocalyptically warning that this world will soon pass away. The Gospel of Matthew then becomes a lens through which Marguerite can develop, through reference to contemporary decorative arts, her interrogation and indictment of earthly treasures. She examines with a critical eye their ornate surfaces. While the world views adornment as conferring added value, Marguerite dispenses with ornamentation. It becomes a sign of much in the world that is dispensable, a sign of imminent undoing.

What makes her work distinct from both late medieval Catholic writers and later Reformed writers is the description, but also the *distrust*, of worldly objects in the text.[7] While, as in the theater, things, such as props, move the drama along, Marguerite never forgets that the plot is actually earthly history that the apocalypse will annihilate. This is a text about transitoriness, even as the sheer proliferation of concrete objects seems a solid anchor for the tales in materiality. Like Luther and other evangelical writers, Marguerite's attitude toward objects is profoundly ambivalent.[8] In *Christ and Culture,* sociologist H. Richard Niebuhr develops a paradigm that helps to explain Marguerite's approach.[9] Niebuhr shows that, while Catholics view Christ as above culture, and Calvinists see Christ as the transformer of culture, Marguerite and Luther hold the two in constant tension. The dialectic that Marguerite's text develops between Christ and culture is creative and is explored through various manifestations of creativity. While in the medieval era God's hand was discerned in all elements of the created order, in the early modern era the acquisitive self succumbs to the lure of self-definition in relation to things rather than in relation to God. For Marguerite, consequently, a profound ambiguity exists between self and God, and the continuum between world and God begins to break up.[10]

While Marguerite may not criticize Catholic practice directly in every case, her views are often "contrary to the prevailing ideological climate within the University of Paris at the time [she] was writing."[11] Further, many expressions in the *Heptaméron*, such as *vive foy* or *grace seule*, are characteristic of evangelical theology.[12] Marguerite's evangelical sympathies may also reveal themselves through, for instance, the fact that she rarely portrays or discusses the sacraments. On the other hand, extensive anti-clericalism, a consistent evangelical criticism, is present.

Marguerite's evangelical leanings thus had considerable influence on the *Heptaméron*.[13] As Marguerite penned narratives embedded in the material culture of her time, the *nouvelles* delineate how her metaphysical focus works itself out in relation to, and in tension with, things of the world. The *Heptaméron* describes a dialectic between body and soul, physical world and celestial realm. To represent the material world in her text, Marguerite has recourse to contemporary artistic innovations. The vibrant culture at the court of François Ier informs her literary project.[14] In 1527, François began to collect curiosities; he added to his cabinet throughout his life.[15] A treasure trove of medals, silverplate, figurines, "de petites pièces curieuses … & une infinité de petites gentillesses" ("small oddities and innumerable knick-knacks"),[16] the curiosity cabinet held examples of innovative media, such as genre painting, richly evocative of daily life. Genre paintings are a presence in the *Heptaméron*, as well. Marguerite's metaphysical perspective disposed her to view the beauties of the world around her, and on the canvasses of genre painters, as desirable yet untrustworthy.

As Marguerite drafted the *nouvelles*, her eyes met the showy parade of sumptuous robes proclaiming a *courtesan*'s status; thick curtains and embroidered wall-hangings of a wealthy man's chambers; gilt-edged books bound in leather, intended more for show than for use.[17] The *Heptaméron*'s glittering materiality showcases disguise as deception,[18] as well as undoing it. *Nouvelle* after *nouvelle* is structured in reference to things, objects that both define and damn.[19] Marguerite's selection of material objects as vehicle for her criticism of the illusion of terrestrial self-sufficiency is evangelical. (However, by continuing to employ worldly goods, she avoids the extreme of iconoclasm to which explicitly Reformed attitudes might lead).[20] Yet, while she focuses on images and things, it is only to use them in the narrative to show their unreliability. Marguerite uses images dually: to describe a material attitude, and to offer a metaphysical corrective to the problems of that perspective.[21]

The Material World

Discussion of quotidian objects, and of objects as evocative of human relations,[22] also occurs in Martin Luther's expository technique, which relied on the application of Scripture to daily life through the medium of material objects. This materialist dimension was typical of the age, and particularly of Protestant historiography.[23] Similarly, genre painting situates objects within the frame of a private room or domestic space to create a narrative about those objects, their possessor, and the meaning of life. Borrowing from the interpretive palette of artistic expression, Marguerite draws on genre painters' techniques for treating objects, applying their approach textually and using words in the way that they use images. Genre painters move away from the stylized universe of late medieval art, where things are used symbolically; they now use objects representatively and relationally. The ultimate effect is ironic: things of the world voice a criticism of the world. This stance may encourage the viewer to look away from earthly objects and desires and to focus on a metaphysical ideal. Similarly, the *Heptaméron*'s artifactual components add a theological dimension to narrative.[24] She sets art, and objects, to do the Lord's work. Charles Taylor, in his discussion of Reformed conceptions of daily life, describes such a treatment:

> the instrumental stance towards the world has been given a new and spiritual meaning ... In this religious tradition, it is the way we serve God in creation [that matters] ... it is also what protects us against the absorption in things which would wrench us away from God. We must constantly remember to treat the things of creation merely as instruments, and not as ends valuable in themselves.[25]

Marguerite's strategy interrogates the use of material culture by translating it to the domain of the text, shifting it to a spiritual orientation.[26] Her innovation constitutes an interdisciplinary melding of visual arts, literature, and theology, and shows how new strides in different cultural and intellectual domains were integrated and reapplied in creative ways in other venues.[27] An illustrated book that Marguerite commissioned demonstrates the influence of her artistic milieu, and shows the marriage of art and theology in her new treatment of word and image. The *Initiatoire instruction en la Religion chrestienne pour les enffans*, a Lutheran children's catechism produced for and dedicated to Marguerite, was probably brought into France by refugees from persecution in Strasbourg, and penned by the Würtemberg reformer Johannes Brenz, with whose work Marguerite was familiar.[28] The *Initiatoire* attests to a transitional artistic moment between the Limbourg *frères*' style of blue background illumination and the genre painting style, which featured imbricated enclosures, boxes, classical arches as found in the *Initiatoire*'s frame, pavilions, gateways, checkerboard patterns, and well-delimited interiors (consistent with the evangelical emphasis on the inner man). The *Initiatoire* uses detail and objects much as do genre painters: an accretion of material objects epitomizes the subject's worldliness. The figure's sword, his jewelry, the bystanders' luxurious garments, the gilded statue in the background, the book one woman holds—all combine to form a tactile and realistic space into which the viewer enters.[29]

A glance at a few paintings from the period illustrates variations in this materialist perspective. Marguerite situates herself in reference to such use of material objects. In *Girl Making a Garland* (see fig. 1), by Hans Suess von Kulmbach, German, circa 1490, a young woman plaits a crown of forget-me-nots to send to her lover.[30] The forget-me-nots are symbols of remembrance; they send the message to the absent young man not to forget his mistress. In this painting, things lack heft and substance; they are the ephemeral media of communication.

In a relatively contemporary painting, however, things already begin to assume a material presence and to convey cultural critique. In *Saint Eligius* (see fig. 2), by Petrus Christus, circa 1449,[31] religious objects and relics arrayed on the shelf

Fig. 1. Hans Suess von Kulmbach, *Girl Making a Garland.* 1490. Metropolitan Museum of Art, New York City. Several material objects adorn this image, among them the garland, possibly a *carpe diem* reference, the screen on one portion of the window, and the window frame itself, a motif extensively featured in the *Heptaméron*, often to demonstrate a gap between earthly and celestial standards. Used with permission of The Metropolitan Museum of Art, Gift of J. Pierpont Morgan, 1917 (17.190.21).

Fig. 2. Petrus Christus, *A Goldsmith in His Shop, Possibly Saint Eligius*. 1449. Metropolitan Museum of Art, New York City. The scale motif recurs in the *nouvelles* as a way of judging between heaven and earth. This couple is richly adorned, with great care to self-presentation. A similarly luxuriously attired couple peers in the window, and is reflected in the convex mirror to the right. Mirrors epitomize distortion and the failure of self-knowledge. Marguerite encourages us to know ourselves, and be known, in Christ. Used with permission of The Metropolitan Museum of Art, Robert Lehman Collection, 1975 (1975.1.110).

symbolize aspects of the saint's existence. However, a mirror in the bottom right corner offers an alternate perspective, adding the possibility of a critique of the literal representation. Inside the shop a young pair consults the jeweler about a wedding ring; the mirror shows that outside the shop, another pair peers in, the juxtaposition of the two couples inviting comparison. (Perhaps the couple in the mirror epitomizes later conjugal bliss.) When twinned with the dangling scale—a jeweler's scale, in daily life, but, read theologically, a Last Judgment motif—the mirror may suggest a judgment rendered on one, or both, pairs.[32] Here, things signify in and of themselves, possess traditional symbolic valences, and also participate in what may be a criticism of earthly pleasures.

Marguerite applies such visual techniques to her literary medium. Her assemblages of objects compose images, but also designate directions for interpretation of the narrative. She recognizes that objects are useful in concretizing the viewer's perspective and in eliciting a mood or a response.[33] A three-dimensionality and a quotidian, lived quality result. Through the medium of earthly things, Marguerite shapes stories like parables: they function simply, on the surface, but contain "strange" or dissonant elements that demand a deeper, metaphysical interpretation.[34] Things thus compose layers through which Marguerite encourages her readers to move, to accede ultimately to a metaphysical truth; as Carol Thysell has shown in *The Pleasure of Discernment: Marguerite de Navarre as Theologian*, "the theological convictions of … Marguerite de Navarre called for a genre that might be received on a number of levels."[35] Things therefore also represent the different kinds of awareness of the text available to individual readers.

Other genre painters, informed by the same sorts of evangelical considerations that interest Marguerite, put art to the service of illustrating Reformed doctrine in a way that is similar to, but—due to the later time period—more fully developed than, Marguerite's approach. A century later, the kind of concern over worldly objects culminates in the visual polemic of Pieter Boel, the Flemish master of *An Allegory of Worldly Vanity* (circa 1640).[36] In his title, Boel makes the hermeneutic assertion that earthly objects are inadequate and deceitful. His construction of an allegory points to the potential for misinterpretation: an allegory places objects at one remove from reality, lifting them into the realm of symbol, so that the viewer may not rely solely on sensory faculties to understand them. Boel expresses his theology through his art, describing Catholic reliance on things, images, and emblems of worldly status as represented by a bishop's miter perched atop a heap of worldly treasures devoid of intrinsic value. Bright colors futilely flourish on the palette near the lower right of the painting, suggesting that this artwork, too, will go the way of all flesh.

If genre painting already seems to display an evangelical or even a proto-Reformed perspective, this may derive from the movement of the locus of piety during this period from the church to the home, culminating in the Protestant *paterfamilias* and family devotions centered around Bible reading. In response to this shift, believers had to come to terms with a de-sacralized world, a world in which compartments separating holy objects from worldly things collapse (and no referent is reliable). By conferring a metaphysical role on the material of existence, Marguerite features earthly treasures but then ultimately moves past them. In this sense, she remains within the mind-set of a medieval Catholic who, in venerating a relic, adores the object as an act of witness and a symbol of a higher reality. But she adds the evangelical nuance of more skepticism vis-à-vis the integrity of these objects in and of themselves. The spiritual truth lies beyond the objects. Yet the object plays a vital role in getting the believer to experience that higher reality, and is also itself in some way encompassed by the reality to which it points.

Marguerite's textual treatment epitomizes a literary paradigm shift from an allegorical understanding of the world typical of the Middle Ages and early Renaissance, to a more inner-oriented, subjective appropriation of the divine Word by evangelicals still within the framework of the Catholic church. The *Heptaméron*'s textual treasure trove functions through progression from object to subject status: subject interacting with subject, subject using or reflecting on object, and object juxtaposed with object, and, finally, a renunciation of reliance on objects and the development of a new, evangelical understanding of subject in which subjectivity can only be experienced fully in relation to the Creator. Things are transformed to act as iconic markers designating a higher significance not confined to their function as cryptograms in a structure to be decoded. Their significance is found in sets of relationships outside and beyond these objects and the framework in which they are situated. The message signifies by progression, rather than by stabilizing one precise meaning: it *moves* from Word to word, from Logos back to Marguerite's reflection of it in her narratives.

Textual Materialism

Glass baubles, silk gloves, embroidered stockings, flagons of beer and casks of wine, mullioned window panes and convex mirrors, lap-dogs, lustrous fabrics and leather-bound books ... such objects form the substance of genre paintings, as well as the texture of Marguerite's text. Textual materialist criticism examines the presence of objects within texts, exploring their relationships and the meaning produced by them.[37]

In the *Heptaméron,* Marguerite plants material markers that map out a route toward salvation. This textual itinerary transmutes materiality into metaphor: things become valuable through the new spiritual message with which they are infused. However, they only temporarily retain their value, as their ultimate worth, paradoxically, lies in their undoing. In her evangelical interpretation of objects, Marguerite starts a process; she is a precursor to later, explicitly Reformed ways of looking at the world.

Textual materialism considers collections of objects to be narrative nodal points. The predominantly evangelical and, later, Protestant phenomenon[38] of the *Wunderkammer*[39] or collector's cabinet was meant to be a "résumé du monde."[40] A spatial and materialist representation of the ramification of knowledge, the collector's cabinet often employs a Reformed approach to Scripture: a system of setting things in order that involves the collection of scriptural *loci* (construed literally as "place" rather than as "citation"): a passage from Scripture is thus both Word, and manifestation of what Word evokes. Through ordering schemas, Calvin's and Pierre Ramus's systematic theology elucidates the significance of worldly things in God's plan for history: they investigate the relationships among things: narrative constructions.[41] Such treatment of objects is similar to Marguerite's textual technique, which anticipates it chronologically. The role of such objects,[42] dependent on their arrangement,[43] is to act as what Antoine Schnapper, specialist on collecting, calls "sémiophores":[44] they refer to the invisible reality of which they are signs and which they invoke in a process analogous to the operation of the Hebrew *dabar*: the creation of the material world through the effect of the dynamic Word. The construction of collections of "significant" objects is oriented toward conferring order on a fragmented postlapsarian universe.[45] Similarly, things provide Marguerite with a medium to work with in order to realign the universe with metaphysical mandates.[46]

Marguerite compiles a sort of textual *Wunderkammer*, in which the narrative is built upon earthly treasures, but also undermines their apparent self-sufficiency, compelling the reader to seek elsewhere for meaning. The arrangement of the objects in patterns of significance matters more than the objects themselves. Her exhibit of these objects, further, has a self-consuming goal: creations by humans should turn back toward the Creator rather than encourage any illusion of autonomy.[47]

Similar to genre painters, Marguerite weaves a nearly tactile textual fabric through the proliferation of material objects in the *nouvelles*: silken hose and beaded gloves, heavy coffers and mahogany placards, pieces of bone, golden goblets, calligraphy lettering, crowns and cuckold's horns, tapestries and canopies. The acquisition of wealth and emphasis on things for personal representation and cultural display that is characteristic of the court of François Ier[48] offers possibilities for Marguerite's revision of the role of objects.[49] This accumulative attitude, the jumbling together and juxtaposition of objects, produces a surplus that requires a narrative to impose significance.[50] She chooses each object to convey a specific aspect of her evangelical perspective, her relationship to God and to the world, and the recipient's social standing as well as metaphysical orientation. Marguerite wants to effect a more critical investigation, in which objects are both positive and negative. They stand in a dialectical relationship, bearing the freight of their own materiality and worldliness, as well as suggesting their own metaphysical undoing.[51] Materiality may eventually be rehabilitated, however, as the paradoxical marker of its metaphysical origin.

Marguerite's reading of Luther taught her to decipher the world in Pauline terms. St. Paul called worldly things *sarks*, a Greek term meaning unregenerate flesh prey to sin. In Gal. 5.16–26, St. Paul explains the dialectic entwining fallen flesh with unsullied spirit, a dialectic that the *Heptaméron* also illustrates: "The sinful nature desires what is contrary to the Spirit, and the Spirit what is contrary to the sinful nature. They are in conflict with each other, so that you do not do what you want … Those who belong to Christ Jesus have crucified the sinful nature with its passions and desires." Material presence in Marguerite's text provides a possible resolution to this dialectic of sinful flesh with spirit. Objects are images, but the text is word testifying to the Logos ("verbum tuum veritas est"). Thus, things may designate that which is divine, but may never contain or limit it in any way. So, when St. Paul instructs the faithful to "put on the whole armor of God," he is referring not to literal armor, but to spiritual weapons. However, he mentions in detail all the components of military garb—breastplate, buckler, helmet—evoking them in their full materiality before employing them to designate qualities of spiritual strength. Similarly, St. Augustine instructs Christians to put on saintliness like a cape or cloak. He uses the simile, constructed through reference to the object, to point to a higher concept: one's ability to reconfigure one's spiritual being in accordance with God's will.

The Transformation of Objects

Just so, in the *Heptaméron*, objects witness textually to their own transformation. The proliferation of objects in Marguerite's narrative indicates that humanity has shifted focus away from Christ and has become objectified. This deviation can be rectified by moving beyond things, representative of humanity's lust for the world.[52] A conversion, or "turning toward" Christ, will then be experienced, along with redemption through the development of a new, "sacralized" subjectivity, one always in relation with God.

The *destruction* of an object at the beginning of the storytelling provides Marguerite's storytellers with the pretext for the construction of their collection. The travelers decide to sojourn in the Abbey because a flood has washed out all the bridges to their various destinations.[53] These bridges summarize Marguerite's narrative project: the very *elimination* of their material presence results in a *metaphorical* bridge (the act of narration) linking man and God. Marguerite's *devisants*' stories will perform the same purpose, metamorphizing materiality into spiritual stories, as they express the intention to pass their time telling each other tales that they can then take back home in lieu of the customary pilgrimage tokens. Thus, stories will replace images, rosaries, and material objects. The disappearance of the bridges, human constructions, also symbolizes the consequences that ensue if Christ is not accepted as the bridge between man and God, heaven and earth. By suggesting that the stories that her *devisants* tell will mediate between tellers and hearers, establishing relationships as the Gospel does, Marguerite indicates that her texts have a practical, proselytizing role.

The first story in the First Day of the *Heptaméron* delineates how to explicate the evangelical message in the text. Bodies lie buried at the base of buildings that, designed by evil intentions and scaffolded upon ruin, recall the holocaust of the sinful heart. Right structuring is an evangelical preoccupation. Marguerite recounts how a lover's bones are thrown into the mortar of the house of his mistress, a woman who betrayed him out of self-interest when he threatened to disclose her affair with the local bishop. The dismembering of the lover, du Mesnil, is prefigured in the slippage in vocabulary used for the plot and its outcome: the woman's *mestier* is to hire her lover's *meurtrier*, while he, ill-fated lover, will become *mortier* for the house's foundations:

> Ung nommé Thomas Guérin, qui faisoit mestier d'estre meurtrier ... vint donner tant de coups d'espée à ce pauvre jeune homme ... [on] feit brusler le corps du pauvre trespassé. Les os qui ne furent consommez par le feu, les feit mectre dans du mortier là où il faisoit bastir en sa maison.
>
> ("An individual by the name of Thomas Guérin, a professional assassin ... the poor young man could do nothing

> against the hail of blows from [the] sword, and he fell dead … [the wife's husband] burned the body of the deceased man, and put the bones which had not disappeared in the fire into the mortar he was using at that time to build an extension on his house."—*Hept.* 1.1.14–15; Chilton 74–75)[54]

Bones are later excavated from the mortar, layering truthful testimony over the dissembling text of the cover-up. In another layer, Marguerite embeds herself into the account: the husband and wife consult a magician to eliminate those prosecuting them, and this "invocateur" fashions "cinq ymaiges de bois," one of which represents Marguerite. More layers of testimony accrue when du Mesnil's two servants and the old chambermaid speak out to denounce the murder. *Nouvelle* #1 can be used as an interpretive paradigm, alerting the reader to investigate detail and to delve beneath the surface to find hidden things of significance.

Further, *nouvelle* #1 has a very materialist texture. Objects disappear, are destroyed, or are otherwise discredited in the first *nouvelle*. As we have already seen, this woman of loose morals has slept with three men: her husband, the bishop, and her young lover. The bishop is the character most linked to materiality; the woman allows him to touch her for "avarice [plutôt] que par amour … pour … proffict" ("… [she] continued to do his bidding more out of greed than of love"—*Hept.* 1.1.12; Chilton 71), frequently "making use" of the bishop to obtain commissions for her husband. She uses her lover as a commodity, too: "she had the Bishop for profit and young du Mesnil for pleasure" (Chilton 71; *Hept.* 1.1.12). One day, while the husband is away, du Mesnil arrives at the woman's house for an assignation, only to find that his place is occupied by the bishop. Furious, du Mesnil tells his lover that he must be unworthy to receive her favors, since she has been touching *choses sacrees* ("she had been in contact with sacred things"—Chilton 72). This wordplay exposes her *cas:* she is nude before his knowledge of his unfaithfulness (*descouvert*). Du Mesnil recognizes that the unfaithful woman does not warrant the value that he had assigned to her body. Marguerite shows in this tale men and women being treated as objects in a spurious sexual economy that appropriates, uses, then casts aside.

The tale is stronger than the objects that compose it: after first neutrally describing, the narrative then aligns itself with the function of truth-telling. The investigation into the event, and the collection of testimony, prevail over the assault on du Mesnil's personhood. Although the husband and wife have suborned the few witnesses to the murder and exacted their temporary silence, nonetheless du Mesnil's bones in the mortar are material evidence. Immobilizing the guilty parties in the material aftermath of their crime, Marguerite denies them the redemptive metaphysical possibilities that her *nouvelles* usually offer. The husband and wife are fixed forever as paradoxical partners of the person whom they had murdered, both by his absence and by his presence through his body being incorporated into the foundation of their house.

In *nouvelle* #1, the authorities eventually learn of the crime because of the fragments of bone found in the foundations. Similarly, objects elsewhere in Marguerite's text signal the presence of subtexts. Marguerite's version of textual materialism uses things to represent beyond themselves and, here, to point to the consequences of sin.

The textual dynamics are similar in the story of the muledriver's wife. Here, Marguerite refers to two objects, both of which functionally surpass their description. A virtuous wife is killed by her husband's servant in an attempted rape. In this *nouvelle*, as in the first, clues to the perpetrator of the crime seem absent from the scene: the rapist flees, taking with him his sword, and there appear to have been no witnesses (although we later learn that a young girl did see the crime take place). Only the woman's body remains. However, the way in which the crime is solved transforms the woman's body from *object* of the servant's desire—which he rendered mute, denying her the status of subject by ignoring her pleas for mercy and silencing her cries with blows—to *subject*—through the voice given her by the text that tells the truth about what has transpired.[55] The woman, near death, no longer can speak:

> … trouverent qu'elle avoit vingt-cinq plaies mortelles sur son corps et feirent ce qu'ilz peurent pour luy ayder, mais il leur fut impossible. Toutesfois, elle languit encores une heure sans parler, faisant signe des œilz et des mains; en quoi elle monstroit n'avoir perdu l'entendement.

> ("When they examined her they found twenty-five fatal wounds. They did what they could to help her, but to no avail. She lingered on for another hour, unable to speak, but indicating by movements of her eyes, and gestures of the hands, that her mind was still clear."—*Hept.* 1.2.20; Chilton 81)

Indicating the wounds, letters of agony on the parchment of her flesh, she signifies what has transpired: she makes a text of the marks. Human text is completed by God's definitive account of what has happened, and a textual voice is restored to her:

> Estant interrogée, par ung homme d'esglise, de la foy en quoy elle mouroit, de l'esperance de son salut par Jhesucrist seul, respondoit par signes si evidens, que la parolle n'eut sceu mieux monstrer son intention; et ainsy, avecq un visaige joyeulx, les œilz eslevez au ciel, rendit ce chaste corps son ame à son Createur ... martire de chasteté.
>
> ("A man of the church came and questioned her about the faith in which she died, and about her hope for salvation *through Christ alone.* Although she could only reply by signs, no words could have conveyed her meaning more clearly. And so, with joy on her face, and her eyes turned heavenwards, her soul left this chaste body to return to its Creator."—*Hept.* 1.2.20; emphasis added; Chilton 81)

The body's message, an evangelical creedal statement, testifies to salvation by faith in Christ alone (*sola fidei*): "son salut par Jhesuscrist seul." Marguerite creates a hieroglyph text, a layering of wound and word akin to evangelical martyrological writing in which the transcription of the martyr's verbal testimony counteracts the graphic effects of torture.[56] Marguerite demonstrates that objects should not be interpreted through their appearance, but rather as they are inserted into God's narrative of salvation:

> Car les graces de Dieu ne se donnent point aux hommes pour leurs noblesses et richesses, mais selon qu'il plaist à sa bonté ... et souvent eslit les choses basses, pour confondre celles que le monde estime haultes et honorables.
>
> ("for God's graces are not given to men for their noble birth and for their riches, but according as it pleases Him in His

> goodness ... and those whom He has elected He honours with virtues and crowns with His glory. Often He chooses that which is low, that He might confound that which the world places high ..."—*Hept.* 1.2.21; Chilton 81)

The woman's body is yet inviolate, not penetrated sexually; she is called a "martyr of chastity." Her identity in Christ thwarts the would-be rapist's attempt to reduce her to the status of object.

The thirteenth *nouvelle* in Day Two uses objects to map out the trajectory of misplaced passions, attesting to spiritual misdirection. The story concerns voyages, and has a materialist component as well.

A captain, married, tries to seduce a pious married woman. He tries to legitimize the seduction attempt by equating his passion with the Passion of Christ. In this manner, the captain epitomizes the distorted application of spiritual signs to earthly contexts:

> mais, à fin qu'elle ne s'en apperceust, se mectoit à parler des sainctz lieux de Jerusalem, où estoient *les signes* de la grande amour que Jesus-Christ nous a portée. Et, en parlant de ceste amour, *couvroit* la sienne, regardant ceste dame.
>
> ("in order that she would not notice his consternation, of the places that bore the signs of the holy places of Jerusalem, of the places that bore the signs of that great love which Jesus Christ has borne us. And, by talking about that love, he concealed his own as he sighed and gazed with tears in his eyes at his lady."—*Hept.* 2.13.99; emphasis added; Chilton 169)

The captain tries to legitimize his adulterous passion for the woman, encouraged in this endeavor by his awareness that the lady is "fort devote" (*Hept.* 2.13.97). The lady possesses material wealth; she states that "Dieu nous a donné ... assez de biens" ("God has endowed us with riches"—*Hept.* 2.13.97; Chilton 167). *Biens* means worldly goods, which may be Marguerite's way of characterizing the woman as worldly, for the lady does seem surprisingly susceptible at first to the captain's suit. The verb *couvroit* indicates the rhetorical strategy of deception at work. Jesus' passion superimposes itself, through the captain's manipulation, over the captain's depiction of a possible passionate involvement between himself and the lady: *ceste amour*, meaning Christ's, blurs into *la sienne*, the captain's lust. *Couvrir* recalls *couverture*, a form of camouflage.

The captain sends the lady a letter describing his desire. The letter is a palimpsest, thickly written on both sides, "escriptes de tous costez" ("on both sides of which were closely written the words"—Chilton 170). Paper was costly and, so as to waste no space, margins and edges were customarily written on as well, sometimes with the paper turned in a different direction to enable the letter-writer to capitalize on white space. The captain's lust is represented by this dense cross-hatching of words in which it is difficult to discern meaning clearly: "il s'est faict venu mectre / au beau milieu de ceste myenne lettre" ("right in the middle of my letter ..."; "Yea, he is truly present / ... right in the middle of my letter ..."—*Hept.* 2.13.100–01; Chilton 170–71). Perspective, and the ability to parse the text, are lacking: sent from afar, the letter seeks to undermine the woman's fidelity to her husband through narrative blandishments and distortions. The captain places his desire at the center of the letter, and claims steadfast love: "la mer peult bien bien ce mien corps emporter, / Mais non le cueur que nul ne peult oster, / D'avecq toy, où il faict sa demeure" ("my body might the ocean freely take, / But not my heart—there is no power can make / It leave your side, where always it shall stay"—*Hept.* 2.13.103; Chilton 174), but this hope is vain: she cannot constitute the fixed point of his desire, for she belongs to another.

Thus, the captain's gift to the lady of a diamond ring in token of his "ferme seureté ... pierre de fermeté" ("[Now so that you may better know my heart] ... / my faith so firm and sure, / this diamond take, a stone that will endure"—*Hept.* 2.13.104; Chilton 174) functions ironically: the jewel meant to ensure stability and changelessness instead highlights inconstancy. Further, the lady immediately displaces his desire, sending the diamond ring to the captain's wife with a fond letter purporting to have been written by him. The lady does so because she is aware of the hindrance that material objects may pose to right living and to salvation: "elle se trouva fort empeschée du diamant, car elle n'avoit poinct accoustumé de se parer aux depens d'autres que son mary" ("she was greatly perplexed as she contemplated ... the diamond ... the diamond was an embarrassment. She was not in the habit of wearing jewelry obtained at the expense of anyone other than her husband"—*Hept.* 2.13.104; Chilton 174). She also divests herself of the diamond out of concern for the captain's conscience: she seeks to redress his religious standing, repairing it with the gift of the diamond to the wife to whom it should really have been given: "elle, qui estoit de entendement, pensa de faire profficter cest anneau à la conscience de ce cappitaine" ("being a lady of good sense, she decided to use the ring to the benefit of the captain's conscience"—*Hept.* 2.13.104; Chilton 175). By ridding herself of a material object invested with fraudulent significance, the woman is acting like an evangelical, living out Scripture's injunction to lose the world so as to save her soul, and she refers to the kingdom of heaven ["gaigné ung royaulme"] in so doing: "[elle] se contenta d'estre defaicte de son diamant par ung si proffitable moyen, que, de reunir le mary et la femme en bonne amityé, il luy sembla avoir gaigné ung royaulme" ("she had restored the bond of affection between man and wife, and so pleased was she at having disposed of the ring in this profitable fashion, that nothing, no, not even the wealth of kings, could have pleased her more"—*Hept.* 2.13.105; Chilton 175).

The lady has dramatized a theological lesson: she has transformed earthly treasures by putting them to a higher purpose, and she has refused to allow misleading meaning to be attached to worldly objects. Although the captain had distorted spiritual signs for his own ends, she has righted the balance by deflecting his misdirected system of symbols, turning toward scriptural purpose. The lady's reinterpretation of symbol for other purposes summarizes how Marguerite herself uses the relationship between semblance and reality to lead the reader to a higher or deeper awareness:

> Marguerite ... has seized upon this form of novella logic, which does not proceed on the mere basis that appearances are deceiving and should therefore be ignored or discounted, but that appearances are extremely valuable if you have the

> power to decipher them. Marguerite takes this novella twist and combines it with a form of that celebrated theological concept known as the *felix culpa*, by which bad becomes the servant of good.[57]

The response of the captain's wife, consequently, shows elements both of the distortion and of its correction: "luy monstra l'anneau qu'elle avoit au doigt comme le signe de sa parfaicte amityé … dont la dame … [a vu] que de sa tromperie estoit sailly un tel bien …" ("… she showed her companion the ring that she wore on her finger as a sign of perfect love … the lady saw that her little deception had borne such good fruit"—*Hept.* 2.13.107; Chilton 178). While the ring had not been intended by the captain as a token of true love, the wife interprets it as such ("comme le signe") because of the letter accompanying the ring, the corrective text.

Biens, worldly goods, the problematic focus of most of this tale, are transformed into *bienfaictz*. Thus focus on good deeds is consistent with the evangelical faith system—doing good works in grateful response to having been saved by grace: "il me semble," says Parlamente, "que celles à qui l'on presente de telles choses, devroient desirer en faire œuvre qui vint à aussy bonne fin que feyt ceste bonne dame; car elles trouveroient que les bienfaictz sont les joyes des biens faisans" ("in my opinion, when ladies receive presents like the one which the lady in this story received, it ought to be their fervent wish to turn them to equally good account. They would find that in return they would be filled with the joy that all those who do good receive"—*Hept.* 2.13.108; Chilton 178).

"Joye" is the result of these good actions. Through Parlamente and this story, Marguerite offers what John Lyons has called an "exemplum,"[58] part of her didactic modeling strategy to encourage others to follow suit. It is as though, in offering this particular sort of story, Marguerite were composing an evangelical manual for right living. No longer worldly goods, but rather good deeds, are the focus of the story, which concludes by upholding the ideal of pure goodness (*bien*). The diamond, an instrument of persuasion and duplicity, has been transformed into an agent to work good: "ceste dame … convertit en bien ce qui de soy ne valloit riens" ("this lady …

pu[t] … to good use something that in itself was of no value"—*Hept.* 2.13.108; Chilton 179).

Earthly treasures, objects of worldly desire, are eventually undone in Marguerite's *nouvelles*. Their capacity to signify is limited by their transitoriness as well as by the deceptive use that humans make of them. They must be either erased, to make way for true significance or, as in the case of the ring, applied in a different way and redefined by a new narrative use. Marguerite's metaphysical "elsewhere" constitutes the originating point, the textual pivot, and the destination of her narrative project. Materiality is alchemized into metaphysics.

Chapter One

Telling *Tableaux* and Textual Resurrections

Marguerite de Navarre
and the Evangelical Narrative

A Theater of Testimonial Texts

The Greek word for gospel, *evangelion*, derives from the same root as that of "gossip."[1] Telling stories to narrate the Christian experience is thus both a theological and literary technique, and, appropriately, personal witnessing combined with scriptural references, metaphors, and anecdotes typifies sixteenth-century evangelical expression. Evangelical witness developed from a demand for the scriptural foundation and validation of the conversion experience. This focus infused the daily lives of believers with significance and encouraged the narrating of the relationship of the evangelical with God as he or she perceived it in lay life. The humanist emphasis on textual criticism, a return to sources to determine authoritative texts (*ad fontes*), combined with popular demand for access to Scripture in the vernacular, prompted the Cercle de Meaux in France, and Luther in Germany, to espouse an unmediated appropriation of the Bible and its thorough, intentional application to every aspect of the believer's reality.

As Larissa Taylor has shown, in the decades prior to the Reformation, Catholic preaching often turned to para-biblical texts for homiletic inspiration, with friars drawing examples of heroic faith from the *Golden Legend* and the *Lives of the Saints* more frequently than they referred directly to the Bible.[2] Evangelicals, on the other hand, increasingly strove to find in Scripture, for themselves, in their own terms and without clerical intervention, the guidance they sought for daily life.

The story-lines of the *Heptaméron* thus also offer, whether intentionally or not, a sort of homiletics source-book: the *nouvelles* contain wisdom and illustration useful for evangelical sermons. Often, the *Heptaméron*'s suggestions for how to live life—whether at court, in church, in towns or in villages—develop through negative references to what *not* to do: Marguerite frequently portrays monks and priors, Catholic preachers, and confessors in the *Heptaméron*, but they are invariably shown acting in worldly or wanton ways—raping the daughter of their host, coercing a contribution to their personal finances, disavowing their promises of chastity and poverty. Casting a critical eye on how Catholic priests abuse their functions, Marguerite expresses proscriptions on such behavior as well as prescribing how the message of the Gospel should be conveyed.[3] On this level, the *Heptaméron* exemplifies evangelical expectations for effective preaching.[4] The criteria of authenticity, simplicity, and practicality in preaching were important for evangelicals, who hoped to return to the biblical *stylus rudus*, or plain style. Yet the "scandal" of the Gospel (from the Greek, *skandalon*, or stumbling-block; obstacle) was precisely the straightforward, unadorned language in which its truths were communicated; intellectuals found this unsophisticated, while esthetes tried to dress it up in rhetorical furbelows. Marguerite set herself the task of illustrating biblical truths in a seemingly improbable narrative venue, thereby demonstrating how evangelical preaching could be direct and sincere and also attractive to the listener.

In part to make the Bible more appealing and understandable to their audience, evangelical preachers wove descriptions of, and details from, daily life into their understanding of Scripture. They viewed Scripture as an instruction manual for every aspect of life, in this way fostering a pragmatic attitude toward preaching that removed it from ecclesiastical and clerical dominance, placing responsibility for reception of the Word on the laity.[5] The *devisants*—both storytellers of and audience for the text—are analogous to the new position in which the laity was placed by the evangelical shift toward more accessible preaching in the vernacular: members of the laity could now both read and interpret Scripture for themselves as well as implement its teachings, preaching through the example of their daily lives. The *nouvelles* lead the *devisants*, and evangelical laity, through a process of progressive spiritual enlightenment, providing instruction in how to preach and how to apply scriptural lessons. Readers participate in a conversion process structured at every point on scriptural passages. In this way, their experience mimetically conveys this message of the *Heptaméron*: the point of preaching is to convert the listener.

Martin Luther and the evangelicals who followed him ensconced the Bible, and its treasure trove of inspirational narratives, at the heart both of the individual believer's spiritual experience and of the community of the Christian church.[6] Telling stories became a foundational tool in Reformation theology and ecclesiology. The emphasis on the significance of story, narrative acted out in the world, was akin to the understanding of providential history that typified evangelicals and later Protestants. As God works out His plan in the larger scope of history as well as in the microcosm of each human heart, the plot line is constantly unfolding.

This is a textual dynamic. Such a shift altered the evangelicals' relationship with the material world, as well. Delineating in detail the ordinary experience of individuals, a micro-focus, brought an understanding of God's workings in human lives. The transformation of the believer's heart was what mattered.

> The sixteenth century was ... concerned with the association of miracles with holiness ... very early in the Reformation period a large-scale Protestant rejection of post-biblical miracles began to occur ... Luther pointedly rejected them ... Calvin argued ... [that] the believer's confidence should not rest on signs and wonders, but rather upon the promise of God in the sacred text. [Rather] ... Protestants were fascinated with the idea of divine providence ... special providence, in which God exercised care for specific individuals and groups.[7]

Luther and the Beginnings of Evangelical Narrative

The evangelical narrative includes vignettes in which individuals describe their relationship with God, highlighting their particular way of perceiving the salvation narrative.[8]

> L'idée de la Liberté chrétienne [,] conception paulinienne ... Mais c'était bien Luther, et lui seul semble-t-il à l'époque de Marguerite, qui se plaisait à amplifier cette idée en des

> *tableaux* très concrets et *vivants* qui représentaient l'âme jouissant de tous les bienfaits de la liberté par le moyen de la foi. De tels développements constituent l'une des plus grandes originalités de son œuvre …
>
> ("the concept of Christian liberty, a Pauline conception … But it was indeed Luther, and apparently Luther alone, during Marguerite's time-period, who expanded this idea into very concrete, realistic *tableaux* which represented the soul enjoying all the benefits of liberty by means of faith. Such developments constitute one of the greatest originalities of [Luther's] work.")[9]

Such evangelical evocations rely most heavily on New Testament writings: they gossip about the Gospels. Further, reacting against formulaic prayers that seemed to lack sincerity, evangelicals attempted reform from within by encouraging group confession, to be recited in church in the presence of fellow believers. Such practice gave voice to the sin, dramatizing it in a kind of community theater, rendering it both more individual (each man was responsible for his own sin before God, whether or not a priest or intercessor were to absolve him) and more communal (confession occurred before multiple witnesses). These public confessions developed into personalized dramatic narratives[10]—stories rather than formulaic expressions.[11]

For evangelicals, the act of telling a story about Christ's actions in their lives, dramatizing his saving grace, established an instant network of Christians, peers who shared similar experiences and therefore could confirm, amplify, or critique the story-line. The reader and the author thus already constitute a core of believers,[12] as do the *devisants,* who share in the crafting of a communal narrative that is also, on another level, a salvation narrative. (While what was heard in the Catholic confessional was also a form of story, priests questioning a penitent began by hearing a formulaic request that the confession be received and ended the session with the formula "Ego te absolvo …" Typically, they also asked a prescribed set of questions—concerning the frequency of the sin, the situation in which the sin occurred, and whether true contrition was present—in a programmatic way that precluded full-fledged storytelling or subjective narrative scrutinizing of the sin. Further, the confessional hid the penitent's identity both from the priest and from the rest of the church; in such conditions, the kind of evangelical community that Marguerite recommends was not easily established.)

Luther inaugurates this evangelical narrative genre with his colorful sermons composed of compelling anecdotes, as well as with his earthy *Table Talk,* homey, short, sometimes humorous tales featuring material objects and ribald occurrences bandied about among multiple interlocutors.[13] "Table talk" composes a dialogue about Christ, a narrative recollection of the Eucharistic feast. "Table talk" recites spiritual truths in an ordinary context: around the hearth, among friends, who, eating, joking, and rejoicing, share stories about grace.

Not only theological commonalities, but also stylistic similarities, link Luther and Marguerite's treatment of text: they both craft dramatic, sensual as well as spiritual, scenarios drawn from daily life. A variety of "secretaries" transcribe Luther's comments at the evening meals. The discussion among the different secretaries over their perceptions of Luther's message is functionally akin to the debate among the *devisants* after each tale is told. This interpretive interplay constructs a frame enabling the reader to engage with the narrative. Both Luther's doctrinal formulations, and his anecdotal style, influence Marguerite's prose: "Chez Luther et chez [Marguerite], des expressions parallèles sont données à des idées qui ... *n'ont pas été formulées de la même façon par d'autres à cette époque*" ("With both Luther and [Marguerite], parallel expressions are given to ideas which ... had not been expressed in the same way by others at that time").[14]

Luther's *Treatise to the Christian Nobility* describes a town set on fire by brigands. He envisions a situation in which the townsfolk stand around and do nothing while the town burns to the ground, simply because the mayor cannot be found and they fear to act without his go-ahead.

> Is it not the duty of each citizen to stir up the rest and call upon them for help? Much more ought it to be the case in the spiritual city of Christ, were a fire of offense to break out, whether in the pope's regime or anywhere else. The same argument would hold were an enemy to attack a town ...[15]

Luther uses this *tableau* to make the point that, if the Pope fails as the spiritual head of the church by sponsoring the sale of indulgences, the Christian's response should be outrage rather than indecision. The evangelical criticism of ecclesiastical abuses, reproving these on the basis of biblical authority, becomes comprehensible to the everyday believer through this simple scenario based in real-life experience. This daily-life component is a crucial quality in the elucidation of the evangelical narrative.[16]

Curiously, while Marguerite's prose work uses everyday life experience and objects, crafting an evangelical narrative, her theater is less likely to exhibit this quotidian or materialist component. Marguerite's *Théâtre profane* is allegorical, featuring characters such as "la Superstitieuse" and "la Mondaine." In contrast, the Reformer Martin Bucer urged a non-allegorical, daily-life perspective on the local theater evolving in Strasbourg, stipulating that

> le peuple se pourra esgayer et prendre delectation en choses honnestes et utiles à l'accroissement de vertu. On mettra en avant … les entreprises, les faicts et les evenements des choses humaines … qui serviront pour la correction des mœurs et pour donner instruction de bonne vie.
>
> ("the people can enjoy themselves and profit from worthwhile matters, useful to the development of virtue … One will put forward undertakings, deeds and events from ordinary human life … which will serve to correct their lifestyle and to instruct them … in how to live a good life.")[17]

Marguerite thus functions as a bridge between *mentalités*: late medieval (her poetry and plays) and early modern (her prose texts that develop an evangelical perspective).

"The Words of Your Mouth": Confessing through Speech and Story

Marguerite reaches back through Luther's work to St. Paul. W. G. Moore, in his study of the transmission of Lutheran ideas into France circa 1529, identifies Marguerite de Navarre as one of the "plus audacieuse" imitators of Luther's style and one of the most faithful translators of his theological emphases. These are mostly Pauline: justification by faith, *sola scriptura*, and the free working of grace.[18] Paul's insistence on the "confession of the words of the mouth" (Rom. 10.9–10) appears in the *Heptaméron* in stories that show the speaking of the confessing self in relation to and with Christ.

Marguerite stresses in the *Heptaméron* the significance of speech and story: without the ability to narrate lives, humanity is unable to confess sin, and thereby to be accorded salvation. Anecdotes and stories also proliferate in Luther's writing. In the *Heptaméron*, Marguerite, like Luther, employs an earthy and embodied vocabulary, an appeal to easily understood sentiments, and a stylistic clarity modeled on the *stylus rudus* of the Bible. *Nouvelle* #32 portrays a woman whose shaven head marks her sinful status. She is forbidden to speak and appears to be doomed to perpetual punishment for her sin. Into this seemingly hopeless scenario comes a Christ-like figure, Bernaige, sent from afar. Bernaige encourages the woman to speak and to confess to her act of adultery. When she does, her confession initiates the soteric process, compelling the husband to forgive his wife. Marguerite uses this *tableau* to illustrate a watchword of Reformed doctrine: salvation *by faith alone (sola fidei)*. She also dramatizes how a contrite heart, speaking its sorrow (the *parole*), calls to the *Parole (le Verbe)*, God, who pardons the sinner. Narrative galvanizes this theological intervention.

The *nouvelle* also illustrates the *tableau*-like mini-dramas favored in Luther's anecdotes. The story takes place in Germany, Luther's country, umbilicus of sixteenth-century evangelical theology, thus preparing the reader to accept the evangelical preoccupations of the text.[19] The book of Romans ensures that if one confesses with the words of one's mouth belief in Jesus, and believes in Jesus' resurrection, then one will be saved: the faith of the heart leads to restitution, and the confession of the mouth evokes salvation.[20] *Nouvelle* #32 offers a dramatic illustration of this important Pauline passage.

Before she is able to speak, the woman must learn that she is a theological creature, a child of God. This awareness will come through the visit of a stranger, Bernaige. Like Jesus, Bernaige is "envoyé de loin" ["sent from afar"]; he is the "légat d'un bon roi" ["the emissary of a good king"], and, like Christ, whom St. Paul calls "nostre avocat" ["our advocate"] and "nostre légat" ["our emissary"], he announces a new law, the law of love characterized by mercy. In Marguerite's *Miroir de l'âme pécheresse*, she similarly calls Christ "mon redempteur, / Qui … a restitué / Nostre heritage, et s'est constitué nostre advocat …" ("Jesus Christ, my redeemer / Who by his death has restored to us / Our inheritance, and has made himself our advocate [lawyer]").[21] Bernaige's actions exemplify *prevenient grace,* or grace that "comes before" undeserving sinners, anticipating their needs.

Bernaige arrives at a fortress closed to visitors; nonetheless, he is granted entrance. The châtelaine's appearance moves Bernaige to pity. Why does she go about with her hair shorn, dressed in black, and mute? The woman is anonymous: she has been deprived both of her identity, and of the words that she might otherwise use to introduce herself to the visitor (and to confess her sins). Each time that the woman appears, she draws a curtain, symbolizing her alienation from others, and her relegation to a death-in-life, as well as representing her sin, which separates her from those who have not sinned. She is walled in by her fault.

The *regard* ("gaze") of others tracks and traps her in this objectified, framed position. She is a *tableau*, but not (yet) one that tells a story.[22] Her husband, Bernaige, and the reader watch and assess her: "Le seigneur de Bernaige la regarda bien fort," "tant esbahy de veoir chose si estrange" ("Bernaige looked at her closely," "taken aback at such a strange spectacle"—*Hept.* 4.32.242–43; Chilton 331). At table, the husband obliges his wife to drink from the skull of the lover whom her husband has killed. Historical context and changes in religious practice may shed light on this detail: in 1523, Luther had called for communion to be available to the laity in both *species* (the cup had been withheld previously). In this light, it is interesting to note that chalices abound in the *Heptaméron*, perhaps in illustration of this important innovation. In addition, the husband's order that his wife always use the cup at every meal seems almost excessive. In an entirely different way of interpreting the presence of chalices in the *nouvelles,* it may be that they illustrate the evangelical reforming impulse to discourage the popular—and even clerical, in some cases—belief that the mass needed to be sacrificed repeatedly. Evangelicals held that the numerous masses said every day by priests were ineffectual and extraneous: Christ had died once, for all. Symbolically recalling the death of the adulterous lover by compelling his wife to drink daily from the skull/cup, the husband may parody what evangelicals deemed a pointless repetition of the Sacrifice, since the skull-chalice denies absolution. Consistent with Luther's call for communion in both kinds, the wife, a lay person, takes the cup, yet, administered thrice daily, it still has no effect.

Further, although the lover can no longer return the lady's gaze, she must stare at him all the days of her life. The skull's eyes, plugged up with silver, render literal the husband's reaction upon learning of his wife's deceit: recounting the event to Bernaige, the husband says, "l'experience *me* creva les œilz" ("what happened put out *my* eyes"—*Hept.* 4.32.243; emphasis added[23]). A pair of intersecting stares keeps the woman transfixed: her dead lover's sightless eye sockets and her husband's unrelenting judgmental stare. The reaction to her infidelity remains symbolically perpetuated. The husband expresses the parallelism between the two *regards* in a phrase that both links and opposes the two men: "Afin qu'elle voie vivant celluy qu'elle a faict son mortel ennemy par sa faulte … et ainsy elle veoit à disner et à soupper … l'ennemy vivant et l'amy mort" ("… and so that she should never forget him even when eating and drinking … so that she would have before her both the living and the dead, both him whom through her sin she had transformed into a mortal enemy and [him whose love she preferred to mine]"—*Hept.* 4.32.244; Chilton 332–33). The woman's sin constitutes the link between the two ("et tout, par son peché"—*Hept.* 4.32.244; "and all by her own sin"—Chilton 333).

When Bernaige enters the lady's chambers, he becomes the first character in the narrative to address her directly. In Marguerite's evangelical reading of the situation, she characterizes the husband as having reacted from a stance of Old Testament judgment, while Bernaige, representing dialogue and pardon, shows that mere observance of Law, unaccompanied by grace, is not sufficient for salvation. This is also a primary consideration in Luther's theological writings.[24] Luther stresses the inadequacy of legalistic observance, indicted by Jesus in the Gospels when he inveighs against the Pharisees. Like Luther, Marguerite nearly always ends her stories with reconciliation and restitution, even when great wrongs have been done. These conclusions are consistent with Christ's teaching that the greatest law of all is love. Marguerite identifies the New Testament virtue of love (*caritas*) as the supreme virtue, which caps and completes the Mosaic commandment.

A hint of love remains in the husband's affect toward his wife, despite his cruel retaliation, and Bernaige seizes on this hope. Grace and speech are the two components of the description that the husband offers, nostalgically, of his spouse:

> Bernaige avoit grande envie de parler à la dame, mais, de paour du mary, il n'osa. Le gentil homme, qui s'en apparceut, luy dist: "S'il vous plaist luy dire quelque chose, vous verrez quelle grace et parolle elle a."
>
> ("Bernaige wanted very much to talk to the lady, but dared not do so because of the husband. Realizing this, the gentleman said: 'If you would like to say something to her, you'll see how graciously she speaks.'"—*Hept*. 4.32.244; Chilton 333)

The man's association of grace with speech suggests a possible resolution to the drama. The wife's first words to Bernaige confess her adulterous act, something that her husband, by refusing to speak to her or to allow her to speak to him, had not permitted her to do.

> Bernaige luy dist à l'heure: "Madame, vostre patience est egalle au torment. Je vous tiens la plus malheureuse femme du monde." La dame, ayant la larme à l'œil, avecq une grace tant humble qu'il n'estoit possible de plus, lui dist: "Monsieur, je confesse ma faulte estre si grande, que tous les maulx, que le seigneur de ceans (lequel je ne suis digne de nommer mon mary) me sçaurait faire, ne me sont riens au prix du regret que j'ay de l'avoir offensé."
>
> ("So Bernaige said to her: 'Madame, your resignation matches your suffering. I think you are the unhappiest woman in the world.' Tears came to the woman's eyes, and she spoke with the greatest possible grace and humility: 'Monsieur, I confess that my sins are so great that all the

> suffering that is inflicted upon me by the lord of this house, whom I am not worthy to call my husband, is as nothing compared with the remorse I feel in having wronged him.'"—*Hept*. 4.32.244; Chilton 333)

Finally, she weeps, demonstrating her repentance. But nothing she says appears to touch her husband's heart.

Through Bernaige's intervention, the woman is transformed: she confesses her sins and speaks of her *pénitence* ("contrition"). Bernaige pleads her case before her husband, playing the Christ-like role of mediator by begging the husband to take pity on her. Depicting her as a "poor, virtuous" woman, Bernaige reverses the negative characteristics ascribed to her and rehabilitates her:

> Monsieur, l'amour que je vous porte, et l'honneur et privaulté que vous m'avez faicte en vostre maison, me contraingnent à vous dire qu'il me semble, veu la grande repentance de vostre pauvre femme, que vous luy debvez user de misericorde.
>
> ("Monsieur, the affection I bear you and the honours and kindness which you have shown me in your own house oblige me to say to you that as your poor wife's remorse is so deep, it is my belief that you should show some compassion towards her."—*Hept*. 4.32.244–45; Chilton 333)

The husband's language expresses a revised view of the wife. "Le gentil homme, qui avoit deliberé de ne parler jamais à sa femme, pensa longuement aux propos que luy tint le seigneur de Bernaige … et luy promist que, si elle perseveroit en ceste humilité, il en auroit quelquefois pitié" ("The gentleman, who had resolved never again to speak to his wife, thought for a long time about the things Bernaige had said to him … and promised him that if his wife continued to live in such humility, he would one day have pity on her"—*Hept*. 4.32.245; Chilton 334).

Several sorts of speech are now possible. Not only has the woman avowed her wrong-doing, but, because of her confession, her husband's position has also changed in his decision to forgive her. These changes move the narrative toward closure. Bernaige's presence, the mention of the king—who, as legal authority, represents a higher authority than that of the husband and thereby points to a metaphysical perspective—and the role of the reader as witness, construct a Christian community that hears the woman's confession.

The *nouvelle* thus begins to make the adulterous wife "into a new creation," tracing her passage from death to life. The structure of the text represents a resurrection. First, *nouvelle* #32 acts like a sepulchre: its deepest, interior point is the entombing of the woman in her chambers. Yet after Bernaige's visit, the movement reverses, with the tale opening out and returning to the point of departure (Bernaige's departure recalls his arrival, with which the story began). The king stands, as it were, on the edges of the story, like a theater director in the wings or God looking down on the world: it is the king who set everything into motion by sending Bernaige from France to Germany in the first place. Upon his arrival, Bernaige enters the formerly impenetrable castle, thereby taking a step closer to the drama about to be narrated. The lady enters, they dine, and Bernaige approaches closer to the space in which the adulterous act had transpired. Finally, he enters the lady's chambers, a claustrophobic space wherein the skeleton of the lover hangs. These bones are a form of relic: the lady is forced to live with and by "relics," rather than in the light of truth, which Bernaige—archetypal evangelical—will shed on the situation by referring to the Word of the New Testament. The lady's bedchamber is the point in the text closest to death. The lady and Bernaige together here contemplate the bones of the lover, which the husband has caused to be displayed in an armoire like a "chose précieuse" ("precious object"), as the husband ironically deems them. The bones constitute a perpetual reminder of the lady's sin. The theatrical device of curtain-pulling to reveal the skeleton[25] imitates how the lady draws a curtain each time that she appears,[26] conveying her separation from others due to her sin. The wages of the lady's sin is, as St. Paul instructs, death: she is as dead as her lover, in the eyes of her husband, and no forgiveness is possible. She is dead to life, explains Oisille, the narrator of this *nouvelle* (not surprisingly, since Oisille is usually the mouthpiece for the most evangelical perspectives in Marguerite's work):

> Je suis seure que vous ne ignorez poinct que la fin de tous noz malheurs est la mort, mays, mectant fin à nostre malheur, elle se peut nommer notre felicité et seur repos. Le malheur doncques de l'homme, c'est desirer la mort et ne la pouvoir avoir; parquoy la plus grande punicion que l'on puisse donner à ung malfaiteur n'est pas la mort, mais c'est de donner ung tourment continuel si grand, que il la faict desirer … ainsy que ung mary bailla à sa femme comme vous orez.
>
> ("I am sure that you are all aware that the end of all woes is death, but that since death puts an end to all our woes, it can be called our joy and repose. Man's greatest woe, therefore, is to desire death and not to be able to have it. Consequently, the greatest punishment that can meted out to an evil-doer is not death but continuous torture, torture severe enough to make him desire death, yet not so severe that it causes death. This is just what one husband did to his wife, as you shall now hear."—*Hept.* 4.31.241; Chilton 330)

Structurally, the woman is assimilated to the lover: she shares his place. The husband acts according to the law of retaliation: since the wife welcomed her lover into the private, nuptial space, " … la privaulté qui n'appartenoyt que à moi avoir à elle …" ("I saw him come in with the kind of familiarity to which I alone have the right"—*Hept.* 4.32.243; Chilton 332), the lover's bones remain, in the site of the transgression, perpetually implicating her by their presence.

Nonetheless, this obsessional image, and her guilt, can be erased by the Word. The narrative demonstrates the importance of the woman's confession by using varieties of texts—commentaries, witnesses, anecdotes. The husband relates the adulterous event; the woman confesses her sin and remorse; Bernaige returns to the king and recounts the story; Oisille and her *devisants* discuss and frame, or inflect, it; and Marguerite narrates it so that her readers may meditate on it. The woman's rehabilitation occurs upon the pronouncement of the Word.

After the wife confesses, the space of the text progressively opens out. Bernaige speaks to the husband elsewhere than in the woman's space, thus moving them out of the deathly *tableau*, taking a step toward freedom in Christ. Bernaige leaves the castle, and returns to the king, where all this storytelling had begun. By the end of the text, the wife and the husband are reunited. The lady, significantly, has emerged from her entombment; she is no longer seated alone in her chambers; rather, the husband "has taken her to be with him again" ("son mary … la reprint avecq soy" ; "he … took her back"—*Hept.* 4.32.244–45; Chilton 334), and they now have several children.[27] Producing progeny ("héritiers") is a man's concern, for he does not want his name to disappear.[28] However, many biblical references, among them 1 Pet. 1.5, call those who will enter into the kingdom of heaven "heirs" ("les héritiers"). The castle now opens itself to the world, welcoming guests and permitting communication.

The wife is even permitted to travel—at least in symbolic form—by way of her portrait that the king has commissioned, and which he displays as an example to others. The Latin *protrahere* means not only to paint a portrait, but also to draw something hidden out into the light (*protrahere*: "to pull toward") so as to reveal its essence.[29] In commissioning the wife's portrait, the king has made the determination that she has been cleansed from her sin; she has value as an exemplary exhibit of rehabilitation. Coupled with the woman's confession, the portrait is a sign of her restitution to her husband, to herself, and to a renewed relationship with God. She has become the "new creation" that the Gospels designate as God's "saving work."[30]

The portrait poses a positive image to the negative one of the skeleton in the closet. Marguerite insists on the woman's reinstatement by designating the painter's role as " … pour luy rapporter ceste dame au vif …" ("to bring back her living likeness"—*Hept.* 4.32.245; Chilton 334): so evocative is the rendering that the portrait seems to place her, in flesh and blood, before the reader/spectator. The painter does not cause this resurrection; rather, he records it. The portrait is the memento of this transformation, not the mechanism for it: like the function of other objects elsewhere in the *Heptaméron,* its materiality is used, then surpassed. (Indeed, materiality is used for the very purpose of being done away with.) On the literal level, the portrait will be taken to the king; on the figurative plane, the woman has been redeemed from death and restored to life through the textual technique that the portrait, its final product, places on view.

The power of the word to galvanize the saving process provides the textual motor of the *nouvelle* and of the entire *Heptaméron*: it is a salvation narrative dramatized for the reader. The role of the *nouvelles* is to provoke communication to ensure that words of confession and forgiveness will be spoken in a community of Christians such as this text seeks to discern, or to establish. In this evangelical perspective, it is no longer necessary or even desirable to confess one's sins to a priest; instead, one confides in a community of coreligionists.[31] The text becomes the theater, even perhaps a new sort of church, in which individual awareness of sin may be recounted. The narrative becomes the *tableau* that both witnesses to and enables the reorientation that places each person in right relation to God.

Framing the Textual *Tableaux*

In the *Heptaméron,* framing forms such as windows, curtains, and mirrors sketch in the outlines of a virtual stage. The clutter of stage properties in Marguerite's narrative—ribbons, treasure chests, books, maps, jewelry, and masks—constructs a material component in the text. The *devisants* also play a theatrical role: by prefacing each narrative with their introductions, they serve the "stage-setting" function of a first act; with their commentary after each *nouvelle*, they offer audience response.

Marguerite develops her *nouvelles* through the *tableaux* in them, using the theatrical technique of foreshortening to focus the anecdotes. Generally, she recounts stories fairly economically. She then emphasizes spiritual motivation, often through a strategic grouping of selected objects. The narrative highlights the otherworldly orientation by surrounding it with a commentary, or frame, making references to *fenestres*, *rideaux*, and *miroirs*.

Using the technique of the *corniche* or frame story, Marguerite not only frames her tales with the *devisants'* animated exposition and analysis, she also outlines key moments in the development of the protagonists' attitudes. For example, when a transformation or conversion is about to take place, Marguerite's characters invariably find themselves "on stage"; they may be framed within the liminal space of a window, evocative of both inside and outside; outlined by or hidden behind bed curtains; or reflected in a looking glass. Through these delimiting forms, the text encourages the reader to penetrate through the frame to the drama working itself out within the individual. The internal self is portrayed and discussed through and within these "framing spaces." Such scrutiny conveys the evangelical emphasis on the "inner man," the disposition of the heart, as well as with their concern over what they viewed as the excessive value placed on "externals" such as ritualized worship.

The stage properties of late medieval miracle and mystery plays is similar to the material substance of Marguerite's *tableaux*. Both medieval mystery plays and Marguerite's minidramas place the mystery, not the material artifacts, at the forefront of the audience's attention. However, Marguerite's Lutheran lens eventually causes the visual awareness of materiality to fade from front and center: the real *mise-en-scène* is the dialogued encounter that spotlights the verbal transmission of spiritual matters; the real event is not action but Word. The *Heptaméron* frequently portrays this relocation of emphasis from terrestrial realm to metaphysical sphere: in one instance, monks forsake their duties to hide behind a hedge—a sort of frame, the edge of the storytellers' "stage"—to listen as an avid audience. Their monastic duties must be less uplifting than the theologically informed conversation of lay men and women! (This example, further, illustrates the Lutheran doctrine of the "priesthood of all believers," with no special privilege given to clergy.)

> Parlamente … et, avecq les autres, entra dedans l'eglise, où ils trouverent vespres très bien sonnées, mais ilz n'y trouverent pas ung religieux pour les dire, pource qu'ilz avoient entendu que dedans le pré s'assembloit ceste compaignye pour y dire les plus plaisantes choses qu'il estoit possible; et, comme ceulx qui aymoient mieulx leurs plaisirs que les oraisons, s'estoient allez cacher dedans une fosse, le ventre contre terre, derrière une haye fort espesse. Et là avoient si bien escouté les beaulx comptes, qu'ilz n'avaient poinct oy sonner la cloche de leur monastere.
>
> ("Parlamente … went into the church. They found that although the bell had been ringing heartily for vespers, not a single monk had yet appeared. The fact was that they had heard that the ladies and gentlemen were meeting together

> in the meadow to recount all manner of amusing tales and, preferring their pleasures to their prayers, they had been hiding in a ditch behind a thick hedge, flat on their bellies, so that they could overhear. So attentively had they been listening, they had not even heard their own monastery bell ringing."—*Hept.* 2.20.156; Chilton 234)

In this episode, what matters is the audition of words, not unavailing actions (such as saying mass or lighting candles). Since the monks, concentrating solely on these edifying tales based on Scripture, have neglected their monastic tasks (which, in the evangelical view, are vain, repetitive, and unavailing works that cannot produce righteousness), it is possible that they have begun to think like evangelicals: their hearts have turned away from the world, warmed by the inner working of the Holy Spirit. The monastic community begins to enter through the frame of the storytelling, to be incorporated into the community of Christians, the small group of *devisants* who spend their time talking about life as illuminated through biblical truths.

Marguerite's *fenestres* function much like the *trompe-l'œil* window frames that Netherlandish genre painters painted around their portraits. These are not real boundaries, as the portraits hang in actual wooden frames; instead, the painted frames act as narrative indicators: they show how and where to interpret the image that they delineate. Contemporary frames demonstrate this "textual" trend in the arts. "Typically, panels were provided with finely-crafted frames; the framing devices could be box-like, with a separate covering panel, or panels, sometimes in the form of wings. Frames could carry large explanatory inscriptions,"[32] emphasizing the conjunction of frame (commentator) and inscription (commentary). In such paintings, framing devices may also be used to "stress narrative purpose."[33] Experimentation with different framing strategies accompanies this interest in narrative emphasis derived from Scripture. "Artists such as Lucas van Leyden sought to give a new, sometimes 'invented,' view of the religious narrative, [and] also framed their works in ways that broke out of the traditional rectangular format."[34] The framing technique offers a paradigm for interpretation of the narrative: it encloses a self-reflective text that also encourages the viewer to look beneath and beyond appearances—just as the terrestrial realm is represented, in Marguerite's *nouvelles*, but then refocuses itself to lead toward a metaphysical perspective.[35] To intensify the *trompe-l'œil* effect and compel the viewer to recognize the contrast between verisimilitude and reality, artists often include whimsical, realistic-appearing details such as, for example, a life-sized fly perched on a window sill. Marguerite's text works that way, too: she requires that her reader discern which is "more real": the material world, or the metaphysical depth that ensues from penetrating through the frame of materiality.[36]

The story of Amadour and Floride consists of several theatrical *tableaux*[37] framed by windows. The window frames both an inside and an outside, both a physical landscape and a psychological and spiritual perspective. Floride and Amadour are separated by age, station in life, and marital status. Amadour's passion for Floride becomes a obsession, and although war and politics often constrain him to leave Floride's side, he always returns. Although attracted to him, Floride cannot quite believe his protestations that he seeks no physical consummation of his love for her. An approach-avoidance textual geography choreographs their desire: she sees him "de bien loing"; he experiences "esloignement"; she is aware of the "longueur de l'absence"; he returns to seek her "en tous les lieux" as her eyes strain to perceive him "en tous les lieux où elle le voioit" (*Hept.* 1.10.60–61). This dance of desire culminates in a face-to-face encounter of the two protagonists through the window frame. Tension mounts over the moment when the sill will be crossed.

Two key scenes take place within a frame. These are both moments of transformation that demonstrate the softening of Floride's attitude, an imminent change in her relationship with Amadour. The first time that Amadour confesses his passion to Floride, he is leaning against a window where they had been chatting, as though verging onto the open space that the window overlooks—the imaginative space in which love between him and her might actually in some way be possible.

> … ung jour, parlant à Floride, appuyé sur une fenestre, luy tint tel propos … "Vous me promectrez doncques, dist Amadour, que vous ne serez non seullement marrye des propos que je vous veulx dire, mais estonnée jusques à temps

> que vous entendiez la fin? … Je ne pretends, pour la fin et recompense de mon service, que une chose: c'est que vous me voulliez estre maistresse si loyalle que jamais vous ne m'esloigniez de vostre bonne grace."
>
> ("one day, as he leaned against the window where they had been chatting: 'Tell me, [my Lady], … will you promise that you will not be angry at what I am going to say, but also, if you are shocked, that you will not say anything until I have finished? … I ask only that you might be my true and faithful Lady, so true, so faithful, that you will never cast me from your good grace.'"—*Hept.* 1.10.62–63; Chilton 130–31)

The phrase "jamais vous ne m'esloigniez" expresses Amadour's wish that not only might the actual distance between the two be bridged, but also that a sort of spiritual conjunction might occur so that they would no longer be physically or emotionally "esloig[nés]" from each other.[38]

Floride's face, as displayed by the reference to the window that focuses attention on the lovers' interaction, reflects an intense transformation. Her face colors and her expression changes: "oyant ung propos non accoustumé, commencea à changer de couleur et baisser les œils comme femme estonnée" ("the young lady Floride changed colour at this speech, the like of which she had never heard before. Then she lowered her gaze … her modesty shocked"—*Hept.* 1.10.64; Chilton 131). The word *comme* ("like") translates the staged quality of the *tableau*. She is not really astounded; she was already aware of Amadour's feelings, but now chooses to act modest, following his stage directions (" … que vous serez estonnée"). Reality, as is often the case in the *Heptaméron*, lies beneath and beyond the appearance, and Floride's willingness to play the role he has set for her attests to their intimacy.

After this first "window scene," Floride changes her conduct: "en tous autres lieux, commencea à ne le chercher pas, comme elle avoit accoustumé … cest esloignement …" ("she began not to seek Amadour's company at all in the way she had in the past … she was keeping away from him"—*Hept.* 1.10.65; Chilton 131). Again, a window frames their second encounter. Amadour has been away for a long time, fighting the Moors, and has only communicated with Floride by letter. Her love for him and trust in him have grown, and she misses him greatly. Hearing of his impending return, she runs to the window to watch for him. In such *tableaux*, discrete details and small shifts of emphasis add important nuances, and here, because the windows frame two discussions, the reader is invited to compare variations in treatment. In the first discussion, Amadour's body leaned against the window, opening up a space for imagination and establishing a new proximity to Floride. In the second episode, Floride waits alone at the window. When she leans out joyfully to call to Amadour, she *chooses* him symbolically: her body breaks out of its physical reserve, crossing over the line of self-restraint.

> Floride ... se tint à une fenestre, pour le veoir venir de loing. Et, si tost qu'elle l'advisa, descendit par ung escallier tant obscur que nul ne pouvoit congnoistre si elle changeoit de couleur; et ainsy, ambrassant Amadour, le mena en sa chambre.
>
> ("Floride ... stood at a window to watch his arrival from afar. Immediately he came into sight she went down by way of a staircase, which was dark enough to prevent anybody seeing whether her cheek changed colour. She embraced Amadour, took him to her room."—*Hept.* 1.10.70; Chilton, 138–39)

The transformation complete, Floride now no longer acts a part. Rather, she has so thoroughly become her "character" that there is no hiding her emotions except by taking a shadowy back stairway. The shadows also remind us that Floride and Amadour are adulterers. Her moral canvas is now marked by *chiaroscuro*, as illicit passion darkens her moral purity.

The *tableaux* encapsulate the concerns of the tales, propel the drama forward, and generally deepen the text's ethical dimension. Other frames constructed by objects draw attention to the *Heptaméron*'s exposition of moral and spiritual matters. Open bed-curtains frame a lady awaiting a lover, while drawn draperies conceal an adulterous act. Both are frames for *tableaux*, focusing the protagonists'—and the reader's—attention either on what is enclosed within them, or on what goes on behind them. Sometimes the reader views an action through open curtains, then sees the curtains drawn, hiding the secret to which the reader is already privy at the heart of the text, and providing the reader (outside the narrative, looking in) with a privileged knowledge unknown to another character within the story. The selective inclusion of the reader has an effect similar to the role of theatrical "asides."

Similarly, mirrors not only frame a space for the reader's focus, they are also frames-within-a-frame, in which the reader views the protagonist through the lens of the latter's subjectivity. The protagonist contemplates her reflection, and this acting-out of self-viewing, represents humanity's lack of self-knowledge or distorted discernment. For this reason, mirrors have a spiritually negative valence in Marguerite's *nouvelles*. Because mirrors reveal not only physical marks, but also, in the *nouvelles*, can reveal spiritual deficiencies, they offer an image approximate to the "examination of conscience" that, further developed by evangelical and, later, by Reformed writers of meditations, starts from the standpoint of sin and scrutinizes the self. Outward appearance may be misleading, for sinfulness may be reflected back to the subject through the mirror of self-examination.[39] This focus on self is paradoxical, since self-absorption precludes focus on God.

Marguerite uses the mirror to reveal earthly beauty distorted—or, rather, accurately represented—as spiritual hideousness. In one of several tales of attempted rape, framing devices, including bed-curtains and mirrors, construct a *tableau* in which a young man, besotted by a woman, pays court to her, but, his suit not advancing, loses patience and decides to take her by force. He causes a trapdoor to be installed in her bedroom and hides it beneath tapestries so that the lady is unaware of its existence. Preparing for his amorous adventure, the man perfumes and robes himself luxuriously, and it seems to him, "en soy mirant, qu'il n'y avoit dame en ce monde qui sceut refuser sa beaulté et bonne grace" ("as he admired himself in the mirror, he was absolutely convinced that there was not a woman in the world who could possibly resist such a handsome and elegant sight"—*Hept.* 1.4.29; Chilton 91). The consultation with his looking glass is a framing strategy showing his delusional state and refusal to admit his sinfulness. The mirror demonstrates his tendency to treat himself as a surface or an object: with narcissistic complacency, his mirrored image only reflects his own uncritical arrogance back to himself. Similarly, he admires the woman's beauty but does injury to her being. With the failure of his endeavor already prefigured by his solipsistic tête-à-tête, the man climbs through the trapdoor. The woman, stronger and more repulsed than he would have thought possible, scratches him with her fingernails as she fights him off. Commentators have shown that the woman is actually Marguerite herself, who now embeds herself within her own *nouvelle* in a mirror-like way, reflecting herself back out of the text.

As in other *nouvelles*, the text frames the transformation: defeated and bloodied, the man returns to his mirror, where he views himself in a physically unattractive light that obliges him finally to see his moral degeneracy, as well:

> Il trouva son mirouer et sa chandelle sur sa table; et, regardant son visaige tout sanglant d'esgratineures et morsures qu'elle luy avoit faictes, dont le sang sailloit sur sa belle chemise, qui estoit plus sanglante que dorée …
>
> ("He picked up his mirror from the table and examined himself in the candlelight. His face was streaming with blood from the bites and scratches she had inflicted. His beautiful embroidered nightshirt had more streaks of blood than it had gold thread."—*Hept.* 1.4.30; Chilton 92)

The possessive pronouns ("*son* miroir"; "*sa* chandelle"; "*sa* table"; "*son* visage"; emphasis added) underscore that he possesses mere material objects, but not the woman, object of his desire. The mirror and candle are stage props in an emblem illustrating vanity. Placed on the table in anticipation of his triumphant return, they instead witness to his failure and, then, to his transformation: his face now truly reflects his inner reality; it is the mirror of his soul. Incised with scratches, he must now hide himself from others in the castle so that they will not decipher his culpability: "Et, au matin, voiant son visaige si deschiré, feit semblant d'estre fort mallade et de ne povoir veoir la lumiere, jusques ad ce que la compaignye feust hors de sa maison" ("in the morning, he looked at himself again in the mirror, and seeing that his face was lacerated all over, he took to his bed, pretending that he was desperately ill and could not go out into the light. There he remained until his visitors had gone home"—*Hept.* 1.4.31; Chilton 93). His once-handsome face, encircled by the frame of the mirror, is now trapped within a frame of his own fashioning. The phrase "ne povoir veoir la lumiere,"[40] casts him into the darkness of debased morals and sinfulness.

"Telling the Story"

Marguerite's *nouvelles* are often parable-like in their content, style, and interpretation: in both sorts of story, appearance and inner reality are nearly always contradictory. The reader must search for the true meaning of an ostensibly transparent, but actually opaque, text. Through *tableaux,* Marguerite illustrates scriptural truths in a way that evangelicals will understand and deepen. Similarly, early sixteenth-century Lutheran theater often dramatized parables through the use of everyday anecdotes and *tableaux.*[41] Parables are illustrated usually with examples from ordinary existence; this creates an illusion of simplicity, when in fact they are usually complex and often ironic. Parables propose a metaphysical truth that reverses the worldly order of things.

An unusual decorative arts object from 1523 illustrates how Marguerite's narrative, through strategically placed objects, redirects focus on self to focus on God. This object also acts in a parable-like way, juxtaposing appearance and essence to show the contradiction between the two. The *Recueil Montmer* is an album composed of fifty-one portraits, several of François Ier's mistresses, all but five of which feature identifying labels. Glued-on paper flaps cover the inscriptions scribbled on the portraits' surface, indicating that the *Recueil* may have been used as a sort of sixteenth-century guessing game.[42] The collection thus replicates the search for identity played out in a social format (analogous, in the *Heptaméron*, to the interplay between the characters in the *tableaux*, and the *devisants*' assessment of their actions). As with the *Heptaméron,* we peruse the portrait gallery of characters, then attempt to establish their psychological and spiritual parameters. Like the pasted flaps over the painted portraits, some of the *nouvelles*' characters are hidden from themselves, alienated from God. But although they may hide and deceive, the narrative, like the inscriptions on the paper faces hidden by the flaps, will witness to their true selves and "tell the story" of their deeper identity, which, in the *Heptaméron,* is evangelical—an identity found, revised, or regained in Jesus.

Chapter Two

Evangelical Dimensions in Decorative Arts

Emblems, Earthly Objects, and the Economy of Transcendence

> Command those who are rich in the present age not to be haughty, nor to trust in uncertain riches but in the living God, who gives us richly all things to enjoy.
>
> 1 Tim. 6.17–18

Marguerite develops a hybrid narrative form in the *Heptaméron* by incorporating representations of material culture. Although Scripture labels such objects untrustworthy and illusory, earthly treasures, in the form of art objects and emblems, are very much in evidence in the *nouvelles*. However, this focus on things produces a very un-material effect, and facilitates a theological statement. Working with the Lutheran understanding of the hidden worth of materiality as a sign of what surpasses it, Marguerite uses material objects as markers of metaphysical meaning.

In his 1519 treatise *The Blessed Sacrament of the Holy and True Body of Christ*, Martin Luther stated that

> in the sacraments we see nothing wonderful—just ordinary water, bread and wine, and the words of a preacher. There is nothing spectacular about that. But we must learn to *discover what a glorious majesty lies hidden beneath these despised things*. It is precisely the same with Christ in the incarnation. We see a frail, weak and mortal human being—yet he is nothing other than the majesty of God himself. In precisely the same way, God himself speaks to us and deals with us in these ordinary and despised materials.[1]

Luther's point concerns the paradoxical lack of markers here, rather than the presence of markers in material things: faith requires overlooking a lack of evidence. However, material markers do exist that, while lacking full presence, nonetheless point to complete truth elsewhere. These things can be valuable, but must be treated with caution. Marguerite imitates Luther's use in sermons and other texts of ordinary objects, developing an evangelical approach to writing about these objects, a style with which other evangelical and Protestant writers of the period demonstrate affinities. Evangelical writers distinguish themselves by their drive to move beyond the things on which they first build their texts when portraying the terrestrial realm. Further, evangelical writers use image as icon. Such iconic images act like arrows: they pass through the medium to attain the metaphysical message behind it.

One laboratory for examining some aspects of this new interdisciplinary evangelical idiom is that of emblematic texts. Evangelicals find emblems useful because no single component of an emblem is sufficient by itself; further, the totality must be deciphered, encouraging the reader to look elsewhere for meaning.[2] In the *Heptaméron,* Marguerite de Navarre deploys a number of techniques and displays certain attitudes that are akin to emblematic modes of writing, reading, and thinking. A similarity exists between the emblematic mode of reading and Marguerite's hope to lead readers to spiritual awareness, paradoxically, through the telling of worldly tales. Although the material objects used in her narrative may differ from objects used in emblem books, which are primarily nonnarrative, the manner in which the objects are treated in both is much alike. Evangelicals are skeptical about the truth-value of images. Emblem writers are similarly wary of placing too much emphasis on images without accompanying text. (Although emblems want to be hieroglyphs, this goal is nostalgic and never can be realized fully. The theological explanation for this gap between signifier and signified is that, at the time of the Fall, meaning was wrenched away from materiality. Consequently, no image or thing may entirely or exactly encapsulate significance.) In emblem books, this tension plays itself out through the dialogue among motto, device, and image. This dialogue produces what might be called a fourth emblematic dimension—the interpretive mode used in reading the emblem—

or what Daniel Russell has called the "emblematic process."[3] While the interpretation of an emblem does not influence its construction, it does influence its reception, similar to the conversion process at which evangelical narratives aim. Motto (which can be equated with the *nouvelles*' thesis), image (similar to the objects used in the *nouvelles*), and *devise* (acting like the *nouvelles*' commentary or frame) produce a fourth component that both equals the sum of their parts and surpasses them: the reader's reception.

A secondary meaning of *devise* is a "dividing line," something that limits or sets one thing or perspective off against another.[4] In the *Heptaméron*, materiality contrasts with, but also culminates in, metaphysics. This movement tends in the direction of narrative development rather than of exclusively visual display. The evangelical preference for "historiated" images—paintings framed with textual commentary or Bible verses, or illustrations of biblical narratives made up of textual images meant to be read and not merely viewed—is also similar to the emblematic technique of composition.[5] Marguerite's *Heptaméron,* while not itself an emblem book, thus, at times, resembles emblematic constructions, because it contains multiple, potentially independent yet inter-related, components.[6] Her *nouvelles* contain images, worldly goods produced by craftsmen such as furniture or tapestries, and manifestations of self-image such as masks, disguises, portraits, or mirrors. Marguerite uses these images to render her narrative concrete and literal. For instance, she often develops devices through wordplay. The *devisants* (*devis*-ants) initiate the interpretation of the text, requiring the reader to weigh the significance of its different components, visual and narrative, material and metaphysical. These are characters who *devise[nt]* or discuss, setting in motion (appropriately, given their name, which is formed on a present participle: *-ants*) a series of complex representations called *devis,*[7] which are both images (as in a standard *devis*) as well as *discussions about* those images. The frame constituted by the presence of the *devisants* offers critical commentary. Both inside and outside of the story itself, this frame does to the *nouvelle* what an emblem requires the reader/viewer to do: accept or reject the rendition of reality offered. The emblem-like aspect of the *Heptaméron* may be called evangelical in effect when, as is frequently the case, the *devisants* provoke a strong reaction that may also cause a change in the reader. Similarly, emblematic rhetoric frequently "breaks the frame" to appeal directly to the reader.

Evangelical writers of emblem-like texts differ from their Catholic counterparts in a more pronounced reluctance to ascribe inherent value to things.[8] Generally, rather than treat objects symbolically or allegorically, Marguerite uses objects to evoke possible sets of human relationships and reactions. Her compositions are as a result interactive and dynamic, because they are conversational compositions. Her approach may reflect the influence of the Lutheran emphasis on "priesthood of all believers,"[9] which encourages the literate lay person to interpret Scripture for himself without intermediary or direction from other authority. The frequent use of the second-person-singular address (*tutoyer*) in emblem books, also a characteristic of the exchanges of opinion among the *devisants* in the *nouvelles,* calls for a response from a "reader" rather than passive acceptance by a "viewer." In addition, Marguerite includes herself in several of her stories as a witness or participant, spoken of in the third-person singular, as though to authenticate the narrated experience, as well as to model how a reader might respond to the story.[10]

Just as the *devisants'* dialogue opens up possibilities for understanding the narrative, evangelical emblem-like texts comment on the possibilities for relationship between object and text. The evangelical text pointedly stands on the very foundation that it seeks to prove inadequate, that of material or sensory perception. This awareness becomes increasingly problematic—so much so that later Protestant emblem books often dispense with representational images entirely, using geometric figures instead (as in Beza's later work *Icones, les vrais pourtraicts des hommes illustres*). In the *Heptaméron*, objects do not play a decorative role or fulfill an exclusively aesthetic function: rather, they are punctuation points in a narrative trend toward metaphysical *telos*. For instance, in *nouvelle* #2, the curtains and windows, used as theater-like props, construct a material witness that reaches toward a metaphysical resolution. In this story of a rape, the curtains adorning the victim's bed serve several purposes: they focus the reader on the event; they conceal the woman from her aggressor (by simultaneously rendering her both protected and more vulnerable); they frame the act of violence; and they foreshadow a second frame: that of the window from which a witness to the rape cries out to the village.

In *nouvelle* #8, a man cuckolds himself unknowingly with his own wife, in the dark taking her to be the maid after whom he lusts. Then, sending his friend in to his wife, he doubly cuckolds himself. When the friend displays the wedding ring that he has taken from the man's wife, the husband realizes his mistake. The cuckoldry is interpreted in the light of contemporary evangelical redefinition of the wedding ring. For evangelicals, the ring no longer merely signified sanctioned sexual union; it was instead a sign epitomizing the Protestant ideal of companionate marriage,[11] a deeply intentional relationship between man and wife as Christians. Surpassing ritual, and meaning more than procreation or cohabitation, companionate marriage joined two individuals who committed to a union that would give witness to Christ's power in their lives. Marguerite shows the importance of the ring and its spiritual significance by miming its presence through the story: "*O* le plus meschant de tous les hommes! *O* le cuydez avoir *o*sté? … *O* malheureux …" ("Oh! You're the most dreadful man I ever met! Who do you think you got it from? … You miserable man … Oh no!"—*Hept.* 1.8.46; emphasis added; Chilton 110).[12] The *O* of this statement mimes the *O* of the ring, and signals the violation of the relationship represented by the ring. It also illustrates the emptiness of materialism: a ring that adorns no finger encircles a void. Removed from relationship, the ring is devoid of significance; it is ornament without substance. While earthly love should be safeguarded, what matters most, Marguerite tells us, is the spiritual resolution of terrestrial plight by the undoing of things: "car, si la chose sur quoy nous la fondons default, nostre amour s'envolle hors de nous" ("for, if the whole foundation on which our love is based should collapse, then love will fly from us and there will be no love left in us"—*Hept.* 1.8.48; Chilton 113).

Marguerite also shares with emblem writers the use of images possessing symbolic value, the meaning of which the accompanying textual or emblematic components alter or complicate. In *nouvelle* #4, as we have seen, a mirror—like candles and skulls, which are *vanitas* objects in emblematic literature[13]—becomes both the medium for distorted self-perception (the man's pride in his appearance) as well as for the revelation of his inner reality (he later scrutinizes in the glass the scratches marking his face after the woman has successfully repulsed him). Two-sided mirror-portraits were fashionable in the sixteenth century; one side is a mirror, while the other is painted with a miniature likeness of the possessor, inviting comparison between reality and semblance.[14] The *Heptaméron* acts like the mirror-portrait artifact to offer narrative semblance coupled with the psychological awareness, and theological insight, of a person's true identity in Christ. The mirror-portrait, and the *Heptaméron*, thus indict the discrepancy between appearance and being.

Evangelical Emblematics: Georgette de Montenay and Claude Paradin

The Reformed emblem writer Georgette de Montenay's emblem book,[15] although later than Marguerite's text, adapts and nuances the evangelical emblematic paradigm. Montenay's *Emblesmes ou devises Chrestiennes*[16] (1571) identifies itself as "chrestien" (*Emblesmes* i) in the peculiar way in which evangelicals had employed the term when presenting Christian moral precepts or spiritual instruction. In keeping with the practical, daily-life focus of evangelicals and, later, Huguenots, Montenay wants her emblem collection to be useful ("utile"—*Emblesmes* a2); she composes a grouping of "emblèmes … Que toutesfois pourront accommoder / A leurs maisons, aux meubles s'en aider" ("emblems … which can be used / In their houses, or as aids in furnishings"—*Emblesmes* a4).[17] Crafting her emblem collection pragmatically, as a proselytizing tool, Montenay resembles[18] Marguerite in her directive treatment of objects: like the function of Marguerite's frame narratives, Montenay provides explicit guidance on how to interpret objects in her text. Objects are put to work in service of a larger purpose. It is also significant that Montenay, as the first woman writer of emblems, chooses to write in French, as does

Marguerite in her *nouvelles*. The use of the vernacular ensured the efficacious communication and reception of the evangelical message. (Indeed, Marguerite herself never used Latin in any of her writing, not even in her religious plays.) The fact that in the *Heptaméron* Oisille dispenses with the monks' reading of the offices, and reads the Scripture for each Day in French, is consistent with Marguerite (and Montenay's) decision.

Thematic resemblances also exist. Montenay, like Marguerite, is interested in the notion of the believer's itinerary through the world and journey to God. Several of her emblems feature landscape, geographical information, and the figure of a pilgrim with a staff. The sources of her anecdotes are also evangelical: like Rabelais, Luther, and Marguerite, Montenay often mentions fables, referring, for instance, to "Aesope" and his tale of the cunning crow ("la Corneille [qui] a en soy … finesse …" (*emblesme* #16). Like her precursors, she summarizes Gospel parables, such as the apocalyptic tale of the fig tree in *emblesme* #97; in this way, she conforms to the evangelical understanding of parable as an instructive story cloaked in a memorable anecdote or a word-picture. Montenay frequently cites the Gospel ("l'Evangile"), as in *emblesme* #43, which illustrates the doctrine of Election, while *emblesme* #69 discusses the doctrine of Justification by Faith and *emblesme* #81 shows that salvation comes only through Christ: "Christ, qui seul nous regenere, / Reforme, & et fait que sommes bonne odeur … " ("Christ who alone regenerates, reforms and … makes us into a beautiful fragrance for the Lord").

Her treatment of objects is similar to the evangelical distrust of them. Montenay quotes St. Paul in *emblesme* #50, denying any inherent value in earthly treasures when she shows the world as a bubble filled with worldly objects in *emblesme* #63: "Sage est celluy qui renonce & laisse / Le monde & soy, pour estre riche en Christ" ("He who renounces the world and himself to be rich in Christ is a wise man"). *Emblesme* #71 reiterates this theme: "Sainct Paul le dit: l'avaricieux / Du ciel ne peut voir l'entree propice: / Car ses thresors ont aveuglé ses yeux" ("Saint Paul tells us that the greedy man / cannot see the entrance to heaven / For his treasures have blinded him"). Many of the objects that she employs are the same as those used in the *Heptaméron*: for instance, she mentions "miroir" (*emblesmes* #s 17, 26, 31, 44, 75) and "pourtraict" and "peincture" (*emblesmes* #s 22, 25; and *emblesme* #37).

Claude Paradin's emblem collection also manifests similarities with evangelical emblematics in his treatment of objects. Paradin published his *Devises héroïques* in 1551 at the press of the evangelical printer Jean de Tournes, who also published an Old and New Testament in an emblem-like format. Claude Paradin, Jean de Tournes, and the Reformed artists and engravers Bernard Salomon and Etienne Delaune participated in decorative arts activity intended to illustrate Scripture. In addition, Paradin and Salomon worked with Rosso Fiorentino at Fontainebleau. Salomon, called "le petit Bernard," was active in the 1540s–1550s in Lyons, and he worked with Etienne Delaune on the *Abecedario* of Mariette. When Jean de Tournes published *La Saincte Bible*, Salomon did the engravings for it; these were later reused in a 1557 Geneva Bible. Salomon's biblical engravings were used as patterns for decorative arts projects such as the mural paintings in the Château de Lude, plates from Pierre Courtey's workshop, and ornamentation on furniture. Sixteenth-century biblical designs were among the first pattern books in Germany in the early sixteenth century. Bernard Salomon and Jean de Tournes's biblical woodcuts, published in 1553, were imitated and reproduced throughout Europe.[19]

Paradin was artistically affiliated with these men as well as sympathetic to their theological perspective. Further, like Luther, Marguerite, and Rabelais, Paradin often used evangelical terminology such as "Jhesuchrist, nostre sauveur & redempcion"[20] ("Christ, our savior and redemption") and "nostre Redempteur"[21] ("our Redeemer"). Like Marguerite, Paradin employed objects derived from daily life in the visual component of his *devis*. He also designed "patterns," decorative arts ornamental schemes meant to be applied to furniture and other everyday objects.

Paradin communicated his theology through signs, moving in, through, and beyond materiality in an *iconic* movement, as did Marguerite:

> le cueur de l'homme, qui n'a nul sentiment d'amour aux choses invisibles, ne viendra jamais à l'amour de Dieu par

> la semence de sa parolle, car la terre de son cueur est sterile, [mais] … par les choses visibles, on est tiré à l'amour des invisibles.
>
> ("Man's heart, which has no special love for invisible things, will never come to the love of God by the seed of His Word, for the soil of man's heart is sterile, [but] … *by visible things*, one is drawn to the love of invisible things."—emphasis added)[22]

Visible things representing invisible ideas enable the envisioning of abstract concepts, but do not in and of themselves contain those concepts.

> … [ce sont des] sublimes esprits, les Ombres ou Idees de vertu: ont tant fait s'aydans de cette Peinture, que ja soit que icelles Idees fussent passageres, & merveilleusement mobiles: ce neanmoins les y ont si bien retenues & arrestees, que perpetuellement en ont eu l'heureuse … connaissance.
>
> ("… [these are] sublime spirits, shadows or ideas of virtue: [artists] have been able to do so much by means of such painting, that although these ideas may be fleeting and marvelously mobile, nonetheless [they] have been able to seize [these images] and stabilize them so that fortunate [readers] have perpetual knowledge of them.")[23]

The outward object, physical sign, is translated to the reader's understanding and dwells in him internally as an understanding no longer dependent on external image.

Things used for a spiritual purpose are subsequently undone. For instance, in Paradin's emblem on mercy, the strictures of the law ("ce pesant Ioug legal … ce Ioug servile;" "this weighty yoke … this servile yoke")[24] from which Christ's preaching of Gospel love liberates humanity, are with the image of a shattered yoke. The object has imparted its lesson, and is no longer necessary—indeed, it no longer functions.

Evangelicals transform daily-life objects into statements about spiritual identity. Albrecht Dürer's anamorphotic pen-and-ink studies of pillows offer a later but similar treatment of objects (see fig. 3). At first glance, the pillows appear ordinary, but, examined closely, the pillows contain human profiles. Just as fallen matter retains the impress of its Creator (and, for that reason, can be used by evangelical narrative to point back to

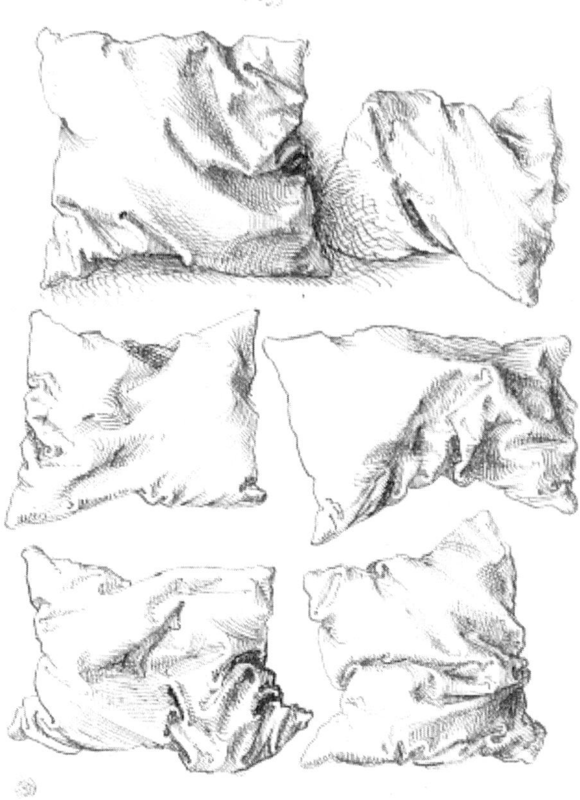

Fig. 3. Albrecht Dürer, *Six Pillows.* 1493. Metropolitan Museum of Art, New York City. Anamorphotic visages peer out of the folds formed in a series of pillows. Dürer, like other Protestant artists of his time, was fascinated by faces, and by the problematics of portraiture. Here, one thing turns out to contain the semblance of another, suggesting that the lineaments of the human face may be as accidental and whimsical as the features discernible in the pillows. Used with permission of The Metropolitan Museum of Art, Robert Lehman Collection, 1975 (1975.1.862).

God), so Dürer's pillows retain an imprint of the heads that rested on them; the material substance of the pillows evokes the existence of the human subjects. In this way, matter points beyond itself and takes on a new significance.

Daily-life objects and decorative art creations have many practical applications, but in evangelical emblematics the most important purpose of objects is to designate their own ultimate extraneousness, when the material world will be dissolved in an eschatological perspective. Such a material metaphorical bridge undoes itself in Paradin's emblem on Elijah, in which the chariot of fire linking heaven and earth self-consumes, demonstrating that objects properly point to a higher reality; they are not self-sufficient or an end in themselves. Elements of earthly experience, Marguerite and Paradin both show, can be used to direct the viewer/reader toward the celestial realm. For instance, in the *Devises héroïques*, Paradin includes Marguerite de Navarre's own *devis*, a *fleur de soucy* turned toward the sun. The sun, in the upper left of the image, breaks through clouds to send rays directly down on the flower. The design creates a link between earth and heaven. Also like Marguerite, Paradin uses objects as signposts, mapping a route out of the world: "à ce que [les] tenans & suyvans tousiours, nous venions à nous tirer hors des dangereuses fourvoyemens des formidables destroits mondeins" ("so that keeping [to them] and always following [them], we may extricate ourselves from the dangerous detours of terrible worldly straits").[25]

Designing Devices

While Marguerite includes *devises*, she often shows distrust of such representations. Devices were used for worldly self-presentation; one represented oneself to others through objects that evoked aspects of character or lifestyle. This self-presentation often says more about individual ego than anything else. Such vanity is problematic for evangelicals. Further, the changeable nature of objects is one that both evangelicals and emblematists acknowledged even as they relied on stock images to convey established meanings.

The emblematic goal is to create equivalence between word and thing, emulating biblical "plain style," which was considered to render meaning exactly. However, the realities of emblem production themselves made such cohesion an ideal rather than a reality: any object used in an emblem might be reinserted into another emblem, producing an entirely different significance. This interchangeability exacerbated the evangelical concern over the unreliability of objects as signifiers. Evangelical emblematists realized that objects could be interpreted variously, depending on context, circumstance or reception. Too many options leave more room for bad choice; too much emphasis on things deflects from the proper spiritual orientation. The emblematist has been described as "nearly a pure *bricoleur*," while the reader of emblem books is viewed as "not yet independent, but no longer passive; he is active in finding and appropriating the point of view that gives access to a meaning."[26] To guide the reader, Marguerite and other evangelicals always juxtaposed objects with the Word in a dialectic relationship, compelling a critical interrogation of the image or picture constructed, and thereby encouraging a specific interpretation. Evangelical theology, while urging the individual to read and reflect on Scripture for himself, nonetheless expected that a standard meaning would result.[27]

Many evangelicals questioned just how much trust could be invested in things. Marguerite, like other evangelicals, often uses similes when describing objects. The simile shows the instability of that thing: its meaning in any given situation can only be apprehended through comparison to another object.[28] Marguerite also employs *enumeratio,* a list or collection, to underscore the inadequacy of worldly things despite their apparent plenitude. In *nouvelle* #15, she compiles a long list of possessions—mirrors, books, a table, a sword, a cape, furred slippers, a coat, a crucifix, money, a letter, a diamond, and a ring—to underscore the contrast between a rich woman and the poor man who courts her, weds her, and wastes all her wealth ("il jouyst de son bien …"; "he drew on her wealth for his own pleasures" —*Hept.* 2.15.116; Chilton 189). The woman's fortune was the foundation for her identity and also ensured her future—but both have now vanished.

Another example of concern over excessive emphasis on things is the tale of the man who worships his mistress's glove. This story shows a disassociation of object from subject. The glove is construed as a substitute, or partially fetishized representation, of the woman, who has been deprived of her personhood and is treated like an object. Glovemakers lavished decoration on their wares in the early modern period. The *nouvelle*'s description of the glove shows an eye for fine detail that seems to give more importance to the embroidery than to the glove itself. Similarly, surface and ornament are in relationship in Marguerite's texts, and may complement or contradict each other, depending on the direction that the story takes.

The glove and its decoration offer a case study of the similarities between Marguerite's text and evangelical emblematic compositions. Gloves are decorative arts objects to the sixteenth-century viewer, not merely apparel. Emblems, paintings, and engravings all frequently contain gloves.[29] For example, in Dürer's engraving *The Imperial Glove,* the shape of the glove seems a pretext for its elaborate ornamentation with cabuchon rubies, sapphires, heraldic figures, pearls, and golden thread. The ornamental additions make the glove precious; the detail on it suggests a significance beyond utilitarian use as clothing. Further, the thin slip of lacing at the bottom of the glove invites the viewer's speculation: was the glove just removed? Why does the glove lie flat, without creases, almost as though it were not meant to be worn, while the lacing strip, more substantial, seems to have been toyed with? The object comes to life when it is explained through story.

A similar phenomenon occurs in two narratives, one by Marguerite, the other told by the Sieur de Brantôme, in which gloves play an important role. The two stories possess several similarities in how the glove is displayed and how its significance is discussed, but there is at least one difference, that of Marguerite's use of the frame narrative. Like Dürer's image of the glove, boxed in by the borders of the page and modeled for more relief against a beige and tan background, Marguerite adds dimension to the glove in *nouvelle* #57. She demystifies its presence, drawing on one element of the story to produce a metaphysical perspective. *Nouvelle* #57 recounts the tale of a lovesick man who errs by trying to substitute a thing for a person, fetishizing his loved one in this manner. Clutching the lady's glove, which had slipped off when he gripped her hand to prevent her from leaving, the man acts as though the glove contained her essence. Marguerite shows in this story her concern over the veneration of relics. During his unsuccessful suit for the lady's love, the man held her hand to his heart, but she pulled away ("Je luy tins la main dessus mon cœur, laquelle estoit gantée … et … luy serra la main contre mon esthomac, en luy disant, 'Helas, ma dame, recepvez le cueur …' Quant elle entendit ce propos que luy tenois, le trouva fort estrange. Elle voulut retirer sa main"; "Then, pressing her hand to my side, I said, 'Alas! Madame, take this heart …' Taken aback by these words, she tried to withdraw her hand"—*Hept.* 6.57.354; Chilton 458). The man keeps the woman's glove: "le gand demeure *en la place de* sa cruelle main" ("as she pulled away her cruel hand, the glove remained"—*Hept.* 6.57.354; emphasis added; Chilton 458); he then decorates the glove with jewels, places it over his heart ("que depuis il enrichit de pierreryes et l'attacha sur son saye, à costé du cueur"; "I affixed this glove as a sticking plaster, the most fitting I could find, to my wounded heart! I have adorned it with the richest rings in my possession" —*Hept.* 6.57.353; Chilton 458). Unable to have her, he symbolically enacts a successful outcome to his desire by reducing the woman's body to an accessory, the glove, then placing it in contact with his own body. The man's action, attaching the glove to himself ("attaché") demonstrates a desire to hold on to what is not rightfully his. The man listening to this tale avers that he would have "mieulx aymé la main que le gand d'une dame" ("preferred the hand to the glove of a lady"—*Hept.* 6.57.355), and, indeed, the protagonist has gained little by the substitution: he holds merely a bedecked shape of the lady's hand, divorced from its possessor and purpose. Further, he adorns ("enrichit") the glove, decorating it as one would adorn a sacred object for display. Ornament facilitates distortion,[30] and the man admits that "je voy bien que vous trouvez estrange de ce que si gorgiasement j'ay accoustré ung pauvre gand" ("I can see that you find it strange that I have decorated a mere glove so richly"—*Hept.* 6.57.354; Chilton 457). So ornate has he made the glove that it is no longer serviceable as a glove: with jewels encrusting even the spaces between fingers it would be unwearable: "un petit gand … à crochetz d'or; et dessus les joinctures des doigts y avoit force diamanz, rubis, aymerauldes et perles, tant que ce gand estoit estimé à ung grand argent" ("a small glove, a lady's glove ... fastened with gold hooks ... and the fingers were covered with diamonds, rubies, emeralds and pearls. The value of that glove was thought to be very high"—*Hept.* 6.57.353; Chilton 457). While *gorgias* ("gorgiasement") can mean beauty, it often connotes ostentation or vanity. Marguerite thus makes the glove a sort of *vanitas* emblem: the man's over-adornment of the glove attests to the futility—and arrogance—of his attempt to substitute a thing for a person. The excessively ornamented glove becomes an anti-reliquary: it harbors nothing at all and is ornamented out of recognition. Rather than represent the woman, it assimilates to the man's body, where it is fixed as a bandage ("emplatre") over his own emptiness.

Without Marguerite's frame, the tale would conclude with the portrait of a fetishist. The frame adds another dimension, however, using the man's attempt to find meaning in things of the world to illustrate how humanity, alienated from God, similarly pursues illusions of presence and significance. Had Marguerite not added the interpretive element of the frame, the glove could, perhaps, have served as a *devis.* But that would not have worked, either, since the glove, embellished, no longer represented accurately its former possessor. By adding the frame, Marguerite creates an emblem-like text, one that includes the image of the glove, the man's story about it, as well as directions for interpretation. The frame is actually very down-to-earth, instructing the reader that the man's action is inordinate and that one should not seek to subscribe ultimate meaning to any person or thing, as all such human relationships are faulty: "'Il semble,' dist Parlamente, 'que vous avez oy la plaincte de quelque sot deçu par une folle, car vostre propos est de si petite auctorité'" ("'It seems to me,' said Parlamente, 'that you have heard some stupid man complaining about being duped by some frivolous woman. What you say carries so little weight ...'"—*Hept.* 6.57.356; Chilton 460). After all the elaborate fetishizing of the glove, the *devisants'* brusque dismissal of the story makes the man's attempts to secure meaning in an object look, not romantic or inspired, but merely foolish. His search for significance was profoundly misdirected, as the commentary provided by the frame informs the reader.

The *devisants* convey evangelical ambivalence about the veneration of objects. The verb Oisille uses is *adjouster*, connoting an unwarranted addition to Scripture, which is already complete and sufficient. "A Dieu ne plaise … que nous doubtions de la saincte Escripture, veu que si peu nous croyons à voz mensonges … c'est de jamais ne mectre en doute la parolle de Dieu et moins ne adjouster foy à celle des hommes" ("Heaven forbid … that we should doubt Holy Scripture, for we are far from believing in your lies. … never cast doubt on the word of God, and even less … give credence to the word of men"—*Hept.* 6.57.356; Chilton 460). *Adjouster* is the same verb, along with the verb *accoustrer*, that the man had used to describe his technique of decorating the glove. In each case, the addition is unnecessary and would be a distortion. Leaning on God's Word for sufficiency will discourage trust in worldly objects, which are unable to sustain the freight of such expectations. This metaphysical perspective frames and limits the potential deviance of materiality.

Brantôme's treatment of a glove in *Les dames galantes* has some similarities with Marguerite's, but in general differs from Marguerite, and he supplies no frame. The man in the *Heptaméron* intended the glove to substitute for the woman. In Brantôme's tale, the glove is a substitute for the man. Unlike Marguerite's *nouvelle* #57, Brantôme's story never fetishizes the glove. Rather, Brantôme's glove suggests what might have happened; it is therefore a fiction, and the glove is a trace, a kind of vestigial writing or account of an imagined event. The glove is left behind in the bed linen by a nobleman eagerly groping at his friend's wife's body:

> … feu M le marquis … devint grandement amoureux d'une fort belle dame; si bien qu'un matin, pensant que son mari fust allé dehors, l'alla visiter qu'il la trouva encores au lict; et, en devisant avec elle, n'en obtint rien que la voir et la contempler à son aise sous le linge, et la toucher de sa main. Sur ces entrefaittes survint le mary … et les surprit de telle sorte que le marquis n'eut loisir de retirer son gand, qui s'estoit perdu, je ne scay comment, parmy les draps.
>
> ("The late Marquis … fell much in love with a very beautiful woman; so much so that one morning, believing that her husband had gone out, he went to visit her and found her

> still in bed; and, while talking with her, got nothing from her except to view and contemplate her at his leisure under the bed-linens, and also to touch her with his hand. While this was going on, her husband came in … and surprised them together, so that the Marquis did not have time to pull his glove back out, which had gotten lost, I don't know how, between the sheets.")[31]

The husband misconstrues the glove as a sign of both the marquis's and his wife's guilt:

> le gentilhomme … par ce cas fortuit trouva le gand du marquis perdu dans les draps … faisant la mine froide à sa femme, [il] demeura longtemps sans coucher avec elle ny la toucher.
>
> ("the nobleman … [having] found by luck the Marquis's glove lost in the sheets … acting coldly toward his wife, he went for a long time without sleeping with her or touching her.")[32]

However, the husband has misread. The glove is arguably a sign of the wife's attempt to preserve her innocence: she allowed the Marquis to look at her and to touch her because, since he was gloved before putting his hand between the sheets, she could believe that he himself never actually touched her body. The glove is ambiguous: a sign of his desire, it has also shielded her virtue. The glove is also a pretext for an epistolary triangle among the husband, wife, and admirer: having found the glove, the husband leaves a poem about it where the admirer can read it on his next visit. The Marquis then pens a response, explaining that he never violated the husband's trust: "Mais Dieu ne me puisse ayder si jamais j'y ay touché!" ("But may God damn me if ever I touched her!"),[33] whereupon the husband reconciles with his wife.

There is no metaphysical message in Brantôme's story, and there is no directive commentary or analytical framework. Instead, the glove offers a conceit for four narrative developments: the would-be lover's wishful version; what actually happened; the husband's speculation about what might have happened; and the poetry that tells the truth. The glove is, as Brantôme frequently summarizes the aim of his stories, "pour faire monstre" ("to show something"): a virtuoso display. Typical of Brantôme, materiality short-circuits metaphysics.

This glove, as far as we know, possesses no jewels, embroidery or distinguishing details, unlike the elaborately adorned glove in *nouvelle* #57. While its presence has been misconstrued by the husband, it has not itself been altered as was the glove by the wistful lover in the *Heptaméron*. It therefore possesses no overlay of detail to cause it to signify something more than itself. Brantôme, not an evangelical, is not overly concerned to discuss the distortion caused by objects invested with too much meaning; he does not develop a frame narrative through which to inflect the story so that the reader will interpret material objects through a metaphysical lens.[34]

Evangelical Emblematic Messages: Mottoes and Wordplay

Another component of emblematic compositions is the motto, or *inscriptio,* which, among other purposes, summarizes the image's message. Sometimes the motto points the reader/viewer to specific details of the image while excluding others. The emphasizing of one or two elements over, or to the exclusion of, other elements is itself a form of interpretation. Wordplay in the evangelical narrative operates in a similar way. Generated by reflection on an image or object, one phrase, reminiscent of the motto's concision, expresses the wordplay. This phrase may be reiterated at key moments in the narrative. For instance, Claude Paradin portrays the emblem of Saladin, Sultan of Babylon and Damascus and King of Egypt, as a shirt hoisted on a lance. The motto reads "Restat ex victore Orientis," and the message is that earthly goods are ephemeral: "le Roy de tout orient est mort, et n'importe non plus de tous ses biens" ("the King of all the Orient is dead, and matters no more than any of his earthly possessions").[35] The text develops the motto, explaining that the lavishly worked silk chemise represents the king's wealth, which now means nothing. Left behind, like a futile standard-bearer blowing in the wind, the shirt shows that the king cannot take his possessions with him when he dies: "ainsi nu hors ce monde" ("thus naked, he goes out of this world").[36]

Marguerite uses brief phrases similarly to summarize her narrative point. For instance, *nouvelle* #3 plays with the words *couronne* ("crown") and *cornes* ("horns"), prefiguring the tale's *dénouement.* The king courts in secret the wife of one of his gentlemen. Wordplays provide clues to his lascivious intentions, associating the royal phallus with the scepter: "le Roy … duquel la lascivité estoit le sceptre de son Royaulme" ("the king … whose well-known lasciviousness was, one might say, the very scepter by which he ruled"—*Hept.* 1.3.22; Chilton 83). While visiting the lady at her home, the king mockingly deems a set of antlers mounted on the wall a fitting component of a cuckold's decorative scheme ("bien sceante"; "… went very well with …"—*Hept.* 1.3.26; Chilton 88). The gentleman, more astute than the king realizes, erects a sign stating: "Io porto le corna, ciascun lo vede; ma tal le porta, che no le crede" ("I am wearing horns, as anyone can see; but someone else is wearing them [cuckolded], who will not believe it"—*Hept.* 1.3.26).[37] When the king asks the meaning of the caption, the nobleman responds with a wordplay on vassal ("serf") that works off of the image of the stag ("cerf"): "Si le secret du Roy est caché au serf, ce n'est pas raison que celluy du serf soit declaré au Roy … tous ceulx qui portent cornes n'ont pas le bonnet hors de la teste" ("If the King doesn't tell his secrets to his subjects, then there's no reason why his subjects should tell their secrets to the King. And so far as horns are concerned, you should bear in mind that they don't always stick up and push their wearers' hats off"—*Hept.* 1.3.26–27). The cuckolding king has himself been deceived, his crown metamorphoses into antlers, emblem of a *trompeur trompé.* In a corner of Pieter Boel's *Allegory of Worldly Vanity* (1622), a gilded stag rears atop a pile of transitory treasures, leaping up over ecclesiastical vestments, drawing the eye into a heap of ephemeral signs of wealth and power. A fade-out to the left of the picture attests to their evanescence. In emblematic paintings and still lifes, stag horns commonly connote vanity and pride. And in Marguerite's *nouvelle*, the stag's horns represent the king's abuse of power. The nobleman places his sign above the lintel of the door to his house, so that each time the king enters he unwittingly situates himself under the indictment over the doorframe.[38] An ornate image of a crown was carved into the top of an oaken door panel at Fontainebleau around 1530. Bearing the initial "F," the crown represented François Ier. By situating the inscription indicting the crown above the door in her tale, Marguerite may have been warning her brother of the dangers of adultery.[39]

Nouvelle #23, explicitly evangelical, uses wordplay in ways similar to emblematic mottos. A *cordelier* ("Franciscan monk"), a *corde* ("rope"), and a *lict* ("bed") construct the pun. A friar sleeps with his host's wife, and in the dark the wife mistakes the friar for her husband. The husband finds out and rushes to avenge his wife's honor. She, however, has already killed herself. The wife's brother, arriving late on the scene, misinterprets the situation, and assumes that his brother-in-law has killed his spouse, then fled.

> Le beau frere luy respondist: "Mais quelle occasion vous a meu de faire mourir ma seur … pendue et estranglée à la corde de vostre lict?" Le gentilhomme … lui feit le compte du meschant Cordelier.
>
> ("'what can have caused you to put to death my sister … and … to strangle her and hang her with the cord from your own bed?' … The husband … told the whole story, and the part the Franciscan friar had played in it."—*Hept.* 3.23.192; Chilton 272)

The wife has hanged herself with the rope that had tied the mattress to her bed: *la corde-du-lict*, which discloses the malefactor through the pun on *cordelier* (*Hept.* 3.23.191; Chilton 272). In their commentary, the *devisants* mimic the wordplay, reviling friars "qui par mariage nous *lyent* aux femmes, et qui essayent par leur meschanceté à nous en *deslier*" ("who tie us to our wives in the bonds of matrimony, and then they're low enough to try to undo those bonds and make us break the very vows they made us take in the first place!"—*Hept.* 3.23.193; emphasis added; Chilton 273). The rope and bed form an acoustic rebus pointing to the murderer and communicating Marguerite's anti-clerical perspective. The evangelical issue of correct interpretation comes to the fore, as the outcome of the tale depends on the deciphering of the wordplay.

The *inscriptio* on an emblem, beyond summarizing content, may also indicate a more theoretical dimension.[40] In another example of wordplay encapsulating narrative message, *nouvelle* #33 uses cloaks and coverings (*manteau*, *couverture*) to describe displaced desire and the misuse of things. A monk impregnates his own younger sister. To deflect the accusations of suspicious townsfolk, the brother and sister construct an elaborate wordplay designed to exculpate themselves. As the villagers try to "read" the situation and pierce the façade behind which that guilty pair hides, the reader learns to distrust the guilty parties' language. The monk, "*tenu pour* ung sainct homme" ("regarded as a very holy man"—*Hept.* 4.33.247; emphasis added; Chilton 337), advises his sister to exculpate herself through veiled language:

> elle ... asseuroit tout le peuple que jamais elle n'avoit congneu homme.
>
> ("she said that no man had ever touched her, *any more than her brother had ...*"—*Hept.* 4.33.247; Chilton's emphasis; Chilton 338)

She is not exactly lying through her *équivoque*: she has not, in fact, ever slept with a *man*; she was virginal until she slept with her brother the *monk*. Blasphemously, she suggests that she may have been inseminated by the Holy Spirit: "et qu'elle ne sçavoit comme le cas luy estoit advenu, sinon que ce fut œuvre du Sainct Esperit" ("unless it be by the grace of the Holy Spirit who perform[ed] in [her] what he pleases"—*Hept.* 4.33.247; Chilton 338). The townsfolk demand that the monk put her to the test: she must swear on a Eucharistic wafer that she is inviolate. She responds with another evasive wordplay, answering: "Je prendz le corps de Nostre Seigneur, icy present devant vous, à ma damnation, devant vous, Messieurs, et vous, mon frere, si jamais homme m'a toucha [*sic*] *non plus que vous*" ("I take the body of Our Lord, present here, before you, Messieurs, and before you my brother, to my damnation, if ever a man has touched me any more than you"—*Hept.* 4.33.248; emphasis added).

Now that the sister and the brother have camouflaged themselves linguistically, Marguerite uses Pauline language to decipher the wordplay. Both St. Paul and St. Augustine used the metaphor of clothing, describing the cloak of holiness, which, while representing a spiritual quality, should be donned like a vestment, and Paul exhorted the faithful to don the accouterments of "the full armor of God" (Eph. 6.11–17). In Marguerite's tale, however, clothing is used negatively, as disguise and deception. Such cover-up is also associated with another wordplay, this time on *monstre:* ostentatious display, or monstrosity. The narrative describes the monk as "soubz si sainct *manteau* ung *monstre* si horrible" ("he wants to cover up his wickedness under this enormous piece of deception"—*Hept.* 4.33.249; emphasis added; Chilton 338). The twinning of the terms *manteau* and *monstre* conveys strong criticism of clerical sham. The image of the cloak demonstrates that the monk tried to cover his crime inappropriately with priestly garb; nonetheless, he can be disrobed of his subterfuge:

> ... les ypocrites, combien qu'ilz prosperent quelque temps soubz le *manteau* de Dieu et de saincteté ... quant ... Dieu lieve son *manteau*, il les descouvre et les mects tous nudz. Et, à l'heure, leur nudité, ordure et villenye, est d'autant trouvée plus layde, que la *couverture* est dicte honnorable.
>
> ("hypocrites, although they thrive for some time under the cloak of God and of holiness ... when God takes off the cloak, He uncovers them, and makes them totally naked. And at that time their nakedness, filth and sin is found even more ugly, in that their covering is deemed honorable."—*Hept.* 4.33.249; emphasis added; Chilton 338)

The commentators finally sort out all the wordplays, instructing the reader not to rely on false signs constructed of objects. Rather, the reader should penetrate to their true sense of the sign:

> Voylà, mes dames, comme la foy ... ne fut vaincue par signes ne miracles exterieurs[:] ... nous n'avons que ung Saulveur [qui] ... n'[a] laiss[é] poinct de lieu à ung aultre successeur pour faire nostre salut.
>
> ("So that, ladies, is how ... faith remained firm against outward signs and miracles [:] ... we have but one Saviour who ... [left] no way open for any [other] to bring us salvation."—*Hept.* 4.33.249; Chilton 339)

Marguerite's use of artifacts constructs inscriptions, in which each object composes one part of a semantic rebus that causes the apparent significance of a story to deepen, swerve, or undo itself. By analogy with the emblem, the anecdote developed in each *nouvelle* (the prose narrative) is equivalent to the third component of the emblem (the narrative poem): both confirm or rework the emphases of the first two components, the image and the *inscriptio,* and their structural equivalents in the *Heptaméron*. Marguerite adds another, new element in her emblem-like text, however: the directional framing that offers an interpretive paradigm. Appropriating a visual arts genre (the emblem) often found on decorative arts objects (such as tapestries, historiated plates, and embroidered table linens[41]), she imports this genre into the domain of narrative space. In so doing, she suggests how to understand her innovative application of one medium to another and her textual treatment of image, motto, and story. Her ordering schema fits into the context of collectors' cabinets as microcosms of the wonders of the world, as well as the evangelical program of restoring prelapsarian order. Collector's cabinets offer another sort of "frame" for interpreting the world; they create relationships among disparate objects and their system of arranging those objects hints at a narrative understanding of them that creates a syntactical unity out of semantic fragments. Similarly, Marguerite's *nouvelles* relate cases of divisiveness, advise against disorder ("il avoit envie de mectre division entre luy et sa femme"; "the servant was trying to sow discord between his wife and himself"—*Hept*. 4.36.261; Chilton 353), and counsel against separation ("puisque le soupson vous a separé de mon amityé, le despit me separera de la vostre"; "As your suspicion has destroyed my love for you, now your love for me will be destroyed by my anger!"—*Hept*. 5.57.314; Chilton 412). The ultimate hope is earthly restoration, an order that will prefigure heaven:

> Par ce compte … vous regarderez deux fois ce que vous vouldrez refuser, et ne vous fier au temps present … parquoy, congnoissans sa mutation, donnerez ordre à l'advenir …
>
> ("This … is a tale that will teach you to think twice before you refuse something. It will teach you not to place trust in the present, hoping that things will remain the same for ever, but to recognize that the present is in constant change and to have thought for the future."—*Hept*. 7.63.383; Chilton 491)

The *devisants*' frame often helps to confer order by corralling diverse interpretations and settling on one meaning as normative. The frame does not nullify any of the options, but rather discusses possibilities. Once the reader has sifted through the interpretive options investigated by the commentators, Marguerite is confident that the true message will be heard; though the tale may initially be multivalent in articulation, nonetheless univocal reception will inevitably ensue:

> Croiez, dist Oisille, que ceulx qui humblement et souvent la lisent, ne seront jamais trompez par fictions ny inventions humaines; car qui a l'esperit remply de verité ne peut recevoir la mensonge.
>
> ("'Be assured,' said Oisille, 'that whosoever reads the Scriptures humbly and with humility will never be deceived by human fabrications and inventions, for whoever has his mind filled with truth can never be the victim of lies.'" —*Hept.* 5.44.304; Chilton 400)

Marguerite acknowledges multiple perspectives, but affirms one ultimate truth.

How does Marguerite's narrative treatment add to the emblematic genre? Without the frame, the *Heptaméron* might simply be a collector's cabinet crammed with lovely objects. With the frame, the *Heptaméron* narratively explores the dialectical relationship between earth and heaven, earthly experience in tension with scriptural injunction, crafted objects contrasted with ideal or regenerate forms. Marguerite knows that a frame confers focus; she states that truth is often arrived at by peering through windows ("regardans aux fenestres"—*Hept.* 1.prologue.3). Although such a view may seem partial, without any interpretive boundaries at all no viable conclusions can be reached. Thus, Marguerite illustrates the Pauline perspective found in 1 Cor. 13.12: "For we see through a glass darkly," says St. Paul, "but then, clearly, face to face."

"Fenestres" open throughout the *Heptaméron*, often marking the moment of a character's conversion, which confers the newfound ability to see and to understand what had formerly been unclear. Windows are analogous to drawn curtains delimiting action in the theater. The *devisants* not only comment on the stories in the *Heptaméron*; they also, to some extent, identify with the characters, as do theatergoers; they "estudie[nt] leur rolle" ("study their scripts"—*Hept.* 4.prologue.236–37;

Chilton 324). Responding to these roles, the *devisants* also model how to make psychological and spiritual choices. Their role in the frame is to exemplify a variety of possible reactions to the stories, and to offer these possibilities to the reader: "Vrayement, dist Saffredent ... j'ay en main l'histoire d'une folle et d'une saige: vous prendrez l'exemple qu'il vous plaira le mieulx" ("'Willingly,' said Saffredent, 'the story I have in mind is in fact about a woman who was wanton and a woman who was wise. You may please yourselves which example you follow!'"—*Hept.* 3.25.207; Chilton 290–91). Yet the spectrum of choices in the text is not limitless. Marguerite uses the frame to guide her readers in a hermeneutic path, inculcating distrust for worldly concerns, and desire for spiritual matters.[42] Fittingly, the *devisants* end the presentation of the Fifth Day with a prayer, attesting to their hope that revealed truth will, despite worldly complications, elicit a unitary response: "Allons-nous en louer Dieu, dont ceste Journée est passée sans plus grand débat" ("So let us go and thank God that this day has passed without more serious dispute"—*Hept.* 5.1.326; Chilton 427).

The aim of the frame is to produce consensus and to open beyond itself to the metaphysical resolution of earthly misunderstandings. Marguerite's evangelical attitude favors the interaction of the independent interpreter with the diverse textual constituents, although the interpretive project eventually moves toward unitary understanding. She encourages the full development of the hermeneutic process, rather than foreclosing it. Marguerite intends that spiritual direction and profit will result in this way from the scrutiny of secular things.[43] Like other evangelical writers,[44] Marguerite cites the parable of the talents, showing that the result of reading the *Heptaméron* correctly will be good stewardship—defined by the willingness to use worldly things in service of a higher purpose.

The consequence of the stories, the frame instructs us, is not to produce simple amusement, but rather to generate *joye*. *Joye* is an evangelical term that expresses the certainty of being rightly aligned with God and enjoying his favor; it is a foretaste of the heavenly kingdom here on earth.[45] On the *Heptaméron*'s Third Day, the *devisants* agree that "nous avons passé ceste Journée aussi joyeusement qu'il est possible" ("to render thanks to God for having spent this day so happily"—*Hept.*

3.30.235; Chilton 66). The repetition of forms of *joye* attests to the term's special significance for evangelicals. Oisille states:

> Mes enfans, vous me demandez une chose que je trouve fort difficille, de vous enseigner ung passetemps qui vous puisse delivrer de vos ennuyctz; car, aiant chergé [*sic*] le remede toute ma vye, n'en ay jamais trouvé que ung, qui est la lecture de sainctes lettres en laquelle se trouve la vraie et parfaicte joie de l'esprit, dont procede le repos et la santé du corps.
>
> ("My children … when you ask me to show you a pastime that is capable of delivering you from your boredom and your sorrow, you are asking me to do something that I find very difficult. All my life I have searched for a remedy, and I have found only one—the reading of holy Scripture, in which one may find true and perfect spiritual joy, from which proceed health and bodily repose."—*Hept.* 1.prologue.7; Chilton 66)

In addition, the stories are situated in reference to a spiritual perspective: "Oisille … leur lisoit le texte et leur faisoit tant de bonnes et sainctes expositions qu'il n'estoit possible de s'ennuyer à l'oyr" ("Oisille … not only read them the text, but she also gave such sound and devout expositions that no one could possibly find it boring"—*Hept.* 4.prologue.236; Chilton 324). Oisille, like her fellow evangelicals, reads carefully, using biblical exegesis and exposition to explain Scripture. She teaches ("enseigner") her fellow *devisants* this method of reading and interpretation (*Hept.* prologue.1.7). Biblical exposition is the broadening of the text's import to apply it to daily life. The *Heptaméron* also relates Scripture to ordinary people and to everyday things and events. In the *Heptaméron*, through the use of material culture, Marguerite devises a prototype for an approach to literature that interprets it in reference to spiritual standards through material documentation.[46] Although Marguerite is aware that created objects foster misuse, the *Heptaméron* furnishes a proof case for the argument that predominantly secular literature, well applied and interpreted, may serve exemplary and theological functions. Biblical literature supports this contention: St. Paul states in his letter to Timothy that the ordinary life of the believing Christian "en-texts" him, enabling him to serve as a "letter writ large," a life illustrative of scriptural mandates (1 Tim. 4.12; 2 Tim. 1.13). Marguerite urges that the *Heptaméron* be read through the frame of Scripture, using daily life to generate a discussion of Scripture, forging a bond between her new genre of *nouvelle* and the *bonne nouvelle* of the Gospel. Oisille clearly indicates that such is the purpose of their "passetemps":

> Et, si vous me demandez quelle recepte me tient si joyeuse … c'est que … je prends la Saincte Escripture et la lys, et, en voiant et contemplant la bonté de Dieu, qui pour nous a envoié son filz pour anoncer ceste saincte parolle et bonne nouvelle, par laquelle il permect remission de tous pechez, satisfaction de toutes debtes par le don qu'il nous faict de son amour.
>
> ("and, if you ask me what the prescription is that keeps me happy and healthy in old age, I will tell you. As soon as I rise in the morning I take the Scriptures and read them. I see and contemplate the goodness of God, who for our sakes has sent His son to earth to declare the holy word and the good news by which He grants remission of all our sins, and payment of all our debts, through His gift to us of His love."—*Hept.* 1.prologue.7; Chilton 66)

The lure of the secular tales is their appeal to the senses and to worldly sensibilities. Fashioning a realistic context populated by ordinary objects and people, Marguerite's stories are engaging and believable, as the *devisants* point out: "Et qu'est-ce à dire, dist Oisille, que nous sommes plus enclins à rire d'une follye, que d'une chose sagement faicte? —Pour ce, dist Hircan, qu'elle nous est plus agreable, d'autant qu'elle est plus semblable à nostre nature, qui de soy n'est jamais saige" ("'And why is it,' said Oisille, 'that we are more inclined to laugh at foolish acts than at deeds which are wise?' 'Because,' replied Hircan, 'folly is more amusing insofar as it resembles our own nature, which in itself is never wise'"—*Hept.* 4.34.252; Chilton 343). The *devisants* know what the characters in the story need to be taught: signs constructed by things of the world can, and usually do, mislead: like our own errant nature, "de soy … jamais saige," worldly things are unreliable. In *nouvelle* #35, for instance, an amorous woman misconstrues her priest's posture:

> Desjà estoit la my karesme, que la dame ne laissa, ne pour Passion ne pour Sepmaine saincte, sa maniere accosutumée de mander par lectres au prescheur sa furieuse fantaisye. Et luy sembloit, quant le prescheur tournoit les œilz du costé où elle estoit, ou qu'il parloit de l'amour de Dieu, que tout estoit pour l'amour d'elle.
>
> ("Mid-Lent arrived, and the lady was still writing to the preacher about her wild passion. It seemed to her that every time the man looked in her direction, or talked about the Love of God, he did it for love of her, and she did her best to express her thoughts in her eyes."—*Hept.* 4.35.257; Chilton 348)

The role of the *devisants* parallels the work of the emblematist; by framing an image with commentary, Marguerite incorporates the figures and function of the *devisants* into the structure of the narrative itself so that ambiguities may be resolved. In addition, like the pattern books consulted by emblematists, the *Heptaméron* describes virtually every sort of earthly interaction. A weaver or a cabinetmaker might select an image from the catalogue of emblematic treatments to apply to their handiwork; similarly, the *Heptaméron* selects images that will stimulate an awareness of a specific spiritual resolution to a particular earthly problem. Andreas Alciati describes emblem books serving as models for craftsmen working in a wide array of trades:

> toutes et quantesfoys que aulcun vouldra attribuer, ou pour le moins par fiction appliquer aux choses vuydes accomplissement, aux nues aornement, aux muettes parolles, aux brutes raison, il aura en ce petit livre (comme en un cabinet tres bien garny) tout ce qu'il pourra, et vouldra inscripre, ou pindre aux murailles de la maison, aux verreries, aux tapis, couvertures, tableaux, vaisseaulx, images, aneaulx, signetz, vestements, tables, licts, armes, brief à toute piece et ustensiles, et en tous lieux.
>
> ("Any time that anyone wants to attribute, or at least by fiction apply to empty things, completion; to naked things, adornment; to mute things, speech; to stupid things, reason, he will have in this little book [as in a well-furnished cabinet] everything he can or will want to inscribe, or paint on walls of the house, on glasswork, on tapestry, on coverings, paintings, vessels, images, rings, signets, clothing, tables,

> beds, arms, in brief on every thing and utensil, and in every place.")[47]

They bring to their product a contribution found in another domain, just as Marguerite sets materiality to the service of metaphysics.

Marguerite's goal is to move in and through these quotidian scenarios, providing a theological critique of them in so doing. The frame curtails humanity's capricious nature. Marguerite describes her interpretive program through reference to a mirror: "quant vous avez bien regardé en ce mirouer, en lieu de vous fier à voz propres forces, vous aprendrez à vous retourner à Celluy en la main duquel gist vostre honneur ("it is, as it were, a mirror, and once you've looked into it, I think you will learn to turn to Him in whose hands your honour lies, instead of relying on your own powers"—*Hept.* 4.35.260; Chilton 351). Marguerite's mirror-text reflects subjectivity, which is contained within and known through the frame of spirituality. Similar to this goal is the Protestant writer Henri Estienne's suggestion that a lady place her *devis* on the frame of her mirror—in this way, she would always be reminded, while making her daily toilette, of the moral ideal to which she should conform.[48]

The *devisants* construct a frame-within-a-frame, as Scripture is the absolute template that models proper reception. The commentators mimic the babble of fallen words, sifting through multiple interpretations, finally arriving at the standard upon which Oisille has always insisted (unitary in intention and in reception, although not absolute literal rendering): "à tout le moins l'intention de mon histoire ne sortira poinct hors de la doctrine de la saincte Escripture" ("but at least the intention of the story that I shall tell you will not be out of keeping with the teaching of Holy Scripture"—*Hept.* 6.prologue.328; Chilton 428). The *devisants* never compel consensus in their commentary, but nonetheless seek to move, in community, to commonality.

Embroidering the Evangelical Emblem and Text

The decoration on objects in the *Heptaméron*, similar to the ornamental elements featured in Paradin's emblems, are like embroidery: they pick out discrete details, rather than the entire object, as significant. In both texts, the earthly object does not count in and of itself, but only as it is *undone,* allowing theological truth to overlay or adorn it. Images function as things of value in a material transaction: de-valued in a spiritual economy, images take part in processes rather than pose as static portraits.[49] The composition of a collection results from a quest for truth in the arrangement of things—a search that must learn its own futility.

Decorative arts objects that play roles similar to emblematic components in the *Heptaméron*—masks, mirrors, glove, books—demonstrated that daily-life objects had a very specific, and somewhat unconventional, purpose and meaning for sixteenth-century French evangelicals.[50] Through the objects in her emblem-like text, Marguerite conveys the need to work through and beyond these things—representative of humanity's turn away from God and to the world—to effect conversion and redemption. The result is a dispossession, then a paradoxical resumption, of subjectivity: one in which creatures know themselves in Christ.

Chapter Three

A New Medium for a New Message

Evangelicals and Decorative Arts

In This World But Not of It: Evangelicalism and the Arts

The presence of Lutheran theology in France during the 1520s and 1530s influenced Marguerite to develop an evangelical narrative. This new narrative form also encompassed certain trends in contemporary decorative and fine arts.[1] Art historians recognize that "Fontainebleau was truly a school for the new culture in France. Fontainebleau also had an impact on the literary style of French culture."[2] For a new message, a new medium is required. Similarly, the Gospel urges that new wineskins be found in which to store new wine. Realizing that the translation of Gospel truths into everyday language warranted a new format and idiom, Marguerite presides over the marriage in narrative of theology and decorative arts, forging an innovative composition and technique.

Evangelical artists of the period incorporated objects into narrative in order to illustrate the didactic and moral focus of a spiritual truth. The Lutheran Albrecht Dürer's engraving of *Knight, Death and Devil* (1513), for instance, embodies concerns that echo those that Marguerite develops in her narrative. The Dürer image derives from a text, Erasmus's evangelical *Enchiridion, or Manual of the Christian Soldier,* which, like the *Heptaméron*, relies extensively on objects and artifacts, delineates a landscape within the narrative, and is didactic in tone. Considerable interdisciplinary collaboration thus existed among evangelicals working in an array of artistic media at this time.[3] Martin Luther also encouraged the use of anecdote for the teaching and discussion of biblical scenes.[4] Art could be a vehicle for faith, abolishing what Calvin, among other

Reformed theologians, had seen as an art/faith dichotomy.[5] The incorporation of daily-life artifacts in Marguerite's prose therefore offered a legitimate technique through which to dramatize spiritual truths. By incorporating things of the world into her narrative, as well as by retaining a creative ambivalence toward them, Marguerite could obey the Gospel mandate to be both in this world yet not of it.

Evangelicalism encourages reference to daily life,[6] perhaps because of its emphasis on the priesthood of all believers and the vocation of the laity. Material objects associated with the exercising of one's calling in the world could thereby have instrumental significance.[7] The fifteenth-century *ars nuova* in Northern European painting prefigured this emphasis on daily-life experience. A shift in the focus of artistic activity occurred around 1500 north of the Alps: efforts centered increasingly on the production of artifacts, with heightened interest in illuminated manuscripts, stained glass, increasingly life-like sculpture, detailing on tombs, ornate pulpits, and jewel-inlaid devotional images. The stylistic alterations demonstrated by such artists were "based on a clear observation of the physical world … [with] more time and attention [given to] the particulars of their earthly existence … [increased] visual realism is evident."[8] Evangelicals borrowed from this focus and technique. Of necessity, to some extent, the new media crossed borders between belief systems; not all artists espousing novel approaches to textual exposition were evangelicals or Protestants. However, the contours of certain artistic developments put to service in the evangelical program began to appear. Evangelicals endeavored to articulate their version of truth and tried to find a particular voice and style fitting to evangelicalism's message. Interdisciplinary collaboration is a hallmark of this venture. In addition, the ability to display two levels or layers of meaning—earthly reality and heavenly ideal—is characteristic of evangelical artistic production.[9] An example of prose that applied the Gospel paradigmatically to everyday experience is Willem van Branteghem's *Dat Leven ons heeren* (Antwerp, 1537). This text, called a Gospel "Harmony," includes more than 200 woodcuts framed by a foreword instructing the reader in how to apply scriptural lessons to daily life. Its teachings are especially strong on the evangelical doctrines of *sola gratia* and *sola fidei*.[10] Marguerite similarly benefits from the latitude implicit in the evangelical perspective,[11] concluding that things of the world in and of themselves are not flawed; rather, human lust for, and inappropriate use of, those things can render them problematic.

Marguerite's perspective coincides with, and profits from, productivity in the field of decorative arts.[12] With this new emphasis on decorative arts came several new artistic genres that emerged during the sixteenth century: the portrait; a more expansive treatment of landscape often displaying an itinerary and, thereby, enumerating the stages of a story; and, toward the end of the century, the still life. Significant changes in ornamental schemes, such as strapwork, also appeared.

Art historians recognize that portrait production during this period increasingly manifested an evangelical perspective.[13] Landscape, still life, and new ornamental schemas can also be linked to a new form of evangelical expression. Marguerite includes descriptions of some of these phenomena in the *Heptaméron*. Marguerite's *nouvelles* borrow from these repertoires of artistic innovation, incorporating and reworking contemporary cultural elements.[14] She configures narrative as a structure to be decorated with a network of objects. By absorbing thing into word, such adorned narrative embodies the reified matter from which the evangelical, and the reader, must move away, rejecting an exclusively terrestrial existence and endorsing a celestial emphasis.

When the artists whose work prompts Marguerite's narrative innovations were evangelical or Reformed artists, similarities were ever more striking. An example of the artistic treatment of corporeal matter by a fellow evangelical is found in Bernard Salomon's engravings. Salomon's elongated figures, reaching heavenward, become increasingly attenuated, as if, were they stretched further, light would shine through them. For instance, in Salomon's *The Creation of Eve*, an illustration for Paradin's *Quadrins Historiques*, God's anthropomorphic representation is unusually slender yet gigantic in stature, acting like a vertical arrow drawing up to the skies. He pulls Eve up out of sleeping Adam's side. Their musculature, dimly delineated, nonetheless lacks three-dimensionality. Instead of possessing the heft of fleshly humanity, the figures seem porous, almost transparent, like filmy veils between one form of reality and another, as though, before the Fall, the laws of gravity had no effect. Adam and Eve seem not entirely earthbound, seeming to hover between the two spheres. Materiality thus cooperates in the depiction of a metaphysical perspective in this illustration.

Daily-Life Details: Evangelicals Employ Earthly Experience

An investigation into the presence of the figure of Joseph, husband of Mary, has enabled art historians to ascertain the evangelical sympathies of certain artists. Joos van Cleve, active at the court of François Ier and painter of the king's portrait, evinced an evangelical perspective. Van Cleve emphasizes Joseph's role as patriarch in the painting *The Holy Family* (1512–13). The Lutheran model of the "holy household"[15] elevated the father and husband as patriarchal authority of biblical morality, responsible for family devotions and spiritual correction. Similarly, in *The Holy Family* (see fig. 4), "Joseph is no longer banished to the background, reduced to playing a marginal role, but now takes his place as Mary's equal partner in the upbringing of the Christ child."[16] Joseph constitutes a significant figure supporting the figures of Mary and Jesus. Joseph reads aloud from a scroll, perhaps a proleptic page of the Lukan Gospel in manuscript. He holds his spectacles, indicating spiritual insight. In other paintings, the omission of figures customarily included indicates a different theological emphasis. For instance, in *The Last Judgment* (1520–25), Van Cleve's elimination of the figures of Mary and of John has been interpreted as representative of a Reformed viewpoint.[17] Further, van Cleve's evangelical sympathies infuse most of his paintings with a portrayal of ordinary experience and the objects of daily life.[18]

For evangelicals, focus on the material world is unavoidable, even necessary, but problematic. 1 Cor. 7.29–31, a common proof-text for evangelicals, instructs Marguerite that "the time is short … Those who use the things of the world [should live as if] not engrossed in them. For this world in its present form is passing away." In *nouvelle* #21, Marguerite decorates her

Fig. 4. Joos van Cleve, *The Holy Family.* 1512–13. Metropolitan Museum of Art, New York City. This image by Joos van Cleve reacts against the late medieval tendency to minimize or marginalize Joseph. Now a significant, patriarchal figure, consistent with the Protestant emphasis on the father's role as leader, pedagogue, and minister of household devotions, Joseph is portrayed about to scrutinize a text, the importance of his meditative, scrutinizing gaze highlighted by his prominent pair of spectacles. Appropriate, also, to a proto-Protestant emphasis on the vocational value of daily life, quotidian details such as the scarred, wooden *trompe-l'œil* windowsill feature in this painting. Used with permission of The Metropolitan Museum of Art, The Friedsam Collection, Bequest of Michael Friedsam, 1931 (32.100.57).

narrative with many material objects, among them clothing, silver, *biens* (worldly goods), a ring, a window, a book entitled *The Knights of the Round Table*, a head-covering, and a crimson shade. However, the story demonstrates that things are unreliable signifiers. Instead, honor and transcendent love should inform life, along with a detachment from earthly possessions: "car s'il y a du bien, on le doit attribuer à Celluy qui en est la source, et non à la creature" ("if there is good in him, one should attribute it to Him who is its source, not to those whom He has created"—*Hept.* 3.21.175; Chilton 254). In *nouvelle* #19, Marguerite recounts how a young man, disappointed in love, converts his earthly appetites into love for God and enters a monastery. While he had loved his mistress, named Poline (perhaps recalling the focus of the Pauline intertext on *sarks*, or sinful flesh) idolatrously, placing his love *in* her ("la devotion qu'il avoit *en* Poline"; "his devotion to Paulina"—*Hept.* 2.19.144; emphasis added; Chilton 221), he now renounces the world and things of the flesh. He notifies his lady of his decision, sending her a spiritual song that summarizes many of the concerns of the *Heptaméron*: "Laissons les biens / Qui sont liens / Plus durs à rompre que fer … / Ne crains à prendre / L'habit de cendre, / Fuyant ce monde ennemy" ("Then put behind / The joys that bind / In iron bonds so dire and fell! / This worldly fame / That leads to shame / Black souls through pride to depths of Hell! / Let us shun lust and vanity …"—*Hept.* 2.19.147–48; Chilton 225).

In the *Heptaméron*, the accumulation of, and value placed on, worldly goods contrasts with moral mandates. In *nouvelle* #12, a duke lusts after his friend's sister. Naïvely trusting in friendship, the latter offers all he has to the duke,

> "… estant *seur* que ce qui sera en ma puissance est en vos mains." A l'heure, le duc commença à luy declairer l'amour qu'il portoit à sa *seur* … [et] par son moyen [il devait] en avoi[r] la jouissance.
>
> ("'… all that I have … has come from you … whatever is in my power to perform shall be …' So the Duke started to tell him how he was in love with his sister … and his friend [must] make it possible for him to enjoy her favours."—*Hept.* 2.12.91; emphasis added; Chilton 159)

The unreliability of things is symbolized by how this phrase opens and closes with near-homonyms (here spelled identically): the puns show that certainty ("estant seur") is, in fact, illusion. The brother's chaste love for his sister ("sa seur") is *not* sure; rather, its security is imperiled by the duke's bribes. The brother's trust is as misplaced as any other dependence on worldly assurances or objects:

> D'un costé, luy venoit au devant l'obligation qu'il devoit à son maistre, les biens et les honneurs qu'il avoit receuz de luy; de l'autre costé, l'honneur de sa maison, l'honnestesté et chasteté de sa seur.
>
> ("on the one hand, he was aware of the strength of the obligations he owed to his master for all the honours and material benefits he had received from him. On the other hand, there was the honour of his family name, the chastity of his sister."—*Hept.* 2.12.91; Chilton 159)

Marguerite dramatizes the brother's moral tension as he struggles to maintain his loyalty to his sister and to disregard the tokens and titles that the duke has given him. The sister incarnates a system of values that is opposed to the text's manifestation of worldliness. Coveted by the duke as only one of many worldly goods he covets, she embodies for the narrative, even more than for her brother, an *ideal* value, a virtual virtue (because unrealized in the narrative despite Marguerite's commendation of it). The sister will not be presented or treated as a commodity. One criticism of worldliness centers on the display of objects and on the Duke's desire, which tries to objectify the sister in order to possess her.

Catholic texts mention objects, too. Jacobus Voragine's *Golden Legend* includes objects representing a saint's extraordinary deed or special mode of suffering. Evangelicals, however, use objects narratively rather than evocatively or symbolically. Evangelical narrative considerations include questions over which objects are chosen, how they are distributed, what relationships their juxtapositions suggest, how their possessors employ them, and how the evangelical text works out its own theological ambivalence toward them. Saints lived exemplary lives and died heroic deaths. For the most part, evangelical laity lived discrete and ordinary lives, lifting up everyday work and experience to God, and reclaiming some ownership of the church through their scriptural understanding. Consequently, objects in evangelical narratives more frequently confer a daily-life texture on lives expressed in literature.[19] The Catholic and evangelical treatments of objects thus differ in method, iconography, and interpretation.

Marguerite uses earthly things to speak of a "chose differente … nouvelle" ("one difference … in the story … that it be truthful"—*Hept.* 1.prologue.9; Chilton 68), thereby associating "the Good News," and new ways of writing, with a novel use of objects in narrative. Evangelicals sometimes select objects with a conventional meaning, then revise them textually to redetermine those objects' meaning and function, thus permitting reference to materiality if it can be configured to point to metaphysical significance. An artifactual example is a Lutheran communion cup, a glass beaker (instead of a metal chalice) incised with the following verse: "What shall I render unto the Lord for all His benefits toward me? I will take the cup of salvation and call upon the name of the Lord. Psalm 115." The material of the glass underscores the transparency of the chalice: its substance opens to a reality beyond itself. The inscription stipulates that the chalice is "to be drunk from for necessity, not for pleasure."[20] Similarly, in van Cleve's *Crucifixion with Saints and a Donor* (circa 1520; see fig. 5), the landscape is crammed with detail. Along with biblical *topoi* rendered visually, the artist includes illustrations of daily life, among them a band of horsemen, pilgrims wending their way past a station of the cross, and boats riding at anchor. Evangelical and Reformed theology developed the ideal of a secular vocation, philosopher Charles Taylor contends; he calls the emphasis on lay experience "the affirmation of ordinary life," and notes that, because of Luther's "priesthood of all believers," the Gospel message might be shared equally; no priestly mediator intervened between man and God, and any lay occupation could be viewed as a vocation: "the rejection of the sacred and of mediation together led to an enhanced status for daily existence."[21] In *The Annunciation* (circa 1525; see fig. 6), van Cleve "dispose[s] objects unobtrusively within the domestic

Fig. 5. Joos van Cleve and a collaborator, *The Crucifixion with Saints and a Donor*. Circa 1520. Metropolitan Museum of Art, New York City. Although this is a theological subject, and probably an image used for devotional purposes, there is a very earthly and material backdrop to the scene. Daily-life details proliferate, including travelers, artifacts such as books, a crowd swarming in the distance, a bridge spanning a river, and a variety of dwellings such as castles and farmhouses. Used with permission of The Metropolitan Museum of Art, Bequest of George Blumenthal, 1941 (41.190.20a–c).

Fig. 6. Joos van Cleve, *The Annunciation.* Circa 1525. Metropolitan Museum of Art, New York City. Many daily-life details can be found in this sumptuous painting of what remains a primarily Catholic subject. Van Cleve may have had evangelical sympathies (the date is 1525, a time of intense interest in Luther). The genre painting from which Marguerite borrows techniques displays quotidian objects as one of its trademarks. Mary's chamber is comfortable and inviting, as light streams in, a window frames a bustling outdoor scene, and Mary pages through the proleptic account of her encounter with the Angel Gabriel. Used with permission of The Metropolitan Museum of Art, The Friedsam Collection, Bequest of Michael Friedsam, 1931 (32.100.60). Image © The Metropolitan Museum of Art. All rights reserved.

interior in much the same way as 16th century domestic viewers of the painting might have arranged them in their own homes,"[22] spotlighting the customary uses for these objects through his pictorial rendition of the evangelical privileging of daily life. Gérard David was an evangelical artist active at François Ier's court. David's *Prayer Wings* (1490) features everyday objects and encourages a metaphysical interpretation of them: the painted objects interrelate with the text, which acts like a frame surrounding them.[23] In *Virgin and Child with a Bowl of Porridge* (1520), David shows a secular side of the Virgin: she offers a model for human behavior, rather than posing as a solely sacred figurehead. This more down-to-earth portrayal also "protect[s] Gérard David from the [potential charge] of idolatry or image-worship,"[24] since the Virgin is not depicted as an intercessor, but simply as a good mother.

The decision to include, then to question, and finally to surpass material objects, has an artistic analogue in the *trompe-l'œil* aspects of van Cleve's painting *Virgin and Child* (see fig. 7): the surfaces from which the viewer delineates the parameters of reality are illusions. *Virgin and Child* has a real frame, then a *trompe-l'œil* frame-within-a frame, the bottom of which looks like a stone windowsill. Someone has placed cherries and half an orange on this virtual frame, as though it were solid; the effect is to highlight the frame's pretense.

In the *Heptaméron*, *trompe-l'œil* plays a textual role. Windows can be *real* demarcations as well as suggest liminal zones for psychological change. At times windows allow interaction between characters, as when Rolandine speaks to her lover in secret through a window. At other times, they frame and focus relationships, as with Amadour and Floride. Windows also open onto a new way of conceiving of, or "framing," reality. If our interpretive referents deceive, like the *trompe l'œil* frame impossibly supporting the clutter of objects in van Cleve's painting, our ways of understanding the world may similarly require readjustment. Social convention may in this way be reoriented, consistent with spiritual standards. For instance, separated by a window whose casement visually reinforces the social proscription against their liaison, Rolandine and her lover nonetheless attain physical propinquity: she and her lover

Fig. 7. Joos van Cleve and a collaborator, *Virgin and Child*. Circa 1525. Metropolitan Museum of Art, New York City. While pointing to the Word, the Virgin leans against a balustrade separating her from a convoluted landscape. The details of the background spread themselves out waiting for the slumbering Christ child to assume headship of the world. It is a commonplace, rural scene, with oxen and horses in fields, trees, craggy rocks, and a route wending its way to a lake or, perhaps, the sea. All aspects of earthly geography are thus summarized in this painting. Used with permission of The Metropolitan Museum of Art, The Jack and Belle Linsky Collection, 1982 (1982.60.47).

lodge in adjoining houses, their close angles suggesting sexual congress.

> ceste dame avecq son filz furent logez en la maison du Roy; et estoit la chambre de ce jeune prince *advancée toute entiere oultre le corps* de la maison où le Roy estoit, tellement que de sa fenestre povoit veoir et parler à Rolandine, car les deux fenestres estoient proprement à l'angle des deux corps d'une maison.
>
> ("this lady and her son were accommodated in the part of the building occupied by the King, and it so happened that the young prince was given a room which projected from the rest of the wing in such a way that it was quite possible for him to see and speak to Rolandine herself, since their windows were situated in the angle formed by the two parts of the building."—*Hept.* 3.21.163; emphasis added; Chilton 241)

Rolandine walls off the windows with a crimson silk bed-curtain, creating a double separation or frame-within-a-frame reminiscent of van Cleve's *trompe-l'œil* frames:

> Elle se mist à faire ung lict tout de rescul de soye cramoisie, et l'atachoit à la fenestre où elle vouloit demorer seulle.
>
> ("she had set about making an open-work bed cover in crimson silk, and this she would hang up in the window where she wanted to be left alone ..."—*Hept.* 3.21.164; Chilton 242)

In this private theater, "elle entretenoit son mary" ("she would talk with her husband"—*Hept.* 3.21.164; Chilton 242). The lovers are united by God's validation of their love, which erases their former separation by removing the metaphoric—and legalistic—"sill" separating them:

> Elle leur feit responce ... ce que Dieu avoit assemblé, les hommes ne le povoient separer ... car ... amour et bonne volunté fondée sur la craincte de Dieu sont les vrays et seurs lyens de mariage ...
>
> ("Her reply ... was ... that which God had joined together, no man could put asunder ... for ... love and honest intent

> founded on the fear of God were the true and sure bonds of marriage."—*Hept*. 3.21.171; Chilton 250)

The window has encouraged movement from one state of being to another and galvanized the "translation" from terrestrial to celestial. Further, Marguerite provides here a portrait of the evangelical notion of "companionate marriage": two individuals who stand "right with God" enter into a covenant, as contrasted with the Catholic convention of a sacramental bond.

Marguerite's evangelical understanding also dovetails with that of many Reformed artists in the shared project to reform art by refocusing it, concentrating primarily on elements of structure and narrative, and only secondarily on issues of representation. Dürer "intended to use his formidable artistic … power to present religious truth in a newly refined and austere simple style."[25] His *Last Supper* (1523) puts the objects in the composition to the service of doctrine. By emphasizing the simple setting of the meal, Dürer illustrates Luther's contention that Communion was not some ornate and mysterious reiteration of Jesus' sacrificial death (as Luther believed the Catholic church construed it), but rather a re-enactment of a real event, and one-time sacrifice, that occurred in the incarnate life of Jesus as a man and as a Jew partaking of the Passover meal. The pared-down quality of the image highlights the humble room and the disciples' divestiture of worldly possessions in order to follow their master. The starkness of the depiction also draws attention to the objects in the foreground. The plate on which the sacrificial lamb would ordinarily be displayed to symbolize the Eucharistic feast is instead empty, attesting to Dürer's Reformed (and more "memorialist") leanings. The lunette window over Christ's head imitates the shape of the plate, while the emptiness of the window underscores the platter's emptiness. Luther taught consubstantiation rather than trans-substantiation: according to Luther, while Christ was really present at the mass, the elements of bread and wine remained in their earthly forms; they were not transformed nor were their substances altered to become Christ's body and blood, as the Catholic church taught.

Spiritual Landscapes and Theological Topography

The most influential landscape painter of the 1520s was the Italian Patinir. Both Joos van Cleve and Gérard David were influenced by developments in Italian landscape painting, many motivated by Patinir. These innovations are reflected in how Marguerite understands textual topography, and are also found in the works of other evangelical and Reformed artists such as Claes Jansz Visscher (1586–1652), Esaias van de Velde, Gillis van Coninxloo, Jan Victors, Hendrik Hondius, and Salomon van Ruysdael.

Reformed theology and landscape painting were mutually influencing. "Perhaps Protestants were more open to landscape regardless of its mode or idiom, because it was a relatively new genre that had no ties with traditional Catholic belief and iconography"[26] and that could be personalized as evangelical or Reformed. Features found in evangelical narrative also turn up in the work of Reformed artists: these include fine detail in renderings of landscape, fidelity in mapping, and the incorporation of realistic scenes from daily life in landscapes.[27]

> Calvinism determined the rise of a realistic landscape genre in Dutch seventeenth-century art ... Calvinism ... viewed nature, i.e. Creation, as the "second book" of God (the Bible being the other book), reflecting the omnipotence, wisdom, goodness, and grace of God ... Calvin himself, in his *Institution de la Religion Chrestienne* ... licensed the depiction of landscape ... Therefore, landscape was a perfect subject for a Protestant painter ... These "Calvinist cartographic interests" prompt a "fundamentally scriptural reading" of such landscape art.[28]

They provide a sort of "God's eye view," reading the world in a sweeping panorama, standing outside and beyond it, but also acknowledging the daily-life interactions and topography of earthly existence. Because such representations proliferate with daily-life objects, some critics refer to sixteenth-century landscapes as versions of *Wunderkammeren* "encompass[ing] virtually the entirety of known global culture, past and present, foreign and domestic."[29]

While genre painters were both Catholic and Protestant, as were landscape painters, it tended to be evangelical and

Reformed artists who placed a greater emphasis on landscape with itinerary: an iconic movement out of the landscape toward an imagined, ideal space. Landscapes provide an apt vehicle for Marguerite's evangelical examination of the world. In *nouvelle* #10, Amadour leaves his own *pays* to go to "lieux estranges" ("faraway places"—*Hept.* 1.10.56). His frustrated love for Floride expresses itself geographically in terms of distance, frontiers, and boundaries,[30] and Amadour describes his hope to win Floride from her husband in terms recalling a form of territorial occupation.[31] Similarly, in the first chapter of *Pantagruel*, the evangelical Rabelais sketches out a "landscape narrative," enumerating many nations in a list that delimits the known world, just as Reformed landscape artists broadened the parameters of their painting, presenting the totality of the world as if displayed before God's gaze.[32] Like the *passetemps* of Marguerite's *devisants* waiting for the flood to subside, enforced leisure is Rabelais's pretext for such narrative re-creation.

> Ce ne sera chose inutile ne oysifve, veu que sommes de séjour, vous ramentevoir la première source et origine dont nous est né le bon Pantagruel: car je voy que tous bons hystoriographes ainsi ont traicté leurs chronicques, non seullement les Arabes, Barbares et Latins, mais aussi Gregoys gentilz.
>
> ("It will be no idle or unprofitable matter, seeing that we have leisure, to remind you of the fount and origin from which the good Pantagruel was born to us. For I observe that all good historiographers have thus dealt with their Chroniclers, not only the Arabs, Barbarians and Romans, but also the gentle Greeks."[33])

The mention of other ethnic groups broadens the geography of his text, just as the topography of many of the *nouvelles* in the *Heptaméron,* originating in depictions of domestic space, moves outside into a larger landscape. This landscape, like Rabelais's, remains abstract.[34] Rather than actually represent terrestrial demarcations, evangelical writers customarily evoke it by enumerating places and names of lands.[35] As such, earth itself is not lifted up as intrinsically valuable; rather, it forms the arena in which a pilgrimage may take place and redemption may ensue subsequent to the pilgrim's voyage through that landscape. Such an itinerary in narrative may parallel a contemporary development in landscape art; this innovation, called the *Andachtsbild,* told story through landscape, requiring the viewer's scanning eye to reconstitute the progressive narrative moments. Similarly, in the *Heptaméron*, the *nouvelles,* self-contained entities, nonetheless may be viewed as linked; they delineate a movement from earthly to celestial, terrestrial to metaphysical.[36]

Narrative, as Marguerite conceives it, becomes an itinerary through the world, the *peripetiae* of story and the vicissitudes of life, to its endpoint, God. In the *Heptaméron*'s varied scenarios in diverse locations, Marguerite models a myriad of possibilities for how to negotiate worldly pitfalls. The *Heptaméron* thereby composes a narrative map of metaphysical orientations. As we have seen, Amadour and Floride are not only geographically separated; they also experience psychological distance, attempting to bridge that emotional gap in order to achieve union.[37] As boundaries blur, and psychological space shifts, Marguerite constructs an idealized space—within the context of everyday existence—for spirituality, much as Reformed landscape painters represent the working-out of God's plan for history on big canvases decorated with daily-life details. Marguerite's message is cautionary: the great psychological and physical distance that Amadour travels in order to be joined with Floride is also a distance of moral transgression, for his journey toward adulterous union contradicts divine precepts.[38] A similar treatment of such a message can be found in Patinir's

> horizontal narrative treatment of his subject … the Holy Family's journey was interpreted by contemporary viewers as a metaphor for pilgrimage, in particular the pilgrimage of every human life, confronting at each step along the way the choice between the easy path of a sinful existence and the more difficult one of virtue and godliness.[39]

The itinerary compels both physical movement and moral discernment: a traversing of outer, physical reality and inner, spiritual space akin to the dimensions that the *Heptaméron* illustrates. Other similar treatments include The Master of the Female Half-Lengths's *The Rest on the Flight into Egypt* (circa 1525; see fig. 8), Patinir's *Triptych: The Penitence of Saint Jerome* (circa 1518; see fig. 9), where the bends and curves of the river guiding our eyes through the landscape recall the

Fig. 8. Attributed to the Master of the Female Half-Lengths and a collaborator, *The Rest on the Flight into Egypt.* Circa 1525. Metropolitan Museum of Art, New York City. Landscape painting was a sixteenth-century development closely associated, although not exclusively, with Protestantism—especially in northern Europe. This landscape possesses curves and turns in the road similar to the Master LC's and Patinir (their model)'s textlike landscape topographies. Used with permission of The Metropolitan Museum of Art, H. O. Havemeyer Collection, Bequest of Mrs. H. O. Havemeyer, 1929 (29.100.599).

Fig. 9. Joachim Patinir, *Triptych: The Penitence of Saint Jerome*. Circa 1518. Metropolitan Museum of Art, New York City. The conspicuously twisty and turning paths that meander through this landscape at various points seem to construct itineraries, narratives complete with points of pause and punctuation, as is the case with the central figure resting against the wall, and also suggests routes resumed and pursued. The *nouvelle* of Amadour and Floride rehearses a similar itinerary. Used with permission of The Metropolitan Museum of Art, Fletcher Fund, 1936 (36.14a–c). Image © The Metropolitan Museum of Art. All rights reserved.

twists and turns of narrative plot, each sinuosity suggesting a *peripetia* in the plot,[40] and in Gérard David's Nativity triptych, which "invit[e us] to wander, like the Holy Family, through the isolated forest of the exterior wings,"[41] constructing a shadow-box effect that places interior and exterior landscape in juxtaposition.[42] Marguerite's *devisants* wander through an elaborate textual topography leading to God, a map marked with physical locales and place names: "vous trouverez en ce desert la beaulté qui peut estre en toutes les villes; car qui congnoist Dieu veoit toutes choses belles" ("you will find even in this wilderness all the beauty a city could afford. For a person who knows God will find all things beautiful in Him, and without Him all things will seem ugly"—*Hept.* 1.prologue.8; Chilton 67). Marguerite causes her characters to wander through this world, visiting villages like Périgord and "Tollette" (Toledo; 5.40.315) and beyond frontiers such as "la frontiere de Perpignan" (1.10.55); on the high seas (2.13.97) and into monasteries (2.20.156). The amorous captain of *nouvelle* #13 sends his love a poem mapping his real maritime displacements as well as his soul's spiritual wanderings. He constantly uses references to traveling, leaving, returning, ports of call, and destinations; his earthly journeys are circumscribed by the spatial referents of Arctic and Antarctic:

> … en lieu dire que je l'aymois,
> Je luy parlais des signes et des mois
> Et de l'estoille Arcticque et Antarcticque.
>
> ("Yea, when I longed to tell her of my love, / I spoke of signs and times, the skies above, / And of the Arctic or Antarctic star!"—*Hept.* 2.13.101–02; Chilton 172)

Marguerite situates each *nouvelle* at narrative distance from the others; each takes place in a new location—Paris, Amboyse, Naples, Flandre, Nyort—encyclopedically evoking the landscape of Europe and of the known world. In addition, since this landscape is the stage setting for a drama about adultery, it attests to the alienation of earthly places on a map from their true spiritual location. Just as the Reformers perceived the visible church to be disjoined from the invisible church, Marguerite's map shows how the worldly maze of desire misses the mark of its metaphysical referent.

Strapwork Thematics: the *Heptaméron* and Innovations in Ornamentation

Marguerite and other evangelical writers and artists respond to the influence, and incorporate aspects, of decorative arts and objects of handiwork. For instance, the Florentine artist Rosso Fiorentino established the School of Fontainebleau.[43] "Religious painters at the court of François Ier followed the mannerist tendencies of the School of Fontainebleau, and … there was a close parallel between the visual and literary arts in France from 1520–1580." One of Rosso's imitators was Etienne Delaune, who adapted some of Fiorentino's drawings by adding gilded components that made the illustrations look more like jewelry or decorative objects. One example is Delaune's *Sacrifice,* which was modeled on a subject from a Rosso fresco in the Galerie François Ier. Delaune was also known as a *compagnon orfèvre* responsible for the production of decorative arts objects such as cups and bowls. His *Design for a Covered Cup* demonstrates that his engraving technique, characterized by fineness of line and attention to detail, could readily be transferred to ceramics, metal, or enamel working. For this reason, this style is often deemed a hybrid of that of a goldsmith and an illuminator.[44] Many of Delaune's sketches, studies for decorated artifacts, borrowed from similar conceptions sketched by Protestant artists such as Jacques Androuet du Cerceau, suggesting that Delaune may have had evangelical leanings; for example, his study of a covered bowl with its foot resting on three angels' elaborately ornamented heads is very much like an engraving of a salt cellar designed by du Cerceau. Another distinctive aspect of Delaune's particular drawing is its apparent impracticality: his objects are so lavishly detailed that they seem improbable fantastical inventions never intended to be constructed or used. On the other hand, their intricately detailed surface may be a way to represent the material world as it is being transformed for a metaphysical purpose: this cup looks like the Eucharistic *ciborium*, which had a ceremonial use: through this artifact, materiality is thus lifted out of context and redeemed through its incorporation in ritual.

Such illustrations offer a visual epitome of how to undo the material world; they are analogous to Marguerite's manner of using, then surpassing, material objects. Delaune's use of anecdotal realism in his drawings and paintings, notably in scenes drawn from daily life, such as the hound scratching itself in the engraving *Jacob Shown Joseph's Bloody Coat,* also parallels Marguerite's textual strategy. The flea-bitten hound seems more central to the composition than the story itself, perhaps because the tale being told to Jacob is a lie or fiction. Delaune here illustrates an Old Testament theme, typical of evangelical artists.[45]

Evangelical and Reformed artists often lived and worked together, collaborating to create a specific evangelical style in decorative and fine arts. Hugues Sambin (active in Dijon, 1520–1621) and Antoine de Recouvrance, his son-in-law, were later examples of Protestant engravers and illustrators; like their evangelical precursors, they incorporated considerable detail and daily-life imagery into their work. Both of them also imitated and revised some of du Cerceau's artistic conceptions.

From 1520 to 1540, ornamental friezes of grotesque figures were popular[46] as illustrative bands of stucco along mantelpieces, urns, ceilings, or around the edges of paintings. However, as the grotesqueries multiplied, their eccentricity undermined their ornamental value: as each was more quirky than the other, the effect was to make surface and base seem less and less related, the ornamental schemas disruptive rather than decorative. Around 1533–35, Rosso Fiorentino[47] began to create narrative-like relationships among figures in his paintings, interweaving them by means of an innovation called strapwork. Strapwork resembles lengths of black, navy blue, or dark brown leather straps, belt-shaped, that wrap around figures and shapes, buckling them together in groups. Strapwork constituted "an *entirely new decorative system*, in which the surrounds and *links of bands* … are almost more important than the … scenes for which they serve as framework."[48]

Strapwork also is an ornamental innovation contemporary with the *Heptaméron*'s composition.[49] An affiliation between the frame-story and strapwork decoration is likely, due to their similar narrative effect. The illustrative importance of the *devisants'* commentary—both ornamental excess and deigetic addition—forms the equivalent of straps linking the various parts of the *nouvelle* together as a unit. Numerous textually significant artifacts in the *Heptaméron* suggest that decorative arts techniques such as strapwork, applied in a compositional way, may have featured in Marguerite's experiments in applying artistic innovations to a new, textual venue.

Throughout Europe during this time period, strapwork cartouches on chimney-pieces were extremely popular. The *Design for a Fireplace in the Council Chamber of the Town Hall at Zwolle* (1650), possibly by Hans Vredeman de Vries of Antwerp (active circa 1549), exemplified such ornamental schemes. De Vries also published many prints with variants of strapwork style. Strapwork was often associated with historiation, the inclusion on an artifact of word conjoined with image. Historiation aimed at telling a story more fully, and both strapwork and historiated images were much used by evangelical artists, as shown, for instance, by a silver drinking cup from 1569 illustrated with strapwork motifs highlighting the parable of the Prodigal Son.[50] Devised by Coljin de Nole around 1539, a Utrecht chimney-piece also showed Rosso's influence; it incorporated scenes from the Bible and featured strapwork elements. Here, as is often also the case in the *Heptaméron,* either the ornament or the frame took center stage, seemingly more significant than the surface that it adorned:

> the lucid structure of the chimney-piece is largely hidden behind the profuse decoration applied at many levels. The architecture ... fails to come out clearly. As a result, it serves primarily as a support for the reliefs and the freestanding statues.[51]

The story is found in the details, rather than in the larger image or structure.

Rosso's strapwork technique remained in vogue for many years, and can be found on "virtually all applied art objects"[52] and in many interdisciplinary venues such as that of the *Heptaméron.* In Rosso's paintings, compositional motifs interweave, leading the eye through narrative patterns delineated by strapwork outlines. In his *Descent from the Cross* (1521), Rosso unifies a cluster of figures through the lines of the cross, the two ladders flanking the cross, and the lines delineated by the spectators' gesturing arms. Alternating chiaroscuro portions of the composition tie together thematically, despite their seeming contrast or tonal opposition, linked by strapwork running through the entire painting. Rosso provides miniaturized versions of the convention of strapwork, such as the belting on the central figure's waist in the foreground and the intricately draped dark belt around the middle of the background figure to the lower right. He also distributes the body parts of the protagonists so that they form directional lines like strapwork bands: a muscular arm stretches in a nearly straight line to grasp the columnar calf of Christ and an outstretched arm in partial darkness reaches toward Christ's torso from the left. In addition, the horizontal bars of the ladder, along with their vertical stays, create through strapwork a pronounced effect of unity.

> Everything is subordinate to the play of graceful linear rhythms created by the tightly interlocking forms. These patterns unify the surface.[53]

Strapwork thus seems to fill a *narrative* function in a decorative project, enabling diverse elements to be aligned with the interpretive framework.

Other Protestant creators also used strapwork in numerous ways. The Huguenot goldsmith Etienne Delaune decorated a *surtout de table* with such motifs, and Jean Bérain, deemed the "master *ornemaniste* of his age,"[54] used strapwork extensively. For Rosso Fiorentino, strapwork operates as a relational device, much as Marguerite creates inter-referentiality among the often seemingly autonomous *nouvelles* through the background device of the commentators. A resemblance exists between strapwork and surface, the structural role of the frame, and the ribbon of *devisants*' interpretation winding through the *Heptaméron*: strapwork plaits together the various *nouvelles*. In the *Heptaméron*, Marguerite creates a multiplicity of viewpoints through the many voices and perspectives of the male and female *devisants*. Yet, their conclusions steer the narrative in a more unitary sense, creating an overall text rather than fragmentary *nouvelles*. Similarly,

> Rosso's work has two characteristic aspects: he incorporated human figures into his framework—sometimes they seem to be imprisoned in them—and he let the bands curl at the ends, in a way reminiscent of leather straps.[55]

Strapwork functions to unify what might otherwise be disparate or apparently unrelated elements. For instance, herm figures are practically lashed down in a straitjacket of unusually thick and highly stylized belts, and the grotesqueries that swarm around the herms are also tied in place with strapwork in many of Rosso's decorative cartoons. Cornelius de Bos's satyr caught in strapwork imitates Rosso's use of strapwork, capturing the figure within a web of lines and lashings.

Similarly, Oisille models the method for textual exposition, instructing the *devisants* that "de … paour de faire mauvaise election à tel passetemps …il falloit remectre cest [*sic*] affaire à la pluralité d'opinions" ("she was afraid the pastime … might not be a good choice … the question should … be judged after an open discussion [and] point[s] of view"—*Hept.* 1.prologue.8; Chilton 67). Nonetheless, common assessment and accord are the goals: "laissons là les passetemps où deux seullement peuvent avoir part et parlons de celluy qui doibt estre *commun à tous*" ("Let's leave on one side all pastimes that require only two participants, and concentrate on those which everybody can join in"—*Hept.* 1.prologue.9; my emphasis; Chilton 68). Although a wide variety of events and characters are featured in the *nouvelles*, unity prevails because of the commentators' inter-referentiality.

In the *Heptaméron*, each Day ends with a tallying of narrative accounts and of moral profits; thus each Day commences with a reiteration of the conversational framework. These organizational components are analogous to the beltlike lashings tying together Rosso's swarm of grotesque figures, creating some impression of relationship despite disparity and deformity. Marguerite's use of narrative strapwork harnesses chaotic elements of an image, bringing worldly things into line, and conferring order by framing them and constructing patterns of relationship among them.[56]

Evangelicals worried about the proliferation of things in a burgeoning market economy. Strapwork offered a way to organize surplus and to minimize the impact of such surfeit, much as the evangelical perspective sought to limit things and their effect by subordinating them to a larger narrative revelatory of *true* value.[57] Similarly, Marguerite's protagonists are nearly always caught in terrestrial traps of their own construction—

possession, desire, ambition. Yet the trailer to these, the equivalent of the loose belt ends in strapwork, offers hope, a pathway out of the world's bondage toward salvation.

Protestantism and Portraiture: Marks of Sin and Salvation

Many *portraits historiés* incorporate strapwork features, attesting to the evangelical tendency to produce artifacts representing the influence of diverse artistic media. For instance, Marguerite uses mirrors to reflect the notion of personages pondering their identity or their fate. The sylistic technique of the frame narrative also has a mirroring effect: the commentators extrinsic to the stories look in on them, explicate and extrapolate, finding something within the framed tales that reflects their own preoccupations, while, implicitly, the characters of the imbricated story react to issues posed by the discussants. Many Renaissance portraits were painted on mirrors. However, in some cases, such as the popular "bull's eye" mirror that created a distorted reflection, Renaissance mirrors did not always render a viewer's image accurately.[58] Debora Shuger claims that

> In the Renaissance, the self's internal mirror angles outward … What Renaissance persons do see in the mirror are instead saints, friends, offspring, spouses, magistrates, Christ. The mirror reflects these likenesses because they are images of oneself: one encounters one's likeness … in the mirror of the other.[59]

She further remarks that

> the preponderance of evidence suggests that the Renaissance self lacks reflexivity, self-consciousness and individuation and … differs … from … the modern self.[60]

We may hypothesize that, to some extent, the presentation of "self" in sixteenth-century mirrors is collaborative: one adds details about one's appearance from information provided by observers outside the mirror's frame, effectively constructing a "composite," in order to produce a full representation.

Subjectivity may thus be experienced more relationally than reflexively, as a manifestation projected outward rather than a notion contained inwardly. Appropriately, then, in the *Heptaméron* the external frame commentators explore each character; the *devisants* have the final say on how the components of the character's subjectivity will be assembled. This is the case in the fourth *nouvelle*, in which the would-be rapist must confront a truthful version of himself as rejected suitor, failed lover, and thwarted rapist. He contemplates in his mirror the indictment that *others*, not himself, will pass on him. He views his temporary disfigurement in an actual mirror, while also intuiting society's reaction to his act around the margins of his reflection (as if in a bull's eye mirror). His "self" bulges out from its confines, having been distorted by desire, and such distortion is now visible outside himself in a phenomenon akin to the *trompe-l'œil* technique used in Van Eyck's *Arnolfini Marriage* (see fig. 10). Here, the artist is reflected back to himself in his own work through the device of the convex mirror. Van Eyck uses a *trompe-l'œil* technique, through the medium of the convex mirror, to inscribe himself within his own painting: his face is found in the bulging glass.

In a similar way, Marguerite often writes herself and her own experiences into her stories. The *Arnolfini Marriage* acts as does the narrative portraiture practiced by Marguerite: many strata of meaning and symbolism are constructed through material objects; these latter are intricately detailed, inter-related, recount a story and, sometimes, a sub-version of that tale. Van Eyck also often painted framing outlines on his portraits themselves. The *Arnolfini Marriage* is recessed, boxlike, while other contemporary portraits featured separate panels, *trompe l'œil* frames, or inscriptions that acted as frames. It was also customary in many portraits of the period to provide an explanatory text in banderoles, or on the image itself, to assist in deciphering the details of the image. Marguerite may be adapting these conventions, uniting them through frame and framelike ornament, crafting a richly imaged text wherein, ultimately, image yields to the definition and direction supplied by the Word.

The Reformed practice of self-examination, without the Catholic expedient of the confessional or a priest, may be a

Fig. 10. Jan van Eyck, *The Portrait of Giovanni(?) Arnolfini and His Wife Giovanna Cenami(?) ('The Arnolfini Marriage')*. 1434. The National Gallery, London. Van Eyck uses a *trompe-l'œil* technique, through the medium of the convex mirror, to inscribe himself within his own painting: his face is found in the bulging glass. In a similar way, Marguerite often "writes herself into" the diegetical content of her *nouvelles*. The "double portrait" also represents a version of "narrative portraiture" practiced later by Marguerite, in which many strata of meaning and layers of symbolism constructed through material objects, are complexly related to recount a story and, sometimes, a sub-version of that tale. NG186. Image © The National Gallery, London. Used with permission.

factor contributing to this somewhat narcissistic focus on the self.[61] Reformed portraiture aims at displaying an acceptable public self, all the while remaining deeply suspicious of the inner person.[62] Like Van Eyck, Marguerite places herself at some distance from herself as though to scrutinize her acceptability. She writes herself into her text by giving her name or by referring to her role in a story that includes her, as in the story of the attempted rape. This strategy recalls the evangelical Dürer, who, more than any other northern artist "exhibited … an intense and repeated fascination with his own face."[63] Dürer, a devout Lutheran, typified the Reformed tendency to focus on the self with both fascination and suspicious scrutiny. Dürer painted many self-portraits as well as innumerable quick sketches studying himself.

As in the case of Dürer's selection of biblical scenes chosen to represent certain of his own autobiographical moments, Marguerite's explication of key evangelical passages in her *nouvelles* constructs another sort of self-portrait, that of a woman of faith. Her use of material objects as markers of humanity's fallen nature creates genre-painting-like backdrops for her portrait, just as, in early modern portraiture, the innovations, called *ars nuova*, were "based on a closer observation of the physical world … [with] more time and attention [given] to the particulars of … earthly existence … [than had formerly been the case]."[64]

Marguerite's density of imagery and self-reference, the concatenation of often inter-referential *nouvelles,* develops a technique for narrative portraiture. While art historians acknowledge the first recorded northern European self-portrait of and by a woman to be that of Caterina van Hemessen (1528–87) of Flanders, Marguerite, her contemporary, parallels van Hemessen through her narrative portraits and self-portraits.[65]

Still Life: Spirituality in Stasis

Marguerite selects her images in consideration of the narrative role that they will play, and she composes her story as a form of portrait from the perspective of sinner in relation to God. Marguerite's narrative self-portrait has the *devisants* as its frame. Her self-portrait is also a *vanitas* image: unless twinned with the Gospel, her symbols of self indict their own insufficiency. As in the would-be rapist's portrait, *vanitas* still-lifes feature several conventional items: mirror, candle, and skull. The portrait of the assailant is thus composed of the candle with which he lights the glass; the mirror itself; and his bloody face staring in self-scrutiny, fixated on its failure and mortality.

The still life, another artistic innovation contemporary with Marguerite's crafting of her new narrative form, was still a fledgling genre in the sixteenth century. Its emphasis on the impermanence and inadequacy of earthly treasures often produced anamorphosis, or a deceptive semblance. To construct her textual still life, Marguerite catalogues the interior decoration of the châteaux in which her characters dwell. The lists of material furnishings include veils, books, jewelry, locks, swords, and tapestries. From this artistic perspective, each *nouvelle* reads like a theater manager's set of properties, objects that evoke ways of acting or encapsulate roles to be activated. In *nouvelle* #43, for instance, we find this list of props: "craie; ung pourpoinct de satin; une robbe fourrée; une garderobbe; une cornette; ung touret de nez; des habillemens … de veloux …" ("velvet clothes … A private room … a piece of chalk … crimson satin doublet and the robe edged with lynx fur … a mask … her cap …"—*Hept.* 5.43.296–301; Chilton 395–97). So extensive are these enumerations that often the effect seems confined to material description rather than producing a representation of selfhood: "Voyez-vous bien cestuy-là, qui a ce pourpoinct de satin cramoisy, et ceste robbe fourrée de loups cerviers?" ("do you see that gentleman … with the crimson satin doublet and the robe edged with lynx fur?"—*Hept.* 5.43. 297; Chilton 392). However, Marguerite steers each narrative in and through these surfaces composed of material substances; she causes one of her characters to say that "tous les biens que l'on sçauroit donner à personne ne me sçauroient destourner d'un pas du propos d'où je suis" ("there is … no gift in the world that could make me stray from my chosen path"—*Hept.* 5.62.292; Chilton 386).

Marguerite incorporates a form of still life into her narrative by using the theatrical technique of the *tableau,* an early-modern charade or pantomime. The pretext for storytelling in the *nouvelles* is, frequently, the enumeration of objects, which are then juxtaposed, grouped, displayed in various configurations and relationships. This process initiates the construction of significance. At the same time, it begins the process whereby earthly meaning will be undone: the objects are rendered extraneous by the narrative itself. In still-life-like compositions, Marguerite poses characters in symbolic transactions, allowing the message of a *nouvelle* to be suggested by these *tableaux*. For example, in *nouvelle* #41, Simontault comments on the deceptions that a lubricious confessor has practiced on a maiden and her mother: he has attempted to coerce the girl into allowing him to beat her nude body. Yet Simontault excuses the priest in this way: it was Christmas, and the confessor was play-acting Joseph's role in the nativity story.[66]

> tenant la place de Joseph auprès d'une belle vierge, il voulloit essayer à faire ung petit enfant, pour jouer au vif le mistere de la Nativité.
>
> ("because he was in the same situation as Joseph—in the company of a beautiful virgin, and he wanted to beget a child so that he could truly play his part in the mystery of the Nativity!"—*Hept.* 5.41.285; Chilton 379)[67]

In such a narrative still life in the *Heptaméron*, at least two textual layers coexist and comment on each other. Similarly, Pieter Aertsen's *Vanitas Still-Life with Christ in the House of Mary and Martha*, a work painted at the peak of the Lutheran Reformation, illustrates Scripture through the use of ephemeral objects and extensive ornamentation. A Scripture scene, framed, to the far left of the painting, is overshadowed by a hefty joint of meat, accompanied by quotidian objects such as jugs, flagons, flowers, and a loaf of bread. The inset figure of Christ is diminutive in comparison with the objects in the foreground. Christ's instruction is that his followers should divest themselves of all such earthly attachments and attractions that loom perceptually so large, yet Aertsen has dramatized the tension between things of the world and things of the spirit by placing

> a complete "vanitas" ... emphatically in the foreground, leaving only a little vista in which Martha is corrected by

> Jesus. Here too an abundance of earthly riches is contrasted with Christ's message, the temporal against the eternal values of the Gospel.[68]

Similarly, earthly treasures obstruct, yet eventually yield to, a theological perspective in the *Heptaméron*.

Marguerite's Narrative "Passetemps": Interdisciplinary Interplay in the *Heptaméron*

Marguerite profited from the latitude implicit in the evangelical perspective: things of the world are not flawed *in se*; what is problematic is human lust for, and inappropriate use of, earthly objects. Marguerite is thus freed to experiment with narrative discussions of doctrinal issues, illustrating them through the incorporation of real-life objects, and communicating her perspective through a dialogue with contemporary innovations in the arts. In the prologue to the *Heptaméron*, Marguerite explains how Oisille gathers the circle of *devisants* together so that, stressed and disoriented by the great flood that has interrupted their voyage, they may re-create themselves through story. She uses a specific word to describe these stories: calling them "passetemps," she interprets this term in relation to theological vocabulary. The frequent corollary of "passetemps" in evangelical and Reformed writings is "proufict." Scripture often refers to the "profit" to be gained from following biblical precepts; the book of Proverbs and the synoptic gospels are particularly illustrative of this concept. Calvin also used this term in a theological, rather than exclusively economic, way—a technique that mirrors Marguerite's use of materiality to prompt metaphysical discussion.[69] He says, "à fin que les lecteurs puissent mieux faire leur profit de ce present livre, je leur veux bien monstrer en brief l'utilité qu'ilz auront à en prendre" ("So that the readers might better profit from this book, I want to show them briefly its usefulness").[70] These "passetemps" "puiss[ent] delivrer de vos ennuyctz ..." ("[they] can deliver you from your worries"); they will be "le remede de toute [votre] vie" ("the remedy for your entire life"); and are constituted by "la lecture des sainctes lettres" ("the reading of holy stories"). Calvin reflects on aspects of the "saincte parolle et bonne nouvelle" ("the holy Word and Good News"—*Hept.* 4.prologue.7).[71]

This notion of textual re-creation is a form of Gospel re-enactment, a recalling of theological truths such as that of the Resurrection, culminating in a theatrical and visual feast that encourages readers' participation in the evangelical message:

> Oisille sceut très bien sercher le passaige où l'Escripture reprent ceulx qui sont negligens d'ouyr ceste saincte parolle; et non seullement leur lisoit le texte et leur faisoit tant de bonnes et sainctes expositions qu'il n'estoit possible de s'ennuyer à l'oyr.
>
> ("Oisille knew how to find the passage in which Scripture reproaches those who are negligent in listening to the sacred word. She not only read them the text, [but] she also gave such sound and good expositions that no one could possibly find it boring."—*Hept.* 4.prologue.236; Chilton 324)

Marguerite constructs relationships among the numerous tales by means of a single frame. Her narrative becomes a laboratory in which each *nouvelle* is assayed as a space for the development of evangelical *practical* application ("experimentée") of Scripture: "Elle *experimentoit* ce que Dieu commande, de faire bien à ceulx qui font mal" ("she was practising God's command to do good to those who wrong you"—*Hept.* 4.38.271; emphasis added; Chilton 362).

Randle Cotgrave's *A Dictionarie of the French and English Tongues* gives one of the meaning of the term *passetemps* as "recreation." Marguerite's creative collage of materials—artistic, theological, literary—is taken in a Christian sense as a re-creation: a re-making, and a redemption, of the fallen world. Cotgrave's terminology further delineates the sensual qualities of ordinary life implied by early modern understanding of *passetemps*; he includes sample expressions such as "to passe [one's] dayes in *all fullnesse of sensuall contentments* … to follow … his *delights*."[72]

A common recreation or *passetemps* of early modern women was embroidery and lace-making, *passementerie*, in which ladies created a finely worked object: the object itself is thus symbolic of all the days spent in its fashioning. Material objects share this function in the *Heptaméron*, also, and *text* and *textile*—found in the *nouvelles* in the forms of curtains, clothing, bedclothes, sumptuous fabrics, copies of books and letters—are linguistically related: they both derive from *textus*, a term meaning "to weave," whether it be a tapestry or a tale.

Further, the phrase *passement de tesmoings* designates "an examination of witnesses,"[73] just as the *nouvelles* witness to a reality beyond themselves. Earthly objects, clearly, participate in this process of redemption. When Marguerite calls her narrative a *passetemps*, she is demonstrating its application of everyday life aspects and objects in a collaborative process with her message of salvation: *passetemps* also means "solace."[74]

Chapter Four

Of Tableware, Chalices, and Axeheads

The Evangelical Narrative and Transitory Treasures

> Vous n'estez le premier de ma congnoissance qui, trop toust voulent estre riche, devenir et parvenir, est à l'envers tombé en pauvreté: voire quelquefoys s'est cassé le coul.
>
> ("You're not the first man I've met who's wanted to get rich too quickly and make his way in the world, but who has fallen down into poverty, and sometimes even broken his neck.")
>
> François Rabelais
> *Quart livre*[1]

The evangelical writer explicates characters and relationships in reference to things of the world; however, narrative problems arise from their presence, because the evangelical author remains ambivalent about objects, and cultivates an attitude of distrust about them. Charles Taylor explains the evangelical attitude toward objects in this way:

> God placed mankind over creation and made the things of the world for human use. But humans are there in turn to serve and glorify God, and so their use of things should serve this final goal. The consequence of sin is that humans come to be concerned with these things not for God's sake but for themselves. They come to desire them as ends and no longer simply as instruments for God's purposes. And this upsets the whole order of things. Humans were meant to bring the rest of creation to God.[2]

Evangelical writers find license to use earthly objects in narrative when they attempt to realign them with this higher purpose.[3]

Luther, Marguerite, and Rabelais draw on shared prototypes in crafting their evangelical genre. Luther and Rabelais both mention Aesop's *Fables*,[4] while Luther, Marguerite, and Rabelais all incorporate proverbs, parables, and aphorisms in their narratives. The most frequent recourse to a narrative model among the three is, however, the gospels, especially Jesus' use of the parable, coupled with the writings of St. Paul. Luther set the tone for Marguerite and Rabelais. Translated into French around 1524 to 1534, at least three of his *Treatises* circulated in diverse social groups throughout France. Among the most popular of his writings were the *Petit catéchisme de Luther* (1520) and the *Petit livre de prières* (*Betbüchlein*), translated in 1522, as well as several of his introductions to St. Paul's letters, and the *Treatise on Christian Liberty*. At this time, few French evangelicals dared to profess their faith openly.[5] Nonetheless, the French translations of Luther's texts possessed a pronounced French tenor, attesting to interest in evangelical piety and a desire to incorporate Lutheran thought in France.[6] Such conformity in idiom, as well as ideology, especially manifested itself around the time that Marguerite began to write the *Heptaméron*. Louis de Berquin had translated the majority of Luther's works into French. These translations were condemned by the Sorbonne from 1523 through 1525. In 1529 Louis de Berquin was burned at the stake for having propagated evangelical doctrine. The translations nevertheless went into print and circulation because François Ier himself granted publication, a concession obtained through Marguerite's intercession.

Other evidence explicitly associates Luther and Marguerite. The evangelical printer of Luther's works in France, Simon Du Bois, participated with Marguerite in evangelical circles.[7] Prior to 1530, Du Bois had published a translation in Alençon of Luther's *Petit catéchisme*.[8] Du Bois dedicated several volumes that he published to Marguerite's interlocutor, Jacques Lefèvre d'Étaples,[9] and Du Bois also printed several of Marguerite's works.[10]

Luther and Evangelical Storytelling

> Riches are the most insignificant things on earth, the smallest gift that God can give a man. What are

> they in comparison even with physical endowments and beauty? What are they in comparison with gifts of the mind? And yet we act as if this were not so! The matter, form, effect and goal of riches are worthless.
>
> Martin Luther
> *Table Talk*[11]

Table Talk was written over several years in the 1530s, prior to, but contemporary with, the writing of the *Heptaméron*. However, it was not published until 1566. Although *Table Talk* came out in print too late to have influenced Marguerite's composition in any explicit way, its technique for textual exposition derived from Luther's commentaries and tracts that were already known to Marguerite. *Table Talk* thus provided a parallel to Marguerite's project: it used biblical interpretive strategies and applied them to a predominantly secular narrative.

Table Talk, like the *Heptaméron*, employs the frame format and *devisants* to discuss issues in the stories recounted. These interlocutors speak in an informal setting, usually before or after a meal, and express their opinions, much as the friends assembled around Luther's supper table contribute anecdotes, ask questions, and discuss issues. The banquet meals in *Table Talk* also symbolically reenact the celebration of the Eucharist and the agape feast, similar to the representations of the Andouilles episode of the *Quart livre.* Rabelais also includes the banquet with King Sainct Panigon and the one with the Chiquanous. Other evangelical works of the period employ the banquet scenario similarly as a structuring device: Erasmus's *Colloquies* contains banqueting episodes, and Béroalde de Verville's *Le moyen de parvenir* is structured on an identical textual conceit, recalling Plato's *Symposium* and Marsilio Ficino's Neo-Platonist commentary on it. Luther's *Table Talk* is one of the first evangelical narratives to use the banqueting conceit explicitly to dramatize a Christian discussion.

Despite the influence of Luther's theology in France,[12] *Table Talk* circulated in a troubled context. In 1523, the Faculty of Theology in Paris wrote a *Determinatio* against Luther, condemning the study of Lutheran thought. In 1525, Lefèvre d'Étaples and Gérard Roussel, noted evangelicals and popularizers of

Luther in France, fled to Strasbourg. This tense climate perhaps accounted for the often veiled quality of theological expression in evangelical texts. To some extent, and for similar reasons, Marguerite's fictional prose offered camouflage for her religious convictions. Another consequence of this context was that considerable textual weight was placed in details, the fine points that, explicated and interpreted, revealed the work's evangelical perspective.

A similar phenomenon occurred in contemporary art. Significant details might inflect a painting in the direction of an evangelical or, later, an explicitly Reformed message. For instance, the Netherlandish painter and creator of woodcuts, Cornelis Anthonisz, depicted a *Fides* figure carrying a crucifix. (This motif was typically more evangelical than Reformed; Calvinists usually showed the cross, when they did so at all, devoid of the *corpus*.) However, Anthonisz's context (1536–54) was still Catholic, albeit in transition, so this *Allegory of the Prodigal Son* used details such as the crucifix so as to be acceptable on the surface to a Catholic, while making an evangelical statement. It was therefore no doubt significant that Anthonisz did not sign this piece.[13]

The puzzle-like quality of some of the ornamental schemas of both Northern European fine arts and decorative arts pieces requires a certain amount of deciphering. These pieces had considerable influence on contemporary French art. The artist's subjectivity—and spiritual perspective—caused the elements of a work of art to be envisioned in a new way, forming ever-new compositions. Using an artistic technique in narrative venue, the *Heptaméron* similarly engages the reader in an imaginative attempt at participatory composition, inviting the reader to divine the meaning hidden beneath the surface.[14] An evocative or unusual detail in a painting, on an object, or in a story may generate discussion about matters of faith. An aura of incongruity or a feeling of being misplaced often signals such details; they alert the viewer/reader to an extrusion or an element of editorializing. The detail may be the tip of a subtext that, when interpreted, may reveal itself to be the *primary* text.

Art works, prints and engravings, and texts themselves were subject to such treatment, as evangelicals sought ways to use objects and images in a way different from statues and conventional religious iconography. For instance, printmaking was the primary artistic medium that met the demand for nonidolatrous religious imagery.

> In about 1510, … Lucas van Leyden … engraved a … Baptism of Christ … He arranged the composition in a way that became something of a trademark in his later works. Lucas van Leyden "inverted" his composition, placing the traditionally prominent, main religious figure of Jesus in the background, and populating the foreground with large, anonymous bystanders [making] … the event … seem incidental, part of a larger narrative or discussion. *This is not a presentation of doctrine so much as a conversation about its meaning and purpose.*[15]

In this engraving, the Reformed artist van Leyden followed the evangelical and Reformed practice of adding—or, in this case, omitting—significant details, such as the dove of the Holy Spirit. Reading literally, he did *not* choose to include the dove, because it was not mentioned in Scripture at the very moment of baptism, but rather at a slightly *later* narrative moment. He also *added* other details, such as the child near the front pointing to the baptismal scene: art historians feel that this figure may allude to the Reformed stance advocating adult over infant baptism.[16]

Luther's narrative technique shows that things of the world can possess meaning when placed in relation to their origin and rationale: metaphysical reality. Luther summarizes this "bridging" strategy of materialism by insisting that "the sign and the promise [must] … be tied to each other, not torn from each other."[17] Marguerite uses the frame narrative to similar effect: the commentators contain and curtail interpretation, explicating in a scriptural sense. Further, Marguerite's narrative technique foreshadows the redemption of things of the world. Material objects, because of their artificiality, are marked by the contrivance and incompleteness characteristic of fallen nature; however, through the incorporation of worldly objects in a narrative that revises their use and meaning, materiality can be rehabilitated.

A similar phenomenon also occurred in publishing history: from 1525 to 1566, it was forbidden to print the New Testament in French.[18] However, Robert Estienne, a Huguenot printer living in Paris, continued to publish the New Testament in Latin with his own Latin marginalia manifesting a Reformed perspective. His New Testament, then, was also a framed text using a technique similar to the one employed by Marguerite in framing her seemingly secular *Heptaméron*. Marguerite's new narrative form may have influenced the Reformers' "marginalia Bibles." These were composed of scriptural text framed by reader's comments jotted in the margins, and were published in Geneva some twenty years after the publication of the *Heptaméron*.[19] The *devisants*' commentary appears similar to the Reformed glossing of the text. Marguerite initiates a discussion among the commentators and within the frame that they constitute, an interaction that acts as a *mise-en-abyme* for process and technique of correct interpretation, a significant Reformed concern.

The stories that Marguerite and Luther tell are explained by figures outside the narrative, and are framed in terms of moral instruction: "let us speak about good things and godly matters. Our Lord Jesus Christ is the one about whom one can never say enough that is good," declares Luther.[20] Luther aims at imparting precepts, while Marguerite hopes to initiate a discussion—one that will also, ultimately, teach a lesson. *Table Talk* collects Luther's statements, but usually does not offer any framing discussion or record of response, while Marguerite relies on the dramatic dialogue format of the *devisants*.[21] This space between audition and reception in the *Heptaméron* mimes the intellectual process of acceptance and spiritual assent to a reality higher than earthly norms, inviting the reader thereby into the dynamics of conversion. Just as a specific audience is envisioned for each story, the material objects chosen to represent that story will also have significance for particular constituencies: "one should preach about things that are suited to a given place and given persons," Luther counsels.[22] Luther's use of detail and anecdote in the friendly supper-time chats transcribed in *Table Talk* renders doctrinal matters into daily-life terms.[23] He refers to quotidian objects, relating homely stories to crystallize and summarize them in a memorable way, then encourages discussion about them. Luther, Marguerite, Rabelais, and other evangelical and Reformed writers all manifest aspects of this narrative approach.

Table Talk spans the years 1531 through 1543. Luther often gathered with family, friends, and followers, sharing the evening meal at which he presided as patriarch, illustrating Scripture, and instructing about doctrinal matters. Marguerite's *devisants* congregate each day *before* the evening meal to share stories, expounding on the narrative's meaning before, during, and after their meals. Both Marguerite and Luther characterize Scripture as the "bread of life" that nourishes both body and soul. Further, they both consider earthly objects as possible vehicles to a fuller knowledge of God. However, objects are never deemed to possess full significance in themselves, nor are they containers of the divine. For instance, Luther says that what matters most at the Eucharist is God's ability to work in the world, not the question of whether the wafer's substance itself is physically altered: "[As for] trans-substantiation ... I think that the bread and wine remain ... Yet it is in truth the power of God, as Paul calls it."[24] Luther also hypothesizes how materiality may paradoxically lead to a metaphysical insight: "Grace does not entirely change nature, but nature as it finds it,"[25] he states: materiality may be a starting point or tool, although not an end in itself. Nature in its current state is fallen away; God's action is required to restore it to its full and original integrity so that materiality may map the way to the domain of metaphysics.

The principle, the abstract concept, the right theology, is paramount for Luther, and he explicates these emphases through concrete imagery and practical illustration. Luther refers to the Psalms, which enumerate many daily-life objects. He describes a treatment similar to Marguerite's evangelical hermeneutic, in which objects signify up to a certain point, but then are stripped of ultimate significance:

> Faith separates the vanity from the substance. David used a bow, a sword, and weapons, and he said, "Not in my bow do I trust" [Ps. 44:6], but he didn't spurn the weapons. So believers say, "My wife, children, gold, etc. won't keep in heaven," but they don't throw them away; they separate vanity from substance ... So vanity is to be put aside, not substance.[26]

In this anecdote, Luther does not advocate a policy of radical renunciation—that could backfire, and cause one to covet that which one claims to do without, making things into idols. Rather, he advocates a reasoned protest against materiality as the exclusive focus of existence. This pragmatic approach to daily life illustrates Luther's understanding of religion: "True theology is practical."[27]

The rehabilitation of daily life as possessing possible elements of vocation is a contribution that the Reformation, and particularly Luther, made to the early modern mentality. There are several explanations for this focus on the quotidian.[28] First, the shift from trust in the clergy to concentration on Scripture as lived out by a faithful body of unordained people created a new emphasis on the role, and reliability, of the laity. This change was also accompanied by a shift from the actual practice of piety in church, to the quintessentially Protestant patriarchal model of domestic piety or the "home church."

Interestingly, this change in focus and venue was roughly contemporaneous with the surge in influence of Netherlandish and Flemish genre painting in France, and the genre painters' typical concentration on detailed interior spaces.[29] Secondly, Reformation strictures on the depiction of sacred imagery may have forced religious art into other venues. Art of the Reformation tended to secularization, more often depicting ordinary scenes and characters accompanied by daily-life objects. This was also the case with genre paintings.[30]

Lutheran theology influenced Marguerite to move religious discussion out of an exclusively theological venue and into secular arenas. Luther, like Marguerite, innovates by using the primarily secular story as a vehicle for theological exposition. He discusses the question of "whether the tools of the arts and nature are useful to theology," and determines that "one knife cuts better than another." Consequently, "good tools—for example, language and the arts—can contribute to clearer learning … A thing must be distinguished from its misuse."[31] Luther's storytelling strategy (as well as his sermonizing technique) takes daily-life reference as its point of departure, showing subsequently how a metaphysical *telos* transforms that object or event:

> Ah, what does reason understand? It can't comprehend how man is made from a drop of blood, how a cherry grows from

> a blossom, how bone and flesh came into existence. The world is full of everyday miracles ... But what happens daily is counted of little consequence. God produces wine from stones and makes butter and bread out of sand. So He once formed man out of the ground, and now He creates men every day out of drops of blood.[32]

Luther emphasizes God's marvelous adoption and transformation of created substances. By mentioning blood, cherries, bread, butter, Luther incorporates the mundane aspects of everyday existence into a theological discussion, demonstrating how things may point to salvation. Luther does not interpret things allegorically, as do Catholics, but rather *narratively*: things can suggest, prompt, or summarize a story, but are not placed in a schema requiring decoding. Luther, like Calvin, who calls allegorists "jugglers" and "street magicians," worries that allegories can mislead, and are either too complex or too simplistic, creating the potential for error in interpretation.

> "When I was a monk," he regrets, "I was a master in the use of allegories. I allegorized everything. Afterward, through the Epistle to the Romans, I came to some knowledge of Christ. I recognized then that allegories are nothing, that it's not what Christ signifies but what Christ is that counts. Before, I allegorized everything, even a chamber-pot, but afterward I reflected on the histories ..."[33]

Luther explains why he eschews allegorical interpretation by referring again to a thing: the allusion to the chamber-pot underscores that worldly objects should not be granted any deep significance in and of themselves.

Luther tells a tale about himself to demonstrate the proper use of material objects. The story essentially is a theory in miniature, one that Marguerite also follows. Luther states,

> When I was young I was learned, especially before I began to study theology. At that time I dealt with allegories, tropologies and analogies and did nothing but clever tricks with them. If somebody had them today they'd be looked upon as rare relics. I know they're nothing but rubbish. Now I've let them go, and this is my last and best art, to translate the Scriptures in the plain sense. The literal sense does it—

> in it, there's life, comfort, power, instruction and skill. The other is tomfoolery, however brilliant the impression it makes.[34]

Material objects become the concrete manifestation of the biblical "plain style," especially when they are genre painting-like: simple, uncomplicated, sensual, grouped in meaningful patterns and their instrumentality readily comprehended by the average person.[35] They are not truth, but a vehicle leading to it.

Conformity to Scripture is essential, both for Luther and for Marguerite. Marguerite's constant concern to "donner ordre" in the *nouvelles* is similar to Luther's reforming impulse: "the papists … have invented a multitude of [rituals and doctrines] … We must therefore restore everything to its right shape—that is, to conformity with the Word of God." Just as the telling and the hearing of Gospel stories can spur conversation and conversion, so, too, stories energized by a material motor can have a constructive effect. Things become text, as material substance shadows forth metaphysical truth: "He gave thought to the pleasant weather of the month of May, whose blooms are a *parable* of the resurrection of the dead."[36]

Just as the telling and the hearing of Gospel stories can spur conversation and conversion, so, too, stories energized by a material motor can have a constructive effect. Things become text, as material substance shadows forth metaphysical truth: "He gave thought to the pleasant weather of the month of May, whose blooms are a *parable* of the resurrection of the dead."[37] Things hold stories within themselves; they are mute witnesses to a truth that both permits and surpasses them—until the narrative activates their potential. From a narrative perspective, such an awareness is equivalent to the Reformed focus on the individual: Protestant theology stipulated that each human was accountable for himself to God, received no intercessory dispensation, and had to "work out" his own salvation. Luther doles out stories like pharmaceuticals for the diseases of the soul:

> the Gospel for the third Sunday after Trinity is an excellent portrait … of how God is disposed towards sinners and how solicitously he seeks them out. The subject and theme of the gospel is repentance, for it speaks of contrite and penitent sinners, to whom this gospel should be preached.[38]

Elsewhere, Luther links wealth and riches to a narrative format, observing that the rich must give a scrupulous accounting, for "to whom much is given, of him much will be required [Luke 12: 48]. Wealth, talent, beautiful form are like fine gifts of God, but we misuse them badly."[39] Luther understands his own life experiences through narrative forms. He cites Aesop's *Fables* extensively, deeming them "next to the Bible ... the best."[40] As in Aesop's *Fables*, Luther often chooses daily-life objects, consistent with the Bible's discussion of the most mundane details of life in reference to matters of faith. "Things in Scripture ... are like the plot of a story which a writer ... adopts and to which he adds character and circumstances."[41]

Marguerite and Luther both apply the daily-life criterion because it is immediately relevant and understandable to contemporary readers. They make the object chosen work in an iconic way, pointing beyond itself rather than to itself so that the image will not lure with its purported self-sufficiency. To illustrate this point, Luther recalls how the Jews wandering in the desert wanted to worship the golden calf and other things evident to the eye: "so they see only the serpent held up on a pole in Numbers 21 and not the Word."[42] The goal is eventually to do without the object: to build up treasures in heaven—spiritual, abstract, invisible, nonmaterial—rather than on earth. This dispossession of material evidence is the very essence of faith; it is also the technique for textual interpretation advocated by evangelicals.[43] Like Luther, Marguerite and Rabelais revise parables, often from the Gospel of Matthew, which they then shape into contemporary anecdotes. One example is the apocalyptic pronouncement of Christ's Second Coming, in which two women are milling in a field, sifting wheat from chaff, yet only one shall be taken up in the Rapture while the other shall remain in the field. The milling or sifting activity points to God's activity of discrimination, of separating sinners from the faithful. Luther recalls Scripture in his allusion to the daily-life object of the millstone to exemplify a doctrinal perspective: he intertwines teaching with text, theology with anecdote:[44]

> The teaching of law and gospel are altogether necessary, but they must be distinguished even when they are conjoined ... [there is] an upper and lower millstone. The upper

> millstone rumbles and pounds. This is the law. It is very well set up by God so that it grinds. On the other hand, the lower millstone is quiet, and this is the gospel. Our Lord God has suspended the upper millstone in such a way that the grain is crushed and ground only on the lower stone.[45]

Here, Luther distinguishes between the top and bottom components of a grinding mechanism. His analogy is between the top as the Mosaic law, in which retribution is meted out according to the misdemeanor, and the bottom as the Gospel, or the mandate of love, which is not legalistic but endlessly forgiving. While both are needed to crush grain, Luther points out that it is only on the *lower* stone that the grain is *transformed* into a new substance, that of flour. The Gospel transforms its hearers into people with a metaphysical mission, just as the millstone transforms an inedible and raw product into a nourishing foodstuff. This anecdote, a parable, may appear to be an allegory, but it is not. Parables are wisdom literature, and their advice goes beyond the bounds of worldly knowledge; their truth is granted to the special few who discern it, not through a system of deciphering, as with allegory, but through an appeal to the heart.

Luther illustrates the principle of evangelical narrative: the practical application of Scripture to the daily life of the ordinary believer. Luther expresses his standard in this way:

> In my preaching I take pains to treat a verse, to stick to it, and so to instruct the people that they can say, "that's what the sermon was about." When Christ preached he proceeded quickly to a parable and spoke about sheep, shepherds, wolves, vineyards, fog, trees, seeds, fields, plowing. The poor lay people were able to comprehend these things.[46]

The object encapsulates the message for the listener's memory, but he who has truly heard and understood the message grasps the kernel of truth rather than needing to retain the object itself. Luther's strategy—like that of other evangelical writers after him—is pragmatic and experiential in its narrative application.

Rabelais's Evangelical Fables

Following this model, Rabelais opens the *Quart livre* with a sort of parable, the instructive tale of a woodsman, Couillatris, who loses his axe. This fable-like tale illustrates the evangelical distrust of excessive reliance on, or desire for, things. Rabelais's narrative treatment of objects is very similar to the way in which Luther and Marguerite write about objects, as Rabelais's story about Couillatris the woodsman demonstrates how not to misuse things. The story has a prophetic overlay: the same mishap that befalls Couillatris also happened to Elisha, "a son of the prophets in Israel," in the Book of 2 Kings (6.1–7);[47] this intertext highlights Rabelais's evangelical concern to illustrate Scripture. Having lost his axe, Couillatris prays to Jupiter to restore it to him. Jupiter decides to test Couillatris, offering him axes of gold and silver. Couillatris, however, remains adamant: he wants his own, humble, axe with its wooden handle, and none other. Rabelais's text is ambiguous here: it is not clear whether Couillatris lost his entire axe or only the axehead. However, Couillatris's personal identifying mark would have been incised, as was the practice among woodsmen, into the wooden handle. Further, *coignée* can mean either the head of the axe that fits into the handle or the entire axe. The wordplay on the axe handle is sexual; *coignée* may suggest intercourse, since the axe penetrates into the gripping sheath of the handle.[48] Consequently, the choice of the appropriate axe is meant to be personal and organic, just as the ability to make good choices is an essential part of one's identity, crucial for knowledge of oneself as part of an ontological order (and, as with the Elisha reference, absolutely necessary if one is to speak the Word of the Lord with accuracy.) It is acceptable for Couillatris to want to have restored to him something that he uses daily and that bears his *marque*,[49] while it would be arrogant were he to covet a more expensive golden axe. Other woodsmen, hearing of the precious goods with which Jupiter is tempting Couillatris, throw away their own axes on purpose, hoping to cash in on a similar deal.

> "Hen, hen! (dirent-ilz) ne tenoit-il qu'à la perte d'une coignée que riches ne feussions? Le moyen est facile et de

> coust bien petit … Hen, hen, ha! par Dieu, coignée, vous serez perdue, et ne vous en desplaise!" Adonques tous perdirent leurs coignées … Tous choisissoient celle qui estoit d'or, et l'amassoient … mais sus l'instant qu'ilz la levoient de terre … Mercure leurs tranchoit les testes.
>
> ("'Ho, ho! My dear hatchet, you're going to get lost, if you don't mind. Lost you shall be, by God!' So they all lost their hatchets … Each one chose the gold one, picked it up … But as each one was lifting it from the ground, Mercury cut off his head."—Rabelais, *Quart livre* 557–58; Cohen 447–48)

Their heads, appropriately, are turned down, toward the earth; rather than lifted to contemplate a higher gain, they are pulled down by their lust for treasure, at which they greedily grab. They suffer the penalty of death, the fate predicted in the Gospel to those who do not renounce the world. Couillatris, however, having made the right decision, prospers. His axe is eventually restored to him, and he is happy. Rabelais uses the evangelical terminology, *joye*, associated in Luther, Marguerite, and Rabelais with Gospel joy[50] or the "peace which passeth all understanding," to show that Couillatris, by rejecting the temptation of earthly *thresors,* lives in alignment with scriptural expectations:

> Puis prend en main la coignée de boys: il reguarde au bout du manche, en icelluy recongnoist sa marque et, tressaillant tout de joye … dist: "Merdigues, ceste-cy estoit mienne! … me la voulez laisser."
>
> ("Then he picked up his own hatchet, looked hard at the wooden helve, and recognized his mark on it; upon which he bounded with joy … Said he, 'This one's mine … leave it for me.'"—*Quart livre* 556; Cohen 446)

Not traduced by treasure, but rather content with his lot, he responds appropriately to the grace and mercy symbolized by the restitution of his axe by offering sacrifice to the divinity. Rabelais underscores the moral of the tale by reiterating the evangelical turn away from riches and earthly treasures: "Soubhaitez donc médiocrité: elle vous adviendra, et encores mieux deuement" ("So wish in moderation. What you ask will come to you, and better things too …"—*Quart livre* 559; Cohen 448). While moderation in all things was a humanistic goal deriving from Greek wisdom, the emphasis here is typical of evangelical narrative, first, because a story is used to impart the precept, and, secondly, because worldly objects and treasures are renounced. The result is a very concrete and practical lesson rooted in reality, rather than an abstract recommendation of moderation.

Like Luther and Marguerite, Rabelais enumerates and describes in detail worldly objects in his narrative. He lists many decorative arts pieces, precious objects, and serving utensils:

> vous, maistre d'hostel, prenez ce bassin d'argent: je le vous donne … prenez ces deux couppes d'argent doré … donnez-leur mes beaulx plumailz, avecques les pampillettes d'or … je vous donne ce flacon d'argent … ceste corbeille d'argent … ceste nasselle d'argent doré … ces cuillères d'argent et ce drageouir.
>
> ("Master Oudart, this silver flagon is for you … these two dishes I give to the porters … this silver basket is for my valets. This silver-gilt bowl is for the grooms … there are ten porringers … silver spoons and [a] comfit-box … a large salt cellar …"—*Quart livre* 600; Cohen 480)

These elaborate and ornate objects circulate in a propitiatory potlatch ("je vous donne … donnez-leur"), part of narrative exchange or *passe-temps*. In addition, like Marguerite and Luther, Rabelais uses the strategy of comparison. Through simile, he builds up lists of references that do not sustain the weight of the relationship in which they find themselves; in this way, he underscores the fragility of objects when too much meaning is ascribed to them.

This is the case, for instance, with Rabelais's description of Quaresmeprenant, who is more "meprenant" ("mistaken") than self-denying ("Caresme," or Lent). While Rabelais seems to be constructing a portrait of the giant, this is ultimately an Arcimboldesque endeavor in which Rabelais amasses things unrelated to the object being formed in order to create a *trompe-l'œil* portrait. While the illusion of coherence may exist, the separate objects have no relationship each to the other;

their selection is idiosyncratic and without rationale. Only the frame—that of the portrait ultimately limned—holds them in any sort of relationship, and the illusion threatens to revert to the initial chaotic state of nonrelationship at any time.[51] While Arcimboldo uses elements of the created order to portray features on a face, for instance, Rabelais's objects are more frequently artificial (*un châssis*; *un bourdon*; *un tabouret*—a wooden frame, a bagpipe, a stool)[52] and without relationship to each other, let alone to the face they purportedly construct (unlike Arcimboldo who, for "Winter," for example, appropriately builds a face out of winter root vegetable features).

The similarities between Arcimboldo and Rabelais suggest deliberate stylistic imitation. Arcimboldo, like Marguerite and Rabelais, also employs the framing strategy to harness the disparate elements of his construction. Marguerite's *devisants* clarify and elucidate relationships among people and things in the *nouvelle,* and this framing discussion inflects the reception of the story. Arcimboldo makes frames within a frame: for "Summer," for instance, he fashions a border of loosely framed blossoms. This frame seems unnecessary, since the canvas will be framed in actuality; however, the painted frame creates thematic coherence internal to the portrait and which would otherwise be lacking. Like the *devisants'* usually practical and reasoned debates (prose different from the often emotional expression of the *nouvelles*), "Arcimboldo's frames feature a different style from that of the figure."[53] The interplay between the two idioms encourages the reader/viewer to construct meaning, as is also the case with the *Heptaméron.* Dialogue about content, crucial in Rabelais and Marguerite, occurs through a visual device in Arcimboldo: the portraits of the seasons, depicted serially "in [various] profiles ... suggest that they can be interpreted as dialogues."[54] Each appears to be engaging an interlocutor.

Rabelais uses a metaphysical frame: the evangelical perspective that Gargantua first expresses and that Pantagruel then sustains throughout Rabelais's works. Rabelais, like Arcimboldo, employs a proliferation of ornament and objects.[55] Collections of decorative objects in Marguerite and Rabelais also have considerable narrative significance. Their collation and the attempt to set them in order is a concern for Marguerite; however, she concedes the impossibility of permanently stabilizing meaning in an assemblage of things. Rabelais mimes a similar awareness of mutability: his list of disparate objects decomposes even as it grows. The similes, simply, make no sense. What does it mean, that Quaresmesprenant should have "la géniture, comme un cent de clous à latte" ("his sperm, like a hundred carpenters' nails"—*Quart livre* 645; Cohen 515)? Or "la salive, comme une navette" ("saliva like a shuttle"—*Quart livre* 644; Cohen 514)? The comma in the preceding examples signals a pause between possibility and the realization of impossibility, rather than establishing a logical progression of comparison as it would ordinarily.

Rabelais thoroughly explores the attempt to locate meaning, turning Quaresmeprenant inside out, beginning with his "parties internes" ("internal organs"—*Quart livre* 643; Cohen 513), then proceeding to his "parties externes" ("external parts"—*Quart livre* 646; Cohen 516). He links the giant's construction—and deconstruction—to other deceptions of knowing equivalent to the evangelical critique of relics found in Marguerite's *nouvelle* #32 (featuring the skull goblet and the lover's bones in the closet). For instance, Rabelais asserts that Quaresmeprenant's baby teeth had been preserved, possibly for veneration: "[Il avoit] les dents comme un vouge. De ses telles dens de laict vous trouverez une à Colonges les Royaulx en Poictou, et deux à la Brosse en Xantonge, sus la porte de la cave" ("his teeth were like boar spears; and you will find specimens of his milk-teeth at Coulonges-sur-l'Autize in Poitou, where there is one, and at La Brosse in Saintonge, where there are two hung above the doors of the cellar"—*Quart livre* 647; Cohen 517). The geographic coordinates suggest that the teeth might be visited, similar to going on a pilgrimage to view a relic.

Rabelais's simulation of order and meaning in a monstrous mass is, perhaps intentionally, ineffectual. After a similar inquiry into the nature of Amudunt and Descordance, Frère Jan still questions, "Quelle forme … avoient-ilz? Je n'en ouy jamais parler" ("And what shape were they? … I haven't ever heard of them"—*Quart livre* 649; Cohen 519). It is a misguided endeavor, both Marguerite and Rabelais tell us, to try to know the things of the world *by* the things of this world. The noetic significance of objects is unreliable and inadequate. Reality can only be known fully in reference to metaphysical reality.

If description is never quite possible and exact, and full knowing cannot occur, chaos looms:

> Croyez que ce nous sembloit estre l'antique Chaos, onquel estoient feu, air, mer, terre, tous les élémens en … confusion.
>
> ("Believe me, we felt that ancient Chaos had come again; that fire, earth, air, and all the elements were in rebellious confusion."—*Quart livre* 614; Cohen 491)
>
> le monde [seroit] en dangier évident de retourner en son antique chaos.
>
> ("the world would be in evident danger of returning to its ancient chaos."—*Quart livre* 708; Cohen 564)

Chaos threatens to be the paradoxical consequence of man's quixotic attempt to re-create the world and hope to reinstate order.

Both Marguerite and Rabelais aim at achieving coherence.[56] A deluge impedes the *devisants* from proceeding on their journey; they then re-create themselves, and regenerate their sense of the world, through narrative. Storytelling creates at least the illusion of order and stability. Rabelais mimes the collapse of efforts at representation through his account of a near-shipwreck: "Zalas! Zalas! (dist Panurge), zalas! Bou, bou, bou, bou, bous! … Estoit-ce icy que de périr nous estoit prædestiné? Holos … je naye, je meurs! Consummatum est" ("Alas, alas! cried Panurge, alas! Boo bou, bou, bou, bous. Alas, alas! Was it here that we were fated to perish? Ho, ho, good people, I'm drowning, I'm a dead man … I'm done for"—*Quart livre* 618; Cohen 493). The religious reference ("consummatum est") provides assurance, directing the reader to a metaphysical stability that earthly vicissitudes do not provide. "Prædestiné"—possibly a swipe at those whom Rabelais called "les démoniacles Calvins"—shows that Rabelais rejects the Calvinist doctrine of predestination (since Panurge does not perish in the storm): predestination would foreclose the outcome of the crucial narrative journey in, through, and beyond the world to God.

Joy and Profit: Testing the Worth of Earthly Treasures

> I tell you, use worldly wealth to gain friends for yourselves so that when it is gone, you will be welcomed into eternal dwellings … God knows your hearts. What is highly valued among men is detestable in God's sight.
>
> Luke 16.9

The term *joye* introduces a network of other words and expressions forming an evangelical vocabulary shared among Luther, Marguerite, Rabelais, and others. Rabelais's *Prologue* talks about health (*santé*), and his reference to Luke, physician and Gospel writer, specifies that *santé* really means *salut* (salvation). Rabelais defines *pantagruélisme*, his neologism for his characters' attitude toward life, in Gospel terms: "vous entendez que c'est certaine gayeté d'esprit conficte en mespris des choses fortuites" ("as you know, [this] means certain lightness of spirit compounded of contempt for the chances of fate"—*Quart livre* 545; Cohen 439), then affirms the Christian message: "duquel je révère la sacrosaincte parolle de bonnes nouvelles: c'est l'Evangile" ("God, on whom I rely, whom I obey, whose most holy message of good news I revere"—*Quart livre* 545; Cohen 439). Marguerite's use of the term *nouvelles* for her new genre thus both conveys the impression of immediacy, of news hot off the press, as well as refers to the Gospel. Rabelais hopes that his text will have a salubrious effect on the sinner ("goutteux"), and that it may even aid the reader in finding the path (Marguerite frequently calls it "le chemin") to salvation:

> C'est, goutteux, sus quoy je fonde mon espérance, et croy fermement que, s'il plaist au bon Dieu, vous obtiendrez santé, veu que rien plus que santé pour le présent ne demandez.
>
> ("it is on moderation, my gouty friends, that I base my hopes. I firmly believe that it please the good God, you will get your health, seeing that health is all that you ask for at present."—*Quart livre* 559; Cohen 449)

Other evangelical words link Luther, Rabelais, and Marguerite. Marguerite often refers to the *profict* resulting from the parable of the talents: right reception of the story and correct disposition of the heart. Rabelais also refers to the parable of the talents:

> le moindre de ces moutons vault quatre fois plus que le meilleur de ceulx que jadis les Coraxiens en Tuditanie, contrée d'Hespaigne, vendoient un talent d'or la pièce. Et que penses-tu, ô sot à la grande paye, que valoit un talent d'or?
>
> ("the poorest of these sheep is worth four times as much as the best of those that the Coraxians sold in Tuditania—a part of Spain—for a gold talent apiece, in the old days. And what do you think a gold talent was worth, you prize idiot?"—*Quart livre* 580–81; Cohen 465)

Rabelais also mentions *profict* in the context of merchandise and commodity culture. Commodity culture traffics in things, ascribing value to terrestrial transactions alone, as Rabelais illustrates in his account of the dealings among a farmer, a farmer's wife, and a little devil. This is Rabelais's paraphrase of the parable of the talents in the New Testament (Matt. 13; see also Matt. 25). In the Gospel story, several custodians of a lord's money deal with it in different ways: some by hoarding it, some by planting it and making more of it. The steward who hides the coins and makes no profit—here, no *spiritual* gain—is rebuked and cast into outer darkness:

> ... he who had received the one talent came and said: ... "I hid your talent in the ground. Look, there you have what is yours." But his lord answered and said to him, "You wicked and lazy servant, you knew that I reap where I have not sown, and gather where I have not scattered seed. So you ought to have deposited my money with the bankers, and at my coming I would have received back my own with interest. So take the talent from him, and give it to him who has ten talents." For to everyone who has, more will be given, and he will have abundance; but from him who does not have, even what he has will be taken away. (Matt. 25.14–30)

In Rabelais's narrative, the devil offers to split with the farmer the *profict* resulting from the farmer's labor in sowing a field:

> Bled semer, toutesfoys, n'est mon estat. Pour tant je te laisse le champ; mais c'est en condition que nous partirons le proficț.
>
> ("Sowing wheat is not my business. So I leave you the field, but only on condition that we share the profits."—*Quart livre* 684; Cohen 545)

The devil duplicates the bad steward's actions in the parable by declining to cultivate the fertile ground. He will remain idle and sow no seed; he resembles the biblical steward who hides the talent his master gives him but does not increase it. In fact, the devil hopes that the grain will remain intact under ground, then he will take that for himself. The farmer points out that wheat comes only from the destruction of the seed; he will reap the profit of this transformation, just as a sinner's life is broken, emptied out, then transformed by Christ.

> Vray est qu'en cestuy choys me pensiez tromper, espérant rien hors terre ne yssir pour ma part, et dessoubs trouver tout entier le grain que j'avoys semé ... Mais ... le grain que voyez en terre est mort et corrumpu, la corruption d'icelluy a esté génération de l'aultre que me avez veu vendre. Ainsi choisissiez-vous le pire. C'est pourquoy estez mauldict en l'Évangile.
>
> ("You had the first choice. The fact is that when you chose you thought you were fooling me. You expected that nothing would spring from the earth for my share, and that you would find the seed I had sown intact in the ground. But ... the seed that you see in the ground is dead and rotten, but from its corruption sprang the new crop that you saw me sell. So you made the worse choice, and earned the Gospel curse."—*Quart livre* 685; Cohen 547)

Rabelais's reworking of the parable is stamped as evangelical by its reference to another scriptural intertext ("si le grain ne meurt"). The devil is upset, because the sown seed is moldy and the farmer has all the profit. Yet Scripture instructs that the destruction of the seed is a necessary step in the production of faith: in order for a plant to grow, the seed must first be destroyed. This destruction is transitory, however, and results in productivity and an abundant harvest. The devil lacks the scriptural savvy, and narrative know-how, to comprehend the evangelical etiology of faith.

Rabelais trenchantly indicts earthly treasures in the description of the Papimanes, who idolize the Pope as their "Dieu de bien en terre" ("God of good things on earth"—*Quart livre* 696; Cohen 557).[57] (The term *bien* [often in the plural form] frequently designates, for both Rabelais and Marguerite, materiality and materialism.) The Pope never appears in this story; he is a fictive construct built up of an assemblage of *things* that represent him: his slipper, his keys, a portrait:

> Homenaz tira d'un coffre près le grand aultel un gros faratz de clefz, desquelles il ouvrit à trente et deux claveures et quatorze cathenatz une fenestre de fer bien barrée au-dessus dudict autel: puys, par grand mystère, se couvrit d'un sac mouillé et, tirant un rideau de satin cramoisy, nous monstra une image paincte … y toucha un baston longuet et nous feist à tous baiser la touche …
>
> ("Greatclod drew a huge bundle of keys out of a trunk beside the high altar, and with them opened the thirty-two locks and fourteen padlocks of a strongly barred iron window above it. Then he most mysteriously enveloped himself in damp sackcloth and, pulling back a curtain of crimson satin, showed us an image, which I thought very crudely painted. This he touched with a longish stick, and made us all kiss the point that had touched it …"—*Quart livre* 695–96; Cohen 554–55)

The list of things composes a "great mystery" that is revealed to be a sham. The objects and grandiose ritual, underscored by the theatrical drawing-aside of the curtain, signify nothing: image masquerades as "presence," consistent with the evangelical critique of *monstrance*. The deceptive quality of the display—the occlusion effected by the bars of iron and Homenaz's self-covering—shows that a charade is being perpetuated. No divinity can inhere in earthly objects, evangelicals assert. Pantagruel refuses to accept the object as presence, viewing it as mere representation: "C'est … la ressemblance d'un pape. Je le congnois à la thiare, à l'aumusse, au rochet, à la pantophle" ("It represents a Pope … I know it by the tiara, the furred stole, the surplice, and the slipper"—*Quart livre* 696; Cohen 555). Enumerating the objects composing this "ressemblance," Pantagruel fractures any coherence in representation. His phrase acts like a mini-*blason,* dismantling the assemblage so that only separate fragments remain and the illusion of unity is dispelled. Pantagruel further emphasizes his distrust by mentioning another object—this time taken from daily life and used for bodily functions—showing his evangelical practicality and scorn over such mystification:

> Quand (dist Pantagruel) telz contes vous nous ferez, soyez records d'apporter un bassin: peu s'en fault que ne rende ma guorge.
>
> ("When you are going to tell us stories like that, please remember to bring a basin. That one nearly made me sick."—*Quart livre* 696; Cohen 556)

"User ainsi du sacré nom de Dieu en choses tant ordes et abhominables!" ("Fancy using the name of God in such a filthy, abominable context!"—*Quart livre* 696; Cohen 555), he sputters, linking earthly objects with misrepresentations, and stressing the disjunction between worldly constructions and divine perfection.

At dinner with the *Décrétales*, believers set before the portrait "bassins tous pleins de monnoye papimanicque" ("basins which were quite full of Papimaniac money"—*Quart livre* 698; Cohen 555). Pantagruel's vomit basin has changed into a vessel overflowing with material gains; filled to the brim with money and worldly goods, the basin is gorged with noxious substances. Homenaz celebrates the materiality of this satire of papal idolatry: "O lors abondance de tous biens *en* terre … délices *en* toute nature humaine!" ("Then there will be an abundance of all worldly goods on earth … delights throughout all human kind"—*Quart livre* 700; emphasis added; Cohen 558). The *en* orients the focus to earthly things, showing that the Papimanes do not elevate their doctrine or their hearts to the metaphysical realm; rather, they confine their focus to superficial earthly treasures. Panurge notes, "ouy dea, messieurs, j'en ay veu troys [Papes] à la veue desquelz je n'ay guères profité" ("yes, yes … Yes, indeed. I've seen three of them, and I didn't get much good from it either …"); he repeats, "A la veue du Pape jamais n'avions proficté" ("we've never profited so far from having seen the Pope"—*Quart livre* 690–91; Cohen 551).

The Papimanes do not deploy materiality, as Rabelais and Marguerite would recommend, as a tool to elevate man beyond the world; they remain trapped in its substance. Homenaz insists on the veracity of the Pope's portrait, and on the ability of things to signify "apertement, visiblement, manifestement" ("clearly, visibly and manifestly"—*Quart livre* 703; Cohen 560). However, Pantagruel takes pleasure in disabusing Homenaz of these misguided notions, showing him that

> A Paris … Groignet, cousturier, avoit emploicté unes vieilles *Clémentines* en patrons et mesures. O cas estrange! Tous habillements tailléz sus tels patrons et protraictz sus telles mesures feurent guastéz et perduz: robbes, cappes, manteaulx, sayons, juppes.
>
> ("In Paris … a tailor called Groignet used an old *Supplementary* for his patterns and templates and, strange to relate, all the garments he cut to those patterns were spoilt. Gowns, hoods, cloaks, cassocks, skirts, short coats, ruffs, doublets, petticoats …"—*Quart livre* 702; Cohen 559)

Trust in things is misguided; Pope Clement V's promulgations offer no sure authority, but rather epitomize slippery signifying. "Groignet, cuydant tailler une cappe, tailloit la forme d'une braguette. En lieu d'un sayon tailloit un chappeau …" ("When he meant to cut a hood, Groignet made the shape of a codpiece. Instead of a cassock, he would produce a scalloped hat …"—*Quart livre* 702; Cohen 559). Rabelais jokes throughout about the invalidity of such pronouncements, which, along with the thirteenth-century *Sext* and the miscellany *Extravagantes*, made up the collection of additional rules or *Décrétales*. Worse than adiaphora, they were agents of distortion:

> Jan Chouart … à Monspellier avoit achapté des moines de Sainct Olary unes belles Décrétales, escriptes en beau et grand parchemin de Lamballe, pour en faire des vélins pour batre l'or. Le malheur y feut si estrange que oncques pièce n'y feut frappée qui vînt à profict. Toutes feurent dilacérées et estrippées.
>
> ("Jan Chouart … at Montpellier … had bought from the monks of St. Olary some fine Decretals written on large and handsome Lamballe parchment, to tear into vellum leaves

> to beat gold between. But it was strangely unfortunate that not a single piece he beat came out right. They were all torn and full of holes ..."—*Quart livre* 701; Cohen 559)

Attribution of value to Papal commentaries distorts the true gold of Scripture; coinage is counterfeit; artificed things and reified words can mark and alter their possessor, deforming him as emblematic of the fallen world.

Like Rabelais, Marguerite evokes such deformation by frequently mentioning masks. Masks disguise identity and essence, precluding one from "voy[ant] son cueur comme sa contenance" ("see[ing] his heart as clearly as his face"—*Hept.* 3.24.194; Chilton 275), and limiting awareness to "son dissimulé visaige" ("disfigured face"—*Hept.* 1.10.81; Chilton 148), with the result that the false semblance is mistaken for reality: "le voyant tant beau et bien parlant, creut sa mensonge plus que une autre verité" ("seeing what a handsome, gently spoken young man he was, believed his lies rather than the truth"—*Hept.* 2.18.139; Chilton 215).[58] Rabelais similarly recounts how masks made of the *Décrétales*, which he decries as documents obfuscating true meaning, stain and sear the faces of their wearers, marking them with signs of sickness and sinfulness:

> Mes compaignons d'eschole et moy ... En faulte de ... personate et de papier, des feueilletz d'un vieil *Sixiesme* qui là estoit abandonné nous feismes nos faulx visaiges, les descouppans un peu à l'endroict des œilz, du nez et de la bouche. Cas merveilleux! ... achevéz, houstans nos faulx visaiges, appareumes plus hideux et villains que les diableteaux de la passion de Doué tant avions les faces guastées aux lieux touchéz par lesdictz feueilletz.
>
> ("as we had no arum, burdock, or bugloss leaves and no paper, we made our masks from the leaves of an old *Sextum*, which were lying about there, cutting little holes in them for the eyes, the nose, and the mouth. But, strange to say, when our little capers and schoolboy jokes were over, and we took off our masks, we appeared uglier and more repulsive than the Devil's brood in the Doué miracle-play. Our faces were all sore in the places which those leaves had touched."—*Quart livre* 704; Cohen 561)

As Rabelais develops the evangelical program, akin to that sketched out by Marguerite's use of worldly goods in the *Heptaméron* and also to Luther's use of daily-life objects in *Table Talk*, he uses catch phrases typical of his two models. *Passetemps,* like *masques,* is another such term. For Marguerite, there are two sorts of *passetemps* which contrast with each other: earthly diversion (usually an occasion for sin, although for great storytelling as well) and prayerful activity or meditation on an uplifting subject (what Oisille hopes the *devisants* will do with the *nouvelles*, beyond being merely diverted by them). Rabelais uses the term similarly. He recounts a story in which François Villon, "pour donner passetemps au peuple, entreprint faire jouer la Passion en gestes et languaige poictevin" ("for the people's amusement, he undertook a production of the Passion play in the Poitevin manner and dialect"—*Quart livre* 597; Cohen 478). Evangelical reformers commended such translation into the vernacular, since priests, by insisting on performing the mass in Latin and by barring access to the Bible to the laity, had prevented the people from understanding Scripture. *Passetemps* can also mean, for both Rabelais and Marguerite, "discussion" ("en ces menuz devis arrivèrent en leurs navires"; "thus gossiping, Panurge and his party went down to their ships"—*Quart livre* 593; Cohen 475) or narration ("ceste narration [dist Pantagruel] sembleroit joyeuse ne feust que davant noz œilz fault la craincte de Dieu continuellement avoir"; "that would seem a jolly tale … if we weren't bidden never to let the fear of God out of our minds"—*Quart livre* 606; Cohen 485).

Marguerite, Luther, and Rabelais all find storytelling essential: for it generates debate and conversation, which may lead to conversion. The act of interpretation is deemed potentially salubrious, as when Pantagruel strives to understand the significance of the *parolles gelées*: "Croyez que nous y eusmez du passetemps beaucoup" ("Believe me, we were greatly amused"—*Quart livre* 715; Cohen 569). The Thelemites are characterized by "passetemps et exercitations honestes" ("soberer pastimes or amusements"—*Quart livre* 732; Cohen 582), and Louis Marin identified Thélème as an ideal space epitomizing evangelical expression. Similarly, the Good News of the Gospel is meant to be shared and explored through plain-speaking and clear exposition: "Cessez pourtant icy plus vous trupher et croyez qu'il n'est rien si vray que l'Évangile" ("so now, stop laughing, and believe me that nothing is truer than my tale, except Gospel"—*Quart livre* 666; Cohen 532).

Accounting and Recounting: The Evangelical *Compte*

> The wicked wrongly says in his heart of God,
> "You will not require an account."
>
> Ps. 10.13

Another term, *compte*, often found in the *Heptaméron*, refers to the emphasis that evangelicals place on narrative. In her text *Le miroir*, for instance, Marguerite uses spiritual poetry to elucidate some of the same themes as in the *Heptaméron*, a sort of economics of salvation. This spiritual accounting employs terms that belong to more than one discourse: while they are words borrowed from Scripture, they are also *semes* in daily-life commercial transactions such as "profict" and "pourchatz," "bien and "richesse." Marguerite refers to sins as the equivalent of worldly goods, devaluing both material acquisition and moral wrongdoing: "Doncques ne sont ses thresors que pechéz" ("Therefore his treasures are nothing more than sins"—*Miroir* 6).[59] Christ contrasts with the spendthrift sinner who throws away his salvation, for Christ has "paya sa debte" ("paid [the sinner's] debt") and furnished "tresgrande recette" ("a great receipt"—*Miroir* 6). When the sinner spurns and wastes these spiritual riches ("ou despendu i'ay toute ma substance"; "for I have spent all my livelihood"—*Miroir* 8), Christ yet again supplies ("il multiplie"—*Miroir* 24) a surplus: "tous voz biens receuz en abondance" ("receive all your goods in abundance"—*Miroir* 8). Marguerite tries to do the math ("car qui a faict la substraction"; "for who has done the subtraction"—*Miroir* 19) and render an accounting ("compte") of the sinner's expenses ("n'ont iamais faict si piteux cas entendre, / Comme Celluy, dont compte ie veux rendre"; "I have never heard of such a pitiful case / as that of which I want to render an accounting"—*Miroir* 12).

> Est-il proufit, que lon deust estimer?
> Brief, est-il riens …?
> Helas nenny: car tous ces mondains biens
> Qui ayme Dieu, repute moins que fiens.

> Plaisir/proufit/& honneur sont corvée
> A qui l'amour de son Dieu a trouvée.
> Amour de Dieu est si plaisant proufit,
> Et tant d'honneur, que seul au cueur suffit.
>
> ("Is it profit that one must esteem? / Brief, is it anything? / Alas, no: for all these worldly goods, / He who loves God, will deem less than filth. / Pleasure/profit/and honor are a chore / To he who has found the love of his Lord / Love of God is such pleasant profit / And so much honor, that it alone suffices the heart."—*Miroir* 18)

The ultimate effect is a mystical one in which Marguerite disburses, or empties herself out (as is customary in mystic spirituality, where the goal is *néant*: the annihilation of the self to self, to live fully in God: "du thresor Divin la seule bourse" ("of Divine treasure the sole purse"—*Miroir* 24). Marguerite has spent all her spiritual capital.

Thus, *compte* and *conte* play off of each other, each underscoring a form of transaction. *Compte* may be a mercantile transaction, such as the transfer of a commodity or the recording of a sale, or it may signify *conte*, a narrative transaction and non-commodified interaction, through which storytelling elevates the reader/listener to a higher state: "comme sont motz de gueule entre tous bons et joyeulx Pantagruelistes" ("as gay quips are among good and jovial Pantagruelists"—*Quart livre* 716; Cohen 569). The Protestant *topos* of the book in which saved souls are recorded in heaven (and, contrarily, the damned are listed in their separate column) is similar to double-entry bookkeeping, an innovation developed during this period. In the *Heptaméron*, a woman of questionable morals furnishes the pretext for a tale (*conte/compte*), and is also herself the recipient of a moral reckoning (*compte*): "la dame de qui avez faict le compte" (["the lady of whom you made a moral accounting"]; "the lady in the story you have just told"—*Hept.* 6.49.360; Chilton 465). Shortly after Pantagruel acquires luxury items and exotica on his trip, he writes to his father, sending him these curios in token of something surpassing their individual parts: his filial love and devotion. The list of precious objects is both a narrative enumeration, and one displaying moral significance in the evangelical economy of love in which gifts are abundantly bestowed regardless of merit.

> Ainsi pourray-je dire que l'excès de vostre paternelle affection me range en ceste angustie et nécessité qu'il me conviendra vivre et mourir ingrat. Sinon que tel crime soys relevé par la sentence des stoïciens, lesquelz disoient troys parties estre en bénéfice: l'une du donnant, l'aultre du recepvant, la tierce du récompensant; et le recepvant très bien récompenser le donnant quand il accepte voluntiers le bienfaict et le retient en soubvenance perpétuelle.
>
> ("I can say in the same way that by the excess of your paternal affection I should be reduced to the painful straits of having to live and die in ingratitude, were I not acquitted of this crime by a maxim of the Stoics. They used to say that a kind act is made up of three parts: firstly, the giver's, secondly the recipient's, and thirdly the rewarder's; and that the recipient amply rewards the giver if he willingly accepts the gift and keeps it perpetually in his memory."—*Quart livre* 571; Cohen 458)

Pantagruel is describing the gift of grace. Using the language of commercial transaction (and also, perhaps not coincidentally, of trinitarian conversation—"troys parties"), he speaks of an abstract attribute rather than of an earthly thing. In this evangelical exchange, three parties trade, suggesting the triune operation of salvation: judgment, atonement, and consolation (Father, Son, and Holy Spirit). The presents that Pantagruel sends to his father—the tapestry, the three unicorns—stand in for his own higher emotions and aspirations. This, Rabelais tells us, is how things of this world *should* be used: in what might be called an iconic movement, that uses, then goes beyond and renders unnecessary, earthly objects. And this is what the evangelical *conte* aims to render as a recounting or *compte*. Like Pantagruel's sea voyage in the *Quart livre,* life is meant to be a pilgrimage, what Pantagruel calls "nostre pérégrination"[60] ("this voyage of ours"—*Quart livre* 572; Cohen 459) through, then out of, the world. Evangelicals seek to turn things of this world into material markers of the way to heaven.

Finally, both Marguerite and Rabelais draw distinctions, as does Luther in his sermons and commentaries, between "true" and "false" Christians. The coded phrase for the former is "hommes de bien" or "gens de bien." The singular *bien* is intended to contrast forcefully with the plural, *biens*, meaning material possessions. The singular *bien* evokes an abstract and spiritual attribute, removed from fatal focus on fallen things. Through the repetition of "choses," Rabelais underscores that trust is not to be placed in things:

> Vous aultres gens de bien, si voulez estre dictz et réputéz vrays chrestiens, je vous supplie à joinctes mains ne croire aultre chose, aultre chose ne penser, ne dire, ne entreprendre, ne faire.
>
> ("As for you, my good people, if you wish to be called good Christians and to have that reputation, I beseech you with clasped hands to believe no other thing, to have no other thought, to say, undertake, or do nothing."—*Quart livre* 707; Cohen 562)

Gaster, the omnivorous stomach, epitomizes for Rabelais the abusive adoration of things. Rabelais describes Gaster "masquéz, desguiséz, et vestuz tant estrangement … [en] diversité et desguisement" ("strangely masked and disguised … oddly dressed"—*Quart livre* 721; Cohen 573), he calls Gaster "une effigie monstrueuse, ridicule, hydeuse, et terrible" ("a monstrous, ridiculous, and hideous effigy"—*Quart livre* 722; Cohen 574). Gaster is an artificial construct, "mal taillé et lourdement paincte" ("badly carved and clumsily painted"—*Quart livre* 722; Cohen 574). Rather than idolize objects, true Christians should listen to the Word and speak with each other about Scripture's significance.

To that end, Rabelais demonstrates thematic, stylistic, and linguistic similarities with Luther and Marguerite, crafting the evangelical narrative so that it uses and displays the things of the world. Their goal is to analyze these objects in order to undermine confidence in them, then to surpass them, showing, by an emphasis on ornate and glittery surfaces, that meaning does not lie in or beneath things, but rather above and beyond them. Rabelais shows that, instead of the act of *collecting*, the process of *communication*, of sharing through story, is what conveys significance:

> La joye ne feut petite, tant de nous comme des marchans: de nous, entendens nouvelles de la marine; de eulx, entendens nouvelles de terre ferme.
>
> ("there was great rejoicing, both on their part and on ours, on ours since they brought us news of the sea, and on theirs

> because we could tell them of *terra firma*."—*Quart livre* 573–74; Cohen 460)

The subject matter forms a diptych, in which one part of the conversation completes the other in a stylistic gesture of reciprocity. In a representation typical of evangelical ambivalence toward commodity culture, the desired transaction is not the circulation of commodities, but rather the exchange of discussion, of experience, and, ultimately, the sharing of faith perspectives.

Gisèle Mathieu-Castellani, in *La conversation conteuse: Les "Nouvelles" de Marguerite de Navarre,* discusses the various functions of objects in the *nouvelles*. Castellani claims that

> dans le décor, tantôt un même objet revient avec insistance … tantôt un autre objet à fonction identique se substitue à lui … les objets eux-mêmes inversent leur fonction.
>
> (" in the decorative scheme, sometimes the same object recurs … sometimes a different object with an identical use substitutes for the former … objects themselves reverse roles.")[61]

An example of similar treatment in narrative, and the development of an evangelical focus, substantiates the paradigm discernible in Marguerite and in Rabelais's work. The use of a carefully selected word, *beluter*, constructs the similarity and conveys a biblical message. Randle Cotgrave's *Dictionarie of the French and English Tongues* defines *beluter* as "to boult," while *belutage* is "a sifting, or bolting of meale" and *beluteau* is a "boulting cloth." There are other such synonyms, such as *vanner*, that Rabelais or Marguerite could have employed, but did not; first, Marguerite would be more likely, in her daily-life focus, to use *beluter* because it is an activity (sifting the flour) that can be done at home while *vanner* (winnowing) is done in the fields; secondly, *beluter* is the verb that the Geneva Bible uses. *Beluter* for both authors recalls the apocalyptic pronouncements of the Gospel of Matthew, in which the Second Coming of Christ comes without warning and overthrows worldly standards. Much of Marguerite's writing speaks of the imperative of re-establishing order and much of Rabelais's *Quart livre* depicts a *monde à l'envers*,[62] a world turned upside down, requiring the restitution of order: "Mais vrayement voicy un mesnage assez mal en ordre. Bien. Il nous faudra réparer ce briz. Guardez que ne donnons par terre" ("But truly we're in sad disorder. All right. Then we shall have to repair the wreck. Mind out that we don't run aground"—*Quart livre* 627; Cohen 501).

The narrative will restore order, as Rabelais shows in his anecdote about *belutage*. The Gospel of Matthew instructs believers that no one can predict the Day of the Lord, and sketches as illustration the scenario of "two women [who] will be grinding with a hand mill; one will be taken and the other left. Therefore keep watch, because you do not know on what day your Lord will come" (Matt. 24.41–42). Both Marguerite and Rabelais recount episodes having to do with making a choice, the discernment that Scripture terms "the separation of wheat from chaff." They are pursuing a strategy characteristic of Reformed artists of the period: in his analysis of Protestant painting, art historian Craig Harbison calls the technique he finds there "compositional inversion," which involves inserting a religious story or significance beneath an overlay of quotidian detail with the goal of "raising questions" about the relation between the two. Harbison defines "compositional inversion" as "visual imagery [which] ... could be a forum for discussion, especially in a time of flux and change ... [the painter was] raising questions, through the inclusion of telling details and, above all, through challenging compositional developments."[63] Marguerite thus applies a painterly technique to the narrative domain. Her daily-life embroidery on her homey version of Mathew's scene[64] shows how objects can be used by the evangelical program. These objects construct relationships and create scenarios, yet do not signify *in se;* rather, they designate a message outside themselves. Regarding both episodes, the reader is invited to ask: which customary details have been omitted? employed? Are there any idiosyncratic details that have been included to construct a sort of "signature piece"? And, finally, what is the effect of all these details and objects?

Rabelais's anecdote about *belutage* is found in the section on the Chiquanous. The Chiquanous indulge in an odd practice of offering themselves to others to be beaten. The narrative describes this practice in mercantile terms as a phenomenon of exchange. Blows are inflicted and endured, delivered by means of padded *gantelez* or *gants*: "Donnez luy coups sans compter à tort et à travers" ("beat him right and left without counting the blows"—*Quart livre* 595; Cohen 477). The scene before the beatings describes the actions of Loyre, who is kneading bread dough ("Loyre poitrissoit sa paste"; "Loire was kneading his dough"—*Quart livre* 600; Cohen 481), his wife, who is bolting or sifting flour ("sa femme belutoit la farine"; "his wife was sifting the flour"—*Quart livre* 600; Cohen 481), and others engaged in various everyday tasks. Suddenly a messenger arrives, announcing that "Chiquanous estoit en pays" ("suddenly everyone realized that there was a Bum-bailiff in the land"—*Quart livre* 601; Cohen 481). Immediately ("lors"), "Loyre et sa femme prendre leurs beaulx acoustremens" ("Loire and his wife [hopped off] to don their finery"—*Quart livre* 601; Cohen 481); they dress and grab their padded boxing gloves. It is, in fact, the eve of a Chiquanous wedding, and Loyre and his wife have donned bridal garments ("acoustremens nuptiaulx"; "wedding clothes"—*Quart livre* 602; Cohen 602), perhaps a reference to Christ who also is portrayed, just after the milling anecdote, returning to earth unexpectedly, clad as a bridegroom (Matt. 25.1–7). A transaction transpires with the contract being drawn up and witnessed: "le contrat est passé et minuté" and an exchange effected: "D'un cousté sont apportéz vins et espices, de l'aultre, livrée à tas, blanc et tanné; de l'aultre sont produictz guanteletz secrètement" ("the contract was signed and sealed; wines and spices were brought in through one door; quantities of orange and white favours through another; and through a third the gauntlets were quietly introduced"—*Quart livre* 602–03; Cohen 483). As we have already seen, gloves symbolize the fidelity of a Christian marriage.[65] The couple is thus beaten over the head with literalized representations of their wedding vows. They are depicted on the verge of a decision, of making a choice; *belutage* connotes separating themselves from a former phase of existence and entering into a new state in life. This new state is the result of an apocalyptic awareness: "le monde … approche de sa fin. Or tenez: des nopces, des nopces, des nopces!" ("the end of the world's approaching. Now come on—The wedding, the wedding, the wedding!"—*Quart livre* 603; Cohen 483). The blows rain down on the fiancés of the Chiquanous without care for distinction between male or female as, married, they now compose one entity ("sans choix ou election de membres"; "without choice or distinction of limbs"—*Quart livre* 604; Cohen 484), just as, when the Second Coming occurs, there will be no apparent rationale as to who is chosen for the Rapture and who remains. The other change that transpires in the story has to do with material wealth: the Chiquanous learn to place value elsewhere than on money and earthly possessions. They had entered into the marriage arrangement as though it were a financial transaction: "Basché prie Chiquanous assister aux fiansailles … et en recepvoir le contrat, bien le payant et contentent" ("Basché then invited the Bum-bailiff to be present at the wedding of one of his officers, and to draw up the contract, for which he promised him good and proper pay"—*Quart livre* 602; Cohen 482). Now, however, they learn to despise money: "De là en hors feut tenu comme chose certaine que l'argent de Basché plus estoit aux Chiquanous et records pestilent, mortel et pernicieux que n'estoit jadis l'or de Tholose …" ("from that time, it was firmly believed that Basché's money was more pestilential, deadly, and pernicious to Bum-bailiffs and beadles than was the gold of Toulouse in ancient times"—*Quart livre* 606; Cohen 485). They value higher things, forgiving the evil treatment they have received: "pour l'amour de Dieu on leurs pardonnast" ("forgive us, in God's name"—*Quart livre* 605; Cohen 484). Although Chiquanous is defined in Cotgrave as "a litigious pleader, craftie pettifogger,"[66] these Chiquanous have changed their ways (perhaps an evangelical conversion) through the medium of the narrative process. They have risen above legalism to comprehend the evangelical doctrine of Jesus as "nostre seul advocat" ("our only advocate/lawyer"), a phrase also often used in the *Heptaméron*.[67] The Chiquanous "records," or "gardes de justice" ("bailiffs"), so officious and overbearing at the beginning of the episode, no longer preside over the scene; rather, they are apologetic, even struck dumb: "le records démandibulé joingnoit les mains et tacitement luy demandoit pardon, car parler ne povoit-il" ("the beadle with the broken jaw clasped his hands and speechlessly begged his pardon—for he could not speak"—*Quart livre* 604; Cohen 483). Rabelais here illustrates, as does Marguerite in so many of the *nouvelles*, the Pauline precept that love, the greatest law, triumphs over a censorious, legalistic attitude: "Love one another, for he who loves his fellow has fulfilled the law" (Rom. 13.8).[68] Interestingly, like the parables from Matthew that both Marguerite and Rabelais illustrate, Paul follows this statement with an apocalyptic utterance: "Our salvation is nearer now … the day is almost here … " (Rom. 13.12). The law of love reverses world order and helps to bring it to an end. Just so, earthly treasures collaborate in indicting the circumstances of their production and possession.

Marguerite's narrative demonstrates similar preoccupations. *Nouvelle* #69 develops from the props of a *sarot,* or worker's blouse, and a *crumeau*, or wimple, as well as the activity of *belutage*. The *nouvelle* involves an advance, a deception, and a choice. A king's squire has married a good woman who has borne him several children, but who now seems old and undesirable to him. She hires a new maid who is eager to retain her mistress's favor. Knowing that the husband courts the other chambermaids, when he propositions her, this maid reports it all to her mistress. One day, while the maid is working bolting flour ("bluter du blez"), she puts her blouse over her head, presumably to shield her from the sun:

> ayant son sarot sur la teste, à la mode du pays (qui est faict comme ung crumeau, mais il couvre tout le corps et les espaulles par derriere), son maistre, la trouvant en cest habillement, la vint fort bien presser.
>
> ("she was wearing her smock over her head as they do in that part of the world—it's a garment like a hood, but it covers the shoulders and falls full length at the back. Well, along comes the master, and seeing her in this attire, he eagerly starts to make overtures."—*Hept.* 6.69.398; Chilton 510)

The blouse depersonalizes her by covering her head (the site for a portrait, and the customary locus of represented identity). By presumably obscuring a portion of her face and certainly making her unrecognizable from behind, the capacious covering presents the maid only as a portion of a body, not as a full person. The master desires her even more when her subjectivity is not apparent; his lust centers on the object, on the garment, "ceste habillement" that frames her anatomy in a way that inspires lust. In addition, the blouse resembles a nun's headdress ("crumeau") in this new position, hinting at a potential violation of a religious person. The extensive covering of the body underscores the indiscriminate and anonymous nature of the man's desire, as well as preparing the eventual means of his comeuppance. What he hopes to conceal, will be revealed. The maid pretends that she will yield to him, but first asks permission to verify that her mistress is not nearby. Under the pretext of keeping up appearances, she asks him to don her garment and to continue working in her stead. She then finds her lady, urging her: "Venez veoir vostre bon mary, que j'ay aprins à beluter pour me deffaire de luy" ("Come and have a look at that husband of yours … I've shown him how to sift, to get rid of him!"—*Hept.* 6.69.399; Chilton 510). The man, who has lacked discernment, now stands in the place of the maid, continuing her work of separating wheat from chaff, a comic emblem of his unwitting training ("que j'ay aprins") in moral discernment. Significantly, the maid refers to the husband ironically as "bon," when he is precisely the opposite, and ascribes the possessive "vostre" to him ("vostre bon mary") at the very moment that he is striving to cheat his wife of that possession. His attempt at seduction and subterfuge has had unexpected consequences, requiring him to occupy the place of one who sifted good from bad, and chose good. The maid's garment now frames the master, and limits his activity, denying him the full subjective exercise of his lust. He becomes an object lesson in the text, just as he had sought to objectify her.

By describing the maid's clothing, then having the husband wear it, Marguerite has crafted an instructive tale that teaches how to discern what is good and what is evil. She has embedded the biblical reference to women milling or bolting flour as the sub-text to her anecdote, employing the "compositional inversion" already seen to be typical of evangelical painters. Marguerite's daily-life description comports with the Reformed emphasis on practical piety, and the simple scene, which contains numerous evangelical motifs, recalls the technique and focus of many genre paintings that "contained within [them] intimations of … many of the issues that led to the Protestant Reformation."[69]

Daily-life objects, furniture, clothing, exotic souvenirs from foreign climes, money, earthly possessions, all will be rendered unnecessary; they will be surpassed and transmuted by the coming judgment. Marguerite prepares for an apocalyptic change by showing that trust cannot be placed in things of the world. Those who learn this lesson will have their hearts properly prepared for the Day of the Lord. "They will be mine, says the Lord Almighty, in the day when I make up my treasured possession" (Mal. 3.17), referring, of course, not at all to earthly treasures, but to the treasure of salvation.

Chapter Five

The Evangelical Narrative

Des Périers, Du Fail, and Yver

Bonaventure Des Périers: Telling Tales in Wartime

Other evangelicals[1] used strategies similar to those that Marguerite de Navarre devised in the *Heptaméron*. Bonaventure Des Périers, secretary to Marguerite de Navarre, shared her evangelical sympathies.[2] His *Cymbalum mundi* was condemned by the Sorbonne in 1537 for "impieties." In this and in other works can be discerned illustrations of evangelical theology, the influence of Marguerite and the influence of Rabelais. In the *Nouvelles récréations et joyeux devis* (1558), in particular, stylistic similarities with the *Heptaméron* are evident. Very popular, the *Nouvelles récréations* went through thirteen editions between 1561 and 1615. Conceived during the Wars of Religion, it used storytelling as a device both to distract from the turmoil of those times and, in some measure, to explain them.

The context for the sharing of stories is the attempt to while away the time until peace returns, much as, in the *Heptaméron,* the *devisants* decided to pass the time until the flood waters subsided and their journey could be resumed. Des Périers states this in his *Préambule*, "je vous gardoys ces joyeux propos à quand la paix seroit faicte" ("I will keep these joyful tales for you until peace has been made"—*Nouvelles* 1). The stories possess a dual purpose: to "cause public rejoicing" and also private joy ("resjouir publiquement et privément"—*Nouvelles* 19). As we have already seen, "joye" is a signature term for evangelicals, signifying beyond earthly contentment to heavenly peace. Indeed, Des Périers deems joy "la meilleure chose que puisse faire l'homme" ("the best thing that man can do"—*Nouvelles* 20). Thus, as is the case with Marguerite and

Rabelais, these stories have an eschatological orientation: while grounded in earthly existence, they await fulfillment in Christ: "pour vous donner moyen de tromper les temps, meslant des resjouissances parmy voz fascheries, en attendant que [la paix] se face de par Dieu" ("to give you a means to pass the times, mixing rejoicing with your sorrows, while waiting for peace to be made by God"—*Nouvelles* 19).[3] Storytelling creates a transition by filling the time between reality and the ideal: "et, pour cela, vous faut-il desesperer? Ne vault-il pas mieux se resjouir en attendant mieux?" ("and, for all this, should you despair? Wouldn't it be better to rejoice while waiting for better [times to come]?"—*Nouvelles* 20). When peace comes, sin will end and evildoing will be forgotten: "je vous asseure que je suis deliberé de mettre en oubly toutes les faultes du temps passé" ("I assure you that I have decided to forget all the wrongdoings of the past"—*Nouvelles,* "Un bassecontre de Rheims" 41).

Further, like the motivation of the Gospel narratives, the purpose of the tales is to heal the sick: "je me suis avisé que c'estoit icy le vrai temps de les vous donner, car c'est aux malades qu'il faut medecine" ("I decided that now was the right time to give [the stories] to you, since medicine is for the sick"—*Nouvelles* 19). In fact, Des Périers does allude to many of the Gospel stories, among them that of the "Good Thief": the criminal crucified next to Jesus who confesses his sin and commends himself to Christ.[4] Scriptural references are also often the occasion for Des Périers to communicate evangelical doctrine. For instance, the story of the "Good Thief" demonstrates that one makes one's confession individually to Christ, without need of priestly intercessor: the thief says, "je feray mes recommendations moy-mesme," and Des Périers comments, "que voulez-vous de plus naif que cela? Quelle plus grande felicité?" ("I will commit myself to God myself … What could be more simple than that? What greater happiness?"—*Nouvelles* 24).

The manner in which the tales are recounted is similar to the style of the Gospels, as well as to the version of it that Marguerite and Rabelais produce; Des Périers aims at *stylus rudus*, or biblical simplicity: "vous n'aurez point de peine de demander comment s'entend cecy, comment s'entend cela; il n'y ha fault ny vocabulaire ne commentaire: tels les voyez, telz les prenez" ("you won't have any trouble or need to ask, what is this or what does that mean; no glossary or commentary is needed: what you see is what you get"—*Nouvelles* 21). In this way, he will obviate complicated deciphering, as could be the case with late medieval contemporary allegorical narratives. Like Marguerite, Des Périers insists that his tales are "gospel truth": "lisez hardiment … il n'y a rien qui ne soit honneste" ("read boldly … there is nothing [in them] that is not good/ true"—*Nouvelles* 22).

Another similarity is the equation quickly established between tale-telling and accounting from a mercantile standpoint: *compte* often puns on both activities "pour mieux faire valoir le compte" ("to make the tale/accounting worth even more"—*Nouvelles*, "De l'asne" 108). It is surely no coincidence that many characters in the tales are merchants, among them the merchant who did a good trade ("un marchand d'assez bonne traffique"—*Nouvelles* 55) and a young clothier ("un jeune homme marchand de draps"—*Nouvelles* 72). Nothing in this world is perfect: "or, pour ce qu'il n'y ha chose si excellente qui n'ait quelque imperfection" ("Now, there is nothing in this world so excellent that it does not still have some flaw"—*Nouvelles,* "De l'asne umbrageux qui avoit peur quand on ostoit le bonnet …" 104). Objects traded commercially symbolize earthly ephemerality:

> les nouvelles qui viennent de si loingtain pays, avant qu'elles soyent rendues sus le lieu, ou elles s'empirent comme le safran, ou s'encherissent comme les draps de soye, ou il s'en pert; la moitié comme d'espiceries ou se buffetent comme les vins, ou sont falsifiées comme les pierreries, ou sont adultérées comme tout. Brief, elles sont subjettes à mille inconveniens … les nouvelles ne sont pas comme les marchandises, et qu'on les donne pour le pris qu'elles coustent. Et … pour cela j'ayme mieux les prendre près, puisqu'il n'y ha rien à gagner.
>
> ("new things which come from far away, before arriving here, may spoil as does saffron, or increase in cost like silk sheets, or half may be lost as can be the case with spices, or be shaken about like wine, or counterfeited like precious stones, or be adulterated as can happen to all things. In short, these things are subjected to a thousand difficult cir-

> cumstances ... stories are not like merchandise, and they are sold for the price that they actually cost. That's why I like to take those found close to hand, for there is no [commercial] profit to be made on them."—*Nouvelles* 22)

Des Périers opposes the experience of the story to the merchandise traded. Commodities may inflate or depreciate in value; they are unstable signifiers. The repetition of "comme" to create similes underscores this aspect of trade goods ("comme le safran ... comme les draps de soye ... comme d'espiceries ... comme les vins ... comme les pierreries ... comme tout"): they are viewed as the simulacrum of the lust to purchase and possess them; they do not incarnate truth, but rather represent the misdirection of greed. They tantalize, but do not assuage, desire, and consequently they compel the would-be purchaser to chase continually after earthly ephemera, as in the following anecdote:

> quand elle eut commencé à gouster un petit que c'estoit des joyes de ce monde, elle sentit que son mary ne la faisoit que mettre en appetit; et combien qu'il la traistat bien d'habillemens ... de bonne chere .. toutesfois cela n'estoit que mettre le feu auprès des estouppes.
>
> ("when she had begun to taste a little what earthly pleasures were, she felt that her husband was just giving her enough to whet her appetite; and however much he treated her well by giving her good clothing .. and good food ... even so this was just tempting her desire."—*Nouvelles,* "Du mary de Picardie" 44)

On the other hand, stories found close to home do not charge interest and do not change in value. They are sold wholesale, as it were, and are not subject to usury. They are, therefore, trustworthy, having escaped the fate of other sorts of exchange commodities. Their reliability contrasts with situations in which commodities represent moral shades of grey; in one tale, a man's wife is seduced, but he accepts this without complaint when a fine place setting of Spanish linen and silver is given to him as a bribe: "Il fut contraint de s'appaiser pour une couverte de Cataloigne" ("he was brought to accept this by [the gift of] a Catalan place-setting"—*Nouvelles,* "De celui qui acheta ..."

58). Like Marguerite's focus on decorative arts objects and daily-life activities, Des Périers primarily bases his stories on everyday events and describes ordinary objects as narrative focal points. He uses what is at hand: "n'ay-je pas mieux faict d'en prendre les instrumens que nous avons à nostre porte, que non pas les aller emprunter si loing?" ("haven't I done well to take the tools that we have at our disposal rather than to go far away to get others?"—*Nouvelles* 21).

Money is the root of discontent in the *Nouvelles récréations*. Des Périers tells the tale of a man who led an exemplary life, always happy except for one time when he found an old pot crammed with antique gold and silver pieces. After finding this treasure trove, he became obsessed with money. However, once he decided to throw the pot away, he again became legendary for his happiness. His epitaph, in fact, commends him as he who "… en son temps rien n'amassa" ("who never built up any wealth during his lifetime"—*Nouvelles*, "Du savetier" 80). Des Périers shows that the imperative is to make an accounting of one's life to God, not to balance the worldly ledger.

Des Périers shares with Marguerite and Rabelais a typical evangelical distrust of clergy. Many of the *nouvelles* demonstrate anti-clerical sentiment, among them the tale of the priest who did not know his Latin and who was shown his true worth—not much!—by an educated young man ("Du jeune filz qui fit valloir le beau Latin"; "Concerning the young son who caused true Latin to be valued"—*Nouvelles* 85); the story of a priest who had been married (*Nouvelles* 86); and the anecdote about a preacher who, untutored in Scripture, understood nothing of it, and so compensated for his lack of comprehension by reiterating the name of Jesus: "et combien qu'il ne sceust du latin que par sa provision, encores pas, toutesfois il faisoit comme les autres et venoit à bout de ses messes au moins mal qu'il luy estoit possible" ("and being as he only knew enough Latin for his own needs,—not even that—, nonetheless he acted like the other [priests] and got through his masses with the least harm possible"—*Nouvelles*, "D'un prestre qui ne disoit autre mot que Jesus en son Evangile" 86). This latter tale is particularly interesting, as it reverses and parodies the evangelical call for *sola scriptura* and injunction for reliance on Jesus alone for salvation: the priest does not believe in Jesus, as the evangelicals would hope, but rather invokes his name thoughtlessly; he admits, "quand je dis la messe ... en l'evangile il y a des mots difficiles à lire, Monsieur, je les saute ... mais je dy Jesus au lieu" ("when I read the Gospel there are words that are hard to understand, Sir, so I skip them ... but I say 'Jesus' in their stead"—*Nouvelles* 87–88). The Gospel is something he has only glanced at a few times: "l'evangile ... n'estoit pas bien à l'usage du prestre, car il ne l'avoit jamais dit que 3 ou 4 fois" ("the Gospel [reading] wasn't something that the priest was familiar with, for he had only said it three or four times"—*Nouvelles* 86). Des Périers criticizes poor preaching: the evangelical model of the scripturally literate and effective preacher—of which Marguerite develops a detailed paradigm, as we shall see later—is apparent *en filigrane* in this caricature of a priest who cannot prepare a compelling homily:

> C'estoit un monsieur le curé, lequel, un jour de bonne feste, estoit monté en chaire pour sermonner; là où il estoit fort empesché à ne dire gueres bien ... quand il se trouvoit hors propos (qui estoit assez souvent) il faisoit des plus belles digressions du monde ... On trouve peu qui soyent dignes de monter en chaire; car, encores qu'ilz soyent sçavans, ils n'ont pas la maniere de prescher.
>
> ("There was a certain priest who, on a holy day, went to the pulpit to preach. But there he really struggled to speak well ... when he found himself off the topic [which was fairly often] he made the most impressive digressions imaginable ... One finds few who are worthy to preach, for even if they are learned, they don't know how to preach."—*Nouvelles*, "Dc maistre Jean du Pontalais" 112–13)

Some preachers rely on scandalous rhetoric rather than plain style, like the preacher who used big words to impress his simple audience, but for that reason never succeeded in communicating with them:

> Il y avoit un prestre de village, qui estoit tout fier ... usant des mots qui remplissoyent la bouche, afin de se faire estimer un grand docteur. Et mesme en confessant il avoit des termes qui estonnoyent les povres gens.

> ("there was a village priest who was very proud ... using words that filled the mouth so that others might deem him very learned. And even in the confessional he used words that astonished humble folk."—*Nouvelles,* "Du prestre et du masson" 138)

Des Périers shows that simple folk will deride such arrogance; as in the Gospel, those who seem weakest are actually strongest. In this anecdote, the pretentious priest hears the confession of a day laborer, but the latter bests the priest by using an evangelical technique that pushes "plain style" to its logical conclusion: he employs literal interpretation. When asked by the prurient priest "Es-tu concupiscent?" he responds, "nenny" ("Are you lustful?"—"no"). Having received a whole series of such denials, the frustrated priest, desperate to identify the vice, finally asks him, "Et qu'es-tu donc?" to which the man replies simply and, probably, infuriatingly, answering with simple truth that misses the priest's voyeuristic point entirely, "Je suis ... masson; voicy ma truelle" ("Well, what are you then? [What sin characterizes you?]"—"I am a mason; here is my trowel"—*Nouvelles* 138). Des Périers cites other such examples of how scriptural literacy makes truly pious folk smarter than their adversaries (the Gospel enjoins that the Christian should be "crafty like the serpent"), as in the story of the peasant who defeats a judge's argument by being a better reader and interpreter than he:

> ... advint un jour qu'il entra en dispute d'un passage de la Bible avec un bon apostre, qui estoit bien ayse de faire batteler monsieur le juge.
>
> ("it so happened that one day [the judge] got into an argument concerning a passage in the Bible with a good apostle, who was quite happy to make Mr. Judge juggle."—*Nouvelles*, "D'un juge d'Aiguesmortes" 193)

In this case, Des Périers concedes ironically that "il fault dire qu'il sçavoit toute la Bible par cueur, fors le commencement, le milieu et la fin" ("I have to admit that [the judge] knew the entire Bible by heart, except the beginning, the middle and the end"—*Nouvelles* 194). Des Périers demonstrates that those who would be thought wise by the standards of the world are revealed to be woefully inadequate for the world that is to come.

Priests who can't preach are bad enough, but Des Périers goes on to excoriate pastors who set poor moral examples, as in this tale of a manipulative and deceitful cleric who sleeps with his maid:

> le dit curé avoit une chambriere de l'aage de vingt et cinq ans, laquelle le servoit jour et nuict, la povre garse! dont il estoit souvent mis à l'office et en payait l'amende; mais, pour cela, son evesque n'en pouvoit venir à bout. Il luy diffendit une fois d'avoir chambrieres qui n'eussent cinquante ans pour le moins. Le curé en print une de vingt ans, et l'autre de trente.
>
> ("this priest had a chambermaid aged 25 who waited on him day and night, the poor girl! For this he was often reprimanded and got off by paying his fine; even so, the bishop wanted him to stop. The bishop forbad the priest to have serving girls of fewer than 50 years old. [So] the priest hired one aged 20, and one aged 30."—*Nouvelles*, "Du mesme curé" 123)

In true evangelical fashion, Des Périers is upset that a sinful act can be permitted once a fine is paid, a penance imposed, an indulgence purchased, or a dodge devised, such as this priest's solution of hiring a girl aged 20 and one aged 30 so as to meet the bishop's imposed age requirement of 50.

Because these are tales told during wartime, Des Périers alludes to their troubled context. He hopes for a reader who will emulate moral probity, but who will avoid controversy and dissension. His description of religious strife makes clear his pacific temperament:

> Il y ha une maniere de gens qui ont des humeurs cholericques, ou melancoliques … la fumée monte au cerveau, qui les rend fanaticques, lunaticques, erraticques, phanaticques, scismaticques, et tous les autres aticques qu'on sçauroit dire, ausquelz on ne trouve remede.
>
> ("There is a type of person who has a choleric humor, or a melancholy mood … smoke rises up in his brain, rendering them fantastic [of imagination], lunatics, in error, fanatics, schismatics, and all the "atics" that can be named, and for

which there is no remedy."—*Nouvelles*, "Du gentilhomme qui crioit la nuict" 140)

Des Périers's text shows stylistic and thematic affinities with those of the other evangelicals whom we have examined, and exemplifies a moment somewhat later in time, documenting how an evangelical reacts to conditions of stress and strife. Storytelling ameliorates and redirects the tense situation, pointing the way to a positive, metaphysical resolution.

Noël Du Fail's Proto-Protestant *Propos rustiques:* A Narrative of Nostalgia

One evangelical writer who shows a pronounced resemblance both to Marguerite and to Rabelais is Noël Du Fail. In 1548, Noël Du Fail published the *Propos rustiques* and the *Baliverneries*. These are both somewhat disparate collections of stories composed of series of rural, intimate tableaux. The tales purport to transcribe discussions among elderly peasants full of Gallic humor and good sense who reminisce about the good old days under the village elm tree. They praise the past, when all was well, speaking nostalgically of the period before the church became corrupt: "Lors Dieu estoit aymé, reveré … appeler ces temps passés: temps de Dieu" ("then was God loved and revered … Call those past days: 'God's days'"—*Propos rustiques* 2.609). Clearly, Du Fail dreams of social and religious reform in these texts.[5]

It is uncertain whether Du Fail had yet, at the time of the publication of these two texts, developed a Reformed perspective, but certain aspects of the *Propos rustiques* seem to indicate that he was already influenced by them, and that he was at least on the way to espousing evangelical beliefs. Further, it is a matter of historical record that some years later, while serving as *conseiller* to the Parliament of Brittany, Du Fail was barred from office, excluded by virtue of his Protestant adherence, from 1573 to 1576. By this date, he had officially converted to Protestantism, and even went so far as to advocate the marriage of priests. The *Propos rustiques* demonstrates many stylistic similarities with other evangelical and Protestant authors, among them the use of dialogue and antithesis or dialectic. Like Marguerite, Du Fail would have received Calvin's censure for a "Nicodemist," or covert, stance concerning his religious beliefs. Perhaps aware of the need to express his opinions carefully in a troubled climate, he states that he will proceed by referring to something through mention of its opposite:

> les philosophes et Juriconsultes ont cela assez familier de déscrire lun contraire par lautre, en baillant par iceluy plus seure et solide congnoissance que silz laissoyent lumbre diceluy pour de prime face traicter leur supposé subject … ils discourent par leurs opposites.
>
> ("philosophers and lawyers tend to describe one thing by its opposite, giving by this [strategy] a more certain, solid acquaintance [of the former] than if they had left it in shadow to treat their supposed subject … they discourse by the opposites [of those things]."—*Propos rustiques,* "Au lecteur" 601)

Like Marguerite and other evangelicals, Du Fail also praises, and seeks to emulate, biblical "plain style"; he eschews complicated and contorted rhetoric and values truthfulness, adhering to simple things and simplicity, as Luther had recommended in *Table Talk*:

> … de escrire choses basses et humbles, ne requierent style eslevé, ne grand façon de dire … il n'y avoit fard ne couleur de bien dire, fors une pure verite.
>
> ("to write [of] lowly and humble things, no elevated style is needed, nor any grand manner of speaking … there was no cosmetic or color [needed] to speak well; truth alone [sufficed]."—*Propos rustiques* 1.607)

In this narrative marked by nostalgia, Du Fail traces the etiology of original sin, which results in alienation: "mais il y avoit un mal en luy (comme nous sommes tous imparfaictz)" ("but there is an evil in him [as we are all imperfect]"—*Propos rustiques* 12.653). He describes the consequences of Adam's sin ("le monde est devenu mauvais garçon") as being not only separation of man from God, but of man from his neighbor ("chascun … distinct et à part"; "each man … distinct and separate"): "Toutesfois, depuis que le monde est devenu mauvais garçon, chascun ha en son lict distinct et à part, et pour cause ..." ("all the same, ever since the world became a bad boy, each man keeps apart in his own separate bed, and for good reason ..."—*Propos rustiques* 6.624).

Not only laity, but also clergy, have become alienated from God. Because of this separation and estrangement, clergy, who should unite God's people, instead foment division and dissension: "à ces Couvents Monachaux se departent les Paroisses pour prescher ... pour ... rapporter tout au commun butin" ("in these monastic convents they divide up the parishes for preaching ... in order ... that all may profit from the booty in common"—*Propos rustiques* 10.635), Du Fail observes, equating corrupt priests with beggars and scoundrels who cheat others for a living. Describing their deceptions, Du Fail tellingly employs a lexicon of terms associated with religious observance, referring to "reliques," venerated "images," "Patenostres" and "pardons." Du Fail describes priests counterfeiting ("contrefaisoi[ent]"—*Propos rustiques* 10.635), or disguising, themselves in order to turn a profit, just as beggars simulate the loss of a limb to turn a trick.

This separation becomes a sadly salutary necessity, as in the following scenario, when clergy defile the marital bed:

> pourque, depuis que Moynes ... (à raison quen ce bon vieux temps chascun se contentoit de son païs) commencerent à peregriner, jetter le froc aux choulx, vicarier, se emanciper hors leur territoire, on feit par commun advis licts plus petits au profit dacucuns mariés ... et merveilleux interest pour les femmes ... Maudict soit le chat, sil trouve le pot descouvert, qui ny mette la patte ...
>
> ("For this reason, that since Monks, (all the more reason that in the good old days each man was content to stay in his own region) began to make pilgrimages, to throw their habit off, to travel around to other's parishes, to free themselves of their own territory, people began by common accord to make smaller beds for the benefit of certain husbands ... and to watch out for the wives ... Any cat who finds the pot without its lid is bound to dip his paw into the pot ..."—*Propos rustiques* 6.624)

The use of the proverb ("maudict soit le chat ..."), coupled with the customary attributes of daily life—the pot, the cat, the bed, the cabbages—as well as the distrust and disgust expressed at the priests' behavior, are all characteristic of evangelical narrative.[6]

Further on, Du Fail expresses his discomfort with the disjunction between how things once were—and should be—and how they have become, again invoking a proverb to show the separation between desired state and actual reality (a contradiction that, as Luther and Marguerite have also found, proverbs are often especially well-suited to encapsulate): "lhabit (lhomme tu sçais) ne fait pas le Moyne"; "the habit ([this means:] the man, you know) doesn't make a monk"—*Propos rustiques* 8.632. Here, Du Fail feels the need to explicate the expression. By clarifying the metaphor by inserting "lhomme tu sçais," Du Fail also epitomizes how "plain style" no longer prevails in a fallen world—although it remains the evangelical ideal.

Banquet Theology

The way in which Du Fail treats material objects aligns him with the norms of evangelical narrative that we have been delineating. He professes contentment with the possessions that he already has, looking askance at acquisitiveness: "pensez vous que je me vueille damner pour les biens de ce monde?" ("do you think that I want to damn myself for these worldly goods?"—*Propos rustiques* 8.632). Du Fail's characters decline to deal in commodities ("les porte[r] vendre") for a profit:

> Où est le temps (ô Comperes) qu'il estoit mal aysé voir passer une simple feste, que quelcun du village ne eust invité tout le reste à disner, à manger sa Poulle, son Oyson, son Jambon? Mais comme aujourdhuy se fera cela, quand quasi on ne permet ou Poules, ou Oysons venir à perfection, quon ne les porte vendre … a lun pour traicter mal son voison, pour le desheriter …
>
> ("Where is the time, oh friends, when it would have been hard to turn away from a simple feast, when someone from the village would have invited everyone else to dine, to eat [with him] his chicken, his goose, his ham? But today this is no longer done, today one hardly allows his chicks or goslings to grow to maturity, but rather takes them to sell … to

> someone, to treat his neighbor poorly, to disinherit [his neighbor]."—*Propos rustiques* 1.610)

Commerce is associated with doing ill to one's neighbor, of pitting one against the other for profit ("pour traicter mal son voisin, pour le desheriter"). Du Fail, like Marguerite's *devisants* discoursing after supper or Luther and his neighbors talking at table, contrasts the banquet with the commercial market; the banquet offers a venue for the free exchange of ideas, an almost utopian scenario that elicits comparison with the Eucharistic feast ("eut invité tout le reste à disner"). In fact, Du Fail suggests a "theology of the banquet": banquets contain good doctrinal principles, and nourish both soul and body:

> banquets et festins de noz antecesseurs se offrent ... estoyent de bonne doctrine ... je vueille mesurer la consequence dun banquet ... quelles choses tant s'en fault quilz nourrissent le corps de lhomme.
>
> ("banquets and feasts of our [ancestors] were offered ... these were of good doctrine ... I want to measure the results of a banquet ... such things were needed as nourished man's body."—*Propos rustiques* 1.611)

Like Rabelais, Du Fail fashions neologisms as needed to communicate his message: *antecesseur* could mean "ancestor," "intercessor," or "ancestors as intercessors." Du Fail seems to equate ancestors with intercessors here, perhaps an implicit criticism of priestly intercession and a nostalgic wish for clerical probity that also may look forward to the Protestant patriarch, a figure who did not intercede, but who did instruct, as well as catechize ("le bon pere de famille se interrogeoit diligemment"; "the good father of the family examined his conscience diligently"—*Propos rustiques* 4.619). We can also detect some ambivalence on Du Fail's part toward priests, which we have also discerned in Marguerite and which is typical of evangelicals, whose reforming impulse nonetheless did not prompt him to leave the Catholic church. Here, in his portrait of the (significantly deceased) "Messire Jean," Du Fail harks back to an idyllic time when the parish priest did faithfully fulfill his functions and was a beloved member of the community. (Of course, much of Marguerite's disgust with Catholic clergy can be similarly explained by such a nostalgic turn back to the time when priests were worthy of veneration).

> Messire Jean, le feu Curé de nostre Paroisse … interpretant, ou l'Evangile du jour, ou sur iceluy donnant quelque bonne doctrine, ou bien conferant avec la plus ancienne matronne, pres luy assise … le bonhomme de curé, se mettant aucunefois aux champs, le tout à la bonne foy, se vantant de belles besognes … ou à chanter du contrepoinct, ou bien et rustrement faire un prosne; et que sil estoit question de Latin (neantmoins quil y fust un peu rouillé) il se y entendoit tout oultre et autant que petit compaignon du quartier …
>
> ("Master John, the deceased priest of our parish … [would be] interpreting the day's Gospel, or giving some good doctrinal explication of it, or indeed conversing with the oldest of the [village] matrons, seated next to him … that good man [would] sometimes go out in the fields, doing everything in good faith, bragging about such good tasks … or [he would] sing harmony, or well and simply do a sermon; and if any Latin was needed (even though his was a little rusty) he could understand it as well as everyone else in the neighborhood …"—*Propos rustiques* 4.612)

Du Fail depicts the good Curé partnering with his parish members in daily-life activities—harvesting wheat, singing harmony—as well as preaching (in what is significantly described as plain style: "bien et rustrement faire un prosne"): a sort of hybrid conflation of the Catholic model of the exemplary parish priest with the Protestant elevation of quotidian activities and lay involvement as also constituting a vocation ("le reste de la famille ouvrant chascun en son office"; "the rest of the family working each at his own task"—*Propos rustiques* 5.620). In fact, Du Fail explicitly designates work in the fields as a form of calling ("ceste bienheureuse *vacation* de agriculture"—emphasis added), developing the focus on practical, homely, daily-life experience on which Luther and Marguerite also focus in their texts:

> Mes enfans, puisque le Seigneur Dieu vous ha appellés à ceste bienheureuse vacation de agriculture … et il est bien raisonnable que soyez diligens et prompts à lexercer par vertueux faicts, bons et louables actes …

> ("my children, since the Lord God has called you to this sainted vocation of agriculture … and it is indeed reasonable that you be diligent and quick to ply your trade with virtuous actions, good and praiseworthy deeds …"—*Propos rustiques* 4.614)

Du Fail appears also to anticipate a sort of doctrine of election: his use of the words "preudhommie" and "gens de bien" seems to indicate a special status to be earned by the diligent believer who focuses on the divine ("le surplus"—a term used similarly by both Rabelais and Marguerite) rather than the things of the world. This (to use the Calvinist term) "elect" status will be visible through "certains signes" as in Protestant theology:

> le surplus parfera une espece de preudhommie que je voy apparoistre en vous, avecques signes evidens de estre à l'advenir gens de bien … le bon Dieu nous ha (comme en toute choses) merveilleusement fortunés en ce.
>
> ("the surplus will perfect a sort of 'good man status' that I see [beginning to] show in you with evident signs [that you will be] in the future 'good people' … Gracious God has [as in all things] marvelously graced you in this."—*Propos rustiques* 4.614)

Such awareness of election must necessarily be preceded by a conversion process, a change of heart such as that envisioned by Luther and Marguerite: "en fin recognoissant ses deffaults (et ainsi contraint) est devenu homme de bien" ("finally recognizing his faults [and compelled to do so] he became a 'good man'"—*Propos rustiques* 4.615). Part of the preparation for this conversion is the recognition that material profit must be superceded by spiritual profit ("nostre profit et bien"), those gifts granted by God that have enduring value:

> il est de besoing en premier poinct aymer, reverer et craindre Dieu, comme celuy qui souffre que devenions en mille adversités, pour nous monstrer quil est le maistre, et celuy qui ha procréé toutes choses pour nostre profit et bien.
>
> ("it is necessary in the first place to love, revere, and fear God, as He who suffers us to be in a thousand trials, to show us that he is Lord, and he who has created all things for our profit and good."—*Propos rustiques* 4.615)

The inflection given to the term *profit* is distinctive to the evangelical narrative and its distrust of exclusively earthly treasures, as we have already seen. As evangelicals construed it, profit was uniquely spiritual and was a deposit to be safeguarded against entrance into heaven; this profit could also be passed from father to son; Du Fail calls it (using the language of the Gospels) a "heritage" (*Propos rustiques* 4.616). This profit accrued from proper instruction, and Du Fail's texts participate in that activity: Du Fail uses "compte" as do Marguerite and Rabelais—to translate both "accounting" and "a tale well told": "Le compte nous est mis devant les yeux (ô Compere) que proprement me semble y estre et voir le bon homme" ("the tale is put before our eyes, oh my buddy, so that I actually seem to be in it and to see the good man"—*Propos rustiques* 4.619).

The conclusion of the *Propos rustiques* is prayerful: "Fin puis que ainsi est" ("The end, because that's how it is / amen"—*Propos rustiques* 13.658). In this way, Du Fail expresses the wish that his reader will heed the teachings represented in the text, be aware of the gap between past and present, appearance and reality, profession of faith and actual deeds, worldly gain and spiritual profit, earthly existence and heavenly destination. His final words are to invite his readers to a banquet which will be a spiritual feast:

> Au moyen de quoy servez à Dieu, et le craignez, et ne vous souciez du reste: car cest peu de cas que biens et telz poincts de fortune ausquelz nous confions. Faictes donques grand chère, mes petits Enfans.
>
> ("by this means serve God, and fear him, and don't worry about the rest: for worldly goods and those things in which we put our trust are worth very little. Therefore be joyful [eat a lot], my little children."—*Propos rustiques* 13.658)

The role of his writing, Du Fail tells us elsewhere, is to direct the reader to something higher that surpasses earthly concerns: "ces … escriptz, m'invitant à tascher je ne sçay quoy de plus hault qui sentist ma vacation" ("these writings, inviting me to try [to attain] something higher—I know not what—that could be my vocation").[7]

Just as in the *Heptaméron*, the evangelical narrative reorients the reader's perspective by describing "un contraire par lautre": earthly treasures gradually shift aside, showing spiritual significance.

Jacques Yver: Evangelical Author and Imitator of Marguerite de Navarre

Jacques Yver was born in Niort in 1520 to a bourgeois family. He died in the 1570s, and most of his writings, composed shortly before his death, were published posthumously. Jacques Yver, Noël Du Fail, and Guillaume Bouchet met in Poitiers, forming a group of writers interested in practicing an evangelical narrative genre similar to that inaugurated by Marguerite de Navarre; Yver later frequented the circle of Marguerite. Sympathetic to Protestantism, during the Wars of Religion Yver sided with the Politiques.

Yver's best-known work, the *Printemps,* appeared in thirteen editions from 1572 to 1618, enjoying an enormous popularity and influence. In the *Printemps*, Yver constructed a narrative scenario similar to that of the *Heptaméron.*[8] Critics have assessed the *Printemps* as a work that "complète ou … nuance l'*Heptaméron*" ("completes, or deepens, the *Heptaméron*").[9] Built around five days of storytelling, the *Printemps* described the life of six noble interlocutors, analogous to Marguerite's *devisants* in their role as framing commentators, in a Poitevin castle during a truce in religious hostilities. It is a *livre d'actualité* that offers documentation concerning daily life during the time period as well as a theological awareness of the arguments subtending the conflict. The first story begins in August of 1570, just after the peace of St. Germain, which ended the third War of Religion, while the fifth *nouvelle* takes place in the Saintonge, a hotbed of Huguenot sentiment, and makes explicit reference to specific battles in the Sainctes, La Rochelle, and Brouage region during the third War of Religion (circa 1570).

Like Marguerite, Yver shows some reminiscences of late medieval narrative: his characters, even more than hers, demonstrate this influence, as they possess allegorical names such as Bel-Accueil, Fleur d'amour, and Ferme-Foy, and the château is itself named Printemps, so that what transpires in the space of the text is also circumscribed by the architectural space of the castle's four walls. Printemps is an ornate castle whose walls are painted with figures representing memorable stories "avec mille subtiles enigmes, emblesmes ou armoiries et devises" ("with a thousand subtle riddles, emblems, coats of arms, and devises"—*Printemps* 1.1136), recalling Marguerite's interest in evangelical theory of emblematics and offering a theater for storytelling that is, itself, a *mise-en-abyme* of the taletelling process. The castle is surrounded by beautiful gardens and grottoes augmented with statuary and sculpture, another similarity with Marguerite's focus on decorative and fine arts:

> nature avoit en debat et contention avec l'excellence de l'artifice ... bref, de tout ce où la main industrieuse monstre le plus beau son mesnagement ... comme l'orfevre pour l'honneur de son mestier, met en de l'or bien élabouré quelque pierre de grande valeur ...
>
> ("Nature there debates and contends with the excellence of artifice ... in short, everything where the industrious hand best shows its work ... like the goldsmith, to give honor to his craft, sets in well-worked gold a stone of great value ..."—*Printemps* 1.1136–37)

The lady of the castle, tellingly, is named Marguerite.

Like Oisille in the *Heptaméron,* the lady of the castle discourses on the topic of the inconstancy of worldly things and the instability of human nature, adopting as her own Yver's—and Ecclesiasticus's—message: "toutes choses par la loy humaine sont sujettes à changement" ("all things are likely to change, due to human nature"—*Printemps* 5.1226). She instructs the other five nobles concerning the nature of sin and the degeneracy of humanity:

> La Dame print occasion de discourir fort profundement de la nature de l'homme, et de son ingratitude mère de sa misère, commençant depuis Adam, jusques à progrés special de ces derniers temps, si pervers et corrompus, qu'il semble que tout doive retourner en l'ancienne confusion.
>
> ("the lady took this opportunity to speak profoundly about the nature of humanity and of its ingratitude, source of humanity's misery, beginning with Adam, up to the present time which, so perverse and corrupt, made it seem as though

> all was returning to its former chaotic state."—*Printemps* 1.1139)

Her "lesson" sets the stage for the didactic quality of many of the tales, purveyors of spiritual wisdom as well as of secular entertainment. This theme is especially acute in Yver, perhaps because of the immediate cessation of the hostilities right before he drafted the tales (or, as he may have suspected, their impending resumption).

Yver adopts the Gospel strategy of storytelling as a restorative tool in reestablishing harmony on earth while also pointing to a higher reality. He describes the strategy of consolation and re-creation through the sharing of stories as "cette charité" (*Printemps* 1.1135), and describes the process in this way:

> je peux bien assurer que, entre tous les François, les habitants du pays de Poitou retournèrent avec extrême joie en leurs désolées maisons, pensant entrer en nouveaux ménages, où ils réputoient pour gagné ce qu'ils trouvèrent de reste et qui étoit échappé aux insolents soldats; si qu'après s'être accommodés tellement quellement selon que la nécessité pouvoit permettre, n'eurent rien en plus singulière recommandations, que de s'entrevoir les uns les autres, consoler et communiquer entre eux leurs pertes et se consoler par la pratique d'un devoir d'amitié en leur commune misère.
>
> ("I can indeed assure you that, among all the French, the inhabitants of the Poitou returned with great joy to their devastated houses, thinking to come into a new household, where they figured counted as gain anything that was left that had escaped that rude soldiers; and indeed, after having settled themselves as best they could given the circumstances, their best strategy was to see each, to console each other, and to communicate among themselves their losses and to console themselves by practicing the duty of friendship in their common misery."—*Printemps* 1.1135)

Stories are both the substance of their interaction, and their cure.

How the stories are interpreted is also a concern:

> Lors chascun commença à dire son opinion, sur l'interpretation du songe … l'autre par un sens plus hautain et sur-

> naturel … un autre interpretoit moralement, et chascun selon son divers instinct.
>
> ("then each began to give his opinion concerning the meaning of the dream … another [interpreted it] in a more elevated, supernatural way … another interpreted morally, and each according to his various instinct."—*Printemps* 5.1220)

Such delusional reading patterns are typical of the world: "aussi tel se fait fort et se vante de tenir la vraye verité, lequel, s'il avoit les yeux bien ouverts, verroit que ce n'est que vanité et mensonge" ("therefore such a man brags that he holds true truth; that same man, if he had his eyes wide open, would see that it is nothing but vanity and lies"—*Printemps* 5.1217). However, the framing provided by the commentators, as is the case with the *Heptaméron*, will now ensure that right reading will ensue. Further, a reliance on evangelical "plain style" rather than flowery rhetoric will henceforth stabilize the meaning and make the text transparent to its reader. Yver states that such a tactic is necessary, since far-flung poetic language and interpretations ("disent nos Poëtes, couvrans la verité des mensonges"; "say our Poets, covering the truth with lies"—*Printemps* 5.1215) are enough to make even the simplest matter seem complex and esoteric: "je ne m'estonneray plus, si en nostre langue champestre, une question qui sembloit si claire, est si debatue" ("I would no longer be surprised if, in our rustic tongue, a matter which seemed so clear, was debated"—*Printemps* 5.1217).

As in the *Heptaméron*, the "passetemps" of storytelling exercised in this way is profitable, and the eventual metaphysical orientation of the tales results in Gospel *joye*: "ilz passeroient le temps joyeusement" ("they spent time more joyfully"—*Printemps* 1.1137). To the strife and division of wars, Yver opposes the evangelical motif, taken from St. Paul, that enjoins that all are members of the same body (1 Cor. 12):

> Ce n'est pas chose étrange qu'un total bien conjoint et assemblé se maintienne par son union, voire s'accroisse en force et puissance … Nature ne se sert d'autre moyen pour détruire et ruiner toutes ses créatures, que de discorde et disjonction.

> ("it is no strange thing that a whole, well joined and assembled, holds together by its union, indeed even increases in strength and might … Nature uses no other means to destroy and ruin all her creatures than that of discord and disjunction."—*Printemps* 1.1144)

Yver's aim is that storytelling will reinstate that organic union and wholeness, when identity is found in Christ, rather than in strident separate selves.

Sacred and secular interweave, as the quotidian occurrences of the characters' lives take place on days of spiritual significance. Like the *Heptaméron,* the feast of Pentecost is important for the *Printemps*, as the first *nouvelle* takes place on that day: the telling of tales coincides with the day of speaking in tongues. The cycle of storytelling parallels the division of the day into periods of work and prayer; the first thing the protagonists do in the morning is pray:

> après avoir presenté à Dieu leur premiere œuvre concernant le devoir de piété et devotion requise, non seulement requise pour le bon reiglement d'une famille bien instituée, mais selon le tribut que doivent tous Chrestiens.
>
> ("after having presented to God their first act concerning the duty of piety and required devotion, required not only for the good rule of a well-established family, but according to the tribute owed by all Christians …"—*Printemps* 1.1137)

In addition, the activities are often framed by scriptural quotations, a technique that Marguerite also relies on to turn her otherwise seemingly secular stories in a spiritual direction. For example, decrying deception and hypocrisy, Yver puts into the mouth of one of his characters the same words that Marguerite causes Oisille to quote from St. Paul: "Ne trouvons donc impossible qu'un malin démon … se transforme en ange de lumière pour nous décevoir" ("let us not then find it impossible that an evil demon might transform himself into an angel of light in order to deceive us"—*Printemps* 1.1150). A paraphrase of St. Paul comes in the fifth Day, where sin (*hamartia*) is defined as falling short of the mark, or standard, that Christ has set: "car ainsi que de plusieurs archers qui visent il n'y en à [*sic*] qu'un ou deux qui frappent le blanc, et rapportent le prix honorable … aujourd'huy que le monde est si corrompu …" ("for, just as several archers take aim at a mark but only one or two strike the target and take the prize … today the world is so corrupt"—*Printemps* 5.1224).

As in the *Heptaméron*, many of the tales are told while banqueting; as with Rabelais, numerous lists of their activities are provided, including games and dances (*Printemps* 1.1139). The Third Day, for instance, is one told at a banquet; the mistress of the house proposes a debate at table that Yver then likens to a recent abortive attempt to resolve contemporary religious tensions through discussion, the Colloque de Poissy (*Printemps* 3.1181). The Fifth Day also takes place at a banquet, this time one decorated lavishly, recalling the technique Marguerite employed—that of enumerating decorative arts objects and ornate, detailed artifacts—to underscore the transitory quality of earthly treasures: "là les tables furent couvertes … [avec] la magnificence … du service: … les vaisseaux estoyent d'or, et les utensiles dorez … [ou] de corail … [ou] d'argent … [ou] de cristal" ("there the tables were laid with a magnificent place-setting: the vessels were of gold, and the utensils were gilded … or [made of] coral …. of silver … or of crystal"—*Printemps* 5.1218).

Another characteristic that the tales of the *Printemps* share with those of the *Heptaméron* is a realization that relationships matter more than things. In fact, things are untrustworthy because of humanity's tendency to place too much trust in them or inability to interpret them accurately; "tellement qu'une chose peut sembler estre qu'elle n'est point, comme monstrent ces tableaux" ("just as a thing may seem other than it is, as these tableaux show"—*Printemps* 5.1222). *Tableau* recalls both Luther's and Marguerite's tendency to illustrate a precept through stories in which objects are carefully arranged in a sort of didactic theater, or *tableau*. One of the statues in the castle's gardens bears this inscription: "Mais l'homme mescognoit les biens que tu [Seigneur] luy faits" ("But man does not recognize the goods that you, Lord, provide for him"—*Printemps* 1.1139), contrasting worldly goods with the treasure of heaven. In the first *nouvelle*, merchandise and trade form the thematic focus. Yver describes a town where

> le commerce et trafic l'enrichit merveilleusement et lui fait part des commodités étrangères … là, deux familles de marchands remarquables … pour leurs grands biens …
>
> ("commerce and trade enriched [the town] marvelously and enabled it to take part in foreign goods … there, two merchant families were noteworthy for their extensive possessions … "—*Printemps* 1.1144)

However, while wealth seems a solid foundation on which to base one's hopes, money and worldly possessions prove a corrupting influence. Despite the anticipated marriage arranged between the scion of one trading house, Herman, and the daughter of another, Fleurie, a "facteur," or trader, named Ponifre decides to take Fleurie by force:

> l'amant épioit toutes commodités d'effectuer son dessein … il s'avisa que c'étoit une grande folie à lui de se consumer ainsi à crédit en une langueur perpétuelle et en dépenses excessives.
>
> ("the lover spied out all sorts of commodities whereby to realize his goal … he decided that it would be crazy of him to consume himself on credit in this way in perpetual languor and in excessive expenses."—*Printemps* 1.1147)

The vocabulary is marked by mercantile terms such as "commodity," "consume," "credit," and "expenses," which indict the worldliness of a man who treats the woman and her desires as simply another thing to be acquired. Further, he aggravates his crime by turning to a pimp ("maquerelle"—*Printemps* 1.1148) to "faire trafic de telle … marchandise" ("trade in such merchandise"—*Printemps* 1.1148). The pimp is assimilated to the figure of priest as intercessor, since the pimp instructs Ponifre to meet him after mass so that they may pursue the deal. Ponifre attends mass in a most inappropriate state, thinking only of his lust and of worldly matters: "durant laquelle ses yeux, avarement fichés sur sa belle maîtresse, lui rendoient, comme on dit, la peau premier qu'avoir pris la bête" ("during [the mass] his eyes, greedily fixed on his beautiful mistress, put, as the expression goes, the cart before the horse"—*Printemps* 1.1148). He then rapes Fleurie while she is unconscious; Fleurie gets pregnant and, dishonored, is married off to Ponifre by her mother, who cannot give Herman "damaged goods." When Herman finally marries another woman whom he does not deeply love, after a brief interlude he wants to return to work: "il est desormais besoin (mignonne) que pour l'entretien de mon devoir … je commence à lever quelque trafic … [pour] rapporter quelque gain" ("il is henceforth necessary [darling] that I attend to my business and begin again to trade … to make some profit"—*Printemps* 1.1155). The manipulative term of endearment *mignonne*, cunningly placed in parentheses, shows that he is not fully considering her wishes, but is lured by commercial activity rather than bound by love. Carite, his wife, reproaches him for not being content to stay with her. She opposes Scripture to his worldly, tradesman's reasoning, quoting from the Bible to justify her position: "Que s'il estoit ainsi que l'homme et la femme n'estant qu'un corps, et j'eusse la moitié en vous comme vous avez une moitié en moy" ("that if it were so that a man and a woman were but one body, and I half of you as you were half of me"—*Printemps* 1.1156); interestingly, however, she quickly switches over to mercantile language, mixing metaphors, as it were, and showing how worldly preoccupations can suborn spiritual standards: "je requerois que me laississiez au moins jouyr de la moitié qui m'est deue et acquise sur vous" ("I would request that you at least let me enjoy that half which is due to me and which I have acquired [by law] over you"—*Printemps* 1.1156), a sort of contractual language meant to show that he is reneging on his marital obligations. This bargaining does not work, however, and Herman leaves for six months. While he is traveling, the news spreads around Europe that Ponifre had bragged about having raped Fleurie before marrying her. Carite, learning of this, decides to test Herman's love for her by sending word to him that she, Carite, has died and that Fleurie is now free to wed (Ponifre having been put to death after his boast came to Fleurie's parents' attention). While Herman is returning to his hometown and his true love, however, Fleurie, having glanced one last time at her child, kills herself, demonstrating the author's moral aside that "les choses de ce monde sont inconstantes" ("the things of this world are unreliable"—*Printemps* 1.1162). In the commentators' framing analysis of the tale, they equate merchant activity with infidelity, among other assessments: "quand [Herman] voulut aller voir les foires d'Anverrs … en fin il tourna ses amours à l'envers" ("when Herman wanted to go [sell his wares] at the fair … he ended up by turning his love upside down"—*Printemps* 1.1167).

Money is judged to be at the root of all the evil in this tale—and all the others of the collection—and earthly treasures are devalued and distrusted. Yver exalts the incorruptibility of celestial treasures, however, at the end of the *Printemps*, requiring a final reorientation toward a metaphysical interpretation of the world and of his book: "l'homme est faict … de deux belles parties: / La première est l'esprit; la seconde est le corps / Le corps garde cachez, les superbes thresors, / Et de l'esprit divin les graces infinies …" ("man is made of two beautiful parts: the first is the soul, the second is the body. The body has contained within it the superb treasures and infinite graces of the divine Spirit"—*Printemps* 5.1274).

Chapter Six

Earthly Treasures

Marguerite's *Mondain* Monstrances

> Monstre: f. A patterne, scantling, proofe, example, essay; also, a muster, view, shew or sight; the countenance, representation, or outward appearance of a thing; a demonstration; also, a watch, or little clocke that strikes not; also, the glassie box that stands on the stalls of Goldsmithes, cutlers, &; and generally, any thing that shewes, or points at, another thing; whence, la monstre d'un horloge. The hand of a clocke. La monstrance d'un maquignon de chevaux. The place wherein a horse courser shews his commodities ... Monstrüeux ... exorbitant, unnaturall, or most contrary to nature.
>
> Randle Cotgrave
>
> *A Dictionarie of the French and English Tongues*

With the exception of theological applications, Randle Cotgrave's above definition of *monstre* enumerates the uses that Marguerite finds for objects in the *Heptaméron*. The definition also implicitly suggests ways in which her evangelical distrust of those things has developed. Its several categories all relate to artifacts. *Monstre* exalts appearance over essence: it is "the outward appearance of a thing." It is unnatural, "most contrary to nature." Artificed, something produced through technological expertise ("a demonstration"), *monstre* often designates a decorative arts object: "... the glassie box that stands on the stalls of Goldsmithes, Cutlers, &," or a timepiece: "a watch, or little clocke"; such objects show that *monstre* is fixed in temporality and is essentially material. While it displays something other than itself, the monstrance as constructed *contains* that thing and in some measure claims structural identity with it, rather than designating something outside itself (such an orientation "beyond" would move in the direction of a metaphysical perspective, and would be therefore acceptable to Marguerite). *Monstre* also "shews ... commodities," objects of exchange or transaction, stopping short of transformation.

For these reasons, and recalling the Catholic view of monstrance as a miraculous manifestation, a containment and a physical showing-forth of a divine attribute, evangelicals distrusted reliance on objects for meaning, to stabilize significance or to embed the sacred in an earthly setting. The Catholic church mobilized monstrances for the faithful to venerate in a sort of theatrical pageant throughout the city; they fixed relics in the frontals of high altars and encased them under transparent glass bubbles as objects of devotion. Evangelicals, influenced by scriptural injunctions against representations of the holy, confined their worship to what they found in the Bible rather than accepting purported evidentiary displays of the holy in the form of a physical embodiment, image, or object, such as a reliquary or statue. Evangelicals questioned the practice of devotion to icons, saints' bones, and relics housed in monstrances.

Evangelicals' objections echoed Calvin's writing against relics, Zwinglian and Anabaptist iconoclasm, and were especially akin to Luther's denial that materiality in and of itself could encapsulate sacred significance. As contrasted with transubstantiation, Luther's notion of *consubstantiation* maintained that the elements of bread and wine evoked the real presence of Christ but nonetheless remained earthly substances: while a spiritual transformation of the heart of the worshiper should occur, the bread and wine were never themselves lifted out of materiality, although their material substance was temporally "overlooked."[1] The words of the consecration spoken at the Eucharist generated for Luther a symbolic transformation—with, nonetheless, *real* matter (bread, wine)—to which the believer acquiesced, so that metaphysical message surpassed material substance. However, the material substance was not itself believed to be transformed in such a way as to become holy (as in the doctrine of Transubstantiation); rather, it was provisionally lifted up, to recall a higher reality, then resumed its base essential state. While in the Eucharist, bread could not possess immanence, in Luther's view it could act as a vehicle to invoke or to enable one to envision transcendence.

Ambroise Paré, a physician with Huguenot sympathies,[2] wrote *Des monstres et des prodiges* in reaction, at least in part, to the Catholic practice of venerating objects or fragments of objects, deemed to be holy. While he believed that God allowed monsters and marvels to occur in nature, Paré stressed that such manifestations should always be interpreted as *signs,* not as *presence*: they were phenomena intended for instruction, warning, or enlightenment. Through their misshapen materiality, they shocked the viewer into perceiving existence in a new way, thereby alerting humankind to God's purpose for the world. However, they did not possess intrinsic meaning or extraordinary efficacy. In this age of *Wunderkammerer*, Paré conceived of monstrous manifestations as paranormal phenomena belonging in God's great "curiosity cabinet," created in heaven as well as displayed on earth:

> Let the reader here adore and consider the awesome wisdom and power of the Creator ... I do not want to, nor can I, penetrate any further into the sacred cabinet ... of God's divine majesty ... Moreover, I do not want to fail to write of things both monstrous and wondrous which are created in heaven.[3]

Marguerite, similarly, constructs the *Heptaméron* as a collector's showcase of *mondain* objects construed both as courtly—expensive, gorgeous, used for costuming or ostentation—and as mundane—everyday objects, found in profusion in the reader's ordinary existence. Marguerite includes such objects, but devalues them after having used them in a way that stretches beyond their materiality through a method intended to redeem that matter. Marguerite proposes to employ earthly objects as did Luther: materiality transmutes into a metaphysical statement; the metaphor of earthly existence helps to translate metaphysical concerns.

Luxury and the *Lectio* of *Luxure*

> Command those who are rich in this present world to be good, to be rich in good deeds, and to be generous and willing to share. In this way, they will lay up treasure for themselves as a firm foundation

> for the coming age, so that they may take hold of
> the life that is truly life.
>
> 1 Tim. 6.17–19

Luther insisted that *figura*, or object, was to be interpreted as "material shape." This perspective enabled him to discern providential history through worldly objects that functioned in, and sometimes as, parables.[4] For Luther, images encapsulated or prompted narratives. Evangelicals asserted that an object should not act like a *monstrance*, claiming its own significance. Rather, an object was the pretext to, and provided an impetus for, a story about salvation.

Marguerite's material objects act as similar narrative motors.[5] The eschatological recuperation of the earthly realm takes place in the *Heptaméron* through textual mechanisms that reorient material objects in a metaphysical sense. Artistic images and art objects were fairly rare at this time, and the objects that Marguerite uses are further rarified and confined to a specific context in that they are usually courtly or very costly. François Ier's decision to revise his fiscal policy because of the devastating expenses of the wars in Italy underscores such scarcity. Deficits in worldly goods persisted, in part accounting for the ambivalence toward luxury goods manifested in the *Heptaméron*.

Because of the cost of such objects, it is not be surprising that their possessors viewed them as valuable, and perhaps even significant in their quiddity.[6] Marguerite values such objects on a different level, however. She discerns a potential spiritual use-value in them. "As goods whose principle use is rhetorical and social, goods are simply incarnated signs"[7] that are "incorporated into the definition of the social self"[8] during the early modern period. However, Marguerite explores how the acquisition and collection of goods actually obstructs the full development of the *spiritual* self. Marguerite also tries to find ways in which these objects can cooperate in enhancing spiritual development. For this reason, her choice of objects is nearly always ideological, not merely aesthetic.

Economic context is a factor in this approach to art objects and artifacts. In true evangelical fashion, Marguerite feels that because words are used to promote and sell commodities, words have been torn from their right rhetorical function. In *Les commerces de Montaigne*, Philippe Desan asserts that speech progressively divorced itself from the theological underpinnings of the sixteenth century, and allied itself with the politics of mercantilism. Marguerite wants to counteract the cultural trend toward the commercialization of object, subject, and language, fighting that trend that Desan identified as "la pratique marchande ... [qui] eut pour effet de dissocier les problèmes théologico-moraux de la réalité quotidienne des marchands" ("commercial practice ... [which] resulted in the disassociation of theological and moral problems from daily mercantile reality").[9]

Marguerite tries to reestablish the relationship between language and theology that has become disarticulated due to merchant practice in this commodity culture. This proto-capitalist culture nonetheless exercised a significant pressure on the text. In *nouvelle* #26, for instance (*Hept.* 3.26), a "riche homme" sets out "collations," collects "ymaiges," obsesses about "argent," and arrays himself in magnificent "habillemens" (210–13; Chilton 292–94). Money is the *leitmotiv* of the tale: "Je sçay, Monseigneur, quel tel seigneur que vous, qui avez peres rudes et avaritieux, avez souvent plus faulte d'argent que nous, qui par petit train et bon mesnaige ne pensons que d'en amasser" ("I know, Monseigneur, that noble lords like yourself often have fathers who are harsh and parsimonious and that you are often more in need of money than are the likes of us who live very quietly and frugally and only think about saving" (*Hept.* 3.26.209; Chilton 294). The danger posed by commodities is that "d'autant que nostre cueur est affectionné à quelque chose terrienne, d'autant s'esloigne-il de l'affection celeste" ("for, the more one fixes one's affections on earthly things, the further one is from heavenly affections"—*Hept.* 7.70.418; Chilton 532).

Theological precedents existed for such a use of objects, in which the object did not alienate, but rather was an agent in a rapprochement between self or soul and God. The medieval tradition of the *lectio* was a hermeneutic strategy built on things and oriented toward spiritual progress through their instrumentality. In the fifteenth century, devotional manuals employed objects as meditational accessories, to be discarded when a higher state of being was attained. The *topos* of the spiritual ladder, common in this genre, was one example. Objects in Marguerite's narrative may, in some of the *nouvelles*, be viewed in relation to this tradition. However, we must refine that understanding by accounting for the persistence of relics in the *Heptaméron*[10] despite the evangelical reluctance to prize them.[11]

Marguerite's text may delineate a transitional moment in the history of evangelical theology: its early period, in which early evangelicals heeded the simplicity and directness of the Reformed message,[12] but with some ambivalence. Criticism of some Catholic practices was tentative, demonstrating evangelicals' reluctance to provoke a rupture with tradition, its reliance on relics and other ostensible manifestations of transcendence. Marguerite's innovation in genre and interdisciplinary project is, then, appropriately complex: the *nouvelles* are not only texts that employ objects, they are also texts that *produce* objects and, sometimes, anti-objects such as the map of the road that one should *not* take. This route leads to the Fall; it is an itinerary that charts the damage wrought by illicit, and unrestrained, passion. While such *via* typically map the Christian's progress to God, the cartographic, "landscaped," components of some of Marguerite's *nouvelles* offer, instead, a dysfunctional map: a graphing of sinful erring.[13] Knowing that man lacks coherence, aware of the dearth of significance in self, humanity paradoxically puts its trust in objects and in what can be seen, touched, and perceived by the contingent and limited perceptions of the senses. These objects thus concretize the culture that Marguerite hopes her textual reorienting will help to redeem.

The objects in Marguerite's narrative offer neither exact descriptions nor accurate representations of real objects. Instead, they function strategically, propelling the narrative, sometimes working symbolically, at other times literally: they are *processes* and actions rather than things. In this way, they recall the scriptural Hebrew verb *dabar*: effective Word, or self-realizing speech.

Further, they conform to the evangelical ideal of perfect equivalence between what is said and what results from what is spoken. *Nouvelle* #24, which we have already discussed in a different light, offers a model for this process. A nobleman, enamored of a queen, wears a mirror on his breast covered by a cloth. In her presence he unveils the mirror, thereby reflecting her to herself as subject and object of desire, as well as representing his obsessive love for her as a form of icon, almost a tattoo, lying atop and over-determining his own subjectivity. Here, the object functions both *symbolically* (Cupid is his *devise*) and *literally* (her image interposes itself between the two, so it is fitting that he *wears* her in an overlay upon himself). The objects work symbolically by designating his passion, and literally, by mirroring her. In the narrative, objects are transformed or enhanced so as to play a dual role evoking both subject and object: subjectivity is produced by a certain "biography of objects" in Marguerite's text, as things take on the ability to signify independently of their possessor. The "grosse robe fourrée de renardz" ("the coat lined with fox fur"), worn by the gentleman of Alençon who tries to fool another into thinking that a wrapped piece of excrement is a dinner roll, offers another example. The gentleman wraps the stool up in his handkerchief, just as he hides his motives. The fur of the robe—yet another layer—further indicates the depth of the deception; in addition, fox pelts symbolize a duplicitous nature (*Hept.* 6.52.333; Chilton 435).

Historiated objects—things inscribed with narrative scenes, or decoration that tells a story—do not signify simply as objects, but rather provide the pretext, and narrative components, for the telling of a tale[14] that results in the teasing-out of subjectivity. For instance, Dagoucin introduces the story that will become *nouvelle* #37 by speaking of a different sort of "manteau" (coat or cloak) from the fox-fur cloak above, yet one that participates in a similar dialectical play between deception and revelation:

> Et, pour vous monstrer que je me suis estudyé de honorer les vertueuses en ramentevant leurs bonnes œuvres, je vous en voys racompter une … il ne fault poinct tant donner de gloire à une seulle vertu, qu'il faille la faire servir de manteau à couvrir ung très grand vice.
>
> ("And to show you how I have striven to honour virtuous ladies by recounting their good actions, I shall now tell you about one such action … One should not exalt a single

> virtue to such an extent that one also has to make that virtue a cloak from some great vice."—*Hept.* 4.36.265; Chilton 337)

Dagoucin uses the term (*manteau*) both figuratively and literally, developing the object in both senses: for instance, he tells of a woman who dons her "manteau de nuyct" ("dressing gown"—*Hept.* 4.37.267; Chilton 358) while she awaits the return of her cheating husband who, believing her to be asleep, has snuck out of the conjugal bed. Her "manteau" mimes the covering-up, or "costume," which the husband adopts for his infidelity. The wrap is both an actual article of clothing as well as the strategic subterfuge to hide the adulterous act.

The selection and description of objects in the text, as well as the detail adorning those objects, bear ideological freight. Objects are never solely ornamental, but rather provide direction on a deeper level into the significance of the representation. Detail thereby creates a *textual* object, a microcosm of Marguerite's narrative project: "we must … descend into detail … [manifesting] a concern with the particular, the circumstantial, the concrete … [and] the interplay among them."[15] For example, in *nouvelle* #53, so many seemingly insignificant objects are mentioned in proximity and profusion that it becomes impossible to dismiss them: their collective presence situates a horrific event in improbably ordinary surroundings. The murder occurring within such mundane parameters underscores the presence of sin within the hearts and lives of ordinary people:

> Le prince descendit le degré … Il se promena en la court devant ceste porte … A l'heure, pensa le prince que le seigneur … estoit en la chambre de la dame … Se advisa que en la chambre de la dame y avoit une fenestre … qui … regardoit dans ung petit jardin … il luy souvint du proverbe qui dict: "Qui ne peut passer par la porte saille par la fenestre" … appella ung sien varlet de chambre et luy dist: "Allez-vous en ce jardin là derriere, et si vous voyez ung gentil homme descendre par la fenestre … tirez vostre espée et, en la frotant contre la muraille, cryez, 'tue, tue!'"
>
> ("the Prince went down again, but strongly suspected the valet was lying … he walked round in the courtyard at the bottom of the stairs to see if he would return. … The Prince now concluded that the Seigneur ... was in his lady's room

> … It occurred to him that there was a window in his lady's room, overlooking the garden … he remembered the old proverb, 'If you can't get out by the door, get out by the window.' So he immediately called one of his own valets de chambre, and said: 'Go into that garden round the back, and if you see a young nobleman climbing out the window … draw your sword, rattle it against the wall and shout "Kill him! Kill him!"''' (*Hept.* 6.53.339; Chilton 441)

The text requires us to retrace the steps that the protagonists take through their everyday setting, moving them—and the reader—ever closer to an awareness of their own sinfulness. The citation of the proverb ("Qui ne peut passer par la porte saille par la fenestre"), phrased equally in a daily-life way and referring to ordinary objects like the door and the window, reinforces the exemplary and practical value of the tale.

The presence of historiated objects in Marguerite's narrative reflects contemporary context: many varities of sixteenth-century objects featured such motifs, among them copes, table linen worked with the scene of Susannah and the elders, brasses with descriptive intaglio, bronze work featuring historical reliefs, majolica, and exotic objects like cups carved from coconuts, capped in silver, and bearing narrative scenes.[16] Historiated motifs also adorned damask, earthenware painted in polychrome, tiles, glassware, alabaster devotional figures—some with strapwork—and retables with strapwork decorative schemes. In addition, many bed panels featured such historiated ornamentation.

Refining Objects in a Spiritual Sense

> But who can endure the day of His coming? And
> who can stand when He appears? For He is like a
> refiner's fire and like launderer's soap. He will sit
> as a refiner and a purifier of silver; He will …
> purge them as gold and silver, that they may offer
> to the Lord an offering in righteousness.
>
> Mal. 2.2–3

Objects in the *Heptaméron* are encapsulations of the material world's preoccupations; they are also intellectual constructs set to the service of spirituality. The *Heptaméron* deploys several categories of objects, among them constructed or artificed objects,[17] objects used metonymically or metaphorically; objects intended literally—usually drawn from daily life; and objects that act like placemarkers or chalklines on a stage to create boundaries and suggest relationships or interactions. While objects might be seen as "embody[ing] a clash between the terrestrial and the celestial,"[18] Marguerite nuances their presentation: instead of delineating an absolute dichotomy, she discerns a *dialectical relationship* between object and subject, earth and heaven. Apparently in schism each from the other, they are actually—however apparently paradoxically—evocative each of the other. Marguerite moves from the stage of experience (materiality) to the *telos* of faith (metaphysics): "Le monde réel est bien ce monde dominé par les phénomènes économiques … [et] pénétré par des images qui rappellent la matérialité de l'existence. L'homme … pense ainsi un autre monde par le truchement d'une logique économique" ("the real world is actually the world ruled by economic phenomena … and penetrated by images recalling the materiality of existence. Man … is able to conceive of another world through the intermediary of an economic logic").[19]

In tracing this progression, the *Heptaméron* proleptically composes a "Protestant pattern book": Marguerite suggests manifold models in the *nouvelles* of how to negotiate worldly perils, which she scrutinizes in detail as they are represented by a selection of objects in the text. As the reader learns to distrust things, and to rely on the voice and commentary constructed by the interplay among the *devisants*, Marguerite traces a map of metaphysical mandates vis-à-vis the world. By the time that the reader has begun to question and to interpret as do the *devisants*, the reader has already shifted to a position outside—beyond—the world epitomized by objects in the text. In this way, the reader herself is a frame that critiques the world, and, in so doing, the reader inhabits a space of metaphysical awareness. By its very lack of conclusion, the *Heptaméron* keeps open the process of storytelling, commentary, analysis, lesson learned, and application of that lesson in the future. Just so, the final words of the *Heptaméron* offer no conclusion but rather only a deferral to another tale-telling occasion:

> Aussy ay-je ung compte tout prest, respondit-elle, digne de suyvre le vostre, car je parle de religieux et de mort. Or, escoutez le bien, s'il vous plaist.
>
> ("'Now I have a story ready to tell you,' she began, 'and it's a very appropriate one after the one you've told ... So please all listen carefully.'"—*Hept.* 8.72.428; Chilton 543)

The ability to listen and to assess show the reader's newly acquired metaphysical astuteness and capacities of discernment, as well as the ongoing need for such qualities while earthly experience still confines and seduces humanity.

Things in the Stories, and the Shape of Things to Come

Both critical of relics and monstrances, yet, to some degree, still using them in her narrative, Marguerite is truly evangelical in the sixteenth-century sense: her work attests to a transitional ideological stage during which Catholics began to use terms and techniques drawn from Luther and other Protestant thinkers, while still determined not to leave the Catholic church. Through its incorporation and treatment of decorative arts objects, the *Heptaméron* constitutes an important document of this period of change. Catholic saints' lives, such as those in the *Golden Legend* of Jacobus Voragine, customarily included objects in their narratives, populating their portraits with objects that functioned *symbolically* to illuminate significant aspects of the saint. Saints also were represented iconographically by a number of coded objects that encapsulated crucial events in the *vita*: St. Catherine and her wheel are a traditional pair, for example. Late medieval representations of scenes from daily life—prior to the development of genre paintings—focused more on objective particularities of various trades or occupations rather than on devising a narrative of ordinary existence spotlighting an individual's role within it. For instance, the title of Jean Bourdichon's *Labor* (circa 1494) designated the employment, not the person. Although designed in a "realistic" style, the "main interest was documentary. Bourdichon's purpose was to convey a moral lesson, rather than to render the atmosphere and the life of an artisan's workshop."[20] The image was exemplary and illustrative rather than representational.[21] The narrative it suggested was schematic, foreknown, like a brief text to be memorized, not an evolving, dynamic story such as that which Marguerite crafts.

Marguerite's inclusion of objects situates her within some persistent awareness of, and respect for, this genre. Yet several features demarcate her from it, among them her reliance on the frame, her focus on detail, and her incorporation of new artistic techniques recognized by contemporaries as characteristically (although not exclusively) Protestant: the portrait, landscape, and still life. In Renaissance portraits, secularized significant objects—such as the purely quotidian (rather than ecclesiastical) inclusion of a pomander, gloves, and a ring in Maarten van Heemskreck's *Portrait* of Wilhelmina Poling (circa 1545)—evoked symbolic saints' attributes.[22] Marguerite draws on the sacral symbolic saint's attribute, recognizes the sixteenth-century trend toward the representation of commodities, and negotiates her narrative application of objects between these two tendencies. Marguerite exemplifies the Reformation's elevation of everyday life to a status of theological worth: the term *Beruf* meant for Luther both work and vocation, thus incorporating both objective and subjective, mundane and metaphysical, aspects.

Desan has asserted that "jamais civilisation n'a été plus matérielle que celle de la Renaissance" ("no civilization has ever been as material as that of the Renaissance").[23] He further finds a similarity between the open-ended narrative genres popular throughout the sixteenth century—Montaigne's *Essais,* Béroalde de Verville's plastic recitals lacking closure, Rabelais's multivocal *récits*—and innovations in expense accounting that facilitated double-entry bookkeeping:

> l'échange n'est plus fondé sur des transactions isolées … mais représente un processus continuel … Puisque l'échange fait partie intégrante de toute activité humaine et commerciale, on recommande de garder le livre de comptes ouvert […] le compte courant … Raconter et comptabili-

> ser deviennent une seule [chose] … *Compte et conte se confondent …*
>
> ("exchange is no longer based on isolated transactions … but stands for a continual process … Since exchange is an integral part of all human and commercial activity, it is recommended to keep the books open … a running total of accounts … Narrating and counting become the same thing … accounting and recounting merge."—emphasis added)[24]

The exchange that occurs within the *nouvelle* is frequently driven by desire for commodities. In that respect, the *Heptaméron* epitomizes its context. The *nouvelles* reflect the collector mentality of the age, in which precious, exotic, or bizarre objects were bartered or purchased, then hoarded, the activity of collecting indicating a belief in the significance of objects.[25] Bits of meaning, stabilized and arranged, created a narrative.

Collecting objects is akin to manipulating semantic units. And yet, without an interpretive framework or labels pointing to their significance, such objects are only a meaningless jumble. To demonstrate humanity's lack of validity when not in relation with God, Marguerite makes earthly objects alluring, initially encouraging her characters to use and rely on those things. She then points out their ultimate unreliability: "Il me semble que, par ce compte, les gens de bien doibvent apprendre à ne retenir chez eulx ceulx desquelz la conscience, le cueur et l'entendement ignorent Dieu, l'honneur et le vray amour" ("in light of this story it seems to me that decent people ought to learn not to detain in their houses those whose consciences, hearts and minds are ignorant of God, of honour and of true love"—*Hept.* 3.27.223; Chilton 308).

The commentators gaze in on, and frame, the objects of each *nouvelle*, deciphering their meaning, much as a spectator would scrutinize objects in a *Wunderkammer*.[26] "What comes to reside in a wonder-cabinet are … strange things; tokens of alien culture, reduced to the status of … sheer objects, stripped of cultural and human contexts."[27] Similarly, objects in the *Heptaméron* signify humanity's estrangement from the metaphysical master-narrative. Marguerite points the way toward a restorative relationship between the atomized self and a divine story that makes sense of disparate selfhoods, creating a textual miracle-box with metaphysical ramifications. Numerous like-minded Protestant collectors accompanied her in this endeavor. In his study of the phenomenon of collecting, Antoine Schnapper finds that the majority of collectors (at least somewhat later in this time period) were Protestant: "… [ils] sont protestants: on a souvent observé que la curiosité scientifique était plus répandue et plus active chez les protestants; plus libres vis-à-vis de la tradition religieuse" ("they are Protestant: it has often been noted that scientific curiosity was more widespread among Protestants, [who were] freer in respect to religious tradition").[28] He lists, among Protestant collectors, Jules-Raymond de Solier (d.1594), François Gaverol (1636–94), and Pierre Borel (b. 1615); this latter inscribed the lintel of the door to the room housing his collection with the phrase "MICROCOSM, SEU RERUM OMNIUM RARIORUM COMPENDIUM" ("man is a compendium of all rare things"),[29] thereby describing his own subjectivity in reference to objects.

In the sixteenth century, architectural and decorative art ornamentation not only used the framing technique, it also imitated collectors' activity by heaping up objects and thus deriving new forms from these accretions. For instance, the popular *candelabrum* structure was "a piling up of ornamental forms, such as grotesques, symmetrically around a central axis, which could be used to fill a narrow vertical panel or [stand] independently as a pillar or pilaster."[30] Many northern Italian engravers and their German imitators, workers in silver and other metals, constructed such structures. Marguerite's narrative compilation and configuration of objects is similar to the candelabrum—she fills narrative space with objects that then, through their assemblage, suggest new shapes or delineate unexpected relations among themselves and her protagonists. Candelabrum constructions could act narratively and could participate in expressing a theological message, as the work of contemporary artists demonstrates. For example, in Pieter Aertsen's "The Meat Stall" (1551),

> the objects piled up in heaps, or strung from poles, are meant to overwhelm us with their sensuous reality (the panel is nearly life-size). Here the still-life so dominates the picture that it *seems* independent of the religious subject. *The latter, however, is not merely a pretext to justify the painting; it must be integral to the meaning of the scene.*[31]

The transitory nature of all life is the larger message evoked by the slabs of meat. Perhaps because objects were important in this period for cultural or social display, collection, representation in print,[32] and in other media, Marguerite produces a proliferation of objects as her textual pre-text. She then applies an artistic vocabulary to the unexpected venue of narrative.[33]

It was also typical of decorative and applied arts of the period to repeat the same model, with occasional minor revisions. Here, too, Marguerite's textual format follows the contemporary artistic paradigm, in that the structure of the *nouvelles* is repetitive. An example is the formula "je donne ma voix à … " ("I give my voice to / the next speaker will be …"),[34] which creates transitions from one *nouvelle* to the next. This reiterated phrase loops all the tales together in a process of enunciation, audition, reception, and interpretation. Another visual sort of rhetorical *conduplicatio* can be seen in *nouvelle* #13, where the wedding ring ("anneau") worn by the captain's wife is doubled by the ring ("bague") that he bestows on the lady whom he desires.[35] The two rings (one lawful, the other its deceiving copy) circulate among different owners, repeating the experiences of possession and desire, until the would-be mistress imposes order, fusing them by returning the wedding ring to the wife.[36]

Finally, similar thematic treatment shared by two or more *nouvelles* indicates the technique of repetition. For example, the *nouvelle* in which the fox-fur coated man tried to pass off a stool as a dinner roll (*Hept.* 6.52) is doubled by a nearly identical story in which Bertrand du Ha deceives his secretary, making him think that a wrapped "sabot de bois" ("a wooden clog, such as they wear in Gascony") is a "pasté" ("Basque ham pie") to savor (*Hept.* 3.28.225; Chilton 310–11).[37] Objects are nearly always the agents of deception in the *nouvelles*.

Stories—often similar in plot, characterization, and conclusion, and especially alike in the assortment and arrangement of objects contained in them—interrelate, as Marguerite searches for a higher meaning to be derived from the documentation that they furnish. "The passion for collecting … and the search for traces of creation … is also a search for transcendence," Jean Baudrillard asserts,[38] and, as every *nouvelle* is a re-creation of reality, the *Heptaméron* demonstrates a similar project.

Object Lessons: Marguerite's Curiosity Cabinets

Marguerite enumerates an extensive list of objects in her narrative. Among them are literary material including books and manuscripts, jewelry, mirrors, furniture, clothing, dolls, and wax figurines, portraits, dwellings, and theatrical props. Spaces also act like objects: *salles*, châteaux, chambers, closets, walls, wells, and gardens shape the architectural universe of the *Heptaméron*, while the objects contained within them, as well as the patterns of arrangement of things within boundaries, all play a textual role. The Renaissance conception of the craftsman, creator of all such objects, was positive: *homo artifex*, in his making of new forms, was God-like.[39] Consequently, Marguerite's evangelical ambivalence toward valuing such objects must contend with the positive valence given to such objects by her time period.

Jean Baudrillard's categories for interpreting the applications of worldly goods as he develops them in *The System of Objects* is useful in investigating Marguerite's creative ambivalence toward objects. These categories consist of symbolization, significance, selection, arrangement, and recurrence. Baudrillard lists as criteria for classification the size of the object; its degree of "functionality;" the gestures associated with it; the object's form, duration, the material that it transforms; the degree of exclusiveness or sociability attendant upon its use; and what "mental structures are interwoven with—and contradict—[the] functional structures"[40] of such objects. The category having to do with related intellectual structures is the most crucial of Baudrillard's categories for the *Heptaméron*: it encourages the consideration of evangelical theology's contribution, that of a metaphysical perspective on—and revision of—the object. In the *Heptaméron*, a consistent "system of meaning" composed of objects coexists with Marguerite's theological perspective, one that criticizes and corrects the cultural mind-set epitomized by objects.

The inclusion of texts as artifacts, and of epistolary textual material as objects in the *Heptaméron*'s narrative development, emphasizes the creative capacities of story by including story within story, word within word. The use of text as object also suggests a meta-narrative perspective since, while a text can be an object (for instance, a bound book), it is never *merely* an object (because it possesses the capacity to express itself). In the tale of Rolandine, a volume of Arthurian legends furnishes a literary clue to the kind of love that Rolandine experiences: *courtois*, not *mondain*, it aims at a higher ideal than worldly love. This love is also *courtois* in an ironic way, because it is critical of the court (its very source) whose notion of love is based on empty fame, lust, and ambition.[41] Like such texts, letters constitute important concrete intermediaries in the *nouvelles* between object and the narrative in which it is situated, often serving to move the plot in new directions. Occasionally, they act more like objects than texts: what they say may be untrue, and, as such, is a sign of the (objectified) fallen world.

Applied arts objects feature prominently in the *Heptaméron,* delineating through detail a language of objects that helps to structure the text. Baudrillard deems *coffres*, chests in which lovers hide, bones are displayed or treasures are stored, "monumental furnishings": he suggests that, because they are heavy, large, and not easily rearranged, such furniture attests to patterns in human relations, its blockiness causing unchanging choreographies of daily interaction that may then be examined and interpreted.[42] There are many beds, for instance, in the *Heptaméron,* some with curtains drawn, others with them opened for a framing effect; others have historiated bed panels creating a story-within-a-story. Furniture and furnishings are contextually significant for many reasons, among them the "trajectory" of their production[43] (which can trace a form of national—or even international—mapping), their prestige and ceremonial value. Like book production, furniture making was regulated by the king, who controlled the craft guilds,[44] so the "economy of exchange" of such furnishings and the locations that they occupy in the *nouvelles*, can indicate—as well as indict—the social standing of a particular character. Furniture is distributed in narrative space as a language. For instance, beds and gardens are often distorted *loci amœni,* theaters in which desire violates innocence.

Small items attest to patterns of use. Tableware, especially cups, bedecks tables in the *nouvelles,* keeping the banqueting format—the paradigm of exchange and discussion—ever present before the reader's eyes. Chalices are frequently mentioned. In 1523, Luther dissented from Catholic communion practice by calling for communion in both kinds ("species"): both the chalice and the Host were now offered to the laity. Marguerite's Lutheran proclivities inspire her to incorporate numerous chalices—and occasions on which the laity use them—into the text.

The *Heptaméron* frequently features mirrors, another object belonging to the realm of applied and decorative arts. Sixteenth-century mirrors were often used as "portrait covers"; sometimes mirrors had miniature portraits painted on their reverse side. Some mirrors were fashioned with fictive frames printed around their top, sides, and base; these frames might be adorned with strapwork.[45] Luther, like Marguerite, linked mirrors to subjectivity, suggesting that mirrors supply only a superficial knowledge of the subject. The true speculum should be the mirroring effect of Scripture, and how one sees oneself in relation to it:

> When the Word is proclaimed, the Holy Spirit accompanies it and breathes upon your heart. The sophists say that this is reflected knowledge, as an image is reflected in a mirror. When the Word is scattered abroad, the Holy Spirit blows upon us, but he must also breathe upon us inwardly.[46]

Thus, an object may be a point of departure for a character's transformation, but the narrative force must operate from within for the change to be successful. Framed mirrors, like framed portraits, provide a variety of similarities with the function of the frame (*corniche*) narrative: like the frame, they may serve as a reality-enhancement strategy, or constitute a *trompe-l'œil* technique to demonstrate that terrestrial reality is an illusion. Mirrors may also evoke an attempt to construct a credible witness (*témoin*) both internal and external to the text, as does the frame, or participate in the strategy to connect heaven and earth stylistically (in the case of a sinner beholding his fallenness in a mirror, and thereby being prompted to eschew his depravity). Finally, both the mirror and the text's frame offer an invitation for the reader to be inserted into the situation represented.

In portraits, somewhat like the effect of mirrors,

> the compositional relationship between sitter and frame, besides determining to some degree the sitter's pose, also affected the choice of background. Just as parapets and painted fictive frames were useful in explaining the cutting of figures, so similar devices were employed to relate the sitters more securely to the backgrounds and to the actual frames.[47]

Groupings of portraits could thus form variants of narrative compositions, establishing a variety of options for directional lines indicating how to read and interpret the poses. Sixteenth-century portrait collections often functioned in this way.[48] Brantôme availed himself of this possibility when he contrasted portraits of "dames illustres" and "dames galantes." The perceived resemblance among different portraits, justifying their grouping in the same collection, already drafted a rudimentary storyline.

Portraits, usually intentionally public self-representations, are similar to the role of masks in the text. Courtly ballets and charades were customary sixteenth-century entertainments in which masking to vest the identity of another was customary. In the *Heptaméron*, descriptions of articles of clothing accompany such *travestis*, or disguises. Furred robes, satin slippers, silken dresses, pieces of jewelry, silver rings, embroidered gloves, adorn the people and pages of the text. During the Renaissance, some workshop portrait painters often limned their portraits directly onto already painted costumes, which could be used interchangeably, no matter who the sitter was. Or separate pre-painted outfits could be inserted into a frame, on the sitter's whim, to alter the subject's appearance, much as a child's paper dolls today come outfitted with different tab-fastened outfits.[49] *Portraits historiés* were painted, and the commissioned likeness of an individual might then be attired as a character from Scripture or from a historical or mythological event.[50] The *nouvelles* use secular settings to illustrate spiritual truths in a similar way: the *personnages* in the *Heptaméron* operate on at least two levels—everyday life and metaphysical drama. Some of Marguerite's *nouvelles* sometimes work this way: otherwise interchangeable, combinable, the frame glues their diversity together. The discussion then orients the material of earthly existence in the direction of an enduring metaphysical message

Luxury clothing, such as gloves, plays a telling role in this process. Gloves were time-consuming to manufacture. However, they were also difficult to clean, so despite their expensiveness they were often discarded and replaced.[51] Gloves therefore were objects possessing cachet in a commodity culture. Nonetheless, they were treated as expendable. Such ambivalence encapsulates the evangelical attitude toward earthly treasures. Gloves often represented a theological distinction in fine arts: "a pair of gloves, the emblem of the *dextrarum iunctio*, or the nuptial joining of right hands—a detail which, in Catholic culture, had originally signified the sacramental nature of marriage—survived in sixteenth-century Protestantism … as a symbol of the [more personal and relational] marital bond."[52] Slippers, too, were expensive to produce yet frequently discarded. Their luxury status accorded well with the erotic suggestiveness seen in them: a foot, teasingly half-inserted into a slipper, connoted intercourse.[53] Marguerite often focuses on slippers—such as those worn by the would-be rapist in *nouvelle* #4—to redefine their use through narrative. In this tale, the emphasis on the slipper becomes a textual clue to the duplicity exercised—his "souliers de feutre" make no sound—as well as an indication that lust will be thwarted (since his stratagem of secrecy is not successful).[54]

These are objects that can be used to *objectify* the "other." Marguerite shows how such objectification occurs. She also tries to forestall such negative transformation in her text, so that subjectivity, which she understands to be the establishing of the self's identity *in God*, may be safeguarded or encouraged.[55] The use of the doll, puppet, or *poupée* is an example of such objectification. In *nouvelle* #1, when an evil person wishes the death of another, she whittles a wooden figurine, and then shapes one of wax to represent her victim (now doubly objectified, since the actual image used for the punitive enchantment is not even a first-hand rendition, but rather is derived second-hand, shaped from the first wooden template). A representation at one artistic remove, the wax image is, however, not suggestive of subjectivity, as it blurs personhood into functionality for evil ends.[56] Identity, now reduced to a thing, is subject to objectification. These *poupées* represent the entrapment of self in the material world.[57]

As the narrative wends its way to the last Day of the *Heptaméron*—although, since the book is not complete, there can never be full closure—the presence and importance of material objects appear to diminish. The text strives to liberate itself from materiality by emphasizing spirituality; things are less often invoked, while the evangelical message is increasingly pronounced. A scriptural lesson more frequently offers the model for the *nouvelle*, which illustrates or explicates it, as contrasted with many of the earlier *nouvelles,* which possess mixed, or exclusively secular and material, narrative foci. For instance, the prologue to the Sixth Day shows Oisille instructing the group in the tactics of evangelical explication:

> l'intention de mon histoire ne sortira poinct hors de la doctrine de la saincte Escripture, où il est dict: "Ne vous confiez poinct aux princes, ne aux filz des hommes, auxquelz n'est nostre salut." Et, afin que, par faulte d'exemple, ne mectez en obly ceste verité, je vous en voys dire ung très veritable et dont la memoire est si fresche, que à peyne en sont essuyez les œilz de ceulx qui ont veu ce piteulx spectacle.
>
> ("The intention of the story that I shall tell you will not be out of keeping with the teaching of Holy Scripture, where it is written 'Trust not in princes, nor in the son of man, in whom there is no salvation.' And, so that you will not forget this truth for want of an example, I am going to give you one which is true and so fresh to the memory that those who witnessed the pitiful sight I shall recount have hardly yet dried their tears ..."—*Hept.* prologue.6.328–29; Chilton 428)

The décor, a believable, quotidian universe familiar to the reader, has been set according to stage directions that stand in for responses to "reality" ("à peyne en sont essuyez les œilz de ceulx qui ont veu ce piteux spectacle").

Sixteenth-century Protestant theater typically demonstrated a heightened reliance on daily-life objects. For instance, the evangelical Sebastiano Serlio (1475–1554) published an important architectural treatise in 1545, which was essentially a compendium of stage designs accented with props.[58] These designs circulated throughout Europe, and may have prompted

Marguerite to populate her text with objects drawn from everyday existence.[59] The manner in which Marguerite employs objects is consistent with Protestant usage and differs from the symbolic props of medieval theater, in which properties incarnated the essence of a type. In the *Heptaméron*, things mean *more*. They embody potential experience, how a character may react or evolve: the suggested development of subjectivity. The thing prefigures, provokes, or encapsulates the textual problem or relationship.

Similarly, the function of the frame narrators is to treat things differently from their treatment in earlier or non-evangelical texts, with seriousness, commenting on representative objects *narratively*, to elucidate a deeper sense. As they "pass[ent] [leur] temps" in excavating meaning from the strata of objects, the *devisants* produce *profit* both for themselves and for the reader: "une morale de profit intellectuel, analogue à l'économie d'un profit matériel" ("a moral of intellectual merit, analogous to the economy of a material profit"):[60] the transforming of the material world into spiritual significance.

Chapter Seven

Costuming the Christiform Text;

Or, *L'habit ne fait pas le moine*

> I believe that your heart is in the right place. But, to tell you the truth, your hands are still hidden in your gloves. I still do not see any faith and flame coming from your hands. *Take off your gloves*, Milady: it is not enough to feel, to know, and to desire: one must also act.
>
> Guillaume Briçonnet to Marguerite

Guillaume Briçonnet, Marguerite's confessor, urged her to strip off her gloves, to remove the material obstruction to her metaphysical self-alignment.[1] His statement may have suggested a model for how Marguerite uses objects in the *Heptaméron*: the literary texture of the *nouvelles* is always woven from things of the world, but a higher, theological interpretation emerges from the divestiture of earthly garb and accessories. A yearning for a rehabilitated human nature, for the restoration of an Edenic environment uncluttered by earthly dross, energizes the stories of the *Heptaméron*:

> Vous contenterez que jamais n'en feut veu ung plus beau [pré]. Quant l'assemblée fut toute assise sur l'herbe verte, si noble et délicate qu'il ne leur falloit carreau ne tappis …
>
> ("Enough for us to say that a more beautiful meadow there never was seen. When they were all seated on the grass, so green and soft that there was no need for carpet or cushions …"—*Hept*. 1.prologue.10; Chilton 69–70)

Things—artificial constructions of human hands striving to fill some perceived void—are extraneous when there is purity of intention. Yet the stories do develop out of the use of worldly objects.

In a similar paradoxical turn, sinfulness is the essential ingredient in these stories that tell of salvation. Sin is the occasion ("ma faulte est occasion …") for both storytelling and for Bible reading:

> Oisille sceut très bien sercher le passaige où l'Escripture reprent ceulx qui sont negligens d'oyr ceste saincte parolle; et non seullement leur lisoit le texte et leur faisoit tant de bonnes et sainctes expositions qu'il n'estoit possible de s'ennuyer à l'ouyr. La leçon finie, Parlamente luy dist: "J'estois marrye d'avoir esté paresseuse quand je suis arrivée icy: mais … ma faulte est occasion de vous avoir faict si bien parler à moy …"
>
> ("Oisille knew how to find the passage in which Scripture reproaches those who are negligent in listening to the sacred word. She not only read them the text, [but] she also gave such sound and devout expositions that no one could possibly find it boring. Once the reading was over, Parlamente said to her: 'I was angry with myself for being lazy when I arrived, but as my failing has led you to speak so excellently, my laziness has yielded twice the profit'…"—*Hept.* 4.prologue.236; Chilton 324)

An anti-materialist stance yields to a narrative treatment of objects: as Longarine rather wistfully observes, "Et bien heureux sont ceulx que la foy a tant humilliez, qu'ilz n'ont poinct besoing d'experimenter leur nature pecheresse, par les effectz du dehors" ("And blessed are they whom faith has so humbled that they have no need of external effects to have their sinful nature demonstrated to them"—*Hept.* 4.34.254; Chilton 344). In this way, materialism mutates into metaphysics. As Simontault describes the operation of the *nouvelles,* it is "en partant d'une très grande follye [que] nous sommes tombez en la philosophie et theologie" ("we started with folly and we end up with philosophy and theology!"—*Hept.* 4.34.254; Chilton 344). The *follye* is human nature, marred by sin and marked by materiality. But the text transforms nature, like Parlamente's *faulte*, inscribing it as art under the sign of redemption—a "falling into" ("nous sommes tombez en") theology that salubriously reverses the Fall.

The rhetorical strategy of layering is one seemingly paradoxical way in which Marguerite conveys the eventual extraneousness of earthly possessions. Many *nouvelles*, especially those involving misrepresentation or deception, unfurl rolls and reams of fabric (clothing, overcoats, wraps) and successive strata of textual significance—actions that signify in more than one direction, on more than one level. Contemporary decorative schemas replicated[2] such techniques of ornamental overlayering. The relationship between image and narrative was everywhere evident in sixteenth-century France:

> Pictorial layering was clearly among the favorite effects employed by the renowned school of Italian and French painters assembled at Fontainebleau. Il Rosso's acclaimed Galerie François Ier (1528–1540) is rife with examples. When considered as pictorial "units" in their own right, the fourteen bays that fill out this extraordinary artistic program are each a grand picture that accommodates a panoply of other pictures—from the image-charged friezes, cartouches, roundels, and stucco reliefs to the narrative fresco at the center of the whole.[3]

Ornamental arts and narrative development exchanged conceits in this period and were mutually influential. While poets such as Ronsard were ambivalent about the influx of Italian decorators into France during this period,[4] they nevertheless often developed their poetic repertoire through a strategy of accumulation like the candelabrum effect (discussed in Chapter 6) or through techniques similar to Rosso's style. Ronsard's poetry aimed to ravish, lift up, or out of context (*ravir*),[5] much as the Neo-Platonist Marsilio Ficino, an important influence on Marguerite de Navarre,[6] defined beauty in the *Commentarium in Convivium*: "it is that charm of virtue or of form or sounds which calls and *ravishes the soul* through thought, sight, or hearing that is most justly called beautiful."[7]

Catholic, evangelical, and Reformed artists all engaged in varying ways, and with different emphases, in dialogue with contemporary decorative idioms. An agglomeration of adornment, as well as an artistic vocabulary of excess, typified courtly culture and luxury production of the period, and was thus also firmly rooted in, and reflective of, its socio-economic context.[8] Such transforming of commerce typically occurred in "elite economic circles … where an economy of profit [was] justified."[9] However, Marguerite's definition of *ravir* is not limited solely to aesthetics: she distinguishes herself from other contemporary artistic creators by the evangelical template to which her text conforms and which it illustrates.

Marguerite's evangelical project empties objects of their purported animistic content or misplaced value to put them to use in a new sort of textual economy. Claude-Gilbert Du Bois observes that the tendency to use "realistic elements ... as ciphers of ... concepts"[10] was characteristic of the sixteenth century. This is, in part, what Marguerite is doing in her text; undoing, by subjecting to a theological critique what Du Bois terms the court-produced "mythologie quotidienne" ("the mythology of daily life"),[11] in order to teach other, higher values. The reader of epiphenomena, objects, artifacts, and texts must interrogate such cultural displays to determine the ideological motivations animating them in order to elucidate their ideological freight.[12]

Layers, Lies, and *Logos*

> Now listen, you rich people, weep and wail because of the misery that is coming upon you. Your wealth has rotted, and moths have eaten your clothes. Your gold and silver are corroded. Their corrosion will testify against you and eat your flesh like fire.
>
> Jas. 5.1–3

The rhetorical technique of enveloping, layering, wrapping, disguising, and costuming creates an overdressed text, one that both exemplifies and attempts to remedy material reality. The overly ornate text represents the potentially problematic status of the word, which often limits itself to the replication, rather than the redressing, of reality. In the prologue to the *Heptaméron*, a good shepherd (perhaps Christ) intuits Simontault's need: "le bergier, qui en entendoit myeulx sa necessité tant en le voiant que en escoutant sa parolle, le print par la main et le mena en sa pauvre maison" ("the shepherd ... underst[oo]d his plight. He had taken him by the hand and led him to his humble abode"—*Hept.* 1.prologue.5; Chilton 64). Marguerite thus asserts, at the very beginning of the *Heptaméron*, that image and word ("tant en le *voiant* que en *escoutant* sa parolle ..."—emphasis added) may cooperate to suggest a deeper sense or a hidden, but higher, reality.

Things coupled with the Word are redeemed by their conjunction with Scripture, tracing the *Heptaméron*'s programmatic itinerary from materiality to metaphysics: "car qui congnoist Dieu veoit toutes choses belles en luy et sans luy tout laid" ("for a person who knows God will find all things beautiful in Him, and without Him all things will seem ugly"—*Hept.* 1.prologue.8; Chilton 67). The traditional pilgrimage motif was earthbound: late medieval Catholics journeyed through a landscape marked with sacred sites, collecting *ymaiges* called *patenostres* as souvenirs of pilgrimage. With the advent of evangelicalism, however, such pilgrimages became less frequent, as the focus shifted to an inner landscape: the journey toward God taking place within the individual soul.[13] Accordingly, Marguerite's *devisants* plan to tell stories, which they will present to others upon their return, substituting Word for thing, tale for pilgrimage token, unwrapping the earthly covers enveloping the characters in the stories the *devisants* recount to demonstrate that ultimate reality resides in one's relationship to God.

Protagonists and commentators in the *Heptaméron* pass by and through things (*corps*) to get to true significance (*âme*) in a process wherein the *nouvelle* forms a semi-secular material membrane facilitating this transmutation. Storytelling, Hircan says, is "quelque passetemps et exercice corporel" ("some amusement and physical exercise"—*Hept.* 1.prologue.8; Chilton 67). Although each narrative event is submitted to the "pluralité d'opinions" ("judged after an open discussion"—*Hept.* 1.prologue.8; Chilton 67), because it inevitably "doibt estre commun à tous" ("those which everybody can join in"—*Hept.* 1.prologue.9; Chilton 68), it has a unifying goal and manifests a saving grace. The *nouvelles,* in Gérard Defaux's formulation, begin to function as does the *Bonne Nouvelle*.[14]

Evangelicals indicted Catholic ritual as not being biblically "established"; it was an excessive and potentially erroneous layer over the essential rudiments of worship stipulated by Scripture. Marguerite's evangelical perspective causes her to revise the Catholic liturgical custom of dividing the day into "hours" or "offices"; in the *Heptaméron*, the daily round of worship is instead demarcated by *stories*. These tales are so compelling that, as already noted earlier in this study, the monks themselves neglect their routine, and forget to say their prayers while their attention is distracted by the tales being told. Oisille and her evangelical company are also virtually oblivious to the church bells, so intent are they on following the plot: a fitting reaction for evangelicals, who disregard ritualistic accretions, but who attend to the Word. Appropriately, too, all the stories are heard "de vive voix," as contrasted with personal journals ("registres"): stories should be shared, not kept secret, for telling stories in community activates the Gospel message.

Nouvelle #14 contains numerous examples of adornment, among them costumes, masks, and disguises. Components of a protagonist's costume convey, through material medium, a literal sense: as already noted, Bonnivet, would-be seducer, wears *escarpins de feutre* to avoid making noise as he ascends the staircase leading to his victim's bedroom. Cotgrave provides a secondary meaning of *feutre* ("felt"): *feutre* means "covered with"; "stuffed"; "thickened," fitting with his motive in Marguerite's tales.[15] The *escarpins de feutre* are part of Bonnivet's sham; they literalize the subjective misconstruction of a situation.

Dissembling and distortion are concerns of *nouvelle* #14. The proliferation of masks, cloaks, and outer coverings (*manteau*, *scoyofon*, *robe de nuict*); curtains behind which a scene is hidden or only partly revealed; inner chambers reached by hidden staircases (… *gallerye* … *escaliers à petit degré* …); and key-holes through which Bonnivet peers into the lady's bedchamber (*coureil*; *verrou de la porte*): these enclosures and coverings both decorate *nouvelle* #14 and convey the theme of subterfuge and seduction. The text's lexicon reiterates the motif, repeating terms such as *tromperie*, *faignit,* and *faisoit en mensonge*. Bonnivet disguises himself as his friend, for whom the lady lusts, so that he may sleep with her under false pretenses. His footgear is a telling choice; through his shoes, Bonnivet costumes himself as a walking simile, the semblance of another: "à fin que à le toucher on ne peust congnoistre leur difference. Il n'oblia pas les escarpins de feustre et le demorant des habillemens semblables au gentil homme" ("he was indistinguishable from … his rival. Nor did he forget the felt slippers, and other details of clothing that were like the Italian's"—*Hept.* 2.14.111–12; Chilton 183).

The object of his desire sits in her bed, framed by bed-curtains. The loose-weave white linen of the woman's attire symbolizes her purity; she is also adorned with pearls ("toute couverte de perles"—*Hept.* 2.14.112). The layering of his body atop hers recalls another body, that of the would-be Italian lover. When Bonnivet reveals his identity, she requires that he remain in disguise ("en masque") so that she may cloak her shame by hiding his (and her) visage: "car elle sçavoit bien qu'elle auroit si grande honte, que sa contenance la declaireroit à tout le monde" ("She did, however, insist that for a while at least … he [be] in disguise, for she knew that otherwise … her disgrace [would be] written all over her face"—*Hept.* 2.14.113; Chilton 185). The ambiguous antecedent attribution of the possessive adjective (*sa*), suggests both his masked face and her own. Each now wears a mask of a sort, for, when her intended suitor turns up, she poses in a totally different posture, hiding all of her body: "il la trouva levée en son manteau de nuict, avecques une bien grosse fiebvre, le poulx fort esmeu, le visaige en feu et la sueur …" ("he found her out of bed wearing her dressing-gown. She had a high fever, her pulse was racing, her face was flushed and she was starting to break out in a sweat"—*Hept.* 2.14.114; Chilton 185). Gone are the diaphanous white linen garment and the white pearls; her face is reddened from sex, sullied with sweat. The two scenes framed by the bed-curtains form a diptych showing the fall from transparency and innocence into opacity and mendacity.

Varieties of figures of speech compile rhetorical layers in the *nouvelles*. Marguerite often uses simile in her stories. Through the positing of rhetorical relationship, simile multiplies semblances. When the simile breaks down, or illustrates something counter to the way in which a character had initially construed it, simile can also denounce a falsehood. In *nouvelle* #14, the woman, having yielded to amorous blandishments, beseeches her lover to be faithful. But he, having sought only a conquest, will not keep her company for long: "la dame … s'arresta au seigneur Bonnivet, dont l'amityé dura, selon la coustume, comme la beaulté des fleurs des champs" ("she gave herself entirely to Bonnivet, whose love, as usual, endured even as flowers of the field in their beauty endure!"—*Hept.* 2.14.114; Chilton 186). The simile underscores the ephemeral nature of earthly desire, and also alludes to a scriptural intertext (Isa. 40.6–8). It may also make ironic reference to a Gospel subtext, that of the "lilies of the field," for which, Christ reminds his hearers, God provides more amply than any of his listeners can provision himself. The lady's attempts to keep her lover faithful are illusory. In addition, duplicity doubles, since the woman has been unfaithful to her first suitor, while Bonnivet, despite his assurances to her while in another's guise that he would be faithful, doubly deceives her.

The woman is reified: framed by her bed-curtains, she is the object of Bonnivet's artful manipulation; she is passive and powerless to alter her situation. As she is thoroughly objectified, in the *devisants'* discussion of her plight, Geburon appropriately discusses her as though she were a commodity: "croyez … que telles marchandises ne se peuvent mectre en vente, qu'elles ne soient emportées par les plus offrans et derniers encherisseurs" ("Take my word for it … you can't put goods like that up for sale without their being carried off by the highest bidder!"—*Hept.* 2.14.114; Chilton 186). An *encherisseur* is "a raiser or out-bidder of the high price of things." Physical objects, people treated as possessions, and a premium mistakenly placed on materiality, thus form the focus of this tale. The woman is merely an object of exchange in an economy of desire. The *nouvelle* makes evident the moral imperative of stripping off costumes, peeling away masks and cosmetics, and of not posing as "other." The text teaches truthfulness in social interactions, as well as an honest assessment of one's self. Since no real love is displayed in the text, but merely sex as a commodity, the text remains in material fleshliness, rather than rising above base motives to attain an evangelical perspective.

Substitutions, untrustworthy similes, seductions and wordplays characterize the stylistic strategies of *nouvelle* #16. Wordplay is a rhetorical layering technique, for the term selected has at least two meanings on which Marguerite plays to suggest multiple interpretations. The material world depicted in *nouvelle* #16's lexicon of commodities is a vanity fair, at which women's assets, arrayed like wares for purchase, are adorned with yet more commodities. The king commands the presence at court of a widow who is reluctant to attend a gala. In public, others appraise her: "[ils] feirent … ung festin … fut contraincte ceste dame vefve de s'y trouver, ce qu'elle n'avoyt accoustumé en autre lieu … ilz feirent grande estime de sa beaulté et de sa bonne grace" ("they were holding a banquet … and this lady, though a widow and not accustomed to appearing in public, was obliged to be present … they all formed a very high opinion of her elegance and beauty"—*Hept.* 2.16.129; Chilton 204). A wordplay summarizes the plot. The widow is kept in a corner ("separée de la jeunesse en ung *coing*"; " in a corner apart from the young people"—*Hept.* 2.16.129; emphasis added; Chilton 204), and her would-be seducer tries to make her acquaintance. The wordplay hints at another, more menacing, meaning: he tries to corner her: "il avoit envie de l'accointer" ("a-*coin*-ter"—emphasis added). *Accointer* can also mean "to pranke or tricke." The way in which the seducer tries to lure the woman is by cornering her with the ploy of substitution: when the suitor sees the pious widow at mass he tries rhetorically to substitute his body for Christ's: "ainsi que le prestre monstroit le *corpus Domini*, se tourna devers elle, et, avecq une voix doulce et plaine d'affection, luy dist: 'Ma dame, je prends Celluy que le prebstre tient à ma damnation, si vous n'estes cause de ma mort [en me refusant]'" ("just as the priest was raising the *corpus Domini* above his head, the gentleman turned to his lady, and said softly in a voice quivering with emotion: 'Madame, in the name of Him whom the priest holds even now in his hands, may I be condemned to everlasting damnation, if I lie when I declare that it is you who are the cause of my death'"—*Hept.* 2.16.130; Chilton 205). The suitor interposes his physical being between her and her metaphysical focus (Christ's body), by figuratively superimposing his reference to himself over the viewing of the Host, constructing in this way a false likeness or simile ("ainsi que"). Although she rebukes him for this blasphemy ("Dieu ne doibt point ainsy estre prins"; "the name of God should not be taken in vain"—*Hept.* 2.16.130; Chilton 205), he persists.

The stage setting of *nouvelle* #22 also relies on a religious cast of characters and scenarios. Illustrating the truth of the proverb *l'habit ne fait pas le moine*, Marguerite deploys material objects such as costumes and veils, and uses literary devices such as metaphor and simile, to demonstrate the negative effect of earthly preoccupations. It is important, for the purposes of the tale, to note that

> le costume ecclésiastique s'est fixé à la fin du XIIe siècle. Le canon 16 du IVe Concile de Latran, en particulier, en 1215, formule les principes qui vont désormais constituer le noyau de la législation canonique jusqu'à la fin du XVIe siècle: les clercs doivent porter des vêtements fermés, ni trop courts, ni trop longs, et, par esprit de pauvreté, ne pas faire usage d'étoffes rouges ou vertes, de gants, de souliers brodés, ni d'ornements superflus. Tous les règlements insistent sur la prohibition du luxe comme du laisser-aller.
>
> ("ecclesiastical custom established itself around the end of the 12th century. Canon 16 of the 4th Lateran Council, specifically, in 1215 formulated the principles which would henceforth constitute the nucleus of canonical legislation until the end of the 16th century: clerics must wear closed-up clothing, neither too short, nor too long and, in the spirit of [apostolic] poverty, must not wear red or green fabric, gloves, embroidered shoes or superfluous ornaments. All the rules stressed the prohibition of luxury as well as loose-living").[16]

In *nouvelle* #22, a prior has such an inflated opinion of himself that he rationalizes participating in the pleasures of the flesh, despite the renunciation of them that his habit represents. The 4th Lateran Council had stipulated that "l'ornement du prêtre réside dans ses mœurs et que, pour l'extérieur, il doit se vêtir d'habits qui ne soient ni luxueux, ni sordides" ("the adornment of the priest derives from his good behavior; as for externals, he should clothe himself in habits that have nothing luxurious or sordid").[17] In addition, in the Lateran Council's concern for "ornament" and "superfluity," the Catholic church implicitly recognized a link between materiality ("ornement") and potentially corrupt morals ("mœurs"), a connection that evangelicals deplored.

Rather than observing a proper private piety, this prior publicly debases his priestly *persona*. He reckons himself a worldly treasure: "il s'estim[a] luy-mesme le bien public de toute religion" ("he began … to regard himself as representing the general good of the monastic community at large"—*Hept.* 3.22.176; Chilton 255). In a blasphemous rejection of divine authority, the prior elevates his own subjectivity as his moral standard, circling into solipsism reflected by the reflexive structure "*s*'estim[a] luy-mesme." His change in lifestyle, Marguerite alerts us, contaminates his entire being, just as those who focus too much on the world lose sight of a greater goal: "et, à ceste mutation de vivre, se feyt une mutation de cueur" ("now this transformation in his style of life was accompanied by a transformation in matters of the heart"—*Hept.* 3.22.176; Chilton 255).

This *mutation* demonstrates both *dédoublement* and degradation: it constructs several avatars of the same person—who progressively worsens—within the same story. The *pasteur* becomes *loup* ("wolf"—*Hept.* 3.22.176; Chilton 255) and *ranard* [*sic*] ("fox"—*Hept.* 3.22.180), epitomizing the lapse from grace into sin. The fall into flesh is dramatized as, first, arrogance and self-exaltation, subjectivity heedless of spiritual standards; next, as a descent into bestiality (*loup*, *renard*); and, finally, a reification, as subject declines into object or mere simulacrum: "l'on le craignoit *comme* ung Dieu painct en jugement" ("He *might have been* God Almighty in some picture of the Last Judgement!"—*Hept.* 3.22.177; emphasis added; Chilton 256). Marguerite underscores this distancing from the truth through another simile. The pastor is certainly not "comme Dieu." Clearly a falsehood, such similes act like literary versions of the commercial practice of "bait-and-switch." The fine arts dimension of a fallacious portrait ("painct en jugement"—the prior posing as God painted in judgment) further indicts the prior's deviance. He is a counterfeit of exterior piety: a *dead thing*. As in *nouvelle* #14, or as in Rabelais's critique of the Papimanes and the Pope as "Dieu in terris," the priest errs because he poses as another and tries to pass himself off for a sacred reality utterly alien to his lifestyle.

The prior intimidates the nuns under his care. Marguerite calls the sisters "pauvres brebis esgarées" ("poor lost sheep"—*Hept.* 3.22.177; Chilton 256) to emphasize his lupine nature. The prior demands to examine the nuns to ascertain their chastity. Himself venal, he anticipates corruption elsewhere. When a young nun spurns him, he scratches her inner thighs in fury. She rebukes him with an evangelical pronouncement, reversing the improper relationship that he has construed between material world and metaphysical allegiance:

> mais elle lui respondit qu'elle aymoit mieulx mourir en chartre perpetuelle, que d'avoir jamais autre amy que Celluy qui estoit mort pour elle en la croix, avecq lequel elle aymoit mieulx souffrir tous les maulx que le monde pourroit donner, que contre luy avoir tous les biens.
>
> ("but she replied that she would rather languish in perpetual imprisonment than admit any other lover than Him who had died for her on the cross. With Him she would rather endure all the suffering in the world than enjoy all the pleasures in the world against His will."—*Hept.* 3.22.179; Chilton 258)

Her repetition of the term *biens* refers back to the beginning of the tale when the prior "s'estima le *bien* public," equating himself with material objects of suspect or transitory value.

Marguerite continues to employ similes to show the prior's depravity and to express theological indictment of his behavior. Formerly she had described him "comme ung Dieu painct"; now she depicts him, in his display of desire toward the nun, deeming himself "comme celluy qui estoit le souverain reformateur" ("in his self-appointed role of reformer-in-chief"—*Hept.* 3.22.180; Chilton 259). The prior denounces the convent as corrupt. He says that it is in need of reforming, yet he acts contrarily and out of self-interest, claiming the prerogative to hear confessions and to examine for bodily purity. The formulaic way in which he constructs a false parallelism ("ainsy … aussy") suggests an unhealthy similarity between body and soul. This conflation only makes his corruption more manifest: "ainsy que je suis visiteur des ames, aussy suis-je visiteur des corps" ("in my capacity as visitor I not only examine the soul, but also the body"—*Hept.* 3.22.182; Chilton 261). The reversed order of subject and verb (*aussy suis-je*) stylistically mimes the inversion of his focus on spiritual things to an emphasis on earthly matters.

Another aspect of this *nouvelle*, as of many others, is the additional interpretation provided of it. The *devisants'* job is to assess the prior's deception, to hear out the witnesses, and to render an opinion. Significantly, the legal and theological term *tesmoing* recurs in this story, as when the prior demands "preuve" and "tesmoing de sa virginité" ("proof" and "testimony of her virginity"—*Hept.* 3.22.182; Chilton 260). Purporting to judge ("en jugement")—and also to sleep with—the nuns, the prior arrogates to himself the capacity of discernment. The text corrects his wrongheadedness by portraying the *devisants* as an *ad hoc* jury. When the nun calls on God for help, not only God hears her defense; but the *devisants* do, too:

> Dieu est tout puissant pour nous saulver … congnoissant que l'ange Sathan se transforme en ange de lumiere, afin que l'œil exterieur, aveuglé par l'apparence de sainctеté et devotions … ne s'arreste ad ce qu'il doibt fuir … Dieu est juste juge.
>
> ("in Him alone who is almighty to save us unto eternal life … knowing that often Satan transforms himself into an Angel of Light—in order, I say, that your eye should not alight on external things, blinded by the outward appearance of sanctity and devotion and linger on those things that it ought to shun … I know that God is a righteous judge."—*Hept.* 3.22.182–86; Chilton 263)

They repeat her insistence on God's justice contrasted with the prior's travesty of it.[18]

Marguerite's *nouvelles* often possess an additional level of reception: they can be read as the transcription of a legal defense. Through activities associated with costuming and attire, the text dramatizes the imperative of discerning motives so that blame for criminal behavior may be assigned. The reaching under the nun's habit; the raising and lowering of veils and of clothing; the up-and-down flutter of garments, contrast the monk's horizontal *modus operandi* with what should be his vertical orientation:

> Vous ne devez craindre que je visite vostre virginité; parquoy, gectez-vous sur le lict, et mectez le devant de vostre habillement sur vostre visaige.
>
> ("You should have no fear, if my visitation extends to an inspection of your virginity. Kindly lie down on the bed and raise the front part of your habit over your face."—*Hept.* 3.22.182; Chilton 261)

The fabric covering the nun's face mimics the prior's technique of enveloping his statements with deception, distortion, and rationalization; it also adds another textual layer to the story.

The *nouvelle* takes a stand, eventually revealing the truth of the nun's tale, documenting it with a proliferation of texts that vindicate her position. The nun's family becomes concerned when she no longer sends letters home. The *lectres* are called *nouvelles*: "… n'avoit plus de nouvelles d'elle" ("she stopped receiving news from her daughter"—*Hept.* 3.22.183; Chilton 262). Eventually, the letters become even more directly "telling," for the nun manages to pass them clandestinely to her family "par la grille à son frère tout le discours de sa piteuse histoire" ("she wrote the whole unhappy story down on paper and handed it to her brother through the grille"—*Hept.* 3.22.184; Chilton 264). The *grille* sequesters the convent from the outside world. Yet this layer facilitates the passage of a testimonial text into receptive hands. While closed to worldly influence, the convent appropriately proffers a metaphysical corrective to the prior's wrongdoing. The *grille* is the religious equivalent of *fenestre* that Marguerite often uses to herald a change in a tale's focus or an impending transformation in a character or a situation.. The letters provide documentation damning the prior: "elle… avoit mis par escript tout ce qui est icy dessus" ("she had put in writing all that has been recounted here"—*Hept.* 3.22.183; Chilton 263); collectively, they constitute a well-argued legal brief.

The *nouvelle*'s narration duplicates the compilation of documents: "tout ce qui est *icy dessus.*" The young nun's truthful text now overlays ("dessus") the prior's perverse version. This duplication ensures authenticity; it has become the definitive text, obviating any need for further scrutiny beneath textual strata. As well as providing forensic testimony, the letters compose an accretion of "proof-texts" in a form of evangelical witnessing. In applying Scripture to daily life, evangelicals assembled "proof-texts," or *loci,* verses from various portions of the Bible applied as prescriptions to the situation at hand.

While the prior, through misleading similes, had felt himself to be, and sought to persuade others that he was, "le seul reformateur," textual rectification begins when the nun herself becomes a true reformer. In evangelical fashion, and in contrast to the prior's abusive metamorphosis, "elle reforma [l'Abbaye] et vesquit comme celle qui estoit plaine de l'esperit de Dieu" ("she reformed the Abbey, and there she continued to live, full of the spirit of God"—*Hept.* 3.22.185; Chilton 265). The text's rhetorical strategy now uses simile to fulfill its role of accurately comparing one thing to another, since, unlike the prior, the nun is indeed living a holy life. The story concludes with an evangelical moral: "Voylà, mes dames, une histoire qui est bien pour monstrer ce que dict l'Evangile: Que Dieu par les choses foybles confond les fortes" ("There, ladies, is a story which demonstrates what we read in the Gospel [and in St. Paul's Epistle to the Corinthians]—that God chooses the weak things of the world to confound the things which are mighty"—*Hept.* 3.22.185; Chilton 265). This time, ornament aligns with surface in the strategy of layering, with the difference that the *nouvelle* now properly "illustrates," in evangelical fashion, scriptural text. Unlike the prior's distorted reading, Marguerite's reiteration of biblical text in her storytelling faithfully renders Scripture, reinforcing its message. Finally, Oisille offers a scriptural lesson as a transition into *nouvelle* #23;[19] she warns against deviant behavior and misplaced (*divertye*) faith:

> que l'ypocrisye de ceulx qui s'estiment plus religieux que les autres, ne vous enchante l'entendement, de sorte que vostre foy, divertye de son droict chemin, estime trouver salut en quelque autre creature que en Celluy seul qui n'a voulu avoir compaignon à nostre creation et redemption.
>
> ("[let not your minds be] be so beguiled by the hypocrisy of men who consider themselves more religious than others that your faith, diverted from the straight and narrow path, seeks salvation in some other creature rather than in Him alone who is almighty to save us unto eternal life …"—*Hept.* 3.22.186; Chilton 266)

Underscoring the evangelical message through Oisille's lesson, Marguerite again uses the technique of doubling, reminding us that the prior had posed as "ung seul redempteur," while in fact only Christ is our redeemer ("Celluy seul qui n'a voulu avoir compaignon à nostre … redemption"). In trying to substitute himself for Christ, the prior has destroyed himself. Motifs of metamorphosis ("se transforma") and rhetorical doubling convey Marguerite's criticism of worldliness and reliance on materiality.

Figurative speech, wordplay, and chiasmus, coupled with the motif of disguise, feature in the stylistic repertoire of *nouvelle* #26. A woman, her older husband, and a younger lover constitute the *dramatis personae* of this story, which depicts self-absorption as objectification. A chiastic structure locks into inanition and treats as objects the vain young man, the woman whom he ostensibly woos while really admiring only himself, and the husband whose will and rights both ignore. Ultimately, the couple's affair aborts, because their dissimilar motivations block any real development, just as the dance of their courtship describes a holding-pattern:

> Ce que feit le jeune prince, duquel la jeunesse estoit si grande, qu'il prenoit plus de plaisir à saulter et *dancer,* que à regarder la *beaulté* des dames. Et celle qu'il menoit, au contraire, regardoit plus la grace et *beaulté* du dict seigneur d'Avannes, que la *dance* où elle estoit.
>
> ("The Prince accepted readily, but young as he was, he took more pleasure in skipping and dancing than in eying the charms of the ladies. His partner, on the other hand, was rather more interested in d'Avannes's looks than in the dance."—*Hept.* 3.26.209; Chilton 292)

The positions of "dancer, beauté … beauté, dance" lock the actions in a static chiasmus, canceling change in character development in the story. D'Avannes focuses on himself, and she mirrors him, so that no real interaction between them occurs, especially as the young man is portrayed more as a gorgeous object than as a person: "[il] estoit fort gorgias et bien en ordre" ("he cut an elegant figure"—*Hept.* 3.26.210; Chilton 294). Nonetheless, they do begin a clandestine affair (described as an "amitié couverte"—*Hept.* 3.26.210; Chilton 294). The phrase ("couverte") suggests disguises and layers of secrecy.

They live in a frenzy of repetitive accumulation and superficial socializing ("mille passetemps") that precludes personal communication, emphasizing instead display and appearance: "Et commencea, pour l'amour d'elle, à lever mille passetemps, comme tournoys, courses, luyttes, masques, festins et autres jeuz" ("in order to please her, he took to putting on all manner of entertainments—tournaments, races, wrestling-matches, masked balls, banquets and other diversions"—*Hept.* 3.26.210; Chilton 294). He treats women as trophies, objects in an economy of exchange that discourages true relationship: "quant il ne le trouvoit poinct, sa femme bailloit tout ce qu'il demandoit" ("if the rich man was not at home, his wife would supply everything he asked for, and not only that ..."—*Hept.* 3.26.209; Chilton 293). The *équivoque* in "everything he asked for and not only that" supplies a textual layer of false discretion that mimics their social subterfuge. He poses in various costumes in order to be near her, first counterfeiting a *pallefrenier* (*Hept.* 3.26.211), and they deceive her husband by means of masks:

> se voyant seul avecq la dame, se despouilla des habillemens de pallefrenier, osta ses faulx nez et sa faulse barbe, et, non comme crainctif pallefrenier, mais comme bel seigneur qu'il estoit ... audatieusement se coucha auprès d'elle ... [puis] reprenant son masque, laissa la place que par finesse et malice il usurpoit.
>
> ("now that he had his lady alone, d'Avannes stripped off his stable-boy's gear, removed his false nose and his false beard, and, without so much as a by your leave, hopped boldly into bed with her ... then ... he put on his disguise again and vacated the place which with such low cunning he had usurped."—*Hept.* 3.26.212; Chilton 296)

The text calls her a place or a space ("la place") that he has occupied sexually. In this way, the lady's identity is objectified. As in other *nouvelles*, similes that do *not* construct conventional comparisons, but rather act to distort, layer additional deceptions over the text. Invariably in the *Heptaméron* many layers of clothing attire someone who dissembles; here, the repetition of words having to do with a lack of sincerity—such as *faulx*, *faulsse,* and *usurpoit*—points to a similar deception.

Costumes reinforce the mendacity. Having agreed to deceive her husband, the lady appears in different attire and brazen near-nakedness. Yet she continues to wear, in society, the garment and demeanor of a virtuous woman: " elle ... se contentoit bien souvent de ne porter sur sa chemise que une chamarre ... Ainsy vesquist ceste jeune dame, soubz l'ypocrisie et habit de femme de bien, en telle volupté" ("she was now content to wear a simple tunic over her shift … Thus in the hypocritical guise of a virtuous wife, the lady lived such a life of sensual pleasure"—*Hept.* 3.26.212–13; Chilton 297). Eventually, lust so distorts her lover's features that, changed, he needs no mask to hide his identity: "… sans porter masque, on le povoit bien descongnoistre" ("even without his disguise you would not have recognized him"—*Hept.* 3.26.213; Chilton 297).

The young man is put to the test when, his lodging having burned down when he set fire to the town, the lady's husband takes pity on him and lends him clothing to wear—including the husband's own nightclothes.

> trouva le jeune seigneur tout en chemise en la rue, et, le couvrant de sa robbe, le mena en sa maison.
>
> ("he found the young man standing in the street in his nightshirt … he took him in his arms, wrapped him in his robe and led him back to his house."—*Hept.* 3.26.216; Chilton 300)

The husband offers his wife symbolically—through the layers of his intimate attire—to the young man, enjoining her: "traitez-le *comme moy-mesmes*" ("treat him *just as you would treat me!*"—*Hept.* 3.26.216; emphasis added; Chilton 300). The young man hopes to profit from this symbiotic doubling and the implicit permission it suggests:

> ledict seigneur Avannes, qui eust bien voulu estre traicté en mary, saulta legierement dedans le lict, esperant que l'occasion et le lieu aussy feroient changer propos à ceste saige dame; mais il trouva le contraire.
>
> ("D'Avannes, who would have liked nothing better than to be treated like the husband, leapt nimbly into the bed, hoping that an opportunity like this would make the wise lady change her tune. But not so!"—*Hept.* 3.26.216; Chilton 300)

Eventually, lectured by the wife, forced to acknowledge his difference from the husband and the moral wrong inherent in posing as another, the young man has a change of heart. He acknowledges the destructiveness of his literalizing of the flames of lust by setting fire to the town: "car de moindre feu que le mien ont esté ruynez plus grandz et plus fortz edifices" ("lesser fires than mine have ruined greater, stronger buildings"—*Hept.* 3.26.218; Chilton 302).

In one of the more dramatic textual conversions in the *Heptaméron*, the young man begins to live a reformed life, free of "luxure" ("lasciviousness"; this term also refers to his renunciation of the luxurious entertainment in which he had formerly indulged with his mistress). Instead of dressing in disguise, he now "se vest[e]" ("clothes himself") with virtue.[20]

> entendez que Dieu, incongneu de l'homme, sinon par la foy, a daigné prendre la chair semblable à celle de peché, afin qu'en attirant nostre chair à l'amour de son humanité, tirast aussi nostre esprit à l'amour de sa divinité; et s'est voulu servyr des *moyens visibles*, pour nous faire aymer par foy les choses *invisibles*.
>
> ("know that God, whom no man may know but by faith alone, did deign to take on flesh, even the same flesh as the sinful flesh of man, so that in drawing our flesh to the love of His humanity, he would draw our spirit to the love of His divinity. And by means of things visible did it please Him to make us love through faith the things that are invisible."—*Hept.* 3.26.214; Chilton 298–99)

Christ had garbed Himself in sinful nature to save humanity; the reformed lover strips off his sin like a disguise. His costumes (*moyens visibles*) removed, his true essence—identity in God rather than thralldom to lust—can be seen. He can dismantle the text of his deception, calling the *robbe* a cloak of deception. The *devisants* observe that the costumes that nearly all men and women wear in society are equally deceiving:

> l'orgueil cherche plus la volupté entre les dames, que ne faict la craincte, ne l'amour de Dieu. Aussi, que leurs robbes sont si longues et si bien tissues de dissimulation, que l'on ne peult congnoistre ce qui est dessoubz.
>
> ("pride … ousts desire much more than fear, or love of God, and … those long skirts they wear are nothing more than a fabric woven from lies and deception, preventing us from knowing what is hidden beneath!"—*Hept.* 3.26.220; Chilton 305)

Costumes, "tissues de dissimulation," epitomize deceit, just as Adam and Eve had "couv[ert] [leur] nudité de feulles" ("covered their nakedness with fig-leaves"—*Hept.* 3.26.221; Chilton 305).

Through heeding the evangelical message, the youth finally finds a mature subjectivity in his relationship to Christ. Although he was formerly characterized by youth and physical beauty, now his new spiritual identity is paramount. He can now discern the instability of things of the world, but can also recognize that, when construed aright, such objects may point the way to a deeper, metaphysical understanding.

> Aussy, ceste vertu que je desire aymer toute ma vie, est chose invisible, sinon par les effectz du dehors; parquoy, est besoing qu'elle prenne quelque corps pour se faire congnoistre entre les hommes, ce qu'elle a faict, *se revestant* du vostre pour le plus parfaict qu'elle a pu trouver; parquoy, je vous recongnois et confesse non seullement vertueuse, mais la seulle vertu.
>
> ("Thus is that virtue, which my whole life through I desire to love, a thing that is invisible unless it show external effects. It must therefore take on a bodily form, so that it may make itself known unto men. Indeed, it has done so, for it has clothed itself in your body, Madame, the most perfect it could find. Therefore, I acknowledge and confess that you are not merely virtuous, but Virtue itself."—*Hept.* 3.26.214; Chilton 298–99)

The phrase "se revestant du vostre" adds another, redemptive layer to the other strata of subterfuge and costume. This layer epitomizes his yearning after moral probity that the woman exemplifies.

Nouvelle #35 delves into disguises and the misinterpretation of the signs that they compose. Writing participates in deception, contributing "lectre contrefaicte" ("to write a letter to reply in another's name"—*Hept.* 4.35.256; Chilton 347) just as a person who seeks to pose as other than he is by simulating height stuffs cork into the heels of his shoes ("du liege en ses souliers"; "a piece of cork in his shoes to make himself taller"—*Hept.* 4.35.257; Chilton 348). The *nouvelle* indicts the world's problematic propensity to insist on signs[21] and to value things; the story oscillates between the apparent prizing of material reality and appearance ("tenu de tout le peuple pour ung sainct homme"; "regarded by everyone as a holy man"—*Hept.* 4.35.255; Chilton 346), and the realization that "opinions du monde" are erroneous.

In this story, a woman becomes enamored of a handsome monk preaching at mass. She surrenders her selfhood, her integrity, and her spiritual sensibilities to what she misconstrues as a sexual advance: the priest's "parolles penetr[èrent] les oreilles de ladicte dame … et bless[èrent] si fort l'esprit de la dame, qu'elle fut comme une personne ravye" ("the preacher's words penetrated her ears and reached her heart … and wounded her spirit so sorely that she was as someone in a state of ecstasy"—*Hept.* 4.35.255; Chilton 346). *Ravye* can refer to eschatological rapture, the Second Coming of Christ; it may also connote an orgasm or carnal experience. While in *nouvelle* #24, imposture and disguise facilitated illicit passion, here self-deception is involved: the woman deliberately chooses to fantasize about fleshly desires rather than hear the Gospel message. The woman deludes herself by isolating components of the mass and decontextualizing them in a carnal, rather than spiritual, sense. Rather than valuing and trusting material objects, as do many of the characters in the *nouvelles*, she focuses on objects that represent metaphysical abstractions, but then deliberately re-materializes them, layering her own significance over their symbolic function. In this way, the *nouvelle* expresses an evangelical polemic against the way that accoutrements of ritual may be misconstrued.

The setting of the story during Lent underscores the fleshliness of the woman's focus: attendance at mass as a pretext for seduction is inappropriate: "ce feu, soubz tiltre de spirituel, fut si charnel" ("the fire of her passion beneath its spiritual guise was carnal"—*Hept.* 4.35.255–56; Chilton 346). The Pauline, and Lutheran, dichotomy between spirit and body, soul and flesh, exhibits itself as the woman insists on things of the flesh rather than aspiring to a symbolic understanding of things of the spirit: "là assista et print les *cendres* de sa *main* [du prêtre], qui estoit aussi belle et blanche que dame la sçauroit avoir. Ce que [la main] regarda plus la devote, que la *cendre* qu'il luy bailloit" ("she was to take ashes from his hands, hands which were as fine and white as any lady's. And upon these hands the devout lady meditated rather than upon the ash they proffered"—

Hept. 4.35.255; emphasis added; Chilton 346). The chiasmus—"cendres-main"; "main-cendres"—short-circuits movement beyond flesh to a spiritual dimension, and confining the meaning in materiality ("cendres"—ashes, symbol of mortality) and flesh ("la main"—emblem of sin.)

The besotted woman writes to the priest, describing the passion that she feels for him. Instead of experiencing evangelical *joye*, she demonstrates a sexual joy. Her husband, who finds the letters, sees a change in her, but this is not the type of transformation produced by a religious conversion. Rather than eschew fleshly things, she gains weight, becoming plump with passion: "car, en lieu d'enmagrir, pour le jeusne du karesme, elle estoit plus belle et plus fresche que à caresme prenant" ("for, instead of looking thin from the Lenten fast, she was even more beautiful and fresh than [she had been] at Shrovetide"—*Hept.* 4.35.257; Chilton 348). Prospering from passion, the lady deludes herself that the priest is sending her a private message of mutual love via his public preaching. Marguerite illustrates the evangelical message that signs can be misread; things can deceive; we cannot, and must not, place too much credence in things or in our own interpretation ("luy sembloit") of them:

> Desjà estoit la my karesme, que la dame ne laissa, ne pour Passion ne pour Sepmaine saincte, sa maniere accoustumée de mander par lectres au prescheur sa furieuse fantaisye. Et luy sembloit, quand le prescheur tournoit les œilz du costé où elle estoit, ou qu'il parloit de l'amour de Dieu, que tout estoit pour l'amour d'elle.
>
> ("Mid-Lent arrived and the lady was still writing to the preacher about her wild passion. Even at Passiontide, and during Holy Week, she persisted. It seemed to her that every time the man looked in her direction, or talked about the Love of God, he did it for love of her."—*Hept.* 4.35.257; Chilton 348)

The mention of "Christ's passion" in juxtaposition with the narration of the lady's concupiscence highlights the contrast between earthbound lust and redemptive love.

Learning how the lady has layered her own misconstruction of the situation over reality, the husband decides to do a little corrective costuming. In the name of the priest, he borrows the priest's vestments and arranges an assignation with his own wife. The priest protests that a clerical habit should not be used for dress-up ("pour ... masques"; "for fancy dress"—*Hept.* 4.35.257; Chilton 348), but the husband convinces him of the need to do so: "c'estoit pour chose necessaire pour son bien et salut" ("it was for a matter essential to his good and his salvation"—*Hept.* 4.35.258; Chilton 348).

The term *salut* conveys the evangelical criticism of a priest's intermediary role, and the husband does require the expedient of disguise to secure his salvation from the unfortunate situation—despite the priest's intercession, which is thereby shown to be inefficacious. The husband puts cork in his shoes to reach the priest's height and dons a false nose and beard. When in the presence of his wife, he continues the deception by appropriating a religious symbol (demonstrating how such symbols can be misleading), making numerous "grands signes de croix" ("made the sign of the cross"—*Hept.* 4.35.258; Chilton 348). Finally, he beats her with a big stick hidden "soubz son manteau" ("under his habit"—*Hept.* 4.35.258; Chilton 349): a painful substitute for the priestly phallus she had hoped to touch. Still unaware of the imposture, the chastened lady takes to her bed. When the husband returns, he invites the priest to dine with them and to "mec[tre] la main sur elle" ("place your hands on her"—*Hept.* 4.35.258; Chilton 350) to cure her of her feigned illness. When the priest tries to touch her, she bites him, thinking that he was the one who had beaten her; he then douses her with holy water. The husband never reveals his subterfuge, knowing his wife to be cured of her "folle fantaisie" ("her folly"—*Hept.* 4.35.259; Chilton 351). The wife had apparently been cured by earthly expedient: the husband in priest's habit took his revenge and the priest doused her with holy water in a belated exorcism. Yet the real change is interior—a change of heart motivated by fear and suffering that causes the woman to desist from her lustful imaginings. Earthly means have cooperated in effecting a restorative reorientation.

The problem lies in how to subdue the human heart, claim the *devisants*: "Vous ne povez vaincre vostre cueur." Humanity is inclined to sin and to self-delusion:

> Je n'espargneray homme ne femme, afin de faire tout esgal, et voy bien que vous ne povez vaincre vostre cueur à confesser la vertu et bonté des hommes.
>
> ("I shall spare neither men or women, in order to make everything equal.... seeing that you can't bring yourselves to admit that men can be good and virtuous."—*Hept.* 4.35.261; Chilton 352)

The solution that Ennasuite offers is the discipline of self-doubt tempered by certainty in the Lord:

> quant vous avez bien regardé en ce mirouer, en lieu de vous fier à voz propres forces, vous aprendrez à vous retourner à Celluy en la main duquel gist vostre honneur.
>
> ("it is, as it were, a mirror, and once you've looked into it, I think you will learn to turn to Him in whose hands your honour lies, instead of relying on your own powers."—*Hept.* 4.35.260; Chilton 351)

The *devisants* conceive of the *nouvelles* as a material object, a sort of mirror ("ce mirouer") that reflects the protagonists' nature back to themselves, compelling them, in turn, to "reflect" on their own character and motivations. The *devisants*' exegesis constitutes the frame of this mirror. Rather than reflecting back solely the viewer's image, the speculum of the *nouvelles* also reflects a spiritual image, that of God, the only valid metaphysical mirror. In this way, the material object, evoked figuratively by the text, becomes a spiritual tool. The repetition of the term *hand* ("main") also recalls the woman's obsession with the priest's hand (and failure to concentrate on the divine mysteries it was engaged in performing). However, this emphasis on the hand eventually situates everything and everyone in the story in the appropriate space: in God's hand ("Celluy en la main duquel gist [v]ostre honneur"; "Him in whose hands your honour lies"—*Hept.* 4.35.260; Chilton 351).

Nouvelles #43 and #49 both employ layering strategies to examine the nature and veracity of writing. In *nouvelle* #43, costumes and chalk marks reveal amorous deception, while in *nouvelle* #49 clothing constructs a false appearance that provokes lust, showing the corruption of earthly sentiment. *Nouvelle* #43 dramatizes the dissimilarity between being and appearance. Jambicque, a noblewoman, has a reputation for chastity: "elle avoit le bruict d'estre ennemye mortelle de tout amour, combien qu'elle estoit contraire en son cueur" ("she had acquired the reputation of being the mortal enemy of love—although in the depths of her heart she was the very opposite"—*Hept.* 5.43.296; Chilton 392). She tattles on her friends when they have affairs. In her repressed desire and resentment of others' pleasure, she resembles hypocritical Pharisees whom Jesus excoriates as "whited sepulchres"; appropriately, her hypocrisy will be exposed by being marked in white with chalk. She masks herself to meet the object of her affection: thinking to hide her spiritual and physical corruption in material wrappings, she steals a disguise from her mistress's *garderobbe,* placing "sa cornette basse et son touret de nez" ("her cap pulled down over her face"—*Hept.* 5.43.297; Chilton 393). To safeguard her reputation, she agrees to sleep with the man on the condition that he not to ask her identity. He is curious, however, as he touches her clothing and finds that it is velvet, a fabric reserved for ladies of quality, so, the next time that he kisses her, he surreptitiously scrawls a chalk mark on the stuff clothing her shoulder—using a material marker on material substance—in the hopes of learning who she is: "porta avecq luy de la craye, dont, en l'embrassant, luy en feit une marque sur l'espaule, par derriere, sans qu'elle s'en apperceut" ("what he did was to take with him a piece of chalk the next time she sent for him, and while he was in her arms he made a mark on the back of her shoulders without her noticing"—*Hept.* 5.43.299; Chilton 394). Paradoxically, the costume in which she cloaked herself now becomes the medium that will expose her.[22] Learning that the woman is Jambicque, the man resolves to reveal that her chastity is a sham. The *nouvelle* cooperates in this revelation: "aujourd'huy est leu aux œilz d'un chascun ce qu'elle vouloit cacher à ceulx de son amy" ("the story I've told today has revealed to everyone what she tried to keep from the eyes of her lover"—*Hept.* 5.43.300–01; Chilton 396). Truth is *read*, and the *Heptaméron* fights image with word. The *nouvelle* functions as God's omniscient eyes that discern truth by penetrating beneath disguise and layers of obfuscation: "Celluy qui ne donne poinct sa gloire à aultruy, en descouvrant ce manteau, luy en a donné double infamye" ("Honour belongs to

God alone, and He, by tearing aside the veil, has placed her in double disgrace"—*Hept.* 5.43.301; Chilton 396). Although Jambicque makes the sign of the cross to fend off the identification resulting from the sign on her shoulder (she is doubly signed, for the gesture replicates the lover's chalk cross), she is unsuccessful. She had trusted to her costume for concealment, and instead it has betrayed her.

Nouvelle #49 also evokes the power of writing to penetrate through sham. Sin depersonalizes by limiting subjectivity to objectivity: in the *nouvelle*, people stare at a countess for the "nouveauté" of her dress, and the king desires her because of how it frames her as an object of desire. The king sends her husband away so as to meet her alone in her room. Several of his gentlemen, eager to share the good reception she gives him, separately decide to visit her as well. So content is Astillon, her first suitor, with the treatment that he receives from her, that he is willing to hide in a "garderobbe" ("her dressing room"—*Hept.* 5.49.319; Chilton 397) for several nights. While he is still there, another of the company, Durassier, comes to proposition the woman, and on the day that she sends Astillon on his way, she replaces him with Durassier. The cycle of repetition, repeated in precisely the same language with identical results, constructs a rhetoric of layering: ("… lequel avoit nom Durassier. Elle tint telz termes à ce serviteur, qu'elle avoit faict au premier"; "… a man by the name of Durassier … She started off [with him] in exactly the same way as [with the former suitor]"—*Hept.* 5.49.319; Chilton 417–18). She also objectifies those for whom she feels lust ("elle mectoit ung serviteur en sa place"; "she duly installed a second one to serve in his place"—*Hept.* 5.49.319; Chilton 418), layering one male body indiscriminately over another, serially substituting sexual partners as though they were interchangeable. The game continues, with a new man replacing the former, every few days (unbeknownst to them all), until "[tous] avoient part à la doulse prison" ("[all] did their spell in this far from unpleasant captivity"—*Hept.* 5.49.319; Chilton 418). Each thinking himself favored and assuming the others denied, each mocks his friends in his heart until one day, at a banquet,[23] they begin to talk about *prisons* in which they have spent time. Realizing that they all, rather unusually, associated pleasure with what should have been painful, they each "se doubta de la prison qu'il vouloit dire" ("strongly suspect[ing] that they were referring to the 'prison' that he too had been in"—*Hept.* 5.49.319; Chilton 418). Durassier asks Astillon what meat/flesh he had eaten in prison, and Astillon quips that the king himself "n'en a poinct de meilleures ne plus norrissantes" ("doesn't have anything better, nor anything more nourishing!"—*Hept.* 5.49.320; Chilton 419).

Realizing that their amorous prison terms have all been served in relay in the same place, they decide to challenge the woman collectively when she goes to mass the next day. Donning black costumes, placing a large iron chain link about each of their necks, they exclaim before her that they are all her prisoners. Having all been closeted at various times in the *garderobbe* with Jambicque's dresses, they now all dress alike to accuse her. Valnebon alludes to the amorous pastimes that they have all enjoyed with her: "si nous avons mangé de vostre pain si longuement, nous serions bien ingratz si nous ne vous faisions service" ("we have eaten your bread for so long, madame, that it would be most ungrateful of us not to do you service"—*Hept.* 5.49.321; Chilton 421). She pretends not to understand, but realizes that "la chose estoit descouverte" ("the whole affair had been uncovered"—*Hept.* 5.49.321; Chilton 421). In fact, by unraveling her strategy, they have caught her in her deception and effectively exposed her greedy vagina ("la chose"). Oisille states that the lady's is a "horrible cas," using slang for female genitalia. While linked to men by the chains of lust, she is, however, "delaissée de Dieu" ("abandoned by God"—*Hept.* 5.49.322; Chilton 421). Oisille concludes with an evangelical message:

> la personne delaissée de Dieu se rend pareille à celluy avecq lequel elle est joincte; car, puis que ceulx qui adherent à Dieu ont son esperit avec eulx, aussi sont ceulx qui adherent à son contraire; et rien n'est si bestial que la personne destituée de l'esperit de Dieu.
>
> ("the person who is abandoned by God comes to resemble him with whom she is joined. For even as they who cling to God have with them the spirit of God, so they who cling to

> God's adversary are imbued with the spirit of evil. Nothing more resembles a brute than a person deprived of the spirit of God."—*Hept.* 5.49.322; Chilton 421)

The lady's custom of collecting lovers, repeating the same technique as, *seriatim*, a new lover supercedes a former, results in a progressive distancing of herself from God through the build-up of strata of sinfulness isolating her heart from Him.

Nouvelle #56 also deals with layers. In *nouvelle* #56, a sword, a doublet, a gown, a headdress, a crown, and a glove are stage properties in a drama about sin. The *nouvelle*'s lists of properties mimetically evokes the materiality of these objects. Luxurious garments and accessories add to the allure of a young woman whose mother deploys her daughter's charms as a lure to capture a wealthy husband. The emphasis is not on making a love match, but rather on making money: "pour luy amasser du bien" ("she was prepared to do anything to provide her with a fortune"—*Hept.* 6.56.348; Chilton 451). Conflating earthly matters with things of the spirit, the mother requests that their confessor find such a suitor. Using religion for her own purposes, she cites an aphorism: "il valloit mieulx faire mal par le conseil des docteurs, que faire bien, croyant l'inspiration du Sainct Esperit" ("it was better to do something wrong on the advice of the doctors of the Church, than to do a good act in the belief that it was inspired by the Holy Spirit"—*Hept.* 6.56.348; Chilton 451).

The priest is the mother's peer in corruption: he, too, plots for material gain. He learns that the lady has set aside a considerable sum for her daughter's dowry:

> elle avoit amassé cinq cens ducatz pour donner au mary de sa fille, et prenoit sur sa charge la nourriture des deux, les fournissans de maison, meubles et accoustremens.
>
> ("she had saved five hundred ducats to give to the girl's future husband, and also … she would provide the couple with a house and furnishings, and keep them in food and clothing."—*Hept.* 6.56.349; Chilton 451)

He then convinces a young fellow monk to pose as a wealthy suitor. The priest plans to give the girl, her lodgings, and clothing to his friend, keeping the money for himself. Lady and priest both deceive each other in order to gain wealth. Rather than exchange spiritual advice, they engage in corruption and commodification. The fantasy of the lavish material existence that the monk has concocted for himself is evoked by the repetition of the objects composing it: "les fournissans de maison, meubles et accoustremens."

In a parody of his priestly role as intercessor, the priest poses as an *entremetteur*, pimping for his friend with the young lady. By assuming this suspect status, he embodies the evangelicals' worst fears about priestly intercession and mediation: he negotiates affairs of the flesh instead of devoting himself to things of the spirit. Inventing a story to account for why his young friend wishes to marry in haste and in secret, the priest attires the former luxuriously to create the illusion of wealth and prosperity so that the mother will deem him a profitable match: he is dressed in "ung beau pourpoinct de satin cramoisy" ("a crimson satin doublet"—*Hept.* 6.56.349; Chilton 452).

After the wedding, the young man tells his wife that he must leave at dawn; he takes his leave even more gorgeously attired—taking some of the goods with him. His dress and ornament accumulate in description, showing him benefiting from the riches he has received by marriage: now he is clad not only in "ung pourpoinct de satin cramoisy"; he also wears "sa robbe longue, sans oblier sa coiffe de soye noire" ("his crimson satin doublet," "his long robe, and of course his black silk cap"—*Hept.* 6.56.350; Chilton 452). The possessive *sa*, where formerly the clothing was simply described without designating the possessor, shows that he has taken for his own that which rightfully belongs to his wife. Enumeration emphasizes the quantity of his ill-gotten gains.

One morning, the mother and newlywed daughter go to mass, where they realize that the celebrant is the husband! He doesn't notice their presence, so, back at home, they devise a scheme to reveal his perfidy. Their plan concerns articles of clothing. They decide to remove his "coiffe": a figurative and literal use of the aphorism, *l'habit ne fait pas le moine*—for neither does a "coiffe" make a husband. His imposture will be disclosed once the costume composing his pretense at being a husband is removed, for his "coiffe" disguises his "couronne," slang for his monastic tonsure, a hairstyle that reveals his deception:

> ainsy qu'il sera dedans le lict, je l'iray trouver, et ... vous luy arracherez sa coiffe; et nous verrons s'il a telle couronne que celluy qui a dict la messe.
>
> ("as soon as he's in bed, I'll come in to him and you will pull off his cap from behind before he knows what's happening. Then we shall see if he's tonsured like the one who said the mass."—*Hept.* 6.56.351; Chilton 454)

The *dénouement* of this story ends similarly to *nouvelle* #9, in which a priest sleeps with a lady who has been cheating on her husband. Oisille explains this deception aphoristically, asserting "Aussy bien sont amourettes / soubz bureau que soubz brunettes" ("whether frieze or lawn you wear, / Love's fancies free do linger there!"—*Hept.* 3.9.228; Chilton 315). "Bureau" or "bure" is the rough fabric of which monastic habits are fashioned, while "brunette" is a soft, high-quality textile. The aphorism reveals that the wife has slept not only with noblemen ("brunettes") but also with clergy ("bureau"). The assessment of her character is constructed by this evocative layering of fabrics that recalls how different male bodies—from different social estates—have lain atop hers. An equation between deceptive substance, "tissu"—or fabric—and text—the *nouvelle*—displays the deception: the material objects mentioned in the tale are items that can cooperate in disguise, as well as tools facilitating the eventual unmasking.

Layers of clothing may disguise motives and foster fraudulent acts, but when materiality is stripped away, only one's essence remains. Here, façade upon façade characterizes the priest, who is a sham of spirituality and lacks moral substance: "pour vous monstrer que ceulx qui ont voué pauvreté ne sont pas exemptz d'estre tentez d'avarice, qui est l'occasion de faire tant de maulx" ("to show you that the men who make vows of poverty are not exempt from the temptations of avarice—a fact which gives rise to so much evil"—*Hept.* 6.56.351; Chilton 454). Saffredent picks up the phrase "tant de maulx," interjecting, "mais tant de biens!" (*Hept.* 6.56.351; Chilton 451), *biens* connoting material possessions, but Oisille rebukes him for this very earthly miscounting, pointing out that the *nouvelle* ("le compte") has rectified matters in a spiritual sense: "le compte … est faict maintenant" ("and that it is not true is clear from the story we have just heard"—*Hept.* 6.56.352; Chilton 454).

The commentary echoes the assessment made throughout the *Heptaméron* concerning the evanescence of earthly treasures. For instance, in *nouvelle* #24, a woman loses her lover when he chooses God over her. This loss is irreparable; no earthly treasure could compensate for it: "nul tresor … ne luy pov[oit] oster le tiltre d'estre la plus pauvre et miserable dame du monde, car elle avoit perdu ce que tous les biens du monde ne povoient recouvrer" ("no treasure in the realm, no, not even the realm itself, could make her other than the poorest and most desolate lady in the whole world. For she had lost that which no riches on earth could replace"—*Hept.* 3.24.200; Chilton 383).

Nouvelle #65 illustrates the theme of priests perpetuating deception and practicing tricks of illusion. Material objects are involved, and here they are doubly suspect because some of them are simulacra of material objects, such as the copy of the façade of a sepulchre. The story shows that the only way to deal with such layers of deception is by adopting a scriptural stance toward them. The message is that trust placed in images and objects is ill founded.

The *nouvelle* tells of a church in Lyons that possesses an impressive tomb, ornately sculpted, with several figures carved in intaglio upon it. These figures are very life-like: "ung Sepulcre faict de pierre à grans personnages eslevez, comme le vif; et sont à l'entour du sepulcre plusieurs hommes d'armes couchez" ("a stone tomb, on which there are sculpted life-size figures. Around the bottom of the tomb there are figures of soldiers in sleeping postures"—*Hept.* 7.65.388; Chilton 498). A soldier enters the church and, exhausted, falls asleep by the sculpted soldiers on the sepulchre. An old lady then comes to pray by the tomb. She lights a votive candle, placing it on what she takes to be an effigy, but which is in reality the sleeping soldier's head, so closely does art imitate life and vice versa: the *nouvelle* designates in this way the deception of which materiality is capable. Because the wax won't stick to his forehead, the old woman touches the burning tip of the taper to his head to warm what she thinks is frigid stone. The soldier, not an image but a man, cries out, which she construes as a miraculous event: “Mais l’ymaige, qui n’estoit insensible, commencea à crier; dont la bonne femme … se print à cryer miracle” (“but this was no insensible statue, and it began to shout … the old woman was terrified out of her wits. ‘A miracle!’ she shrieked. ‘A miracle!’”—*Hept.* 7.65.388; Chilton 498). People gather round, and the woman points out the soldier to the monks as the sculpture “that had moved” (“l’ymaige qui estoit remuée”—*Hept.* 7.65.388; Chilton 498). Some of the monks realize that they may be able to capitalize on her misprision: “ilz avoient bien deliberé de faire valloir ce Sepulcre et en tirer autant d’argent que du crucifix qui est sur leur pupiltre, lequel on dict avoir parlé” (“the priests … had already made up their minds that they should turn their tomb to account and make as much money out of it as they had from their crucifix—the one that hangs over the rood-screen and is supposed to have spoken”—*Hept.* 7.65.388; Chilton 498).

Although the male *devisants* mock the woman’s credulity, Oisille asserts that the woman has acted by faith; the old lady did not seek to delude or to profit—she merely wanted to pray. Nothing she has done is reprehensible; rather, the monks’ money-making deception is blameworthy. Like Christ’s assessment of another old woman, the widow offering her mite in the Gospel narrative, Oisille says, “je ne regarde poinct la valleur du present, mais le cueur qui le presente. Peut estre que ceste bonne femme avoit plus d’amour à Dieu, que ceulx qui donnent les grandz torches, car, comme dict l’Evangile, elle donnoit de sa necessité” (“I do not look to the value of the present … but to the heart that presents it. It may be that this good woman had greater love of God than those who light huge torches, for, as the Gospel says, she gave of her penury”—*Hept.* 7.65.389; Chilton 499). The formulation “non la valleur du *present*, mais le cueur qui le *presente*” cleverly plays the thing off against the act, noun against verb, showing that the inner being, intention, and realization of that intent matter much more than any material object.

By offering a candle as symbolic of her prayer, the woman cooperated in the distinction between appearance (sculpted soldiers) and reality (the live soldier). However, it is also possible that she inadvertently enabled the priests to play a trick on other worshipers, since the soldier seemed a part of the tomb and, by moving, suggested that a miraculous power had suddenly animated the sepulchre's figure. Perhaps Marguerite cautions here, in her evangelical way, that acts of devotion such as candle-lighting, and material markers of metaphysical orientation—such as candles—are ritualistic accretions, not derived from Scripture, that can distort intention.

Elsewhere in the *Heptaméron,* candles evoke the metaphysical standard of the light of the Gospel. Significantly, they are extinguished when evil is planned. For instance, in *nouvelle* #23, a Cordelier, planning to seduce a woman, lights his way to her chambers with a candle that he then quickly blows out. In *nouvelle* #54, as in *nouvelle* #65, a candle is again at the center of the story. Suffering from a headache, a man named Thogas consults doctors, who advise him to abstain from sexual relations with his wife. He puts her in another bed in the corner of their room. Their habit is to have servants read to them, the book illuminated by a chambermaid holding a candle, until they fall asleep. However, this time the candle throws an unexpected light on the situation and on the husband's motives: it projects a revealing image on the wall, showing the husband making love to the chambermaid while the bedtime story is being read:

> regardant la damoiselle de loing du costé du lict de son mary où estoit la jeune chamberiere qui tenoit la chandelle ... et estoit d'une muraille blanche où reluisoit la clairté de la chandelle, et contre la dicte muraille voyoit très bien le pourtraict du visaige de son mary, et de celluy de sa chamberiere ... elle veit que les umbres retournoient soubvent à ceste union.
>
> ("the side of the chimney, which came out in front of his bed, was white, and reflected the light from the candle. On this wall were clearly cast the shadows of the faces of her husband and the maid, and the wife could distinguish quite plainly what the two were doing—whether they were moving apart, getting closer together, or laughing."—*Hept.* 6.54.343; Chilton 445)

The term "ceste union," describing the merging of the two silhouettes, also evokes the "union" of sexual congress, one which Scripture instructs should rightfully occur only between spouses. The husband, however, has chosen to obey earthly advice—that of his doctors—and has also distorted it: they have told him to refrain from intercourse with his wife—but they have omitted to make any similar proscription about any other woman, so he casuistically derives permission for adultery from that omission. In this way, Marguerite epitomizes the evangelical insistence on reading Scripture carefully and interpreting it in context so as not to distort it through truncation or misapplication.

The light cast by the candle reveals a truth about fallen humanity:[24] the *ombres chinoises*, or silhouettes, of sin. His wife is so astonished at what she sees that she starts to laugh, excusing herself as laughing at shadows: "je rys à mon umbre"; homophonically evocative, since she is actually laughing at her "homme," who should, also, be her "umbre": he is her husband so, in a sense, the shadow that his body casts also belongs to her in the context of their marital union. He, incensed, has a "face umbrageuse" ("shadowy face"—*Hept.* 6.54.343; Chilton 446); that shadow symbolizes his sin. In her commentary on this story, Oisille quotes St. Paul, advising the wife to "aymer, servir et obeyr [son mary] comme l'Eglise à Jesus-Christ" ("love, serve and obey [your husband], even as the Church serves and obeys Jesus Christ"[25]—*Hept.* 6.54.343; Chilton 446), regardless of his reprehensible behavior. However, God sees and rectifies those matters that men try to hide from detection, and the wordplay on shadow, man, and anger ("umbre," "umbrageuse") links the sign to reality, and the sin to its ineluctable disclosure. The candlelight highlights his infidelity, and is the vehicle to communicate St. Paul's message: "Now we see as through a glass darkly [*umbre*], but then, face to face [*ceste face*]." Parlamente reinforces the message by echoing implicitly the Pauline passage mandating how men should rightly act toward their spouses: "il fauldroit doncques, mes dames … que noz mariz fussent envers nous, comme Christ et son Eglise" ("so it follows … that our husbands should be towards us as Christ is towards his Church"—*Hept.* 6.54.344; Chilton 446). The husband's lustful behavior is not in conformity with Scripture.

One of the most frequent ways in which material props, clothing, and layers are employed in the *Heptaméron* is by heaping substance upon substance. Yet no matter how dense the deception, no matter how thick the accretion of layers, God's Word, as the *nouvelles* attest, strips away imposture and deceit, to reveal the pretense and posturing of those who ascribe significance solely to earthly treasures, and points the path toward metaphysical redressing. If the "idea of dress [is] the key to the self,"[26] then these representational constructs reveal costuming and display as both "spectatorial and critical practice."[27] The self is thus image or deception, yet, ultimately, through each tale, the self is critically examined, so as to be relocated within what is no longer an earthly, but rather a spiritual, narrative.

As costume developed as its own aesthetic discourse during the early modern period, simultaneous with excessive ornamentation on sculpture and decorative arts objects, surface was wrenched away from ornament, and costume differed from essence, cloaking rather than disclosing reality. The mimetic pretense of conferring unitary significance on the world by maintaining an equation between subject and display of objects collapsed. When the subject no longer controlled or deployed objects, and when surface no longer directed or justified ornament, an ontological anxiety existed about meaning, identity, and motivation. In this case, art and literature could no longer refer back to real objects, with the result that "art put in to question the reality of the referents for writing's model, and proposed to go beyond that model."[28] When realism and representation no longer sufficed, the metaphysical orientation had to be envisioned. The possessors of material objects then struggled to define themselves not in relation to things, not even in relation to each other (for the "other" had also become a commodity), but to God.

The *Heptaméron*, displaying a textual wardrobe and chest of properties full of costumes and disguises, masks and makeup, is, itself, costumed. However, the *devisants* encourage the reader to peel away the textual adornment, to peek beneath the skirts of the text, and to discern the ultimate Christiform orientation of the stories. An evangelical perspective penetrates the disguise and discerns the message subtending the *Heptaméron*, one that transforms the trappings of materiality into its own indictment.

Chapter Eight

Interior Decoration and External Trappings

Space for the Spirit

> And he told them this parable:
>
> "The ground of a certain rich man produced a good crop. He thought to himself, 'What shall I do? I have no place to store my crops.' Then he said, 'This is what I'll do. I'll tear down my barns and build bigger ones, and there I will store all my grain and my goods. And I'll say to myself, 'You have plenty of good things laid up for many years. Take life easy; eat, drink and be merry.' But God said to him, 'You fool! This very night your life will be demanded from you. Then who will get what you have prepared for yourself?' This is how it will be with anyone who stores things up for himself but is not rich toward God."
>
> Luke 12.16–21

Furnishing the Space of the Spirit

Exterior spaces (gardens, forests, bordered alleys, streets), buildings (castles, prisons, churches, monasteries), and interior spaces (bedchambers, salons, closets) play narrative roles in the *nouvelles*. Their decorative schemes (composed of tapestries, rugs, clothes chests, beds, tables) are also significant. Such objects of furnishing receive different emphases in the text depending on the circumstances of the narrative; they are strategically situated to convey a certain significance.

> [In Ancien Régime France] creating a piece of furniture was not unlike creating a sentence for a native speaker of a language. In both cases the makers of furniture or of speech

> had a repertoire, which consisted of the rules of the trade, or the grammar and vocabulary of a language; a sense of audience, which constrained what could be made or said and how, if one wanted to be understood; and individual creativity, which enabled one to construct unique objects or utterances that were both correct and comprehensible.[1]

Thus, in the *Heptaméron*, some items serve a descriptive function, while others encapsulate the thematic thrust of the tale in which they feature. Furniture and furnishings, as displayed in, and distributed throughout, a defined space, constitute a semiotic reservoir of potential narrative negotiations, summarizing "the communicative capacity of objects, in their exchange and in their use."[2]

As characters work through this trajectory of possibilities offered by the *décor*, objects collaborate in the process of making meaning. In addition, these objects bear witness to the character of their possessor: "in [Ancien Régime France], furniture … stood in for, represented, a man's moral standing; it matched his mode of being in the world."[3] The placement of selected objects in the narrative reveals Marguerite's subtexts.[4] Narrative representations constituted through the act of reading, these textual furnishings are virtual objects; they exist only by virtue of the narrative that houses them. Called into being by the power of Marguerite's words, they also recall creation by the Word; as they gesture toward a metaphysical origin, they require a metaphysical interpretation.

Nouvelle #49 offers a case study of how furnishings may evoke the message of a story, as well as how they elicit the moral furnishings of a protagonist's interior space. This is the story, already discussed in Chapter 7, of the countess who, much admired by the king, accepts in succession several of the king's men as lovers, closeting each in her *garderobbe* during the period of the affair. A *garderobbe* is a small room off a bedchamber. As such, it is a permanent and immobile ancillary fixture of the bedchamber. The *Cent nouvelles nouvelles* and other late medieval texts featured many *bahuts* ("trunks," a variant of "clothes chest" or *garderobbes*); not unlike the purpose to which the countess puts hers, these were frequently used to hide a lover from a husband. But they were objects rather than spaces: large, bulky chests usually crafted from dark, heavy wood, often nearly the height of a standing woman. In both cases, the *bahut* and the *garderobbe* represented the woman's space, either because of proximity to her bedroom or because they contained her clothes, the props from which she constructed her appearance. The repetition of the phenomenon of concealment in this particular *nouvelle* of the *Heptaméron* is striking: not only does the woman hide one lover, Astillon, but also Durassier, and others. The *garderobbe* was meant to store dresses, not serial lovers. The repeated insertion of males into this female space suggests promiscuity. The *garderobbe* substitutes in the *nouvelle* for the woman herself: the opened space, into which the woman installs numerous men, connotes the sex act. Through the use of an inadequately ascribed antecedent ("un"), as in the phrase "quant elle en tenoit ung en cache" ("while she kept one man hidden away"—*Hept.* 5.49.321; Chilton 420), the text's lexicon equates clothing stored in a *garderobbe* with lovers tucked away in secret. Jambicque's *garderobbe* attests not only to her ownership of numerous articles of clothing; it also provides the occasion for her to garb herself with plural lovers, covering her body in another sense. The woman should have been a closed space to all but her husband; instead, the *garderobbe* becomes a signifier of the shaky moral grounds on which her marriage perches as the men pop in and out of what is defined as her space.[5]

In *nouvelle* #37, another *garderobbe* furnishes a filthy back bedroom: "un lieu ord et salle" ("somewhere foul and dirty"—*Hept.* 4.37.267; Chilton 359), while the term *maison* symbolizes the married couple, domesticity, and fidelity. When the husband begins to cheat on his wife, the domestic space offers clues: its appearance alters along with his alteration in affections: "la maison fut bien tost rendue si brouillée" ("the household became so disorganized"—*Hept.* 4.37.266; Chilton 358), and a watchful relative enjoins the wife to watch out for the "proffict de sa maison" ("consider the family fortunes"—*Hept.* 4.37.267; Chilton 358). The *nouvelle* stresses that the lady being wronged is châtelaine of "une des plus riches maisons et des mieulx meublées" ("one of the richest and best appointed [houses]"—*Hept.* 4.37.266; Chilton 358), underscoring the importance of décor and furnishings as a material mark of status. Yet, as Marguerite's evangelical polemic reminds us, a plethora of earthly treasures can lead to their misuse, and worldly possessions carry no assurance of security.

The *garderobbe* in this story is likened to another space: the *retraict*.[6] *Aller au garderobbe*, in fact, often means *aller au retraict*. Here, as in *nouvelle* #11, contamination by insertion into suspect space takes place, as the husband sleeps with an ugly, dirty chambermaid in a space representative of their lack of virtue:

> [l'épouse] le trouva couché en une arriere garderobbe et endormy avec la plus layde, orde et salle chamberiere qui fut leans.
>
> ("she found him in an obscure closet asleep in bed with the ugliest, dirtiest and foulest chambermaid in the house."—*Hept*. 4.37.267; Chilton 359)

The same vocabulary describes the room ("ord et salle") and the loose woman ("orde et salle"). Significantly, the *garderobbe* is situated "arriere," farther back, in a kind of architectural cloacal recess, such as that occupied by the toilets, *le retraict,* which is actually the pretext that the husband provides when he leaves the marital bed at night.[7] In this story, the *retraict* is, thus, simultaneously, a real location, a mendacious pretext, and a symbol of the husband's infidelity. The loving wife recognizes the multivalent referents of the *retraict*, for every time that the husband returns from cheating on her, she provides him with "ung bassin et de l'eaue pour laver ses mains" ("a bowl of water, so that he could wash his hands"—*Hept*. 4.37.267; Chilton 357–58), instructing him, "si estoit-il honneste de laver ses mains, quand on venoit d'un lieu ord et salle" ("it was only decent to wash one's hands when one had been somewhere foul and dirty"—*Hept*. 4.37.267; Chilton 358). As the dirty servant-girl, and the *garderobbe* where she and the husband cheat, are equated with the *retraict*, emblem of physical filth and spiritual wrongdoing, the wife symbolically retaliates against this space and its furnishings: she sets fire to the *garderobbe* "pour [luy] apprend[re] à laisser une si honneste femme pour une si sale et orde" ("she would teach him to leave an honest woman for this foul and dirty creature"—*Hept*. 4.37.267; Chilton 358). Place and props in this way summarize the plot. In addition, by reiterating the adjectives *sale* and *orde* in juxtaposition with her own self-description as *honneste,* thereby justifying herself in contrast with the maid, the wife constructs a chiasmus: *orde* and *salle* reverse to *salle et orde*, making a tight circle of judgment just as the wife symbolically reverses the adulterous situation and restores order to her home. Later she instructs her husband that "en lavant le dehors, vous deviez nectoier le dedans" ("in washing the outside, you should be also inwardly cleansed"—*Hept.* 4.37.267; Chilton 359). This is a precept that she had mimed with the hand-washing practice and had literalized by setting fire to the *garderobbe*: by eliminating the space that had housed sin, sin can be eradicated from the interior, moral space of her husband: "vesquirent ensemble en si grande amityé, que mesmes les faultes passées, par le bien qui en estoit advenu, leur estoient augmentation de contentement" ("they lived together in such great affection, that past misdeeds only increased their happiness by the good that had come of them"—*Hept.* 4.37.268; Chilton 359).

In this and other *nouvelles,* Marguerite at times inserts *herself* into suspect spaces and into situations. In so doing, she writes herself back into the medium for communication that she creates. Like the wronged wife, she is involved in, and struggles to redress, the world's disorder. By miring herself, along with her characters and the *devisants*, in the muck of materiality, Marguerite shows how humanity must progress through the world's deceptions and entrapments—just as the reader mimes this itinerary by reading—to arrive at a metaphysical destination. In the world, Marguerite is analogous to the objects displayed in the text. For instance, she is one of the scarified voodoo dolls fashioned of wood by the magician. However, once known in God, she finds true subjectivity, and is known in and by Him. Thus, decorative art objects participate in ploys of narrative deception, as well as demolish those deceptions. Such objects are "both constitutive and representative,"[8] as is the discourse of the *Heptaméron* that evokes and deploys them.[9] They constitute the material world in which the narrative develops, as well as represent key moments in that narrative; the narrative both composes a terrestrial tale and represents beyond its apparent reality.

In *nouvelle* #45, for instance, a rugmaker, deceiving his wife with serial lovers, uses his trade and its products to perpetuate this deception. All rugmakers know how to dye rugs, just as colors and figures of rhetoric can camouflage a text or construct a lie. Rugs and tapestries facilitate this man's unfaithfulness, while also revealing it to the reader: "luy, qui sçavoit donner couleur à toute tapisserie, pensa si bien colorer ce faict, [pour] bien tromp[er] … sa femme" ("but he was just as clever at embroidering the truth as he was at embroidering tapestry—so clever, in fact, that he ended up by tricking both the next-door neighbor and his wife"—*Hept.* 5.65.306; Chilton 403).

Nouvelle #32 (already discussed in a different light) also demonstrates the narrative use of artifacts and furnishings in a distinctive way; this is one of the few *nouvelles* in the *Heptaméron* in which an object plays an unequivocally positive role.[10] The portrait of the formerly adulterous wife, now reunited with her husband, is unusual in that Marguerite supplies details about the painter's identity, enhancing the interdisciplinary quality of her text and situating it in contemporary context: the portraitist is Jehan de Paris (Jean Perréal), an artist whose work François Ier collected. It is surely significant that Marguerite supplies his name, for she names *him* at the same time as her text confers identity on the *woman.* In addition, Jehan de Paris, like Marguerite herself, was a writer[11] and was cited in literary works of the period. Marguerite here delineates how her text constructs and employs art objects in a representational project in which both literary depiction and artistic rendition cooperate.

Many of the *nouvelles* contain floor plans and decorating schemes meant to delineate and furnish spaces for the work of redemption that the *Heptaméron* envisions. For example, *nouvelle* #38 offers a space for the practical application of Scripture, illustrating the Gospel mandate to "render good for evil." The text extensively enumerates objects and furniture—soft beds and hard pallets ("bon lict"; "mauvais lict"), sheets ("linceux"), bed hangings ("mante") and coverlet ("couverture"), rugs and tapestries ("pour tapisser la chambre"), dishes and plateware ("la vaisselle honneste"), and even a silver goblet ("une coupe d'argent")—along with good food, wine, and sweets ("vin"; "dragées"; "confiture"): a compendium of creature comforts and earthly treasures.

These commodities are linked to carnality, *luxure,* and greed, furnishing an adulterous husband's hideaway. Surprisingly, the interior decorator of such a sensual space is the wronged wife herself, who hopes, by so sumptuously adorning her husband's love nest, to demonstrate *caritas* and concern for his well-being. She has deprived herself in order to do so, removing these decorative pieces from her own house. While the text does not explicitly state that these are her belongings, the lack of partitive construction in "elle luy donna *la* vaisselle honneste" ("she provided good crockery for him to eat and drink from"—*Hept.* 5.38.270) seems to indicate that she gave him her good dishes (or the ones that they had formerly shared) rather than purchasing new ones (which would be "*de la* vaisselle"). "Maison" here connotes, as in *nouvelle* #37 already discussed in this chapter, the orderly home of a married couple. In divesting their conjugal household of furniture, the wife compares her experience of disorientation to the relocation of the familiar furnishings, just as her husband transgresses by occupying another space and the space of another.

Furniture in the sixteenth century was costly and not frequently discarded: it was considered to be an art object as well as a functional accoutrement; meant to be preserved and cared for, it symbolically stood in for its possessor. Leora Auslander notes that, up until the time of Louis XIV, it was not customary to destroy, and certainly not to bestow on others, the king's furniture, for the furniture was assimilated to the king's essence by a process of identification between object and user.[12] This sort of fetishism is consistent with variants illustrated in the *Heptaméron*, as well as in the treatment of saints' relics throughout the tales.

However, developing technology gradually made furniture less expensive, more available, and less personal because it could be produced in shops rather than by one craftsman or by a team of artisans. Accordingly, the transfer of furniture in *nouvelle* #38 to a new location represents how the husband's heart has moved to a new "home" or chosen a new identity. Both in the earthly realm and in the spiritual domain, the wife is a good housekeeper: finding that the space (and, by extension, the woman kept there) is "si froide et salle et mal en poinct" ("so cold, dirty and ill-kept"—*Hept.* 4.38.270; Chilton 362), she proceeds to clean, warm, arrange, and adorn the room. She will similarly treat the interior moral space of her husband. The wife acts out the Gospel imperative of hospitality extended to all without regard for the recipient's worth or lack thereof:

> elle en eust pitié … la dame … donna … une pippe de bon vin, des dragées et confitures; et pria la mestayere qu'elle ne luy renvoiast plus son mary si morfondu.
>
> ("she felt sorry for him … The lady … provided … a cask of good wine, and a supply of sweetmeats and preserves. Then she requested the woman kindly not to send her husband back so run-down in future."—*Hept.* 4.38.270; Chilton 362)

The new dwelling (prior to the wife's decoration of it) represents the deceitful *metayere*: the room "froide et salle," just as the husband's emotional state upon his return from the second house and the second woman is *morfondu*. The wife's reaction to the poorly appointed room ("elle en eust pitié") underscores the equation between place and person, since compassion is an emotion generally accorded to people.

The husband's response reinforces this conflation: he asks his mistress "d'ont estoient venuz tous ses biens" ("where all these belongings had come from"—*Hept.* 4.38.271; Chilton 363), suggesting that he did not expect care for his creature comforts from his mistress (and acknowledging that he recognized these as former furnishings in his home). His process of penitence begins through his association of his wife with these *biens*, and of himself and the maid with shameful acts: "voiant la grande bonté de sa femme, que, pour tant de mauvais tours qu'il luy avoit faicts, lui rendoit tant de biens, estim[oit] sa faulte aussy grande que l'honneste tour que sa femme luy avoit faict" ("the husband realized how good his wife was to do all this for him after the rotten tricks he had played on her, and had to admit to himself that his behaviour was no less wicked than hers was virtuous"—*Hept.* 4.38.271; Chilton 363). His wife's kindness ("la grande bonté de sa femme") is now literalized by the bestowing of the furniture ("tant de biens"). Initially, worldly goods were tainted with infidelity once they furnished the space in which adultery transpired. Now, however, furniture = *biens* = *bonté*. The one piece of furnishing is metonymic for an entire material, formerly suspect, but now associated with positive qualities and epitomizing a new state of mind or spirit. The furnishings represent, for the husband, the wife's forgiveness of his infidelity. They show how material objects can cooperate in producing metaphysical understanding. By redecorating the space of adultery with uxorious care, the furnishings redetermine that space and reorient the husband back to his loving wife.

The repentant husband returns to his wife, confessing his *debte* (sin) to her ("à laquelle il confessa la debte"; "he confessed his debt"—*Hept.* 4.38.271; Chilton 363); this theological language also recalls humanity's indebtedness to Christ for his sacrifice. Like Christ, the woman becomes the medium for forgiveness, and the vocabulary echoes this theological function: "de sa femme … sans le moien de ceste grande doulceur et bonté, il estoit impossible qu'il eust jamais laissé la vie qu'il menoit" ("saying that if she had not acted with such goodness and kindness, he would never have been able to give up the kind of life he had been leading"—*Hept.* 4.38.271; Chilton 363). In worldly transactions, a *debte* owed for *biens* is financial; here, the *debte* and the *biens* are spiritual. The two terms echo the words of the Lord's Prayer: "et dimitte nobis debita nostra sicut et nos dimittimus debitoribus nostris."

Equally Christian in tone is *nouvelle* #40, and specifically evangelical in how it is interpreted, since it is read against a scriptural template. As in *nouvelle* #38, objects are eventually rehabilitated to play a role in Marguerite's theological theater of conversion. The theme in this tale is that of displacement, a continual wrenching out of context that demonstrates that certainty only resides in heaven. A count with an unmarried sister does not want to allow her to marry "par trop aymer son argent" ("because he was too fond of his money"—*Hept.* 4.40.275; Chilton 368). The possessive pronoun ("son") is vague, blurring the rightful ownership of the money by the sister and implying either that the count hopes to augment his own income by retaining that of his sister in the household instead of giving it to her as a dowry—or that he would have to pay a dowry for her out of his own pocket. In either case, the Gospel injunction not to worship money indicts his reprehensible actions, the contrast between his cupidity and his sister's devotion to him, and his self-love that he puts before affection for his sister. The count violates the scriptural intertext of 1 Tim. 6.17–19:

> Charge them that are rich in the world, that they be not high-minded, nor trust in uncertain riches, but in the living God, who gives us richly all things to enjoy; that they do good; that they be rich in good works, ready to distribute, willing to communicate; laying up a store for themselves to be a good foundation against the time to come, that they may have eternal life.

The count values money above his sister. He treats her badly, imprisons her, refuses to hear her pleas, and forbids her to speak to others. While she experiences a sort of sainthood, his refusal to follow scriptural mandates causes his ruin and that of his house. The terms *heritaige* and *heritiere* provide another indication that the tale has a scriptural template: as we have seen, such terms usually refer to the heritage stored up in heaven for the elect. The exclusively female use of the term ("heritiere") here is telling: no such treasure awaits the brother, who has placed all his trust in, and has exclusively valued, earthly possessions.

One of the count's friends falls in love with the sister, and they wed in secret. Marguerite describes this marriage as epitomizing the Protestant model of "companionate marriage": when the sister and the count's friend are together, they live "comme la plus belle couple qui fut en la chrestienté"; demonstrating "la plus grande et plus parfaicte amityé" ("the handsomest couple in Christendom"; "the most deeply and perfectly in love"—*Hept.* 4.40.275; Chilton 368). An ill-wisher denounces the couple to the brother, who rushes in to find them in bed together.

The husband tries to flee by jumping from the bedroom window into the garden below. In the *Heptaméron,* windows often constitute an opening onto a new spiritual state and not simply a view of a different space. Here windows frame a change, but this is a change for the worse prefigured in the description of the surprised couple as "aveuglez d'amour" ("the poor love-blind couple"), and brought to horrific resolution as the wife, all too sighted ("voyant ce piteux spectacle" ["having witnessed this piteous spectacle"]), sees her husband die "devant les œilz" ("even as they watched"—*Hept.* 4.40.276; Chilton 369) at the hands of the count's servants. The count removes the sister from their ancestral home and locks her in a château-like prison isolated deep in a wood. His forcible displacement of his sister is spurred by a sense of culpability rather than of self-justification: he wishes that he had locked himself up, in a sense, rather than having committed such a crime and he also fears being prosecuted:

> Il ... eust bien voulu n'avoir poinct commis ung tel crime. Si est-ce que la craincte qu'il eut que sa seur en demandast justice ou vengeance, luy feit faire ung chasteau au meillieu d'une forest, auquel il la meist; et defendit que aucun ne parlast à elle.
>
> ("he ... would have preferred never to have committed such a crime. So much did he fear that his sister would demand vengeance or justice, that he made a castle-prison for her in the middle of a forest, in which he placed her, and forbade anyone to talk to her."—*Hept.* 4.40.277; Chilton 369)

Although the sister has no earthly defender, her faith in God sustains her. Her faith enables her to imagine a spatial transformation: the terminus in the process of displacement that the count had envisioned, the château/prison, is spiritually enlarged. It becomes for her a retreat and a refuge where she can be alone with God. She figuratively rearranges the interior decoration that has been forced on her, transforming it into a representation of her spiritual state: "avecq l'amour [de Dieu] seul elle vouloit user le demorant de sa vie en son hermitaige" ("I whose [God's] love she wished to abide in the lonely castle that was now her hermitage"—*Hept.* 4.40.277; Chilton 370). The *chasteau* is no longer a terrestrial prison; it has been transformed into a spiritualized dwelling, a *hermitaige.* The sister experiences not only a spatial change, but also a spiritual transformation: "Et elle, convertissant l'ayse qu'elle avoit avecq [son mary] au service de Nostre Seigneur, se povoit dire bien heureuse" ("she could count herself happy indeed in converting the happiness she had enjoyed with her husband to the service of our Lord"—*Hept.* 4.40.279; Chilton 372). Her metaphysical focus enables her to overlook her material circumstances, liberating her spirit: "et, quant à la prison de son corps, je croy que, pour la liberté de son cueur, qui estoit joinct à Dieu … ne la sentoit poinct, mais [l']estimoit … très grande liberté" ("and though her body was imprisoned, her heart was free and united with God and her husband, so that I believe she did not experience her solitude as imprisonment but regarded it rather as the highest liberty"—*Hept.* 4.40.279; Chilton 372).

Justice is meted out on the earthly treasures that the count had sought to safeguard and for which he had murdered his sister's husband: his house—his domestic space and emblematic of his identity—falls into disrepair, paralleling his moral dereliction: "la maison de son frere alloit tellement en ruyne" ("the brother's family declined"—*Hept.* 4.40.277; Chilton 370). While Scripture is the foundation for this tale, an additional subtext underscores the inter-referentiality of the *nouvelles*: the château/prison in the woods is the same prison in which the king had incarcerated Rolandine (*nouvelle* #21) when she contracted her morganatic marriage in defiance of his refusal (motivated by the queen's reluctance to part with Rolandine's "biens," her dowry, a very similar situation to that of the lady in *nouvelle* #40). Rolandine, too, is termed an *heritiere* in *nouvelle* #21. *Nouvelle* #40 divulges that the count's sister is Rolandine's mother, thus establishing a sort of genealogy of biblical inheritance: "l'heritaige demoura, comme vous avez oy en l'autre compte, à sa fille Rolandine, laquelle avoit succedé à la prison faicte pour sa tante" ("in the end it was his daughter Rolandine who remained sole heiress, as you heard in the earlier story, and inherited the prison which had been built for her aunt"—*Hept.* 4.40.277; Chilton 370). The *spiritual* line of heredity, rather than biological provenance and worldly relationship, matters most in the *nouvelles*. However, God's will can rectify the distortion of the material world, even sorting out financial matters: "l'heritaige demoura … à sa fille" indicates that the count's attempts to keep the money for himself have been thwarted. Finally, the genealogical affiliation does not observe chronological order: Rolandine's tale is told *before* that of her aunt, suggesting that God's perspective reverses worldly events and productions.

The story is structured around the sister's wrongful removal from the *maison* and imprisonment in the *chasteau,* as well as the spiritual transformation of the prison into her *hermitaige*.

In the frame concluding the story, the commentators retrace the itinerary leading to spiritual perfection and disregard of earthly suffering. Their itinerary follows the sister; in addition, they "pause" in *faulxbourgs* and take "rest-stops" at inns:

> Qu'appellez-vous les faulxbourgs de la mort? dist Simontault.—Ceulx qui ont beaucoup de tribulations en l'esperit, respondit Nomerfide, ceulx aussi qui ont esté longuement malades et qui, par extremité de douleur corporelle ou spirituelle, sont venuz à despriser la mort ... ceulx [qui] ont passé par les faulxbourgs et vous diront les hostelleriez où ilz ont plus cryé que reposé.
>
> ("What do you mean by 'lingering on the outskirts of death?' asked Simontault. 'I mean those people who suffer torments of the mind,' answered Nomerfide, 'and those who have been ill a long time, and who, because of the extreme nature of their bodily or mental suffering, no longer fear death, but rather find it slow in coming. I mean those people who have journeyed through the outskirts and can tell you the names of inns where they have wept rather than rested.'"—*Hept*. 4.40.278; Chilton 372)

The final space of the text is not a physical, but a spiritual, location, as the sister's soul and body undergo a Pauline split, the "prison de mon corps" now facilitating, rather than inhibiting, "la liberté de son cueur" ("though her body was imprisoned, her heart was free"—*Hept*. 4.40.279; Chilton 373). The inner space of the heart, the crucial space of regeneration, is the last stop on the sister's journey.

While the count's refusal to share treasure (and his sister) is the issue in *nouvelle* #40, *nouvelle* #47 explores the narrative problem of the impropriety of excessive sharing that disregards another person's subjectivity. If men and women all are equal in God's sight, as Scripture instructs, then it is inappropriate not to respect the identity and boundaries of each individual. Reference to physical spaces conveys this overstepping of physical and spiritual parameters. Mention of interior decoration (a house, a bed, a table, and a purse, all shared in common) works similarly. Two noblemen, friends since childhood, love each other with "parfaicte amityé" ("perfect friendship"—*Hept*. 5.47.311; Chilton 410), the same phrase used in *nouvelle* #40 to refer to the count's sister's secret marriage. Here, however, Marguerite uses the phrase ironically, for the crucial element, *chrestienté*, previously placed in apposition to "parfaicte amityé," is lacking. While the two friends in *nouvelle* #47 are still bachelors, their communal lifestyle is not problematic. One of them decides to wed, rupturing their relationship, which had formed one person out of two entities ("ce n'estoit que un cueur"; "they were one in heart and mind"—*Hept.* 5.47.311; Chilton 410; "ilz vivoient non seulement comme deux freres, mais comme ung homme tout seul"; "they lived as if they were one man"—*Hept.* 5.47.312; Chilton 410). Their union and harmony is divided and, even though they place all their possessions in the common pot ("leurs biens estoient tous en commung"; "their belongings were held in common"—*Hept.* 5.47.312; Chilton 410), the addition of the wife to one man's list of possessions, as a "good" which he does not quite fully share with his friend, troubles the latter: "quant ilz estoient en quelque logis estroict, ne laissoit à le faire coucher avecq sa femme et luy: il est vray qu'il estoit au millieu" ("if they ever had to stay in cramped quarters, he did not hesitate to let him sleep in the same bed as himself and his wife—though it is true that he slept in the middle"—*Hept.* 5.47.312; Chilton 410).

The qualifier "il est vray que" adds the recognition of a change in the friends' relationship, that now something is withheld from the formerly mutual experience. The husband, who had instructed his wife to treat his friend as himself "en toutes ses choses" ("treat his friend in all things … just as affectionately as she treated him"—*Hept.* 5.47.312; Chilton 410), had quickly set limits on his statement: "hors mys une" ("in all things but one"—*Hept.* 5.48.313; Chilton 410). The problems of exclusive possession soon manifest themselves, as the husband begins to speak poorly of his friend to his wife. Formerly, "ce n'estoit que un cueur, que une maison, ung lict, une table et une bource" ("as they were one in heart and mind, so in house, bed, board and purse they were as one"—*Hept.* 5.48.311; Chilton 410). While they do still share their money, there now is a *bource* that they do not share: the *bource*[13] of the wife. The friends begin to quarrel, and the friend upbraids the husband for not speaking directly to him if something is wrong: "vous estes bien fort jaloux de vostre femme et de moy, mais le me voullez couvrir, afin que vostre maladie dure … [et] tourne … en hayne" ("you are jealous … I urge you to tell me if you have the slightest suspicion, so that I may set the matter right and so that we do not permit our friendship to be destroyed"—*Hept.* 5.47.313–14; Chilton 411).

Finally, the friend decides to leave. Separation is the key word for this story: "puisque le soupson vous a separé de mon amityé, le despit me separera de la vostre" ("for as your suspicion has destroyed my love for you, now your love for me will be destroyed by my anger!"—*Hept.* 5.47.314; Chilton 412). While pronouns and adjectives distinguishing between the two individuals or their possessions were not mentioned in the earlier story, possessive pronouns[14] now proliferate and create tension. The friends' statements to each other mime the disintegration of the relationship. Whereas formerly the restriction "ne … que" had collapsed the two distinctions into an apparently seamless entity ("ce n'estoit que ung cueur"), further emphasized by the number one ("ung"), rather than by any distinguishing marks of possession: "ce n'estoit que *un* cueur, que *une* maison …," now the two exist at cross-purposes and in disunity.

The material realm reflects the psychological schism. The friend removes from their dwelling the furniture belonging to him, which, until this point, was never so designated: "il … retire sa part de ses meubles et biens, qui estoient tous en commung; et furent avecq leurs cueurs abuse separez" ("he moved out his share in the goods and chattels which they had previously held in common. With this division of their property the union of their hearts was finally dissolved"—*Hept.* 5.47.314; Chilton 412). *Estoient,* the imperfect tense, evokes a long, harmonious past relationship that the past simple tense, *furent,* abruptly and definitively terminates.

Nouvelle #47 constructs a contrastive diptych with *nouvelle* #38. Motivated by her charitable concern, the wife in *nouvelle* #38 brought her own furniture (formerly shared with the husband in the conjugal household) to the suspect space he shared with his lover, in order to decorate that lodging comfortably. However, in *nouvelle* #47, the spitefulness begun by the husband's jealousy culminates in the friend angrily *removing* his furniture from the space of their former idyllic happiness.

The emotional arithmetic of addition and subtraction tilts toward a total of bitterness and failure, along with the tendency to treat people as commodities or to value possessions over people. The friend not only demands his personal share of possessions once shared communally, but, treating the wife as a commodity, "steals" her from her husband by cuckolding him ("… aussi separez, qu'ilz avoient esté uniz, en sorte que le gentilhomme qui n'estoit poinct marié ne cessa jamais qu'il n'eust faict son compaignon coqu"; "as he had promised, the unmarried gentleman did not rest till he had cuckolded his friend"—*Hept.* 5.47.314 ; Chilton 412). Through this vengeful act of cuckoldry, *nouvelle* #47 portrays the consequences of Old Testament legalism ("an eye for an eye") contrasted with the restoration of relationship and personhood enacted in evangelical *nouvell*e #38 through the pardon proffered by the loving wife. In *nouvelle* #47, emotions have become objects, physical obstructions to the continuation of relationships. The interior decoration of the souls of the two former friends is furnished with resentment and distrust, the trappings of a failed friendship.

For early moderns, furniture was considered to be miniaturized versions of architecture: many seat backs, or cabinet tops, had columnar motifs and ornamentation customarily found on building frontals. Some furniture also had ecclesiastical motifs.[15] Thus, materiality, space, and theology often conjoined in early modern furniture. Contrarily, the artifact might appropriate theological motifs, but be used in such a way that it clearly disassociated itself from its initial theological context. Early modern aristocratic subjectivity developed in and through an appropriation of spaces increasingly starkly delineated each from the other, and especially from the spaces of others. *Nouvelle* #47 replicates this phenomenon with the deliberate disjunction between *en commung* and *separez*. The friend's decision to reclaim certain pieces of furniture as "*ses* meubles et biens" demonstrates a walling-up of the self, through a focus on material possessions, against his former friend.

Commodity culture, and the evangelical perplexity over what to do with profit, were issues that increasingly troubled the time period:

> Calvinism and its ambivalence toward worldly wealth shaped ... [other European *bourgeois*] ... whose homes were understood to provide protection against the corruption of the material world (although rooms were beautifully decorated with material things).[16]

The *Heptaméron* illustrates this tension between material profit and spiritual purity.

Nouvelle #55 includes many decorative arts furnishings, among them gilded frames ("dorures") and paintings ("painctures"). This tale concerns a woman who distorts the intention of her deceased husband's will. Motivated by self-interest and avarice, she "reads in" her own meaning: "la veuve d'un marchant accomplit le testament de son mary, interpretant son intention au proffict d'elle et de ses enfans" ("the widow of a merchant put into effect her husband's last will and testament, interpreting its intention for her profit and that of her children"—*Hept.* 6.55.345).[17] The term *accomplit* and the fact that the woman is reading her own meaning ("interpretoit") and desires into the will sets the stage for a drama of deception. The widow's motives are suspect, and she seeks to "save herself" materially by *works*—by distorting through willfully misreading so as to keep the money, rather than through faith (looking to Divine Providence to provide for her and her progeny). Thysell elucidates this importance of the distinction between salvation by faith and by grace, as opposed to "works righteousness," referring to other of Marguerite's texts, and stating that

> ... the problems arise from that which Marguerite de Navarre would characterize as *cuyder*, or the false belief and pride in one's own strength and ability to save oneself or the belief that one's natural desires are inherently good and should not be restrained ... [in] the theology of works [as portrayed by Marguerite] ... self-determination becomes self-destruction.[18]

The "testament" is not merely a document to be deciphered whose intentions are then misread; it is also a text possessing a palimpsest-like relationship to Scripture: it offers a prototype for explication potentially applicable to any text.[19] Thus, the woman not only alters her husband's will; in so doing, she also tampers with God's Word.

The last will and testament also illustrates Marguerite's awareness of a dialectic between materiality and metaphysics: the concerns and circumstances of its drafting conjoin the disposition of earthly goods with preparation for eternal life. Many early modern wills include confessions of wrongdoing, protestations of orthodoxy, and provisions for almsgiving: in essence, a final editing or re-interpreting of one's life, and an attempt to rectify its errors by valuing metaphysics over materiality. Such is the case with the merchant's document: "ung riche marchant, lequel, voyant sa mort approcher, et qu'il ne povoit plus tenir ses biens, que peut estre avoit acquis avecq mauvaise foy, pensa que, en faisant quelque petit present à Dieu, il satisferoit, après sa mort, en partye à ses pechez: comme si Dieu donnoit sa grace pour argent!" ("a rich merchant [who] seeing that his death was near, and that he could not take his wealth with him—wealth which perhaps he had not acquired altogether honestly—he thought that he might make some amends for his sins by making some little donation or other to God. As if God grants his grace in return for money!"—*Hept.* 6.55.345; Chilton 448). The merchant, apparently, was a bit of a shady character in days gone by ("avoit acquis avec mauvaise foy"). Marguerite's use of the term *mauvaise foy* points to the next section of the text, in which the merchant, who has finally begun to heed the Gospel precept of not storing up earthly treasures ("voyant … qu'il ne povoit plus tenir ses biens"), tries to atone for his sins through works-righteousness ("il satisferoit … en quelque part à ses pechez"), a practice distrusted by evangelicals. The trouble is that once a merchant, always a merchant. The sentiment and intent of the will are flawed because the merchant is trying to strike a bargain with God ("en faisant quelque petit present à Dieu"). Marguerite quickly sets the reader straight on that score, indignantly exclaiming, "comme si Dieu donnoit sa grace pour argent!" The exclamation point underscores the bad theology inherent in the eleventh-hour deal that the merchant envisions.

The merchant, compelled by his impending death to cease commercial transactions, is misguidedly trying to "close a deal," in a sort of metaphysical horse-trade. He decides to sell one of his horses and give the money to the poor, and asks his wife to distribute the alms as he specifies. However, after he is buried, his wife decides that such a dispossession of goods would not be to her advantage, and determines not to "perdre les biens" ("los[e] his property"—*Hept.* 6.55.345; Chilton 448). Her solution of how to deal with the *testament* turns on a misinterpretation of it, rationalized via a distorted application of the Pauline distinction between the "spirit" and the "letter" of a text ("for the letter killeth, but the spirit giveth life"): "Si est-ce que je ne vouldrois desobeyr à sa parolle, mais oy bien faire meilleure son intention" ("Not that I want to disobey his instructions. In fact, I want to carry out his wishes even better than he intended"—*Hept.* 6.55.345; Chilton 448). She decides to infuse the literal statement of his wishes with the spirit of her own self-interested interpretation. She will make the will better ("meilleure"), that is, profitable for her.

Next, the merchant's wife shows that she has been an avid pupil of her husband's questionable mercantile enterprises, for she devises a clever plan involving some juggling in accounting. The financial accounting that she proposes parallels the spiritual accounting—coupled with financial consideration—in the *testament* (which she disregards, claiming that her husband had been "seduict par l'avarice des prebstres" ("seduced by priests' greed"—*Hept.* 6.55.345—utterly disregarding her own greed!). She instructs her servants to sell the master's horse for one ducat, and a cat for ninety-nine ducats. The purchaser, "estim[ant] avoir raisonnable marché" ("finding this a reasonable deal"—*Hept.* 6.55.346), readily acquiesces, whereupon the wife gives the one ducat from the sale of the horse to the poor (following the letter of the *testament* rigorously, but certainly not observing its spirit), and keeps the ninety-nine coins from the sale of the cat for herself: "[la] maistresse fut fort joieuse; et ne faillyt pas de donner le ducat … aux pauvres … comme son mary avoit ordonné et retint le demorant pour subvenir à elle" ("the mistress was extremely pleased, and lost no time in giving away the proceeds from the sale of the horse to the poor mendicants. As for the rest, that went to provide for the wants of herself and her children"—*Hept.* 6.55.346; Chilton 449). The schism between the husband's intention and the wife's self-serving construction of it is underscored by the ironic repetition of the assurance "comme son mary avoit ordonné": she has indeed followed the letter, but not fulfilled the spirit, of the document.

The *devisants'* discussion of the transaction develops from their scrutiny of market economy, different kinds of *prouffict,* and the dichotomy between material gain and metaphysical reward. The wife clearly cares more for her earthly well-being than for her moral and spiritual rectitude, as one of the *devisants* sarcastically observes.[20] The widow has made a self-serving deal: she has traded *bien* (moral good) for *biens* (material possessions).[21] In this, she is in morally worse straits than the deceased merchant who tried to buy off God, placating Him with alms for the poor, for she takes no care for the poor at all, seeking only to fulfill her own desires.

Of course, Marguerite stipulates that no efficacy obtains in the merchant's ploy either, which similarly was not the fruit of altruism but rather of self-interest:

> car vous verrez ordinairement les plus grands usuriers qui soient poinct, faire les plus belles et triomphantes chappelles que l'on sçauroit veoir, voulans appaiser Dieu, pour cent mille ducatz de larcin, de dix mille ducatz de edifices, comme si Dieu ne sçavoit compter.
>
> ("It's common to see the world's greatest usurers putting up ornate and impressive chapels, in the hope of appeasing God for hundreds of thousands of ducats' worth of sheer robbery by spending ten thousand ducats on a building! As if God didn't know how to count!"—*Hept.* 6.55.346–47; Chilton 449)

Marguerite keeps the accounting ledger intentionally in the red here: clearly, 10,000 ducats spent on buildings do not compensate for 100,000 ducats stolen (nor would an exact accounting expiate the sin, she implies). The faulty arithmetic underscores the cupidity and underhandedness of the merchant and his wife: even though God doesn't accept such payoffs, the deal proposed would be really bad business, tantamount to trying to cheat God, a sort of shell-game performed with worldly goods. Marguerite emphasizes the erroneous calculation set forth in the example meant to mirror the merchant's proposition by using the term *usurier,* as though the merchant finds 10,000 to be the equivalent of 100,000, once he has skimmed off the interest! She also points out the skewed mathematics that tries to make an equation of artificial constructions as a restitution for moral wrongdoing: the pain and injury caused by extensive *larcin* could never be repaired with a building, however "triomphante" that "chappelle" might be.

The term *triomphante,* in fact, points to the misguided hubris behind the proposed trade-off. Oisille continues the reference to worldly constructions by enumerating precious things and decorative arts objects, which weigh heavily in gold and in prestige yet which, she reminds us, do not impress God: "Vrayement, je m'en suis maintesfoys esbahye, dist Oisille, comment ilz cuydent apaiser Dieu par les choses que luymesmes estant sur terre a reprouvées, comme grands bastimens, dorures, fars et painctures" ("'indeed, I am frequently astonished,' said Oisille, 'that they presume to be able to appease God by means of the very things, which, when He came to earth, He condemned—things such as fine buildings, gilded ornaments, decorations and paintings'"—*Hept.* 6.55.347; Chilton 450).

The equation between "good works" and works of art associates material production with "works-righteousness": good deeds are also a form of human production, cunningly crafted in the mistaken hope of securing salvation. Scripture alone (*sola scriptura*) is the evangelical answer: performative acts and artistic production have no merit in themselves. The only construction of interest to God is the configuration of interior space, the "temple," as St. Paul terms it, composed of the believer's heart—and its interior decoration should feature spiritual attitudes and dispositions such as contrition and humility:

> Mais, s'ilz entendoient bien que Dieu a dict, à ung passaige, que pour toute oblation il nous demande le cueur contrict et humilié, et, en ung aultre, sainct Pol dist que nous sommes le temple de Dieu où il veult habiter, ilz eussent mys peyne d'aorner leur conscience durant leur vye.
>
> ("But, if they rightly understand what God has said of human offerings in a certain passage—that 'the sacrifice to God is a troubled spirit: a broken and contrite heart, O God, shalt thou not despise'—and again, in another passage, what

> Saint Paul has said—that 'ye are the temple of the living God, in which He will dwell'—if they had rightly heard these words, I say, they would have taken pains to adorn their conscience while they were yet alive."—*Hept.* 7.55.347; Chilton 450)

Without reliance on God and attentiveness to Scripture ("s'ilz entendoient bien ce que Dieu a dict"), the work of human hands is unavailing and suspect. The only "interior decoration" worth envisioning, Oisille concludes, is not that found in "grands bastimens," not that composed of gilded wood and painted boards, but rather the act of beautifying the conscience with virtue ("aorner leurs consciences").

After several such *comptes* and calculations, the commentators reach the conclusion that the merchant and his wife should have stopped investing in trade and ceased accumulating possessions, in order to attend to their spiritual selves. Marguerite reinforces the lesson with an image. Tympani of many contemporary cathedrals displayed representations of "Christ in Judgement" dispatching sinners to hell and receiving saints in heaven. Another late-medieval/early modern judgment theme was the image of Christ holding scales like a merchant, weighing heavy sinners and releasing lighter-than-air souls bound heavenward. Figuratively and eschatologically, this image reversed customary commercial practice, which deemed that products weighing more were worthier, and that lighter objects were lesser in value. Marguerite alludes to a similar image in her narrative, speaking the idiom of the marketplace so that the merchant's wife, and those who resemble her, may hear and understand: "Mais Celluy qui congnoist le cueur ne peut estre trompé; et les jugera non seullement selon les œuvres, mais selon la foy et charité qu'ilz ont eues à luy" ("But He who reads men's hearts will not be deceived, and He will judge them not only according to their works, but according to the faith and charity that they have shown towards Him"—*Hept.* 6.55.347; Chilton 450). *Fides* and *caritas* will further lighten the scales in favor of the penitent. The sentence structure imitates this balancing act: *jugera* initiates the image, *œuvres* occupies one side of the scales, *mais* is the division between the two trays of the balance, and *foy ou charité*, two possibilities added to the one side, tip the balance in favor of a salvific outcome.

The Netherlandish painter Quentin Metys, in several of his paintings termed his "banker pictures," explored through the medium of money the fraught relationship between materiality and metaphysics.[22] Metys's treatment of this genre invariably "juxtapose[d] the love of coin with the true redemption of grace and faith."[23] Particularly in "The Money Changer and His Wife," the woman ponders the scales as though assessing the weight of the material world compared to spiritual values—and the relevance of these measurements to her marriage.[24] This "storytelling painting," like many painted by evangelicals[25] is akin to Marguerite's narrative: replete with detail, it features worldly objects as painterly points of narrative development, representing preoccupations similar to those of the *nouvelles* on canvas.

Marguerite repeatedly makes the point that attempts to purchase earthly happiness, as well as attempts to secure assurances of salvation, are as unproductive and as mercurial as the market-place. In *nouvelle* #50, a man unsuccessfully woos a lady by showering her with precious objects. Marguerite uses an unexpected term to describe his attempt. For "court," "woo," or "seduce," she uses *pourchatz* ("to pursue or approach"; more commonly, "to purchase"). By allowing the possible mercantile meaning, Marguerite indicates that the man's suit depends on material objects and that, no matter what gifts he might bestow on the object of his affection ("pour pourchatz qu'il sceut faire, ne povoit avoir d'elle la responce qu'il desiroit"; "no matter how he approached her he could not obtain the answer he desired"—*Hept.* 5.50.323–24; Chilton 424), he will not receive her favor. Marguerite's implication is that his suit will be unavailing, because his approach is wrong: it is founded on earthly treasure rather than derived from a spiritual valuation of the woman he claims to love.

The repetition of *pourchatz* conveys the sense of a commercial transaction, similar to the emphasis placed on monetary value over metaphysical worth in *nouvelle* #55. *Nouvelle* #59 also develops this theme, using as illustration apparel, furniture, expensive objects, and the luxurious space of the court. The woman who possesses all these things adorns herself like a glittering object before the king "pour entretenir sa gorgiaseté et pour suyvre la court" ("so that she could follow the court and maintain her elegant style of life"—*Hept.* 6.59.360; Chilton 465). She demands financial favors and presents from her husband as part of a deal, which he has initiated, that she will take no more lovers: formerly, she cuckolded him with men; now she prostitutes herself for things. The term *gorgias* has already been associated in the *nouvelles* not only with beauty but also with vanity. The term recurs here, as the text transforms the woman into a component in a *vanitas* painting: "elle aymoit si très fort les acoutremens, qu'il falloit qu'elle en eut des plus beaulx et riches qui fussent en la court" ("she loved the precious objects so much that she insisted on having the most beautiful and extravagant attire at the court"—*Hept.* 6.59.360–61; Chilton 465). As the woman makes an accounting of the objects that she claims to need, Marguerite links storytelling and money management by calling this tale not a *nouvelle*, but a *compte*: "la dame de qui vous avez faict le compte" ("the lady in the story you have just told"—*Hept.* 6.59.360; Chilton 465). While the tale is told about the woman by someone at the court—prior to Marguerite's transcription of it, which will transform it into a *nouvelle*—and consequently is rightly a "conte," or oral recounting, "compte" also puns on accounting and financial transactions.

More than one variant of financial bargain, and moral compromise, is transacted in this story. Angry with her husband for refusing to take her to court where he would have to satisfy her cravings for fashionable clothing and costly furnishings, the wife plans retaliation. She has learned that her husband has been propositioning her *femme de chambre*. The wife devises a second arrangement that will be materially advantageous to her; she blackmails her husband: "… elle pensoit bien faire son proffict … la joie estoit qu'elle esperoit prendre son mary en si grande faulte qu'il ne luy reprocheroit plus ses serviteurs ny le demeure de la court" ("it occurred to her that here was an opportunity she could turn to her advantage … she was pleased, because she now hoped to catch her husband out, and place him so much in the wrong that he would never again criticize her for her devoted servants or the time she spent at court"—*Hept.* 6.59.361; Chilton 465–66). She employs commercial language and tactics, instructing her servant to measure out her favors to the husband: "pria ceste fille d'accorder petit à petit à son mary ce qu'il luy demandoit, avecq les conditions qu'elle lui dist" ("she asked the girl to come round little by little to her husband's demands, on certain conditions which she laid down"—*Hept.* 6.59.361; Chilton 466). She gets the better of him in this consumer transaction. A vocabulary of consumer goods characterizes the exchange between the husband and the servant: she tells him she is poor; he reassures her that he'll make her rich ("qu'elle n'eut soulcy de toutes ces choses, car il la marieroit mieulx et plus richement que sa maistresse ne sçauroit faire"; "she was not to worry her head about such things—he would find her a better husband, and a better-off one, than her mistress ever could"—*Hept.* 6.59.361–62; Chilton 466). The servant enters into a separate narrative exchange with her mistress: while parceling out her charms to the husband "peu à peu," she gives to the mistress the entire accounting of their transactions ("entreprinse"): "luy compta tout le discours de son entreprinse bien au long" ("she told her all about the arrangement she had made with her husband"—*Hept.* 6.59.362; Chilton 466).[26]

Because the servant girl has recounted to her the husband's advances, the wife is able to catch him in the act of propositioning the maid. When he spins a yarn to exculpate himself, the wife refuses to bargain or to accept his version instead of the maid's story. She implies that the coinage he offers, and the tale he tells, are counterfeit: "elle, qui se congnoissoit en tel metail, ne le prenoit pas pour bon" ("the wife knew what to make of excuses like that"—*Hept.* 6.59.363; Chilton 468). Her refusal to do business with him in this matter leaves him unable to exculpate himself; as a result, she makes quite a good business deal for her future: he will never again keep her away from court, and he will supply her with every luxury good that she desires so that she may make a grand appearance: "Et, pour faire oblier entierement à la damoiselle ceste follye, la mena bientost à la court en tel ordre et si gorgiase, qu'elle avoit occasion de s'en contanter" ("and he, in order to make his wife forget his foolish aberration, lost no time in taking her to court—in such high style that she had every reason to be satisfied"—*Hept.* 6.59.364; Chilton 468–69). She indeed has reason to be *contante* of how the story (*conte*), and the ledger of moral accountability *(comptant)* registers in her favor. The story is her pay-off for the "hush money" he has offered: in the economy of this *nouvelle*, in which lust (*luxure*) and luxury are linked, the consequences of his ill behavior are represented as commodities.[27]

The reign of François Ier was bedeviled by financial stringency. He appears as a protagonist in *nouvelle* #62, a story that discusses monetary issues and narrative exchange. Marguerite states that the context for this story is "au temps du Roi François premier" ("in the reign of Francis the First"—*Hept.* 7.62.377; Chilton 485). The *nouvelle*'s attentiveness to context attests to the display of riches and power by François Ier; the narrative next demonstrates the illusory nature of material wealth. Telling stories is shown here to be a form of trade. The narrator offers an alternative scenario for envisioning the world; if the listener is compelled by it, learns from it, or finds pleasure in it, he purchases the tale for himself, then recounts it to others. This textual transmission replicates early modern commodity culture typical of François's court, and, unlike earlier oral tradition, is dependent on an object—the printed book—for its circulation.[28] The currency of this "purchase" is the reader's response or reaction to the tale: "bien dire … et en rire."

This *nouvelle* dramatizes how trust placed in things may be ill-founded, since objects here act as the primary vehicles for the disclosure of scurrilous secrets. A younger suitor pursues a virtuous young woman who is married to a much older man. The former determines to undermine the woman's resistance by placing her in a vulnerable position so that she won't be able to thwart his desire. One morning, he goes to her house early, after her husband has left. She is still in bed. He enters her room and climbs, still booted and spurred, into her bed, where he takes her by force. He threatens that if she divulges the occurrence he will claim that she had sent for him in her husband's absence. Two objects collaborate in the drama of disclosure. First, while only the two of them would have known what transpired, one of his spurs, unbeknownst to him, has caught in the sheet. The spur is emblematic of his lust; St. Paul calls lust a spur and a "goad," or a thorn in the flesh. The material proof of the man's misdeed thereby also literalizes his lust.

As his spur catches in the sheets, the *linceul* pulls away, revealing the woman's nakedness to her chambermaids entering the room.

This nakedness, however, also evokes the storyteller's inadvertent self-disclosure: forgetting to disguise the fact that she herself is the lady of whom she tells the story, she commits a *lapsus* and says to her listeners: "jamais femme ne fust si estonnée que moy, quand *je* me trouvay toute nue" ("No woman was ever as embarrassed as I was, when I found myself completely naked"—*Hept.* 7.62.378; Chilton 486). She intends the story itself to be a commodity, a material object to be traded to others. She packages the event in materiality's opacity so as to hide the truth at its core. But she betrays herself by having confidence in the ability of a thing to cover up for the misdeed. Now she tries, yet again, to pull back up over the naked truth the additional layer of third-person-singular narration with which she has sought to camouflage her own identity, a subterfuge that she herself unwittingly thwarts. The *devisants* use yet another material object to point out that, in losing her honor, she experiences a form of death to virtue: *linceul* is not only synonymous with *drap* or sheet; it can also signify a shroud:

> Je vous asseure, mes dames, que, si elle eut grand desplaisir à faire ung tel acte, elle en eust voullu avoir perdu la memoire. Mais, comme je vous ay dict, le peché seroit plus tost descouvert par elle-mesme, qu'il ne pourroit estre sceu, quant il n'est poinct couvert de la couverture que David dict rendre l'homme bien heureux.
>
> ("I can assure you, Ladies, that if this kind of act had been distasteful to her, she would have wanted to erase it completely from her memory. But as I've already said, a sin like hers would be revealed by the sinner herself sooner than it was discovered by other people, unless it were covered with that covering [which makes man blessed] ..."—*Hept.* 7.62.378–79; Chilton 486)

Without the covering that God provides for sin ("la couverture [qui] ... ren[d] l'homme bienheureux"), saving grace, she is lost. The material layer of covering, the bedsheet, metamorphoses linguistically into a shroud, or covering for a corpse, indicating that striving to cover up the truth produces mendacity, a prefiguration of metaphysical "death."

Verbal Adornment: The Scandalous Rhetoric of Preaching Plain Style

> Monseigneur le Daulphin ne voulloit que leur art y fut meslé … de paour que la beauty de la rhetorique feit tort en quelque partye à la verité de l'histoire.
>
> *Hept.* prologue.9

> [Les Cordeliers] parlent comme anges, et sont importuns comme diables.
>
> *Hept.* 1.5.37

> Il ne fault poinct craindre à scandalizer ceulx qui scandalisent tout le monde.
>
> *Hept.* 5.61.286

Preaching the Word with power and persuasion was a priority for evangelicals.[29] Logocentric to the core, channels and strategies for communication were primary concerns for them. Within their context of (and reacting against) clerical abuse, illiteracy, and the often hypocritical sermonizing by Catholic clergy, evangelicals discussed—and prescribed—how Scripture *should* be preached. Martin Luther's commentaries, sermons, and the compendium *Table Talk* all offered recipes for effective preaching.[30] Marguerite de Navarre read and translated several of Luther's tracts and texts. In "The Argument of St. Paul's Epistle to the Galatians," Martin Luther developed his own paradigm of how preaching should produce conversions, a process that Marguerite imitates in the *Heptaméron*:

> First, a man must be taught by the law to know himself, so that he may learn to sing: "All have sinned and fall short of the glory of God" (Rom. 3:23) … Now once a man has thus been humbled by the law and brought to the knowledge of himself, he becomes repentant … he despairs of his own strength; he looks about and sighs for the help of the

> Mediator. Then there comes, at the appropriate time, the saving word of the Gospel ... This is the beginning of salvation.[31]

Heptaméron Homiletics

Marguerite de Navarre's audience generally read the *Heptaméron* as a collection of secular, sometimes scabrous, stories. However, a coherent and well-developed homiletics manual can be discerned *en filigrane* subtending these stories: a how-to book for Protestant preachers. Often, its instructions develop through negative reference to what *not* to do: Marguerite frequently portrays monks and priors, Catholic preachers and confessors, but they are invariably shown acting in worldly and wanton ways: raping the daughter of their host, coercing a contribution to their personal finances, disavowing their promises of chastity and poverty. So when Marguerite does display them in the act of performing the sacraments of preaching, we should pay very close attention. Those occasions do not occur often, but they are telling. By casting a critical eye on how Catholic priests abuse their functions, Marguerite articulates a detailed and well-illustrated manual for how the message of the Gospel should be conveyed.[32] The *Heptaméron* makes thoughtful suggestions deriving from the period prior to the definitive split between Protestants and Catholics, exemplifying thereby the evangelical expectations for effective preaching.[33]

The role of storytelling in the *Heptaméron* serves another purpose: it aims at prescribing a corrective program to ameliorate the preaching function of the Church. This homiletical guidebook is all the more valuable because, like sixteenth-century evangelicals who sought to reform the Catholic church *from within*, it is encased within the larger structure of the *Heptaméron*, which acts as a sort of camouflage, or at least, an attractive wrapping, for its more serious message. While Calvin reproached Marguerite with Nicodemism—the refusal to take a stance publicly on faith issues[34]—it may be that Marguerite's ambitious program for preachers could more easily be accepted because of the unthreatening and appealing nature of its container. Her incorporation of such a "secondary text" is entirely consistent with Protestant strategies of subverting from within—of finding coded ways to make their theological statements even while experiencing overt persecution or at least official disapproval for their faith.[35] Marguerite delineates a "method," in miniature.[36]

Further, it is a Renaissance stylistic convention that texts have many layers and manifold meanings. Often, when a Renaissance writer wants to make a challenging point, he expresses his perspective using the *topos* of the banquet.[37] The *Heptaméron*, with its series of seven Days structured around church attendance, Bible reading, eating, and discussing, presents a similar format for the free expression of possibly problematic views. As the Eucharistic feast is itself a form of banquet, this literary convention nicely dovetails with Marguerite's theological concerns. What kind of conversation should we expect to overhear at this "sacramental" feast? Marguerite answers this question programmatically throughout the book, offering suggestions for effective preaching as well as illustrations of both good and bad expositions of Scripture. Gérard Defaux has demonstrated how closely many of Marguerite's tales conform to the church lectionary, with certain stories occurring on the Feast of Pentecost or the Nativity.[38] Marguerite takes this relationship among church calendar, scriptural intertext, and narrative development further, elucidating a full-fledged theory not only of when and in which venues to speak, but also of what matter and in what manner one should preach.

The Scandal of the Gospel

> But I fear, lest somehow as the serpent deceived Eve by his craftiness, so your minds may be corrupted from the simplicity that is in Christ. For if he who comes preaches another Jesus whom we have not preached …
>
> 2 Cor. 11.3

> Il est temps de parler des scandales auxquels nous avons assigné le second rang. Plusieurs se plaignent que l'Evangile est comme une source de tous discords, d'autant que si tost qu'il vient en avant, beaucoup de contentions s'eslevent, et mesmes les

> hommes s'enterpicquent, comme si une trompette avoit sonné l'arme.
>
> John Calvin
> *Des scandales*

> Il y a de bons, dist Oisille, et de mauvais. Et en fault poinct par que pour les mauvais ilz soient jugez.
>
> *Hept.* 3.30.186

Marguerite does not hesitate to state that there is good preaching and there is bad preaching. She distinguishes clergy who perform their functions well and devoutly[39] from what is, in her opinion, the majority of clergy who, like the cloaca of Cordeliers in the story of Madame de Roncex, epitomize all-too-earthly, bawdy, and bodily preoccupations.[40] She calls for a "prescheur suffisant et homme de bien" ("a competent, honest man"—*Hept.* 5.41.283; Chilton 377).[41] *Suffisant* means more than "adequate"; it implies a competence and an expertise, capacities and credence: Cotgrave renders *suffisant* as "fully; of good satisfaction; of worth" and even "a belly-full," which recalls Luther's very earthy applications of Scripture to daily-life contexts.[42]

Developing the personal and practical desiderata for evangelical preaching, Marguerite stipulates that preaching should satisfy both body and soul: "ma dame Oisille leur prepara ung desjuner spirituel d'un si bon goust, qu'il estoit suffisant pour fortiffier le corps et l'esperit" ("Oisille [prepared for them] a meal so nourishing that it sufficed to nourish both body and spirit"—*Hept.* 5.prologue.282; Chilton 376). Preaching should be tailored to the interests and needs of its audience, demonstrating a real concern for, and attention to, other souls:

> Hircan print la parolle et dist: "Ma dame … il nous fault quelque passetemps et exercice corporel; car si nous sommes en noz maisons, il nous fault la chasse et la vollerye, qui nous faict oblier mil folles pensées; et les dames ont leur mesnaige, leur ouvraige et quelquesfois les dances où elles prennent honneste exercice … vous … nous lirez au matin de la vie que tenoit nostre Seigneur Jesus-Christ, et les grandes et admirables euvres qu'il a faictes pour nous."

> ("Hircan began to speak and said: 'My lady … you must bear in mind that we have not yet become so mortified in the flesh that we are not in need of some sort of amusement and physical exercise in order to pass the time. After all, if we're at home, we've got our hunting and hawking to distract us from the thousand and one foolish thoughts that pass through one's mind. The ladies have their housework and their needlework. They have their dances, too, which provide a respectable way for them to get some exercise. All this leads me to suggest … read to us every morning about the life of our Lord Jesus Christ, and the great and wonderful things He has done for us.'"—*Hept.* prologue.1.8; Chilton 67)

Preaching thus offers earthly recreation, and re-creation in a spiritual sense, and provides a model on which the believer can mold his life.

For this reason, preaching must be truthful and unadulterated, following the mandate of Scripture that no word may be taken away from or added to it. Oisille assures her listener that "l'intention de mon histoire ne sortira poinct hors de la doctrine de la saincte Escripture" ("the intention of the story that I shall tell you will not be out of keeping with the teaching of Holy Scripture"—*Hept.* 6.prologue.328; Chilton 428). Marguerite tells her reader that she "ne dir[a] rien que pure verité" ("and every single one of them will be the unadulterated truth"—*Hept.* 1.11; Chilton 70). Through this statement, Marguerite implicitly equates her role as storyteller with that of preacher. Insisting that every tale she tells is true, she removes the taint of *fingere* (feigning, or lying) from the word *fiction*:

> ne vouluz croire en parolle de prescheur, si je ne la trouve conforme à celle de Dieu, qui est la vraye touche pour sçavoir les parolles vraies ou mensongeres … [nous] ne ser[ons] jamais trompez par fictions ny inventions humaines.
>
> ("I have refused to believe those preachers, unless what they say seems to me to conform to the word of God, which is the only true touchstone by which one can know whether one is hearing truth or falsehood."—*Hept.* 5.44.304; Chilton 400)[43]

It is significant that Marguerite's comments are addressed both to clergy and to laity. She intends that the laity will make their lives conform to, and embody, the message that they hear.[44] Preaching itself becomes a participatory phenomenon: if no conversion transpires, then true preaching has not taken place. In the *Heptaméron*, the personality of the Word—persuasive, plain, personal—is so potent that it erases the privilege customarily accorded to clergy.

Marguerite shows that clergy neglect their institutionalized duties to eavesdrop on the stories being shared (thus making the form of "lay preaching" in which the *devisants* are implicitly involved more compelling than clerical functions). This secretive approach by the monks typifies the covert and shameful conduct of the clergy in general.

> avecq les autres, entra dedans l'eglise, où ils trouverent vespres très bien sonnés, mais ilz ne trouverent pas ung religieux pour les dire, pource qu'ilz avoient entendu que dedans le pré s'assembloit ceste compaignye … et … comme ceulx qui aymoient mieulx leurs plaisirs, que les oraisons, s'estoient allez cacher dedans une fosse … et là avoient si bien escouté les bealux comptes qu'ilz n'avoient poinct ouy sonner la cloche de leur monastere … ce qui paroist bien, quand ilz arriverent en telle haste, que quasi l'alaine leur falloit à commencer vespres.
>
> ("they went into the church. They found that although the bell had been ringing heartily for vespers, not a single monk had yet appeared. The fact was that they had heard that the ladies and gentlemen were meeting together in the meadow to recount all manner of amusing tales and, preferring their pleasures to their prayers, they had been hiding in a ditch … so attentively had they been listening, they had not even heard their own monastery bell ringing. The consequence was that they came scurrying to their places in such a hurry that they hardly had enough breath left to start singing the service!"—*Hept*. 2.20.156; Chilton 234)

The monks are out of breath—they lack "alaine"—which indicates that they lack the in-spir-ation or the guidance of the Holy Spirit *(ruach* is Hebrew for both Spirit and breath) needed to preach well or to perform their functions properly. When the *devisants* entered the church they had found it empty, attesting to the spiritual bankruptcy of the clergy and the paucity of preaching.

Proper preaching, Marguerite tells us, ensues from learning and study[45]: "Madame Oisille ... avoit ... estudié la leçon qu'elle debvoit lire" ("ha[d] spent more than half an hour studying the lesson that she was to read to them"—*Hept.* 3.prologue.157; Chilton 235). Marguerite disparages unschooled and often illiterate clergy: "vous veulx-je racompter ung tour que feit ung prestre ... de toutes ... choses estoit-il si ignorant, que à peyne sçavoit-il lire sa messe" ("I shall tell you a tale about a trick perpetrated by a priest—a priest whose only teacher was love, for the man was so ignorant in all other matters that he was scarcely capable of reading his masses!"—*Hept.* 3.28.226; Chilton 316). This emphasis on the ability to read and to interpret is consistent with the significant contribution that Protestantism made to literacy throughout Europe; because of the need for each person to be able to read the Bible for himself, analphabetism dwindled especially, but not exclusively, in urban areas as a direct consequence of this evangelical intervention.[46] Marguerite observes, further, that learning alone will not suffice: inspiration is required, as well.

Marguerite recommends that the writer should be filled with the Word, just as the Word should occupy fully the space in which it is preached and heard. Usually in the *Heptaméron*, Marguerite portrays an anti-type of this desideratum: churches function more as theaters for social interaction or stages for seduction; they offer secular pretexts rather than spiritual opportunities. For example, a man trying to seduce a lady learns that she regularly attends mass, so he goes daily to church so as to be able to stare at her: "il ne demourast autant à l'eglise qu'il povoit avoir le bien de la veoir; et tant qu'elle y estoit, la contemploit de ... grande affection" ("he would always ... linger as long as possible just for the pleasure of gazing upon her"—*Hept.* 2.16.130; Chilton 205). Marguerite underscores that his attention to her is misplaced and inappropriate, substituting a visual idol for contemplation rather than focusing on the Author of his salvation. At the worst, churches are used blasphemously to facilitate sacrilegious acts or sorcery, as in the case of the wooden images that the magician Gallery instructs an evil-wishing woman to bury beneath the high altar after reciting abracadabras.[47]

While in the case of the man who stared at his object of desire in church, the imagination was wrongfully engaged, Marguerite shows that there is a role for the imagination in preaching. However, she stipulates that, if any figures of speech are employed, they should be directly applicable to the matter being preached, and should please the mind's eye: "A fin … que les signes et miracles, suyvant ma veritable parolle, vous puissent induire à y adjouster foy" ("in order that signs and wonders may prove the truth of my words, and bring you to believe in them …"—*Hept.* 1.8.49; Chilton 114). Preaching needs to be disciplined and well structured; any anecdote or illustration should fit the lesson ("comme vous verrez par l'histoire que je vous voys raconter"; "for such indeed is the case, as you will now see from my story"—*Hept.* 3.prologue.158; Chilton 215), and nothing extraneous, diverting, or wandering from the Word should be condoned: "que vostre foy … [ne suit] … diverty de son droit chemin" ("that your faith [be not] diverted from the straight and narrow path"—*Hept.* 3.22.186; Chilton 266). The preacher must proclaim truth, however tough that truth might be; preaching cannot be casuistical (as in the case of the preacher who told a woman "qu'il valloit mieulx faire mal par le conseil des docteurs, que faire bien" ("it was better to do something wrong on the advice of the doctors of the Church, than to do a good act in the belief that one was inspired by the Holy Spirit"—*Hept.* 6.56.348; Chilton 451) or self-serving (as in the case of the man who tries to seduce a woman by saying that God had found it necessary to reveal Himself in flesh and that therefore, he, the man, finds it necessary to touch divine perfection in her female flesh. The woman responds, ironically, "Monseigneur, je n'entreprendz pas de responder à vostre theologies"; "Monsieur, I cannot guess what state your conscience is in"—*Hept.* 3.26.215; Chilton 297).

Earthly pleasures *properly* employed, however, may lead to metaphysical epiphanies: "Car, par les choses visibles, on est tiré à l'amour des invisibles" ("for it is through things visible that one is drawn to the love of things invisible"—*Hept.* 2.19.152; Chilton 230). There is a progressive movement in the *Heptaméron* away from ritualized religious observance to a reliance on the audition of the Word as both more attractive and more efficacious.

> Oisille leur dist: "Il me semble que ceste Journée soyt passée si joyeusement, que, si nous continuons ainsi les aultres, nous accoursirons le temps à faire d'honnestes propos. Mais voyez où est le soleil, et oyez la cloche de l'abbaye, qui, long temps a, nous appelle à vespres, dont je ne vous ay point advertiz; car la devotion d'oyr la fin du compte estoit plus grande que celle d'oyr vespres."
>
> ("Then Oisille turned to them and said: 'I think it has been a delightful day, and if the remaining days are equally enjoyable, then we shall have seen how swiftly the time can be made to pass in refined conversation. See how low the sun is already. And listen to the Abbey bell calling us to vespers! It started ringing a while ago, but I didn't draw your attention to it because your desire to hear the end of the story was more devout than your desire to hear vespers!"—*Hept.* 1.10.84–85; Chilton 154)

This shift anticipates the Protestant phenomenon in which religious observance increasingly occurs in the home rather than in consecrated space, and the Protestant patriarch leads family prayers and Bible reading.[48] Also very Protestant is the expectation of integrity in the preacher's life, not just in his preaching. The moral and exemplary role of the pastor is underscored, and no donatism is allowed: the priest must be worthy to perform the sacraments and worthy to preach Holy Scripture: "C'est grande pitié, dist Oisille, que ceulx qui ont l'administration des sacremens en jouent ainsy à la pelotte: on les debvroit brusler tout en vye" ("'It is a great shame,' said Oisille,'that men who are in charge of the administration of the sacraments should play about with them in this frivolous way. They ought to be burned alive!'"—*Hept.* 3.23.193; Chilton 274).

Marguerite argued that the life of the preacher of the Gospel (whether clergy or laity) must be above reproach, worthy of the message; otherwise the preaching will be in vain. Indeed, the Word abusively preached will turn on the sinner and indict him rather than save him, as in the case of the Prior of St. Martin in the Fields, whose sexual advances to a young nun he has sought to legitimize under cover of the words of the Gospel, by distorting its precepts and applying them for this own purposes. Marguerite's tale states ironically that this prior "ne se faisoit reformation de religion, qui ne fust faicte par sa *main*" ("there was not a piece of monastic reform for which he did not have some responsibility"—*Hept.* 3.22.176; emphasis added; Chilton 255); indeed, his hand features very prominently in his salacious acts (rather than assisting in the sacraments, as it should): he raises her veil "avecq sa main" to gaze lustfully at her beautiful face; "luy voulut mectre la main au tetin" ("tried to put his hand on her breast"—*Hept.* 3.22.178; Chilton 257), embraces her, throws her on the bed, and "luy meit la main soubz la robbe, et tout ce qu'il peut toucher des ongles esgratina" ("he thrust his hand under her robe and scratched wildly at whatever came in contact with his nails"—*Hept.* 3.22.179; Chilton 258). Other clerics abuse their authority in the *Heptaméron*; Oisille is contemptuous of a Cordelier who tries to seduce a woman who comes to him for confession: "Vrayement, dist Oisille, voylà ung bien meschant Cordelier! Estre religieux, prestre et predicateur, et user de telle villenye, au jour de Noël, en l'eglise et soubz le manteau de confession" ("'Well,' said Oisille, 'that particular Franciscan was wicked indeed! His sin is all the worse because he was a monk, a priest and a preacher, and yet he could still do an evil thing like that, on Christmas day, in church and under cover of the confessional!'"—*Hept.* 5.41.285; Chilton 379).

Instead, appearance and being (*l'être* and *le paraître*) must conjoin for effective preaching to occur. All too frequent are cases like that of the Franciscan who is described as having "la contenance et la parolle toute contraire à son cueur" ("the way he spoke and the expression on his face were the opposite of what he felt in his heart"—*Hept.* 3.23.187; Chilton 267), or that of the Cordelier in the same story who hopes to sleep with his host's wife in lieu of saying his prayers, and who is reproached by the *devisants*' wordplay that judges him as being "plus actentif à la *vie active*, que à la vie contemplative" ("by this time more intent on the active than the contemplative life"—*Hept.* 3.23.189; emphasis added; Chilton 269). Such actions and demeanor are at odds with clerical vows and do a disservice to the Gospel and to its hearers: "souvent l'ange Sathan se transforme en ange de lumiere, afin que l'œil exterieur, aveuglé par l'apparence de sainctеté et devotion, ne s'arreste ad ce qu'il doibt fuir" ("often Satan transforms himself into an Angel of light—in order, I say, that your eye should not light on external things, blinded by the outward appearance of sanctity and devotion, and linger on those things that it ought to flee"—*Hept.* 3.22.186; Chilton 266). In the preceding examples and elsewhere in her text, Marguerite uses a consistent stylistic device, that of antithesis, to describe the disjunction between what is, and what should be. Antithesis was a rhetorical tool frequently used by other Protestant writers to establish clarity in a complex situation.[49]

In this way a more participatory and personalized paradigm for homiletics develops, rather than a top-down, hierarchical transmission from clergy to laity. The narratives of individual lives gain in significance, while traditional exemplary saints' lives are recited less frequently. Every evening, each *devisant* prepares the story planned for the next day:

> chascun avoit son compte si prest, qu'il leur tardoit qu'il ne fust mis en lumiere … Apres qu'ilz eurent ouy la leçon de madame Oisille, et la messe, où chascun recommanda à Dieu son esperit, afin qu'il leur donnast parolle …
>
> ("they had all prepared their stories, and could hardly wait to tell them. They listened to Madame Oisille's lesson and to mass, each of them offering their hearts and minds to God that He might inspire their words and grant His grace to continue their gathering …"—*Hept.* prologue.2.87; Chilton 155)

These tales become a method for describing their own concerns and interests, a textual screen for an awareness of their own, distinct identities.

Appropriately, Marguerite specifies that the Word should reveal what is hidden in men's motives and hearts. "Nous couvrons nostre diable du plus bel ange que nous pouvons trouver. Et, soubz ceste couverture, avant d'estre congneuz, recepvons beaucoup de bonnes cheres" ("We cover our devil with the most beautiful angel we can find. And, under this covering, before being recognized, we receive a lot of good things"—*Hept.* 2.12.96; Chilton 165). An indictment should ensue from such disclosure, one that will incite the hearer to repentance.[50] "Prescheur," as Marguerite uses it (and she only uses the term a few times), has a pejorative connotation, indicating one who says what he does not mean, or who seeks to manipulate through preaching. Marguerite points out such occasions, and hopes to correct them. For example, Geburon advises all women to flee men. He claims that the latter want to capture and use the former, but Hircan reproaches him for this hypocritical statement (Geburon has quite a reputation), labeling him a "prescheur" (which also rhymes with *pescheur*: "sinner") and saying, "depuis quel temps estes-vous devenu prescheur? J'ay bien veu que vous ne teniez pas ces propos" ("since when have you turned preacher? I remember a time when you weren't in the habit of saying that sort of thing"—*Hept.* 2.16.133; Chilton 208).

Preaching and storytelling progressively conjoin in the *Heptaméron*. Preaching is more potent when combined with the personal witness that storytelling adds: "elle sent plus la predication que son compte" ("it smacks more of sermonizing than of story-telling"—*Hept.* 3.26.221; Chilton 306). The *devisants*' commentaries turn all the *nouvelles* into effective sermons, as the tales become illustrations for the tellers' own glosses on Scripture: "Je sçay bien, ce dist Parlamente, que nous avons tous besoing de la grace de Dieu, pour ce que nous sommes tous encloz en peché; si est-ce que noz tentations ne sont pareilles aux vostres" ("'I accept,' said Parlamente, 'that we are all in need of God's grace, since we all incline to sin. Yet the fact is that our temptations are not the same as yours, and if we sin through pride, no one suffers for it, and neither our body nor our hands are tainted by it'"—*Hept.* 3.26.221; Chilton 305).

Further, technique is important so that the tale is well-told, thereby eliciting greater response: storytellers, and preachers, have an obligation not to bore ("ennuyer") their audience.

> Oisille sceut très bien sercher le passaige où l'Escripture reprent ceulx qui sont negligens d'oyr ceste saincte parolle; et non seullement leur lisoit le texte et leur faisoit tant de bonnes et sainctes expositions qu'il n'estoit possible de s'ennuyer à l'oyr.

> ("Oisille knew how to find the passage in which Scripture reproaches those who are negligent in listening to the sacred word. She not only read them the text, [but] she also gave such sound and devout expositions that no one could possibly find it boring."—*Hept.* 4.prologue.236; Chilton 324)

Good preaching requires both *explication* (explanation) and *exposition* (development or application of its teaching based on experience).[51] A balance needs to be reached, however, between experiential exposition and excessive self-involvement: the goal of effective preaching should be to remove the self: "Car amour de soy est une passion qui a plus tost saisy le cueur que l'on ne s'en advise" ("for [self-]love by its very nature is a passion which seizes the heart before one realizes it"—*Hept.* 4.35.260; Chilton 351). Hircan is pejoratively labeled by the others a "prescheur des dames" ("you have started to preach to the ladies"—*Hept.* 4.35.260; Chilton 351), for he has wrongfully used his rhetoric to deceive them, acting out of self-interest. His blandishments are sarcastically termed "ces beaulx sermons" ("these fine sermons"—*Hept.* 4.35.260; Chilton 351), and he is likened to an actual preacher who uses his office and persuasive powers to seduce another man's wife.

Thus, good preaching is not permitted to distort a scriptural passage or wrench a text out of context. Rather, it entails attentiveness and faithfulness to the intention of the Word:

> Il n'y a si beau passaige en l'Escripture, dist Oisille, que vous ne tirez à vostre propos. Mais gardez-vous de faire comme l'arignée qui convertit toute bonne viande en venyn. Et si vous advisez qu'il est dangereulx d'alleguer l'Escripture sans propos ne necessité!
>
> ("There is not a single text in Holy Scripture, however beautiful … that you would not turn to your own ends. But take care lest, like the spider, you turn wholesome meat into poison. Be you assured that it is indeed dangerous to draw on Scripture out of place and without necessity."—*Hept.* 4.36.265; Chilton 357)

The image of the spider ("arignée"), in the context of early modern natural history's understanding of it—that the spider takes good food and makes it into poison—illustrates the dangers of a-contextual preaching, and contrasts with Scripture's own self-characterization as possessing nutritive substances of milk and daily bread ("et, comme celle qui avoit toute consolation en Dieu, porta pour sa saulve garde, *norriture* et consolation, le Nouveau Testament"; "she was a woman who placed all her trust in Him, and for her preservation, nourishment and consolation she had brought her New Testament"—*Hept.* 7.67.393; emphasis added; Chilton 503).

Preaching must have Scripture as its sole foundation. This is the evangelical dictum of *sola scriptura:* "Ils sont ordonnez ... pour nous prescher l'Evangile" ("They are appointed by our prelates to preach the Gospel and admonish us for our sin"—*Hept.* 5.44.303; Chilton 399). Any other pretext is illegitimate:

> Le Cordelier ne s'estonna poinct de ces propos, mais luy dist: "Monseigneur, nostre religion est si bien fondée, que, tant que le monde sera monde, elle durera, car nostre fondement ne fauldra jamais, tant qu'ily aura sur la terre homme et femme." Monseigneur de Sedan, desirant sçavoir sur quel fondement estoit leur vie assignée ... Le Cordelier ... luy dist, "... nous sommes fondez sur la follye des femmes."
>
> ("The Franciscan was not at all taken aback by this, and simply said: 'Monseigneur, our order has a sure foundation, and it will endure for as long as the world endures. Never, as long as there are men and women on this earth, will the foundation on which our order rests fail us.'"—*Hept.* 5.44.302; Chilton 398)

The correlate is that, when preaching is entirely scripturally based, the listeners are to respond with absolute trust in it, as divinely inspired: "nous [sommes] tenuz ... de croire tout ce qu'ilz nous dient ... quant ilz ne parlent que de ce qui est en la saincte Escripture" ("We [are] bound on pain of mortal death to believe what they preach to us from the pulpit"—*Hept.* 5.44.303; Chilton 399).

Obviously, such acceptance occurs within a community of the scripturally literate ("... le Nouveau Testament, lequel on lisoit incessamment"; "she spent her time in reading the Scriptures"—*Hept.* 7.67.393; Chilton 504); it is therefore even more striking that such consensus and commonality of belief can be produced by good preaching. The *devisants* in the *Heptaméron* represent the community of readers and capable interpreters whom evangelical preachers should anticipate addressing: "Croiez, dist Oisille, que ceulx qui humblement et souvent la [la Bible] lisent, ne seront jamais trompez par fictions ny inventions humaines; car qui a l'esperit remply de verité ne peut recevoir la mensonge" ("'Be assured,' said Oisille, 'that whosoever reads the Scriptures often and with humility will never be deceived by human fabrications and inventions, for whosoever has his mind filled with truth can never be the victim of lies'"—*Hept.* 5.44.304; Chilton 400). Literary expertise is an evangelical expectation for both clergy (generally portrayed as illiterate or barely able to read in the *Heptaméron*) as well as for the laity (who were prevented from reading Scripture by the Catholic church in early modern Europe).

Awareness of context also ensures that nothing will be added to, or subtracted from, Scripture: "[Il faut] jamais ne mectre en doubte la parolle de Dieu et moins ne adjouster foy à celle des hommes" ("Heaven forbid that we should doubt Holy Scripture, for we are far from believing in your lies'"—*Hept.* 6.57.356; Chilton 459), Oisille instructs. In the same vein, she cautions against allowing any practices that are not scripturally authorized (a common evangelical criticism of many Catholic practices, such as the veneration of the saints):

> Voylà, mes dames, comment les chaisnes de sainct Pierre sont converties par les mauvais ministres en celles de Sathan, et si fortes à rompre, que les sacremens que chassent les diables des corps sont à ceulx-cy les moiens de les faire plus longuement demeurer.
>
> ("Thus, Ladies, are the chains of Saint Peter turned by corrupt ministers of the Church into the chains of Satan, chains so hard to break that the sacraments which cast devils form the body are for such people as these the means whereby devils are kept in their conscience even longer."—*Hept.* 7.61.376; Chilton 483)

Through such scrupulosity, the preacher will avoid the worldly pitfall that Parlamente warns against: "l'opinion des mauvais hommes qui prennent ung passaige de l'Escripture pour eulx et laissent celluy qui leur est contraire" ("you're as bad as all the other men who take a passage from Scripture which serves their purposes, and leave out anything that contradicts it"—*Hept.* 7.67.394; Chilton 505).

If the primer for preaching that Marguerite provides in the *Heptaméron* is followed, preaching will prove spiritually profitable; it will produce *profit*: "que cest exemple vous soit si profitable" ("as I now hope to show you, with the example ..."—*Hept.* 4.36.265; Chilton 357). This profit will be realized in the reinstatement of moral rectitude: such sermons are "ordonnez ... pour nous reprendre de noz vices" ("appointed ... to preach the Gospel and admonish us for our sins"—*Hept.* 5.44.303; Chilton 399). The encouragement of contemplation, reflection, and discussion will also provide a profit of good preaching: "toute la compaignie fut fort attentive, en sorte qu'il leur sembloit bien jamais n'avoir oy sermon qui leur *proffitast* tant ... ilz ... s'alerent exercer à la contemplation de [ces] sainctz propos" ("the whole company was very attentive, and it seemed to them that they had never heard a sermon so much to their profit ... they went to exercise their souls in contemplation of the holy words to which they had just been listening"—*Hept.* 5.prologue.282; emphasis added; Chilton 376).

Recounting Conversions

Marguerite's *Heptaméron* thus doubles as a homiletics manual for evangelical preachers. The stories told play a dual role: they illustrate worldly issues, and they point to a metaphysical perspective. The stories are, in fact, the bridge that relates the two concerns, for the recounting of the tales stretches a bridge between speaker and listener, Word and word. The time that it takes to tell those tales allows the bridge that had been destroyed by the flood, hampering the travelers from continuing their journey and necessitating their tale-telling to pass the time, to be rebuilt. This bridge, projected for completion within three days, recalls Christ's body, which was raised up on the third day.

In addition, the *Heptaméron* itself represents—mimetically enacts—the conversion process that should ensue from proper preaching. The *devisants* have effectively composed their own, reformed lectionary: each reads his or her *roolle,* or part from the *rota*, and they all read together, as stipulated by Oisille, in the order that follows. The book begins with the worldliest concerns and reflections on lifestyles. These days begin and end with readings from St. Paul to the Romans, and the *devisants* mull over his practical, even stern, admonitions to a moral life. After these issues have been addressed, the reading changes to part of the Gospel of John, the mystic Gospel of love, which seeks to touch hearts. The terrain is prepared for conversion.[52] In fact, several of Marguerite's stories employ the term *pourchatz,* which has "preparation" as a possible meaning, and "eager pursuit … diligent solicitation … vehement following of a matter …" as its primary denotation, showing the zeal with which the interlocutors turn to the Word of God for inspiration, instruction, and emendation of their lives.[53] The nature of the readings again alters; we now hear from the Gospel of Luke, the physician, demonstrating Christ's healing power in lives. Finally, the *Heptaméron* culminates with the end of the Gospel of John and the description of the descent of the Holy Spirit at Pentecost as described in the beginning of the Acts of the Apostles. That very day the Mass of the Holy Spirit is being celebrated in the little church and, at last, the church is appropriately filled with scriptural activity ("l'on commenceoit la messe du Sainct Esperit"; "the mass of the Holy Spirit [was] about to begin"—*Hept.* 7.prologue.370; Chilton 476). Through preaching, teaching, and storytelling, the *devisants* have been molded into a community of believers ("en l'unyon [des] apostres"; "in the union and fellowship in which the apostles themselves prayed together"—*Hept.* 7.prologue.370; Chilton 476). As Oisille commences the final reading of the *Heptaméron* on the Seventh Day, the *devisants* receive the Holy Spirit and are now fully aware of their charge to "preach the Word at all times, both in season and out of season" (they are quite cognizant that this Mass of the Holy Spirit is no coincidence: rather, it "sembloit chose venir à leur propos"; "it was a matter directly related to their conversation"):

> Et, quant elle eut suffisamment leu et exposé le commencement de ce digne livre, elle les pria d'aller à l'eglise, en l'unyon que les apostres faisoient leur oraison, demandans à Dieu sa grace, laquelle n'est jamais refusée à ceulx qui en foy la requierent … l'on commenceoit la messe du Sainct Esperit, qui sembloit chose venir à leur propos.

> ("When she had thoroughly read and expounded the opening chapters of this noble book, she exhorted them all to go into church, in the union and fellowship in which the apostles themselves prayed together, and to seek God's grace, which is never refused to those who seek it by faith ... the mass of the Holy Spirit [was]about to begin. This seemed most appropriate ..."—*Hept.* 7.prologue.370; Chilton 476)

Marguerite here illustrates in narrative form Luther's morphology of conversion:

> The operation of grace was crucial in Luther's explanation of the Reformed doctrine of repentance, which he called the "true meaning of Christianity," and out of his two-stage theory of repentance came a "morphology of conversion" which was, in effect, a model for all the later ones. First, under the work of the law, the sinner saw his sinner and was sorry for it; only then, under grace, was he enabled to resolve or amend his life. That resolution was literally the turning-point or conversion.[54]

Thus, the direction taken by the series of readings, readings which frame the collection of stories within the *Heptaméron* itself, inflect the course of the readers' reception of the tales and prompt a change of heart, the conversion experience called for by evangelical preachers. Not only is the *Heptaméron* a manual for preachers, it offers a model for the effect such preaching should ultimately have: it is both method and message. In this way, the final plank in the bridge stretching from materiality to metaphysics, man to God, is set in place.

Conclusion

From Self to Soul

Treasures of the Heart

> For where your treasure is, there will your heart be also.
>
> Matt. 6.21

The eventual eschatological transformation of materiality manifests itself progressively as the earlier *nouvelles* of the *Heptaméron*, saturated with objects, are replaced in the text by a different sort of object in Books Six and Seven; more explicitly associated with economy, accounting, profit, and commercial transaction, these objects increasingly illustrate the conceits of contemporary commodity culture. However, the stories resolve materiality's unreliability by progressively moving away from reliance on objects as textual motors, so that by the final Day of the *Heptaméron*, the material presence is virtually non-existent.

This shift in emphasis begins as early as the Fourth Day, when the prologue constructs a *rapprochement* between secular stories and sacred narrative. Each narrative type produces its own sort of *joye*, but the former sort of story may only be profitable when re-read and interpreted in the new light of scriptural perspective. Secular stories thus experience the same treatment as do material objects: a useful starting-point, but never the final destination. On the path to salvation, they must either be discarded or transformed by faith:

> quant il congnoist … que ès choses territoires n'y a perfection ne felicité, [il] desire chercher le facteur et la source d'icelles … si Dieu … luy … ouvre l'œil de foy … car foy seullement peult monstrer et faire recevoir le bien que l'homme charnel et animal ne peult entendre.

> ("but once the soul has searched out these things and tried and tested them, once it has failed to find in them Him whom it loves, it passes beyond ... Yet, if God does not open the eyes of faith, they will be in danger of leaving ignorance behind only to become infidel philosophers. For only faith can reveal and make the soul receive that good which carnal and animal man cannot understand ..."—*Hept.* 2.19.152; Chilton 229)

The secular story is analogous to the space of the unrepentant human heart before it has received and responded to God's Word. Using the evangelical phrase *sola fidei*, Marguerite underscores the close relationship between the transformation in the tales she tells and the reforming of subjectivity to a spiritual perspective : "foy ... foy seullement." By turning away from the objects that decorate it, secular narrative imitates the necessary swerve away from self, an objectification, to establish identity in Christ: for an evangelical, spirituality constitutes true subjectivity.

Things function in the stories as components in the construction of a metaphorical bridge uniting man and God, moving from solipsism and self-scrutiny to salvation, a focus on soul that renounces earth in favor of heaven: "l'ame, qui n'est créée que pour retourner à son souverain bien, ne faict, tant qu'elle est dedans ce corps, que desirer d'y parvenir" ("for the soul, which was created solely that it might return to its Sovereign Good, ceaselessly desires to achieve this end while it is still within the body"—*Hept.* 2.19.151; Chilton 229). How does this happen? Creation is a paradoxical phenomenon. It makes concrete and literal a separation from the Creator, and its creatures henceforth can only know, and be fully known, through reintegration with their source:

> Mais, à cause que les sens, par lesquelz elle en peut avoir nouvelles, sont obscurs et charnelz par le peché du premier pere, ne luy peuvent monstrer que les choses visibles plus approchantes de la parfection, après quoy l'ame court, cuydans trouver, en une beaulté exterieure, en une grace visible et aux vertuz moralles, la souveraine beaulté, grace et vertu.
>
> ("But the senses, by means of which the soul is able to have intelligence of its Sovereign Good, are dim and carnal

> because of the sins of our forefather Adam and consequently can reveal to the soul only those things which are visible and have some nearer approximation to perfection. The soul runs after these things, vainly thinking that in some external beauty, in some visible grace and in the moral virtues it will find the sovereign beauty, the sovereign grace and the sovereign virtue."—*Hept.* 2.19.151; Chilton 229)

Objects are thus artifacts attesting to "otherness." Consequently, they must be removed from earthly existence.

Here, the narrative develops a morphology of the transformation whereby the soul, embodied in the self, moves in and through things of the world, realizing that they actually hinder its attempt to find God. At first, physical man perceives himself, and constructs his understanding of selfhood, through experience in the material world. The focus is on the senses (*sens*) because that is what is immediately available and accessible; from information provided by the senses, man "peult avoir nouvelles" of earthly experience as well as intimations of an existence that lies beyond. The *nouvelles* at this stage are firmly tethered to materiality.

However, although sin distorts perception's functioning ("sont obscurs et charnelz par le peché du premier pere"), a reminiscence of soul within the self nonetheless remains ("elle ne faict … que desirer y parvenir"). The soul yearns for things of beauty in the sublunar sphere, for these things dimly recall a lost state of perfection ("court [après], cuydans trouver, en une beaulté exterieure … la souveraine beaulté"). This equation of earthly virtue with spiritual perfection is thoroughly orthodox, deriving from the Pauline perspective of the incompleteness and shadowiness of worldly life, to be resolved someday by incorporation into spiritual wholeness and sightedness. Once the seeker has learned that meaning cannot be found in the earthly treasures that seem to proffer significance, she enters into the final stage, one characterized by the divestiture of material dross ("Mais, quant elle les a cerchez et experimentez, et elle n'y treuve poinct Celluy qu'elle ayme, elle passe oultre").

Nouvelle #19 describes this bridging movement ("passe oultre"; "passé par l'echelle") from apparent earthly sufficiency to absolute heavenly significance by contrasting the piling-up of inanimate objects ("elle estime richesses d'assembler des petites pierres"; "They think that the pebbles they collect will make them rich"—*Hept.* 2.19.152; Chilton 229) and the eventual turn, through a process of spiritual growth ("en croissant"; "and as they grow up"—*Hept.* 2.19.152; Chilton 229), to the need for live creatures, dialogue, the sort of interaction that Marguerite's stories encourage: "mais, en croissant, ayme les popines vives et amasse les biens necessaires pour la vie humaine" ("but, as they grow up, the dolls they love are living people and the things they collect are the necessities of human life"—*Hept.* 2.19.152; Chilton 229).

Finally, the soul is led to the immaterial spiritual virtues vital for salvation. *Biens*, goods, defined in an abstract sense, epitomize spiritual values rather than commodities traded for earthly gain. The *vives popines*, no longer inanimate puppets but now living creatures, prefigure the invigorating power of the Holy Spirit. This profile of how earthly treasures function in Marguerite's narrative program shows them to be material manifestations, or way-stations (*degrés*) on an itinerary that uses materiality paradoxically by dissolving it, at the end, into metaphysical awareness:

> encores je croy que Dieu ne se courrouce poinct de tel peché, veu que c'est ung degré pour monter à l'amour parfaicte de luy, où jamais nul ne monta, qu'il n'ait passé par l'eschelle de l'amour de ce monde.
>
> ("What is more, I believe that God is not angered by sin of this kind, since it is one step in the ascent to perfect love of Him, to which one cannot ascend without passing up the ladder of worldly love."—*Hept.* 4.36.265; Chilton 356–57)

Péché seems a paradoxical way of getting to God, yet by its very nature sin engenders the intense need for God's forgiveness, and, as such, is efficacious; similarly, the world, reinterpreted through story, is revealed as fallen, a perspective that propels the reader beyond illusory finitude.

As the *nouvelles* become less invested in the earthly realm, an increasingly spiritualized exposition is provided of the world, so that, by the Fifth Day, the prologue provides a different, nuanced definition of *nouvelle*: it is "ung desjuner spirituel … suffisant pour fortiffier le corps et l'esperit" ("a meal so nourishing that it sufficed to fortify both body and soul"—

Hept. 5.prologue.282; Chilton 376). This nourishment ("ceste viande si douce"; "this such sweet nourishment"—*Hept.* 6.prologue.328; Chilton 428), is the daily morning round of Bible reading that precedes each session of storytelling. The close association of Scripture and stories causes them to conjoin in effect, as well as implicitly suggests the model of biblical exposition for the interpretation of the tales that follow. *Nouvelle* is linked to scriptural *innutritio*: in both the Old Testament and New Testament, the Word of God offers the essential supernatural nourishment: "man does not live by bread alone, but by every word that proceeds from the mouth of the Lord" (Matt. 4.4). The terrestrial and the metaphysical then conjoin in a didactic moment: on the Sixth Day, Oisille, before telling a tale, reads aloud from 1 John, "l'epistre de Sainct Jehan l'evangeliste." Oisille assures her readers that her selection will not depart from scriptural guidelines. The narrative of the *Heptaméron* thus situates itself as introduced by and modeled upon Scripture, of which it offers an exposition in secular context. This is appropriate according to the evangelical understanding of the proper role of narrative.

The Sixth Day is set under the sign of the Holy Spirit. Pentecost supplies the various tongues needed not only to tell stories, but also to praise the Redeemer: "Au partir de là, s'en allèrent à la contemplation de la messe, où chacun se recommanda au Sainct Esperit, pour satisfaire ce jour-là à leur plaisante audience" ("afterwards they went to the contemplation of the mass, where they commended themselves to the Holy Spirit in order that they might that day satisfy those who would listen to them"—*Hept.* 6.prologue.328; Chilton 428). Another important function fulfilled by the gift of tongues at Pentecost is the recognition of one's identity as fully known only in Christ—those present heard the Word of God "in their own tongues"—a validation both of the human capacity to craft narrative and of the spiritual imprimatur accruing to such narrative properly applied. Earlier in the *Heptaméron*, the role of the *nouvelles* had been, at least in part, compensatory, composing a kind of appeal to humanity's fallen nature, while simultaneously prescribing a corrective to it:

> la malice des hommes mauvais est toujours telle qu'elle a esté, comme la bonté des bons. Tant que malice et bonté

> regneront sur la terre, ilz la rempliront tousjours de nouveaulx actes, combien qu'il est escript qu'il n'y a rien nouveau soubz le soleil. Mais à nous, qui n'avons esté appellez au conseil privé de Dieu … trouvons toutes choses nouvelles [et] … admirables.
>
> ("For the wickedness of evil men is the same now as it has always been. So too is the goodness of good men. As long as good and evil reign on the earth, the earth will be filled with new deeds, even though it is written that there is nothing new under the sun. For [we], who have not been called to God's privy council … [we] find all things new [and] wonderful."—*Hept.* 5.50.326–27; Chilton 427)

While earlier the *nouvelles* were marked by materiality, they now conform to divine story.

The *devisants* have constituted a secular frame for the stories to be discussed and, thereby, linked, within the larger frame of the *Heptaméron* as a collection; Scripture is the final frame that directs the reception of the tales. At Pentecost, which reverses the confusion of tongues at the Tower of Babel, the potential for the proliferation of divergent interpretive perspectives (like the debates among the *devisants*) subsides. Now the unity of the spirit of reception, if not the actual literal reading, obtains, fulfilling the exegetical goal of uniform understanding of a text.[1] It is significant that Marguerite's work, while aiming at univocity, remains polyvocal. The *devisants* do not all see or read or interpret as evangelically as Oisille, Parlamente, or Longarine. But, by allowing such difference through the invitation extended to the "other"—the dialogue engaged in with a different perspective—all humanity is ushered into the ranks of the *Heptaméron*'s readers, where, Marguerite hopes, the evangelical message seeded between its lines will bear fruit in many different sorts of souls. "Ne voyez-vous pas bien, que la terre non cultivée, portant beaucoup d'herbes et d'arbres, combien qu'ilz soient inutilles, est desirée pour l'esperance qu'elle apportera bon fruict, quant il y sera semé? …" ("Do you not see … that uncultivated ground is desirable, although it bears nothing but useless trees and grasses, because it offers the hope that one day, when it is sown, it will bring forth good fruit?"—*Hept.* 2.19.152; Chilton 229). The conclusion of Day Six in the *Heptaméron* represents the narrative ideal, as the tale-tellers go in to supper, "souppa la compaignye toute ensemble, parlant de plusieurs beaulx comptes" ("they ate together, speaking as they did of many fine tales"—*Hept.* 6.60.369; Chilton 475) in a storytelling event that recalls the Eucharistic feast.

Now that the textual aim has been made specific, Day Seven can be even more didactic and explicit in its offerings of *exemplaria* of how to reach that goal. For instance, Simontaut states, "Ce n'est chose nouvelle, mes dames, d'oyr dire de vous quelque acte vertueulx qui me semble ne debvoir estre celé, mais plus tost escript en lettres d'or, afin de servir aux femmes d'exemple et aux hommes d'admiration" ("it is so unexpected to me, Ladies, to hear of you performing any virtuous deed, that when such a deed does occur, it seems to me that it should not be concealed but rather written in letters of gold, in order to serve as an example to women and as a source of wonderment to men"—*Hept.* 7.66.392; Chilton 502). He also delineates the portrait of an evangelical believer who, "n'aiant autre desir que d'exhorter ung chascun à l'amour et confiance de Nostre Seigneur, se proposant pour exemple …" ("desire[d only] to exhort all people to love Our Lord and place their trust in Him, holding forth as an example the great mercy He had shown to her"—*Hept.* 7.67.394; Chilton 504–05).

Day Seven is summarized in this way: "En la septiesme journée, on devise de ceulx qui ont fait le contraire de ce qu'ilz devoient ou vouloient" ("On the Seventh Day, we speak of those who have done the opposite of what they should have done or wanted to do"—*Hept.* 7.prologue.370).[2] This statement directly recalls St. Paul's acknowledgment of weakness in the flesh and fallibility in the will: "for what I will to do, that I do not practice, but what I hate, that I do" (Rom. 7.15). The final *nouvelles* thus embody and explore the quintessential paradox of man caught between materiality and the metaphysical life for which he yearns. The Seventh Day shows the reforming drive of Marguerite's evangelicalism even more clearly as she uses the *nouvelles* to dramatize the disjunction between earthly living and heavenly expectations: "la lecture des Actes et vertueux faictz des glorieux chevaliers et apostres de Jesus-Christ … ces comptes-là debvoient estre suffisans pour desirer veoir ung tel temps et pleurer la difformité de cestuy-cy envers cestuy-là" ("the reading of the Acts, and the righteous deeds of the glorious knights and apostles of Jesus-Christ ... these tales should be sufficient [to make them] long to live in such an age, and weep for the corruption of the present"—*Hept.* 7.prologue.370; Chilton 476).

Earthly treasures are proven unreliable, but Scripture is exalted as *suffisant*, offering the completion and truth that enlightened humanity, shedding self as it mutates into soul, is moved to seek. At this point, the text delineates an *ascesis,* or spiritual formation predicated on the denial of self through the renunciation of the material world. A pause for reflection and meditation, here represented by the *devisants'* habit of retiring alone to their rooms for a rest before storytelling, is necessary preparation for the desire and ability to recount a new sort of *nouvelle*: "... pour nous preparez à racomptez noz nouvelles" ("to prepare ourselves for our stories"—*Hept.* 7.prologue.370; Chilton 476).

By *nouvelle* #63, the text pares down to make merely one mention of materiality. This *nouvelle* details the process of angelizing: elsewhere, in *nouvelle* #67, Marguerite terms this phenomenon to be living a "vie bestiale, et, quant à l'esperit, de vie angelicque" ("her bodily existence no higher than the beasts, but her soul in the sphere of the angels"—*Hept.* 7.67.393; Chilton 504). Angelizing paradoxically elevates base human nature through the medium of characters who revel in their carnal body and the materiality of their environment; this substance is, nonetheless, finally transformed by a yearning for God: "Je n'entens poinct seullement parler de ceulx qui sont par la grace de Dieu tout transmuez en luy, mais des plus grossiers esperitz que l'on voye ça-bas entre les hommes ..." ("I do not only mean the bodies of those who through God's grace have been transmuted into Him, but also those bodies that belong even to the basest spirits we see here on earth among men ..."—*Hept.* 7.63.382; Chilton 490). Marguerite's plotting of vertical points of reference exemplifies the tension, and the distance to be traversed, in this textual and existential dialectic; one is absorbed upward into God ("Dieu ... en luy"), a state that contrasts starkly with existence "here below" ("ça-bas entre les hommes"). Marguerite explicates the dialectic between fleshly experience and spiritual fulfillment.

> vous trouverez ceulx qui ont mys leur cueur et affection à chercher la perfection des sciences, non seulement avoir oblyé la volupté de la chair, mais les choses les plus necessaires, comme le boire et le manger; car, tant que l'ame est par affection dedans son corps, la chair demeure comme insensible … Et ceulx qui ne peuvent experimenter ce contentement sont les charnelz, qui, trop enveloppez de leur graisse, ne congnoissent s'ilz ont ame ou non.
>
> ("you will find that those who have given their heart and affections to the pursuit of the perfection of knowledge, have not only forgotten the pleasures of the flesh, but even the most basic needs, such as eating and drinking. For, as long as the soul is by affection within its body, the flesh remains as if it were insensible … those who can not experience such contentment are men of carnal desires, who, being too much enveloped in their flesh, do not even know whether they have a soul or not."—*Hept.* 7.63.382; Chilton 490)

The details of this description compose a summary of the moral character of the *dramatis personae* of the *Heptaméron.*

Despite persistent worldliness, however, fallen humanity is redeemed by the Spirit; Marguerite concludes that no matter what the faults of humanity, once acknowledgment of the spiritual nature is made, the earthly side can be overcome: "Mais, quant le corps est subject à l'esperit, il est quasi insensible aux imperfections de la chair" ("But when the body is subject to the spirit, [the body] is almost insensible to the imperfections of the flesh"—*Hept.* 7.63.382; Chilton 490). It is surely significant that this strong statement is made in one of the few *nouvelles* that does not rely on objects to drive its textual exposition. Instead of deploying objects narratively, the story develops through reference to universal truth-sayings—proverbs, scripture verses, and aphorisms—which the *nouvelle* literalizes in order to dramatize the vicissitudes of earthly experience. One such aphorism is "qui peut eviter l'offense de Dieu et … l'ire du prince est bien heureux" ("Blessed is he who can avoid offending God and avoid the wrath of the monarch!"—*Hept.* 7.63.381; Chilton 489), setting earthly authority in tension with divine mandate.

Received wisdom, rather than an actual material object, now propels the narrative, thereby moving toward abstraction and farther from the earthly realm. Parlamente exacerbates this disjunction, distinguishing between present experience and the world to come; she mandates a skeptical distrust of the earthly sphere and urges an apocalyptic move beyond it: "Par ce compte ... vous regarderez deux fois ce que vous vouldrez refuser, et ne vous fier au temps present, qu'il soit toujours ung; parquoy, congnoissans sa mutation, donnerez ordre à l'advenir" "this ... tale ... will teach you to think twice before you refuse something. It will teach you not to place trust in the present, hoping that things will remain the same forever, [but] to recognize that the present is in constant change and to have thought for the future" (*Hept.* 7.63.383; Chilton 491). She characterizes the present age as unstable ("sa mutation"), untrustworthy ("ne vous fier au temps present"), and in need of order ("donnerez ordre").

Ordre is one of Marguerite's main concerns in the *Heptaméron.* The jumble of earthly treasures—objects and exotica epitomizing the fallen material world—that the capacious text, like a collector's cabinet, contains and displays, must be reconfigured in harmony with divine purpose. Setting things in order, so that the disarray of the material world may be mitigated, occurs through the telling of the tales in the last part of the *Heptaméron*: "Et, pour y donner ordre, se retirerent chascun en son logis jusques à l'heure qu'ilz allerent en leur chambre des comptes, sur le bureau de l'herbe verte ..." ("and after they had each spent some time in his or her own room, they duly went out to the meadow ..."—*Hept.* 8.prologue.421; Chilton 476). *Ordre* is no longer wishful thinking; this goal is now accomplished in the text ("pour y donner ordre"), as the final Day evokes the imminent return of Christ who will judge all and set all things in order.

Nouvelle #72 features Marguerite herself as a secondary player in the story. She is qualified in this way to verify the possibility of rectifying her characters' disorders: "s'il y a ordre," Marguerite "le trouvera" ("if there is anything that anyone can do, she will do it"—*Hept.* 8.72.427; Chilton 542). This is her role as author: to "keep the books" and to maintain the register that records sin and salvation: "je tiens ce compte de la duchesse mesme" ("This is a story that I was told by the Duchess herself"—*Hept.* 8.72.427; Chilton 542), says Dagoucin, mentioning Marguerite, thereby attesting to the Scripture-like authenticity of the tale.

The space of the story forms the arena in which the eschatological establishment of order should commence. The aphorism participates in this plan by stressing truthful speech: putting an aphorism into effect validates its assertion. The aphorism is a verbal, abstract evocation of a terrestrial truth, the secular equivalent of scriptural mandates for spiritual existence. Scripture should be acknowledged as truth-bearing and normative, and should also be implemented in the daily-life experience of the believer as metaphysics displaces materiality. Parlamente provides a characterization of how *not* to read Scripture (and the *nouvelles*): evoking "Sainct Pol"'s use of contextual hermeneutics to insist that the whole truth, and not a partial perception, has derived from reading Scripture, she indicts "earthly" readers: "Vous vouldriez suivre … l'opinion des mauvais hommes qui prennent ung passaige de l'Escripture pour eulx et laissent celluy qui leur est contraire" ("You're as bad as all the other men who take a passage from Scripture which serves their purposes, and leave out anything that contradicts it"—*Hept.* 7.67.394; Chilton 505).

The final Day of the *Heptaméron* literalizes the metaphor of the bridge, enabling the passage from earthly concerns to metaphysical concentration, referring back to the actual bridges that, by their absence, had provided the pretext for the prologue to the First Day of the *Heptaméron.* The *devisants* had been hindered from continuing on their journey in the Prologue to Book One because a flood had washed out the bridge needed to cross the river to reach the next town. They decided to pass their time of waiting by telling stories: in effect, to construct a narrative bridge between present predicament and future hope. The *Heptaméron* is itself this bridge. Now, in the final Day of the *Heptaméron*, the *devisants* suddenly remember their need to progress on their physical travels, now that they have advanced so far on their spiritual journey: "[ils] s'enquirent si leur pont s'advançoit fort, et trouverent que, dedans deux ou trois jours, il pourroit estre achevé" ("they inquired how work on their bridge was progressing, and learned that it might be completed in two or three days"—*Hept.* 8.prologue.421; Chilton 535). The body of the risen Christ forms another bridge between earth and heaven, one implied in the statement "dedans deux ou trois jours, il pourroit estre achevé," an implication which Oisille reinforces by stating her desire to finish the "Canonicque de sainct Jehan" with them. She alludes to the Resurrection, as well as, yet again, Pentecost; appropriately, inspired by the Spirit, the *devisants* now speak with one voice: "il sembloit que le Sainct Esperit, plain d'amour ... parlast par sa bouche. Et, tous enflambez de ce feu ..." ("the Holy Spirit, full of sweetness and love, seemed to be speaking through her mouth. Inflamed with this fire, they went off ..."—*Hept.* 8.prologue.421; Chilton 535).

In another theological reference, the speakers are *élus*, chosen to speak;[3] they observe a heavenly order despite their terrestrial predicament. Finally, the text surpasses objects, materiality, and commodity culture by making itself the new commerce: in the *Heptaméron,* objects and experiences without value are permanently exchanged for priceless heavenly treasures. Marguerite uses a wordplay to allude to François Ier's Chambre des comptes de Paris[4] here ("en leur chambre des comptes"; "room ... to present their accounts ..."—*Hept.* 8.prologue.421; Chilton 535), but now the accounting is textual and theological, not financial. Accountability hinges on moral rectitude and spiritual insight, not monetary gain; and the accounting occurs through the telling of stories in the open air, the fresh space of nature ("sur le bureau de l'herbe verte") instead of locked in with the money changers.

The topic now and henceforth of the *nouvelles* will not be human folly, associated with lust for material possessions, but rather what St. Paul calls estimable folly: the folly of the Cross, of being "fools for Christ." Parlamente specifies the subject matter: "que ceste-cy soit de toutes les plus grandes folyes et les plus veritables que nous pourrions adviser" ("today should be taken up with stories which are the most foolish and the most true we can think of"—*Hept.* 8.prologue.422; Chilton 536).[5] The final Day was never concluded, appropriately so, since the *matière* of the *nouvelles* should remain inexhaustible in order to express the ongoing need for the transformation of materiality and the renewing of the unfinished text:[6] "pour en oyr ung plus plaisant ... [pour] ... rabille[r] ma faulte" ("for a more amusing story, I hand over to [her]. I'm sure she will make up for my lapse"—*Hept.* 8.72.428; Chilton 543). The *devisants*, Marguerite herself, even the reader have not *failly*—failed or sinned—in a permanent sense, because of the —redemptive nature of the stories they have shared: "vous ne racompterez que de follyes, et il me semble que je n'y ai pas failly" ("You did say … that [we] would only tell stories about foolish things, and I don't think that I have failed in that respect"—*Hept.* 8.72.427–28; Chilton 543). "Failly" and "follye," placed in juxtaposition, show that "not failing" is equivalent to embracing the folly of the cross: consequently, sin is not a permanent failure.

The reader has learned from the *Heptaméron* to attend fully, as a matter of eternal life: "Or, escoutez le bien, s'il vous plaist" ("So please all listen carefully"—*Hept.* 8.72.428; Chilton 543), enjoin the "last" words of the text. While earthly treasures impede the progress of the self toward the soul, materiality is not successful in dead-ending the pilgrimage out of the world, to God. The book provides the narrative space for an evangelical *lectio divina*: as God's Word is read into worldly context, it transforms *in situ*, emptying terrestrial content out and filling the frame with spiritual truth. Formerly inscribed with dark ink, blots of sin, the pages of humanity's text are now emblazoned with luminosity and transparency ("lettres d'or") as worldly experience cedes to a spiritual redemption of it, making the *Heptaméron* into a beautiful, illuminated manuscript. And the text itself, however luminous, is nonetheless self-consuming: it is an artifact that undoes itself in the light of God:

> … me semble ne debvoir estre celé, mais plus tost escript en lettres d'or.
>
> ("it seems to me that it should not be concealed but rather written in letters of gold."—*Hept.* 7.66.392; Chilton 502)

Earthly Treasures Cast Aside

Marguerite's ability to cast a critical eye on the essential, generally valued, aspects of one's own culture requires a complex mind-set:[7] a perception of, to some extent, being set against that world by one's ideology or, in the case of evangelicals, one's own theology. What makes a writer able to stand outside her circumstances in such a way that she is able to shape a critical stance on her own context? Rather than use objects as did her medieval predecessors—as properties in a play, to create a scene, to represent stock characters' professions or estate—Marguerite renounces this homely relationship to the things that surround her. She makes earthly objects *unheimlich*. Wrenching herself out of her cultural determinants,[8] Marguerite becomes a sort of separatist—as did Martin Luther: his self-described terrors over damnation could not be resolved through the confessional or church ritual, but only through a direct, dramatic confrontation with Christ as Savior.[9]

Willy-nilly, early modern evangelicals were compelled to be individuals. Similarly, for Marguerite, the drama is about the individual's encounter with the living Christ, found only in the Word and not through the world. In the *nouvelle* about Marie Héroët, for example, no succor came from the outside, from the world, to assist her against the venal abbot's charges, and no help came even from within her community. The very fact that Marie is cloistered emphasizes that her salvation cannot come to her via the world, but rather only through the Logos. Marie stands up to the abbot and denounces him because she knows Christ; she holds her model of Christ up to the abbot and, in that mirror, the abbot is damned as a flawed spiritual "superior." Only Marie's individual conscience enables her to withstand his advances and calumnies. While, at the end, the tale enacts a neat reversal with Marie herself installed as the order's superior, reintegrated into the community in order to do good within it, she is still named separately, and recognized as a strong individual.[10]

Theologian Carol Thysell concludes that Marguerite's ultimate goal is always to orient salvation toward, and to envision it within, community (that is, in her view, the most important role of the commentators): "one of the strongest implications of [Marguerite's] mystical insight … was the cohesion of the human community."[11] However, we find that Marguerite's evangelical understanding is far more mystical in tenor and effect than communitarian.[12] The fact that the ultimate responsibility to interpret resides with the reader only further attests to Marguerite's status as an early modern individual produced by evangelicalism.

The mystic's ultimate goal is to be undone, to be reabsorbed into the Godhead, but the ontological experiential reality of the mystic is to remain an individual—one set apart from the world, and on the way to God. Mystic speech troubles the hierarchy; it regards the world and its components in idiosyncratic—but creative—ways. Marguerite's use of objects in the *Heptaméron* sounds remarkably like how Michel de Certeau describes the mystic use of figures of speech:

> Behind the various religious conducts or convictions, the possibility was created of making these figures into something else and of using them to serve different strategies—a possibility whose equivalent can be seen during the same era, in the more flexible fields of writing and aesthetics, with the art (baroque or rhetorical) of treating ideas in order to obtain new effects from them.[13]

The various techniques that we have seen Marguerite employing in the *Heptaméron* to use, remake, then surpass the material world, all appear here: to "reform" is, in de Certeau's paradigm, to "remake the forms" and "produce a [new] policy of meaning."[14]

The new sort of evangelical narrative that Marguerite crafts—along with Rabelais, Des Périers, Du Fail, Yver, and others, and enhanced by adaptations of artistic innovations of their time period—illustrates the new sort of meaning that can (indeed, *must*) be conferred on the world and on its objects by just such an individuated writer seeking to exemplify and convey her theological stance. Earthly treasures, representative of material culture, function in a textual economy oriented toward a deep understanding of metaphysical perspective that, of necessity, rejects the very objects encountered on the way to its *telos*.

Notes

Introduction
Objects of Desire: Reading the Material World Metaphysically in Marguerite de Navarre's *Heptaméron*

1. This chapter in an earlier form first appeared in the journal of the Rocky Mountain Medieval and Renaissance Association *Quidditas* 19 (2001): 163–95.

2. Similarly, there is a lot going on in this study. Diverse disciplines offer tools with which to explore these cultural phenomena. Among them are textual materialist criticism; the venues of fine and decorative arts; evangelical thought, both Calvinist and Lutheran; and the technique of *explication de texte*. Textured hybrids result from such pluridisciplinary influences, and various colleagues provide models for discussion of them: Patricia Fumerton and her work on miniatures and other early modern material representations of ideology; Gérard Defaux's work on sixteenth-century French evangelicalism; Roberto Campo's deft exploration of the intersections between Renaissance painting and Ronsard's poetry; Peter Stallybrass's examination of artifacts and early modern oddities such as costumes and theatrical props; Mary McKinley's thesis that the *Heptaméron* is the product of collaborative construction; and numerous others.

3. It is legitimate to use the term *metaphysics* in reference to Marguerite; William Tyndall used it, for instance, in 1528 in the *Oxford English Dictionary.*

4. She nonetheless distinguishes herself from them, and from Lefèvre d'Étaples in particular. D'Étaples still held to a doctrine of "double justification" (faith coupled with works), while Marguerite is more explicitly evangelical in denying the efficacy of the latter.

5. McKeon 41.

6. Abel Lefranc's 1896 article, "Les idées religieuses de Marguerite de Navarre," already provided an *état présent* of the subject, then demonstrated that Marguerite's poetry was penned by an author convinced by the dogma and spirit of the Reformation.

7. She differs from Boccaccio, a certain influence as Donald Stone has already shown, in that ambiguities persist in Boccaccio's text concerning the moral dimensions of worldliness and materiality. Marguerite is clear that both are suspect; not prey to such ambivalence, she uses these elements dialectically, in tension with her vision of an ideal, spiritualized universe. See Donald Stone, *From Tales to Truths: Essays on French Fiction in the Sixteenth Century*.

8. Similar precursor and contemporary projects, which both influenced and probably were influenced by the *Heptaméron*, include Bonaventure Des Périers's *Nouvelles récréations et joyeux devis* (1558), in which the author, like Marguerite, expounds at length, and digressively, on the etymology of *deviser*, and Noël Du Fail's *Propos rustiques* (1547) and *Baliverneries* (1548). These texts are discussed further on in the present study as examples of the new genre of evangelical narratives.

9. W. G. Moore, Henri Heller, and Gérard Defaux all identified distinctly evangelical aspects of Marguerite's work, although none has situated it in reference to other cultural productions, such as artistic media, as the present study will do. Gary Ferguson's study, *Mirroring Belief: Marguerite de Navarre's Devotional Poetry*, also identifies evangelical elements in Marguerite de Navarre's poetry. Ferguson shows that Marguerite evolves away from her traditional Catholicism toward a pronounced sympathy for certain Reformed perspectives: an evangelical Catholicism. He demonstrates that, even in her early works, Marguerite employs many of the ideas and images emphasized by the Reformers and, in particular, by Luther. Such borrowing is especially apparent in discussions of the problem of sin and in articulating ideas about fallen man.

10. See, notably, Henri Heller, "Marguerite de Navarre and the Reformers of Meaux." Heller examines the evangelical position of other reformers such as Briçonnet and Roussel, as well.

11. Heller 273. Particularly concerning justification—whether by faith (Calvin and Luther's perspective: *sola fidei*) or through works (the Catholic stance)—Marguerite took some time to move from the customary reliance on saints, intercession, and works of charity to a Reformed reliance on the sacrifice of Jesus Christ as sufficient and absolute atonement for all sins and proof of salvation. Nonetheless, shift she eventually did.

12. Heller 273. "[*Vive foy*] is [an expression] associated primarily with the evangelicals, and though not eschewed by certain Catholics, it yet comes to be linked more and more firmly with Protestant writers."

13. Gérard Defaux's research and publication in theologo-literary interpretation of Marguerite's *Heptaméron* supports my thesis. See his "De la Bonne Nouvelle aux nouvelles: Remarques sur la structure de *l'Heptaméron*," *French Forum* 2001. (I had not had the opportunity to read this piece prior to completing most of my work on this manuscript, but am gratified to find that we concur: "... la septième Journée était toute entière éclairée et structurée par la référence faite dans le Prologue aux 'Actes et vertueux faictz des glorieux chevaliers et apostres de Jesus-Christ'"—10; "Marguerite a voulu inscrire la 'Bonne Nouvelle' au cœur même des nouvelles de sa cinquième Journée ..."—11).

14. François collected Clouet. See Antoine Schnapper, *Le géant, la licorne et la tulipe: Collections et collectionneurs dans la France du XVII*[e] *siècle* 180. In addition, "[il] appréciait les objets exotiques. On met parfois la création de son cabinet de curiosités en relation avec la visite qu'il fit à Jean Ange à Dieppe en 1527" ("he appreciated exotica. The impetus for the construction of his cabinet of curiosities is often attributed to his visit to Jean Ange in Dieppe in 1527").

15. Schnapper, *Le géant* 180.

16. Le Père Dan (speaking in 1642), qtd. in Schnapper, *Le géant* 182.

17. Clouet's painting of the reformer Guillaume Budé is a case in point. Budé's introspective expression complements his careful penmanship in the book in which he is writing. He has slightly turned the book so that the viewer may read from it. The book is presented as a precious object, with gilded edges and a pink cover, stacked on top of another book. Provenance: Metropolitan Museum of Art, New York, Accession number 46.68.

18. Calvin's image of the deceitful maze, or labyrinth, of the world works much the same way. See William Bouwsma, *John Calvin: A Sixteenth-Century Portrait.*

19. Such a textual approach is consonant with the description of otherworldliness that contemporaries have provided of Marguerite: "He saw in the Queen's eyes, even from a distance, that fervent spirit and the light which God has given her, so clear that it can lead one to the blessedness of eternal life, *without being detained in the impediments of immortality*" (Pier Paolo Vergerio, qtd. in Pinkus 64; emphasis added).

20. Similarly, avoiding the dichotomy that Calvin develops between visible church and invisible church (already implicit in St. Augustine's city of man and city of God), Marguerite—more like St. Paul in his understanding of *sarks*, or fallen flesh, as the housing for the soul which also wages war on the soul—exemplifies the tension between Catholicism and evangelical impulses (at this stage, still internal to Catholicism) that speak of materiality as a flawed screen for metaphysics.

21. In this way, Marguerite's textual materialism is "essentially paradoxical, since its ultimate objective is to proclaim the obsoleteness of literature in the face of the absolute Non-Being" (Miernowski 132).

22. An unexpected effect of this object-based treatment is that gender issues, often problematic for Renaissance culture, can be resolved by Marguerite's text: men and women possess gender differences, yet ultimately their significance lies in their *personhood* as it is, or is not, oriented metaphysically. In the *Heptaméron*, the explanation for such a disregard is precisely the metaphysical perspective. Marguerite may anticipate here the Reformed ideal of "companionate marriage," which forswears sexual relations in favor of a mutual devotion to the adoration of Christ.

23. Protestant biblical scholars tended to concentrate on excavating the material culture of antiquity. "While the largest number of entries in Renaissance biblical commentaries discuss philological matters, antiquities form the second most popular category; miniature essays on such topics as Mary's alabaster box, the nature of hyssop … Pilate's atrium … a scholarly fascination with the material culture of antiquity: the detailed explanations of clothing, pots and pans, burial customs, coinage, table manners, and other such ephemera" (Shuger 42 and 290).

24. Charles Taylor 232.

25. Charles Taylor 232.

26. Watts 251. Early modern evangelicals in England were implementing similar tactics to illustrate their faith: "In a society adjusting to literacy, print was not just print, but was incorporated into daily life by allying itself with other methods of communication—be it the tactile language of gloves and garters, or the oral activities of prayer, proverb, and song."

27. Kroll 39. While these interests and foci are distinctively Marguerite's, it should be noted that it was not unusual during this time period to find literature functioning as a sort of laboratory within which to experiment with social or cultural issues. "Literary genre [is treated by the time period] as an experimental space within which to treat wider discursive issues."

28. Marguerite read extensively. From 1509 through the early 1520s, she read omnivorously. Briçonnet, her spiritual director, took her to task, however, for not reading more selectively or in greater depth. After becoming a writer, Marguerite continued to read Scripture, the writing of Lefèvre d'Étaples, Briçonnet, Rabelais, Ficino, Castiglione, Clément Marot, and, as this present study illustrates, Luther. I owe to John Lyons this reminder of the sorts of reading in which Marguerite indulged.

29. The provenance is the Bibliothèque de l'Arsenal, ms. 5069, folios Av–I. The image is also reproduced in Ladurie 195, illus. 71. Along with her coat of arms to the left, Marguerite herself has been identified in the features of one of the women to the right, and Henri d'Albret holds a daisy, or *marguerite*, a signature of subjectivity that stylistically seems to prefigure the introspective, thoughtful features of Van Eyck or Holbein's subjects somewhat later.

30. Provenance is the Metropolitan Museum of Art, New York City. Accession number 17.190.21.

31. Provenance is the Metropolitan Museum of Art in New York City. Accession number 1975.1.110.

32. "The mirror not only describes the site of the workshop but may also add a moralizing dimension. It perhaps signifies the imperfections of the real world, as represented by the reflection of the vast space outdoors ... [while] the falcon is a traditional symbol of pride and greed, a meaning reinforced by the idea of vanity associated with the mirror [which Marguerite also underscores] and played off against the sense of virtue evoked by the solemn couple in the goldsmith's shop" (*Catalogue of the Metropolitan Museum* [Baetjet 153]). See also Guy de Tervarent, *Attributs et symboles dans l'art profane, 1450–1600. Dictionnaire d'un langage perdu*. The falcon, if hooded, may also symbolize hope.

33. Objects inscribe a sort of visual shorthand: "Well-chosen similes, metaphors, and allegories ... being taken from objects already known, and familiar to the understanding ... are conceived as fast as spoken;

and the correspondence being concluded, the thing they are brought to explain and elucidate is thought to be understood too" (John Locke, *Of the Conduct of Human Understanding*, qtd. in Kroll 275).

34. Marguerite's evangelical peer, Rabelais, might call this the "substantificque mœlle."

35. Thysell 125.

36. Provenance is the Musée des beaux-arts, Lille, France.

37. This theoretical approach calls for studies that will reveal to us "the ways in which the mass consumption of objects of commerce and high culture meet … the specific psychological and cultural needs of dynamic social groups[,] … providing them with a sense of identity" (Ann Bermingham, "Introducing the Consumption of Culture," in Bermingham and Brewer 4).

38. Schnapper, *Le géant* 220. "Notons que, comme bon nombre de leurs confrères, ils sont protestants: on a souvent observé que la curiosité scientifique était plus répandue et plus active chez les protestants, plus libres vis-à-vis de la tradition religieuse" ("let us note that, like a good many of their confrères, they are Protestants. It has often been observed that scientific curiosity was widespread and active among Protestants [who were] freer vis-à-vis religious tradition"). Some later, explicitly Protestant, collectors who continue this evangelical concern for setting the church in order, and thereby the world, include Jules-Raymond de Solier (d. 1594); François Gaverol (1636–94); Pierre Borel (b. 1615).

39. "WUNDERKAMMER: a wonder-cabinet: a form of collection peculiar to the late Renaissance, characterized primarily by its encyclopedic appetite for the marvelous, or the strange, and by an exceptionally brief historical career … for perhaps 100 years such collections flourished, but by the middle of the seventeenth century they were rapidly vanishing" (Mullaney 65).

40. Mullaney 8.

41. While Marguerite and Calvin, unlike Marguerite and Luther, probably have more differences than similarities, the ramified approach to knowledge as apprehended through the logical and careful distribution of portions of knowledge building gradually to a complete view appears to be an approach that they both implement. The demarcations between Catholic and Reformed doctrine in this argument are not meant to be absolute; often there are overlaps and similarities in treatment. Rather, such characterizations are intended to function as schematic tools in establishing a spectrum of narrative possibilities for Marguerite's text.

42. Schnapper states that the project of theorizing the collector's cabinet has yet to be undertaken; his contribution is the first comprehensive historical overview.

43. Mullaney 67. "The objects thus displayed [are] maintained as 'extraneous,' in the Latin sense of the word, lodg[ed] … beyond the bounds of cultural hierarchies or definitions, at least for the time being." Their selected pattern of display will insert them into a new system of signification.

44. Schnapper, *Le géant* 7.

45. Catholics are less concerned with the effects of the Fall on the material world; nature, to them, still seems inscribed with the divine signature. The Catholic use of objects is, as a result, descriptive, while the Reformed treatment tends to be prescriptive and, at times, proscriptive. For Palissy, shells, fossils, odd rock formations, and other natural and artificed oddities and shards delineate God's plan for the world and His mandate for salvific alteration. For instance, on a lead-glazed earthenware dish from his workshop in Paris, circa 1565, Palissy invents ceramic *rustiques figulines*, his neologism for the assemblage of miniature animals, shells, snakes, lizards, and ferns (elements of nature rendered in the creation colors of green, gray, brown, and blue), which he encrusts in collage fashion over all available surface. The effect returns nature to its original state of chaos, a paradoxical way in which to point to the need for a second chance for the fallen world.

46. The curiosity cabinets demonstrating Reformed perspectives differ from those of other Renaissance humanists in that the former not only aim to summarize the world and its treasures, but also to go beyond the world, to seek a hidden significance in a higher sphere unconfined by the box, desk, or room of the curiosity collector. The nature and intent of their collection is cognitive, narrative in purpose, rather than simply acquisitive.

47. "God placed mankind over creation and made the things of the world for human use. But humans are there in turn to serve and glorify God, and so their use of things should serve this final goal. The consequences of sin is that humans come to be concerned with these things not for God's sake but for themselves. They come to desire them as ends and no longer simply as instruments for God's purposes. And this upsets the whole order of things. Humans were meant to bring the rest of creation to God. But when they turn to make creatures themselves the end, then both mankind and the creatures are thrown out of their proper relation to the Creator" (Charles Taylor 221).

48. John Brewer, "Attitudes towards Culture as a Commodity, 1600–1800," in Bermingham and Brewer 346. "This cultural site was characterized by an emphasis upon social display: cultural sites were places of self-presentation in which audiences made publicly visible their wealth, status, social and sexual charms … this was a culture steeped in hedonism and sexual intrigue."

49. A century later, Claude de Vaugelas described the court environment as being "like a store, in which our tongues shop for a quantity of beautiful expressions" (*Remarques sur la langue française* [1647], preface to vol. 2, qtd. in Fragonard 105). This is my translation of "Il est certain que la Cour est comme un magazin, d'où nostre langue tire quantité de beaux termes pour exprimer nos pensées." Montaigne also refers to our imaginative capacities as a *boutique*: our minds are stocked with objects (*topoi*) in situations (*loci*). Montaigne's incessant digressions, revisions, and accumulation of variants could be said to compose his own sort of collector's cabinet.

50. Unlike Michel de Montaigne's technique in "Des cannibales" where he bestrews the essay with exotic objects and ancillary references without discrete attention to each of them, Marguerite does select, discriminate, and analyze. Debora Shuger observes that "Montaigne ... fashions a litany of the variety and strangeness of things found in culture ... The methodology ... is aggregative and paratactic, an encyclopedic 'heaping' of unrelated exotic details. This pack-rat accumulation of curiosities and broken pieces of knowledge characterizes empirical and humanistic studies ... throughout the sixteenth century. It is endemic to the topical organization recommended in Renaissance rhetoric" (50). While Montaigne displays substance, Marguerite hollows it out. Montaigne adapts his tactic to create an overall manifestation of heft and significance in the exotic culture.

51. "The symbol in Lutheran thought was perceived as a materialization, a reification of spirituality, the death of faith itself" (Pinkus 45).

52. Bermingham: "Consumption [can be] figured ... as the exchange of money for luxury goods but [also as an occasion for] the psychological dynamics of fantasy and narcissistic self-absorption" (Bermingham and Brewer 3).

53. See "Prologue," Marguerite de Navarre, *Heptaméron*, ed. Michel François (Paris: Garnier, 1967).

54. All translations are from Paul Chilton, Marguerite de Navarre's *The Heptaméron* (London: Penguin, 1984).

55. Defaux, "De la Bonne Nouvelle" 5. Defaux argues that these 25 wounds point to Jesus, as December 25 is the date of His birth. This suggests a form of textual resurrection for the woman: assimilated to her Lord through her passion and suffering, she will die on the date of His birth, and live eternally with Him. Material presence is thus reoriented to a metaphysical perspective.

56. For the distinction between lives of saints and accounts of their martyrdoms, and evangelical and Protestant martyrological accounts in which lengthy transcriptions are provided of the martyr's last words, see Catharine Randall Coats, *(Em)bodying the Word: Textual Resurrections in the Martyrological Narratives of Foxe, Crespin, de Bèze and d'Aubigné.*

57. Lyons 110.

58. Lyons: "*Exemplum* connotes the relationship between a[n] ... ignorant laity and ... an informed class of preachers" (107).

Chapter One
Telling *Tableaux* and Textual Resurrections: Marguerite de Navarre and the Evangelical Narrative

1. A version of this chapter appeared as "'Tableaux vivants' and Textual Resurrection" in *Religion and the Arts* 3 (1999): 408–27. ©Koninklijke Brill N.V.

2. Larissa Taylor 67.

3. Larissa Taylor pays considerable attention to post-Tridentine changes in preaching practice and to the Catholic Reformation's response from the pulpit to inroads made by Protestant preaching.

4. Erasmus did this in the *Enchiridion*. We may contrast Marguerite's prototype for preaching, in which individuals define their beliefs in dialogue with their interlocutors, all within the conscious framework of Scripture, with that found, for example, in Jean Trepperel's *Mistere de l'Institution de l'Ordre des Freres Prescheurs* (1504–12). The play dramatizes how the Dominican orders were established as itinerant preachers. Rather than exemplifying Scripture *strictu sensu*, the *Mistere de l'Institution* features didactic sermons such as the one with which the drama concludes: this is a polemic against heresy requiring the very sort of compulsory observance of doctrine (without an accompanying virtuous life) against which evangelicals were shortly to react. This comparison demonstrates Marguerite's innovations in the sense of the evangelical exploration of the heart and soul of the individual—and the sort of preaching needed to reach such individuals.

5. This was also a characteristic of orthodox Franciscan preaching, showing how evangelical concerns do not break with Catholicism, but rather enter into a critical relationship with it from within the Church.

6. "Dénoncé par Erasme suivant dans les pas de Jean Vitrier, puis (avec des nuances) par Lefèvre, le culte des saints sera vivement attaqué par ses disciples (Farel notamment) et le groupe de Meaux autour de Briçonnet (Mazurier, Caroli, Roussel). Bientôt on n'entend plus parler que de cette 'idolâtrie' condamnée en chœur par les réformateurs français" ("Denounced by Erasmus following in the footsteps of Jean Vitrier, then, with nuances added by Lefèvre, the cult of saints would be roundly attacked by its disciples [especially Farel, and the group at Meaux around Briçonnet: Mazurier, Caroli, Roussel]. Soon one would no longer hear of anything but 'idolatry,' condemned in chorus by the French reformers"—Beck 227n10).

7. Mullin 12–14. Calvinists termed revelation "closed," meaning that no new miracles would transpire, but rather were limited to the time of the early Christian church, serving the purpose of encouragement of the faithful as evidence of divine power in the life of the Church.

8. Another distinction is that Catholic miracles, morality and mystery plays paraphrased primarily *Old* Testament scripture, and their scripts aimed at a universal, generalized experience.

9. Moore 192–93; emphasis added; my translation.

10. "At stake in the *Heptaméron* is the role of literature in an era increasingly confronted by a withdrawal of the divine order from the observable world. In attempting to establish order without abandoning the divine, narrative can only displace the transcendent function onto some human agency" (Lyons 79).

11. Jean-Claude Aubailly (138) shows that, similarly, sixteenth-century Protestant theater has a "style de représentation tendant au réalisme … [offrant la voix] d'un commenta[teur] critique [du monde]" ("a representational style bordering on realism … offering the voice of a commentator critical of the world"). Marguerite's *devisants* fulfill this function of commentators and critics.

12. In the Gospel of Matthew, Jesus told his disciples that wherever two or more of them were gathered in his name, there he would also be. The evangelical poet and member of Marguerite's coterie, Clément Marot, wrote an epigram from Jesus' words ("Quand en mon nom assemblez vous serez …") in Marot 711.

13. Michel Jeanneret has written about the significance of this phenomenon of sharing stories at table for Renaissance French writers, and makes interesting comments on Luther's role as important exemplar of this practice.

14. Moore 192; emphasis added.

15. Luther, qtd. in Spitz 58.

16. "La subordination … encore plus marquée … à l'objectif idéologique que provoque la confessionalisation du théâtre scolaire … favorise une actualisation par *l'ouverture aux conflits contemporains* … ce nouveau théâtre de laïcs, échappant à l'emprise de l'Eglise … constitue un des éléments déterminants de l'évolution du théâtre allemand du XVIe siècle" ("… the increasingly pronounced subordination … to the ideological goal that the confessionalizing of scholastic theater compels … favors [dramatic] actualization through an openness to contemporary conflicts … this new lay theater, not subject to control by the church, … constitutes one of the determining aspects of the evolution of sixteenth century German theater"—Hartweg, qtd. in Aubailly 121; emphasis added). The *nouvelles* of Marguerite could be construed as the concrete prose narrative form of the contemporary dramatic treatment ("*actualisation*") called for.

17. Bucer, qtd. in Spitz 244.

18. Moore 22.

19. The first Protestant drama to develop and flourish during the early years of the Reformation came, as well, from Germany. In "Le drame scolaire protestant en Allemagne," Frédéric Hartweg entwines theology and didactic ("scolaire") *œuvre*, two traits that the *Heptaméron* shares. While Luther opposes Catholic "jeux de la passion," he is in favor of "représentations des actes de Jésus-Christ … [et] de la représentation de comédies … à des fins didactiques et moralisatrices" ("… plays based on the deeds of Jesus … [and] plays … with didactic, moralizing aims"). Like Marguerite, whose stories often possess an admittedly salacious content, Luther "écarte l'argument selon lequel ces comédies contiendraient [et ne devraient contenir] des passages d'une certaine verdeur, en affirmant qu'il en éta[it] de même dans la Bible" ("he set aside the argument according to which these comedies contain [and should not contain] questionable passages, pointing out that such passages also existed in the Bible"—Aubailly 120n3).

20. Speech is very important for most of Marguerite's characters. For instance, in *nouvelle* #21 Rolandine is forbidden to speak. Rolandine has a secret to hide: she has married in secret, without permission. In *nouvelle* #40, Count Jossebelin adores his sister with an incestuous passion. When he learns that his sister has married secretly, he locks her up in a castle deep in the forest, and forbids visitors to speak to her, although he allows them to speak about her. It is often the case in Marguerite's work that men try to impose silence on women. Women become objects; they are no longer subjects. But we cannot limit this analysis to discerning a form of proto-feminism in Marguerite's work. Certainly the story surpasses what would upset modern feminists—and any sensitive reader—as the horror of the husband's treatment of the wife and lover seems out of proportion, even given her adultery.

21. Martineau: "Cette certitude du salut se greffe sur le thème paulinien de Jésus-Christ avocat des siens" (541–42).

22. Another effective example of how "le regard" reifies is found in the story of Madame de Roncex. She leaves her ladies to heed a call of nature. When she is startled by something, she drops her skirts into a mess of excrement. Having called for help, she is rescued by her ladies who fear that she is being attacked by lustful monks. Her bottom is exposed, covered with dung, for all the world to see. In Pauline terms, Roncex embodies *sarks*: those determined by their fleshly nature to remain risible and sinful, narrated as an object lesson laughingly recounted by others about them.

23. I must note that Chilton's translation here does not do justice to the horror of the husband's reaction. He translates this passage almost in a reversal of its true sense as "I could not bring myself to doubt her, until the moment when my eyes were opened and I saw for myself what I had feared more than death itself" (Chilton 332).

24. Old Testament legalism, Luther finds in *Against the Jews*, following St. Paul (Rom. 10.4), is what makes salvation of the Jews unlikely—and such a tragic missed opportunity. He claims that the Jews, not the Gentiles, are the people of the promise and thus are so close, yet so far, from salvation, in Luther's view.

25. "... Le gentil homme tira ung rideau qui estoit devant une grande armoyre, où il veid penduz tous les oz d'un homme mort ("The gentleman pulled a curtain that was in front of a large closet, where [Bernaige] saw the suspended skeleton of a dead man"—*Hept.* 4.32.244).

26. "Et, ainsy que la viande fut apportée sur la table, veid sortyr de derriere la tapisserye une femme ... après qu'elle eut souppé et faict laver les mains, feit une reverance ... et s'en retourna derriere la tapisserye, sans parler à personne" ("And, when the meat had been brought to the table, he saw a woman emerge from behind the wall hanging ... after she had eaten and washed her hands, she bowed ... and went behind the tapestry, without speaking to anyone"—*Hept.* 4.32.242).

27. This French fairy-tale ending—"et ... en eut depuis beaucoup de beaulx enfants" (*Hept.* 4.32.245), as opposed to the English "and they lived happily ever after," is Marguerite's way of conferring a metaphysical happy ending on the drama. By thus resolving it narratively, she shows how miraculous it is that a beneficial conclusion has been achieved, and glorifies the theological motors that have enabled this resolution.

28. Bernaige appeals to this sentiment when pleading the wife's case before the husband; he says to him: "... et aussy, vous estes jeune, et n'avez nulz enfans; et seroit grand dommaige de perdre une si belle maison que la vostre, et que ceulx qui ne vous ayment peut-estre poinct, en fussent heritiers" ("Besides, you are young, and have no children, and it would be a great shame to lose such a beautiful house as yours, and for people who may perhaps care nothing for you to inherit from you"—*Hept.* 4.32.245; Chilton 334).

29. John Lyons observes a uniquely literary aspect of this phenomenon, which I believe should be linked with a theological process. Lyons: "If a person can learn something about himself or herself, such learning has to pass through a representation from outside" (88).

30. Defaux, "De la Bonne Nouvelle" 14. "To open one's heart to this Word, to receive and lodge it within oneself, to assimilate and make it one's own was ... to allow within oneself the restoration of a nature originally created good."

31. Oisille explains the process in this way: "Mes dames, si toutes celles à qui pareil cas est advenu beuvoient en telz vaisseaulx, j'aurois grand paour que beaucoup de coupes dorées seroient converties en testes de mortz. Dieu nous en veuille garder, car, si sa bonté ne nous retient, il n'y a aucun d'entre nous qui ne puisse faire pis; mais, ayant confiance en luy, il gardera celles qui se confessent ne se pouvoir par elles-mesmes garder; et celles qui se confient en leurs forces sont en grand dangier d'estre tentées jusques à confesser leur infirmité ... [mais] ce que Dieu garde est bien gardé" ("My ladies, if all those to whom a similar thing happened drank from such cups, I'd be really afraid that a lot of gilded goblets would be changed into skulls. God preserve us from this fate, for, if His goodness does not restrain us, there is not one among us who is not capable of doing worse; but those who put their trust in Him, and acknowledge their own inability to keep themselves from sin, He will keep in safety. And those who rely on their own strength are in great danger of being tempted and of having to confess their weakness ... but that which God safeguards is well guarded"—*Hept.* 4.32.245; Chilton 333).

32. Harbison 77.
33. Harbison 135.
34. Harbison 149.
35. In this regard, it is intriguing to speculate that other innovations in the field of fine arts during Marguerite's time, and especially among evangelicals or Protestants, may have been motivated by their new subject matter or technique. For instance, the Protestant Jan van Eyck is widely lauded in the art world for the illusion of transparency that his new technique of composing and applying paints suggests: he uses an oil-based painting medium, which actually suspends particles in it. Harbison: he "allow[s] one to actually look through van Eyck's finely textured surfaces" (33). Could the technique be a part of a larger, theological initiative to encourage the spectator to seek the reality behind the appearance, the spiritual world beyond the material manifestation, as Marguerite's frames and windows function here?
36. This also recalls the framing arches in genre painters' Annunciation scenes, for example. Metropolitan Museum of Art: "… Framing devices are inherited from fifteenth-century models … experiments in illusionism … enhance the realism" (187). See Rogier van der Weyden's *Annunciation* (circa 1465–75), in which Gabriel enters from the left, while Mary quietly reads in the right foreground. Between the two is an arched window. The world appears through the window, while a bound-up bed curtain dangles an oval pendant along the dividing line of the window, representing Mary's chastity.
37. These are actually versions of *natures mortes* fashioned both of people and of things, as we shall see in the later discussion of the sixteenth-century still life (a contemporary innovation), and the Protestant inflection of it. Harbison: "15th century art had demonstrated a great degree of religious homogeneity, but in the 16th that was radically transformed … 'secular satisfactions' … com[e] to the fore; portraits, landscapes, still-lifes, and genre or peasant imagery emerg[e]s … [evoking] the daily, worldly existence of contemporaries" (123).
38. The "loin" resonates with Bernaige's arrival from a far country ("de loin") to enact a *rapprochement* of two spouses separated by sin.
39. This phenomenon appears, for instance, in Théodore de Bèze's *Chrestiennes méditations* where the self, while acceptable in the eyes of the world, is reflected back through the mirror of the soul (his text) as a horrible "crocodile" and sinful beast.
40. This is the case with Floride's descent through the darkened stairway.
41. Aubailly: "pour ce qui est des matières tirées du Nouveau Testament … les paraboles fournissent la matière de nombreuses pièces dans lesquelles sont fréquemment inclus des tableaux représentant des situations de la vie quotidienne" ("as concerns subjects from the New Testament … parables supply the theme for many plays featuring *tableaux* demonstrating scenes from daily life"—123). For instance, Burkhard

Waldis's "De parabell vam verlorn Szohn" (1527) illustrates the doctrine of justification by faith by reworking in theatrical fashion the parable of the Prodigal Son.

42. The *Recueil Montmor* can be found in Aix-en-Provence, rés. # ms20. f.13.

Chapter Two
Evangelical Dimensions in Decorative Arts: Emblems, Earthly Objects, and the Economy of Transcendence

1. Luther, qtd. in McGrath 165; emphasis added.

2. I am speaking specifically about French evangelical writers here. I do not mean to draw the line too sharply between evangelical and Protestant, and Catholic treatments. We know that Quarles, for example, consulted some Jesuit sources. I hope simply to construct useful categories for distinguishing between some of characteristics as related to theological stance.

3. Russell 162. "It is clear that the principal aim of [theorizing about the emblematic forms] was to isolate a pure emblematic form that was *not* the emblem."

4. Cotgrave: "*Devise*: a device, embleme ... Also, a division; bound, meere, or marke dividing land."

5. These paintings, such as Cornelisz's "The Parable of the Bean and the Mole," while also found in the work of Catholic emblem writers, seem more prevalent among evangelicals and Protestants.

6. I do not mean to imply that such an emblematic function is the sole purpose of the frame. Marguerite inherits the frame from Boccaccio, and uses it both similarly and differently from him. However, her evangelical stance does inform the construction and the interpretation of the frame.

7. Cotgrave: "*Deviser*: to commune, talke, discourse ... converse with ... to order ..."

8. The Jesuits' aim of contemplative silence is very different from Marguerite's proto-Protestant goal. She represents her hermeneutic through the figures of the *devisants* and through discussions that take place in a secular setting.

9. Ignatian emblems—generally composed some seventy years after Marguerite de Navarre, and written, at least in part, in reaction to the Protestant Reformation—also try to generate a response from the viewer. However, rather than aim at an abstract elsewhere, they try to rein in the imaging and imaginative capacities of the viewer, to direct constructively what the viewer may see, think, experience, or interpret. A good example is the *Imago primi saeculi societati Jesu a Provincia Flando-Belgica* (Antwerp, 1640). Père Sucquet describes Ignatius's emblematic intention in this way: "For he who uses this method will easily overthrow those two things which tend to make meditation difficult and even fruitless.

The first is the instability of the imagination: after the sin of Adam it became wholly unbridled; the unstable mind was made to wander over the whole course of the earth and was not allowed to stick to pious thoughts. In order to restrain it, it seemed appropriate to fix it, as it were, by means of pious cogitations and by images" (Le père Suquet, qtd. in Freedberg 180). Thus, the Ignatian approach is dogmatic and disciplined, permitting solely a pre-established conclusion.

10. This is a strategy used by many Calvinist writers for self-authentication. Coats, *Subverting the System* 2. This is in fact a narrative strategy modeled by the Gospel writers themselves.

11. Schama, *Rembrandt's Eyes* 32.

12. There may be some parallels with Hans Carvel's "ring," discussed in Rabelais. Geoffrey Tory also uses the "O," developed in this tale, in a strictly emblematic sense.

13. In a series of helpful comments on an earlier version of this manuscript, Daniel Russell pointed out that the mirror as a *vanitas* attribute really dates from the seventeenth century, after the dissemination of Venetian technique had made mirrors more faithfully reflective.

14. Lorenzo Lotto in 1552 used a mirror as the cover for a small portrait; in this instance, the mirror is called a "portrait cover." Brantôme tells how Louis, Prince de Condé, sent his mistress a mirror containing his portrait (Campbell 67).

15. Concerning evangelical emblematics, "Claude Paradin may be quoted as an example, in his *Devises heroiques* (1557) … [of] moderate [evangelical] Catholic views" (Montenay ii).

16. Montenay iii.

17. The translations of Georgette de Montenay are my own.

18. There are certainly occasions when she does use allegory or symbol, however, as in the pillar and globe in "Nuntius Viribus."

19. Paine 129.

20. Paradin, *The Heroicall Devices* 11.

21. Paradin, *The Heroicall Devices* 8.

22. Paradin: "selon la particuliere affection qu'[un chascun] avoit en son idee, … à [la] figurer [en] certeine chose … Telles figures, ainsi inventees, ils apellarent leurs Devises" ("according to the special affinity each person had for his idea, that person represented that idea through a particular object … Such figures, invented in this way, they called their devices"—*The Heroicall Devises* 152; emphasis added; my translations).

23. Paradin, *The Heroicall Devises* 3–4.

24. Paradin, *The Heroicall Devises* 6.

25. Paradin, *The Heroicall Devises* 94.

26. Russell 175–79.

27. In this boundary imposed by the frame, Marguerite seeks to channel free interpretation. Ignatius, later, not surprisingly as he is reacting to the successes of the Protestant Reformation, also strives to guide imagination into acceptable channels. The difference is that he is proposing a primarily visual method of enacting aspects of the Divine Passion: while he refers to Scripture, the primary emphasis is on "word-pictures" constructed by the believer and meant to evoke subjective responses to the Passion. For Ignatius, an initial goal of the exercise is the construction of the image itself, which is deemed to have meaning.

28. In *nouvelle* #10, for example, the use of simile discloses Amadour's deceptive nature and imposture: "l'on ne se gardoit de luy non plus que d'une femme … comme s'il eust esté son propre frère" ("Floride was aware of nothing, except perhaps that she was as fond of Amadour as if he had been her own brother"—*Hept.* 1.10.60; Chilton 128).

29. For example, Corneille de Lyon (1533–75), a Netherlandish artist active in Lyon and Paris and Marguerite's contemporary, painted *Portrait of a Young Man with Gloves.* In the portrait, the first finger of the youth's right hand sports a ring, and he clutches an embroidered doeskin glove. Elements of the representation suggest questions that could be responded to through narrative development: Why does he grasp his glove so firmly? Is he about to take it off or to don it?

30. In *Building Codes: The Calvinist Aesthetics of Early Modern Europe*, I discussed the use of ornament as distortion or as ciphered evidence of an impulse subversive of the status quo, in many Protestant writers of the period, as well as in the architectural treatment of real structures. Evangelicals such as Marguerite use ornament and excessive detail to similar ends.

31. Le sieur de Brantôme 273; my translation.

32. Le sieur de Brantôme 273.

33. Le sieur de Brantôme 273.

34. Contrarily, this may explain why Dürer, a Lutheran, presented his engraved glove to us in such a flattened way: while the jewels draw attention to its surface, the glove seems to lack substance and heft. It remains a virtual or potential representation, although some cross-hatching near the wrist of Dürer's glove suggests some "hand" to the fabric: perhaps were a wearer to don the glove, a practical relationship might exist between subject and object.

35. Paradin, *The Heroicall Devises* 53–54.

36. Paradin, *The Heroicall Devises* 53–54.

37. Chilton includes no translation from the Italian.

38. This technique is used by other evangelical and Protestant writers. The Huguenot Bernard Palissy, for instance, in the *Recepte véritable*, has his *promeneur*, or Everyman, walking in the garden of Palissy's designing, enter through doorways inscribed with scriptural passages, so that the Everyman figure is thereby inevitably inserted into biblical order.

39. The contextual tenor of most of her stories bears out this possibility. Further, Marguerite most frequently inserts herself into those *nouvelles* that are more evangelical in tenor and message, e.g., *Hept.* 3.30.232.

40. The wordplay in *nouvelle* #18 acts similarly. The play on, and contrast between, *conte* (a Count) and *compte* (an accounting, a recounting, or a tale) puns the story into metaphysical sense. A corrupt nobleman supplies the pretext for an admonitory tale that, in due course, exonerates him of his misdemeanors. Paradin also offers another example of this punning strategy; his *devise* of the anchor may also be read as a pun. The anchor, he tells us, is meant "en signe de l'esperance que nous devons avoir de nostre salut, en nostre sauveur Iesus christ" ("as a sign of the hope that we should have of our salvation through our savior Jesus Christ"). This soteric sign is communicated through the *encre* ("ink") that narrates it, teaching that attentiveness to evangelical doctrine may lead to redemption; this belief is encapsulated in the *ancre* that rhymes with the *encre* that describes and defines it.

41. See, for instance, the embroidered damask table napkins from Flanders, circa 1630, at the Philadelphia Museum of Art, displaying three scenes from the Old Testament story of Judith and Holofernes.

42. The terms *enigma* and *emblem* are linguistically closely related. Neither is transparent; both necessitate a process of interpretation. I owe this insight to Daniel Russell, who made the comment in prefatory remarks to his paper presented at the Newberry Library, Renaissance Society of America, Chicago, 29 Mar. 2001.

43. Critics have long acknowledged that this is the intent of Marguerite's poetry and plays. However, her prose works have not benefitted from the same scrutiny along theological lines. Studies tend to be more narrative criticism or gender studies, e.g., Patricia Cholakian's *Rape and Narrative*.

44. See, for instance, Palissy's *Recepte véritable*.

45. Rabelais also uses *joye,* in the *Quart livre*, for example, where he conflates a discussion of *santé* with the goal of *salut*: "s'il plaist au bon Dieu, vous obtiendrez santé" ("if it pleases God, you will gain health/be saved"–prologue, *Quart livre* 559; my translation). Rabelais speaks of "certaine gayeté d'esprit conficte en mespris des choses fortuites" ("a certain joyfulness of spirit, made up of the distrust of transitory things"—545), and links this disposition of spirit to "la sacrosaincte parolle de bonnes nouvelles: c'est l'Evangile" ("the holy word of the good news: the Gospel"—562). The term *joye* recurs in his text ("entrast en joye nouvelle"; "he experienced a new joy"—559).

46. She differs from Calvin in her willingness to use literature, which Calvin had condemned as fiction: *fingere*, or mendacity. Carol Thysell has dealt with this issue in *The Pleasure of Discernment*. See also Coats, *Subverting the System* 1–3.

47. Alciati, qtd. in Saunders 264; my translation.

48. I thank Daniel Russell for this information.

49. Rabelais's list of exotica—the unicorn's horn and the tapestry—acts similarly, in that the collection of objects on its own is not important, but the *act* of collecting *is*.

50. The term *décorateur* only enters the French language at the end of the sixteenth century, and is generally applied to the court, in the sense of designing costumes, exploiting varieties of postures, masks, and crafted self-depictions. It is ornamental, not necessary, disguise. Evangelicals seek to penetrate beyond its play to discern essence.

Chapter Three
A New Medium for a New Message: Evangelicals and Decorative Arts

1. By describing innovations in both decorative arts and fine arts (the distinction was only just beginning to be made at the beginning of the sixteenth century), and by drawing on textual materialist criticism that interprets daily-life objects, their applications, and their possessors' interactions with them as meaningful *narratives*, it can be seen that Marguerite de Navarre, stimulated intellectually and visually at the showcase court of her brother François Ier, the first great "collector king," crafted a new form of narrative. Despite the proliferation of ornate objects possessing narrative significance in the *Heptaméron*, Marguerite has not previously been interpreted from an art historical angle.

2. Baumgartner 199.

3. For instance, the Reformed printer Jean de Tournes penned a preface to the 1553 edition of Claude Paradin's *Quadrins Poëtiques*, an emblem book, stipulating that the purpose of such prose construction is to magnify the divine Word:

> Donques, pour l'importance des Sainctes Histoires, qui est si grande, qu'elles ne devroient estre ignorees de personne: nous avons choisi certeines adminicules de Peintures, accompagnez de Quadrins Poëtiques, tirez de la Bible, pour graver en la table des affections, l'amour des sacrees Histoires, à celle fin que un chacun fust induit à l'amour de ce seul et unique necessaire, qui est la saincte Parole de Dieu.
>
> ("Therefore, because of the importance of Scripture, which is so great, and so that it might not be unknown to anyone, we have chosen certain smallish paintings, paired with poetical quatrains taken from the Bible, to engrave on the tablet of human affections the love for these holy stories, so that everyone might be led to love the one essential thing: God's Holy Word."— De Tournes, qtd. in Rosasco 241)

Paradin also wrote the *Quadrins Historiques de la Bible* (1553), which he published with Jean de Tournes, and which was illustrated by the engraver Bernard Salomon, a Protestant. The 1557 Bible revised by the Protestant ministers of Geneva incorporated Salomon's engravings. "Le petit Bernard"'s enormously popular engravings were also consistently used as "pattern book" illustrations throughout the period among craftsmen and artists, exemplifying the interdisciplinary collaboration that

Marguerite also employs in the *Heptaméron*. Different *métiers* copied Salomon's cartoons, adapting them for furniture, art objects, and bibelots. Salomon's designs enriched varied media such as ceramics (decorated plates from Pierre Courtey's workshop) and *ébenistrie* (slats of exotic woods set decoratively into furniture), providing in this way a parallel to the applications that Marguerite envisions for her narrative. Salomon's images, termed "patrons sur papier de diverses histoires" ("patterns on paper of diverse stories") like the *Heptaméron*'s varied tales, moved artistic innovation into the realm of textual transmission. Salomon, like Marguerite, conceived of text as a container for artifacts, or even as itself an artifact. He writes:

> … en cestuy labeur … si tu n'as le loisir de lire … tu puisses pour le moins tapisser les chambres de ta mémoire des figures d'icelle, plus honnestement selon nous que tu ne fais les chambres, les salles de ta maison, des histoires …
>
> ("… in this work of [representation] … if you do not have the leisure to read [it], … you may at least line the rooms of your memory with its tapestried figures, in a more seemly fashion, in [my] opinion, than the way that you [now] decorate the chambers and rooms of your home with tales.")

He asserts, like Marguerite, that a "plus honnest[e]" Christian direction and content for storytelling exists, in which appropriate objects may be selected for purposes of communication (as opposed to stories "mal convenantes") (Salomon, qtd. in Brugerolles 226–28).

4. Calvin similarly condoned works of art as long as they did not violate the Second Commandment: once removed to a secular sphere, where they could not be blasphemous, artworks did not trouble him. Calvin enjoined, "let them paint or sculpt only those things which the eyes are capable of seeing" (Calvin, *Institutes* 1.9.12).

5. See the discussion of how Rembrandt creates a synthesis between art and his Reformed beliefs in Tanis 395.

6. Harbison 26.

7. Hegel claims a link between genre painters and Protestantism based on the observation that "Protestantism alone enjoys the distinction of infiltrating the prose of life" (562). See also Charles Taylor, "God Loveth Adverbs," in *Sources of the Self*.

8. Harbison 26.

9. This can be contrasted with the collapse of one into the other typically seen in the fifteenth century.

10. Veldman 404.

11. Despite the existence of such texts, it nevertheless remains the case that "the depiction of specific Calvinist doctrines like predestination is extremely uncommon" in literature and art of the first few decades of the sixteenth century (Veldman 404), perhaps because strains of Calvinism possessed strongly iconoclastic sentiments deterring the illustration of dogmatic concepts.

12. Or so we would call it today; the distinction between "fine" and "decorative" arts did not exist in the sixteenth century.

13. "Portraiture is a genre that we customarily associate not just with Protestantism in general, but more specifically with the Calvinist or Reformed branch of Protestantism" (Harbison 18).

14. In order for this cross-pollination to take place, it is not always the case that artists of identical theological persuasion influence Marguerite. Although this does occur, it also happens that Catholic artists experimenting in new venues and with new media bring their work to Fontainebleau where Marguerite sees it, is interested in it, and finds something in it to imitate and incorporate.

15. Roper 34.

16. O'Neill 246.

17. Harbison, qtd. in O'Neill 366.

18. This is an emphasis shared by the early Netherlandish painters, whose work François Ier extensively collected. Hegel noted the close connection between Protestantism and genre painting. Hegel: "Protestantism alone enjoys the distinction of infiltrating the prose of life" (562).

19. Rembrandt's narrative use of objects is a later example of this emphasis.

20. Harbison 164, fig. 268.

21. Charles Taylor 216.

22. O'Neill 364.

23. Harbison 21–24.

24. Harbison 120.

25. Harbison 112–16.

26. Harbison 359.

27. Falkenburg: "Martin de Klijn relates … the rise of realistic painting during the first decades of the seventeenth century directly to the theocentric view of nature in the emerging Calvinist culture of the northern Netherlands" (345).

28. De Klijn, qtd. in Falkenburg 350.

29. Kloek 529.

30. "Et, pour parvenir à la plus grande difficulté, qui estoit la loingtaneté du païs où il demeuroit … avoit tellement hanté ceste frontiere" ("… and in order to overcome the greatest obstacle, which was the distance of the country where he resided, he had spent a lot of time on its borders"—*Hept.* 1.10.56).

31. "esperant que à la longue il gaigneroit le lieu" ("hoping that in the long run he would take [the other's] place"—*Hept.* 1.10.59). As Amadour's desire grows, the pinpoint focus on different real places he had visited, or the fictive sites of his fantasies, broadens to embrace an expanse of space: his lust is now global and pervasive, "en tous lieux" ("everywhere"—*Hept.* 1.10.61).

32. Rabelais, *Pantagruel* 193.

33. Rabelais, *Pantagruel* 193; trans. Cohen 171.

34. Neither Marguerite nor Rabelais represent landscape in a painterly way; rather, they enumerate places and lands. Many Catholic writers do, however, represent landscape more exactly. These include Francesco Colonna and Cervantes, among others.

35. A notable exception is Rabelais's Thélème.

36. In her study *Celestial Ladders*, Paula Sommers interprets the text as belonging to the tradition of the "ladder," a "medieval *topos* describing the stages of spiritual ascension and progressive detachment of the soul from worldly dross. Landscape itineraries epitomize in this context the Christian's progress toward union with God" (11).

37. They both describe their inner states in spatial language that evokes the landscape of attraction. Floride uses terms of proximity to explain to Amadour that she feels very happy when he is near: "elle sentoit ung très grand contentement, quand elle estoit auprès de luy" ("she felt great contentment when she was near him"—*Hept.* 1.10.61), and he disavows the base emotion of lust toward her by expressing in spatial terms his intention to distance himself from such emotions: "de vous aimer d'une amour vitieuse … je suis si loing de ceste affection" ("to love you with a vicious love … I am so far from that feeling …"—*Hept.* 1.10.63).

38. Floride reproaches Amadour, accordingly, that "ceulx qui tentent pour chercher la vertu n'ont accoustumé prendre le chemin que vous avez prins" ("those who try to seek virtue do not usually follow the path that you have taken"—*Hept.* 1.10.75). The text literalizes Amadour's *chemin*, displaying it so that the reader may discern that it is erroneous, a *mis*-mapping of worldly desire.

39. O'Neill 266.

40. This relationship between plot and river has been well exemplified in an analysis of La Fontaine's fable "Le loup et l'agneau" (Chambers 71).

41. O'Neill 279.

42. Medieval paintings often hinted at, or delineated in miniature, landscape as background for a larger setting for a subject and theme. The Catholic treatment in many cases does not differ substantially from that of evangelical artists. Read in conjunction with evangelical narratives evoking landscapes, however, the landscapes by evangelical artists license interpretation as narrative rather than simply as image. These landscapes, when read in relation to the evangelical text, demonstrate a progression and a change in perspective.

43. Sommers 81. See also Donaldson-Evans 210–23.

44. Brugerolles 206.

45. Catholic painters chose Old Testament subjects, also, but their repertory was different: Tobias and the Angel, and similar stories generally taken from the Apocrypha, were more prevalent.

46. I have commented elsewhere on the use of such grotesqueries by artists such as Bernard Palissy and Jacques Androuet du Cerceau, both

Calvinists, and asserted that the broken, bizarre figures epitomize fallen nature, a theological statement in artistic terms (Randall, *Building Codes: The Calvinist Aesthetics of Early Modern Europe).*

47. See Brugerolles 198–204. The *Design for a Covered Cup* (B.n. Département des Estampes et de la Photographie) is reproduced on page 204 of the catalogue.

48. Harbison 91; emphasis added.

49. The need to control, order, and organize the plethora of *exempla* can be seen in Catholic artists as well, but they deal with this urge somewhat differently. Dante's *Inferno* was organized by categories, levels, and types of sin, a more doctrinal concept lacking typology in Scripture and, therefore, devised by man. The Calvinist writer Du Bartas, on the other hand, organized his *La sepmaine* by the rubric of "days": this division is directly derived from Scripture.

50. Another example is storytelling tapestries adorned with strapwork such as *Verdure with Animals* by Willem Anderesz de Raet (1570).

51. Harbison 93.

52. Kloek 91.

53. Janson 484.

54. Lomax, "Huguenot Goldsmiths in England," in Finney 113.

55. Kloek 90.

56. Certainly, organizational techniques were a commonplace preoccupation among both sixteenth-century Catholics and Protestants. Pierre Ramus and Guillaume Salluste Du Bartas, both Huguenots, are probably the two most influential of such devisers of systems. In addition, the Protestant Henri Estienne's *Dictionnaires* were organized alphabetically, an entirely new idea at the time.

57. This is discussed in Simon Schama, *The Embarrassment of Riches*, where he chronicles, among other examples, how Calvinist city fathers tried to corral the ambitious constructions of their wealthy coreligionists, requiring that house fronts be limited to a certain footage rather than present an invasion of space from the street front.

58. Bull's eye mirrors were in vogue, having only recently been invented. Flemish artists favored them because of the technical difficulties posed by accurately reproducing the distorted, or even anamorphotic, likenesses that such mirrors produced. Other mirrors were more reliable, some made of burnished metal and others constructed of glass backed with a slim metal sheet or coating.

59. Fumerton, "'Secret' Arts" 27.

60. Fumerton, "'Secret' Arts" 35.

61. Harbison: "In the Protestant states portraiture flourished" (18).

62. They feel "impuissant[s] à refaire l'image de Dieu en [eux-mêmes]" ("powerless to remake God's image within themselves") and ask, "que suis-je, Seigneur, en moy-mesmes que corruption, qu'injustice, que mort?" ("what am I, Lord, in myself, but corruption, injustice and death?"—Bèze 60).

63. Harbison 22.

64. Harbison 26.

65. Similarly, Van Eyck's *The Arnolfini Marriage* is "composed heraldically: each object or detail is carefully positioned so that the surface of the panel forms a shield-like pattern, a frozen puzzle of artful precision ... [a] manipulated spatial composition ... creati[ing] a compact zone of interaction and meaning" (Harbison 31). This is a representation meant to be interpreted through strategies of reading, inviting the application of such technique to textual constructions.

66. Like other evangelicals, Marguerite criticizes clergy who posture, "tenu pour ung sainct homme" ("regarded by all as a very holy man"—*Hept.* 4.33.247; Chilton 337). She incorporates evangelical creedal statements in her text: "Voylà, mes dames ...sçachant très bien que nous n'avons que ung Saulveur, lequel, en disant: *Consummatum est*, a monstré qu'il ne laissoit poinct de lieu à ung aultre successeur pour faire nostre salut" ("So that, ladies ... knew that we have but one Saviour who, when He said 'Consummatum est,' showed that he was leaving no way open for any successor to bring us salvation"—*Hept.* 4.33.249; Chilton 339).

67. I have already noted in Chapter 1 the similarities in narrative treatment of the *tableau,* a sort of Protestant micro-genre, in both Luther and Marguerite.

68. Harbison 120.

69. Desan, *L'Imaginaire économique*: "dans son 'Argument du present livre qui précède *l'Institution de la Religion Chrestienne*, Calvin insiste pareillement sur le profit à tirer de la lecture de son ouvrage. Les vocables 'proffit,' 'profitter,' et 'proffitable' reviennnent quatre fois en moins de deux pages et agissent tel un leitmotiv" ("in his 'Argument of the Current Book' that preceded his *Institutes of the Christian Religion*, Calvin stresses the profit to be gained from reading his book. The terms 'profit,' 'to profit,' and 'profitable' recur at least four times in fewer than two pages and thus act as a leitmotif"— 217).

70. Calvin, qtd. in Desan, *L'Imaginaire économique* 217.

71. Marguerite de Navarre, *Heptaméron*, ed. M. François (Paris: Garnier, 1967), 7.

72. Cotgrave, "passer le temps."

73. Cotgrave, "passement" and "passementerie."

74. Cotgrave, "passetemps."

Chapter Four
Of Tableware, Chalices, and Axeheads: The Evangelical Narrative and Transitory Treasures

1. Rabelais, *Quart livre* 580.

2. Charles Taylor: "So to take their proper place in God's order, humans had to avoid two opposite deviations. They must spurn the monkish error of renunciation of things of this world—possessions, marriage—for this amounts to scorning God's gifts, which they should instead be bringing back to him through worshipful use ... The other error was to become absorbed in things, take them for ourselves ... It was not the use of things which brought evil, Puritan preachers constantly repeated, but our deviant purpose in using them: ... 'where the world hath got possession in the heart, it makes false to God, and false to man, it makes us unfaithfull in our callings, and false to Religion it selfe'" (221).

3. Calvin even goes so far as to distrust writing, such as verses inscribed on walls, as a potentially idolatrous thing, if such inscription is viewed as having a sort of magical potency (such that writing a verse on the wall is efficacious in and of itself): "*Pace* Calvin, the repetition of God's law within a predestined world is precisely superfluous; the wall-written prayer (and by extension any prayer) is reduced to the statement of an intention to pray. What, after all, following Deuteronomy, should one write on posts, gates and frontlets for the eyes?—nothing more nor less than the injunction to do so. But what has one done in doing this? The answer, even for Calvin, is nothing at all ... Calvin attempts to displace the carnal potential of the writing practices he endorses by displacing it first onto women ... and then on to the Jews ... For Calvin, to believe in the efficacy of words in their material dimension is to commit precisely the idolatry that the passage warns against ... Impossibly, Reformed Christianity structures itself across the problem of the signifier, the problem that is the material dimension of language" (Fumerton, *Renaissance Culture and the Everyday* 340).

4. Luther had such a high opinion of Aesop that he published his own German version of the fables. Luther, *Table Talk* 76n246. See also Rabelais, *Quart livre* 548, where he refers to the "saige Aesope Français."

5. Weiss, "La littérature de la Réforme française": "Ces parties indépendantes sont-elles des manifestations *originales* de la piété évangélique *française* à cette époque où la Réforme n'avait encore dans notre patrie que peu d'adhérents déclarés?" ("Are these independent groups the first manifestation of evangelical French piety during this time in our country when the Reformation still had very few overt adherents?"—37, 161).

6. Weiss, "La littérature de la Réforme française": "La partie la plus originale du livret, celle du moins dont nous connaissons pas d'autre texte, est la troisième. Elle a peut-être été inspirée par plusieurs des premiers traités de Luther, mais c'est certainement une des premières pages qui résument d'une manière populaire les idées et les préoccupations des ouvriers français de la première heure et à ce titre elle mérite d'être reproduite intégralement" ("The earlier part of the booklet, that which appears to have no precursor, is the third, which was perhaps inspired by some of Luther's early treatises. It is certainly one of the first [French] texts to sum up in a popular vein the ideas and concerns of these innovative French precursors [of Protestantism] and, as such, deserves to be reproduced in full"—37: 436).

7. Du Bois shows an interesting similarity with Marguerite's strategy of self-inscription in her *nouvelles,* a technique that may derive from the auto-referential presence in Luther's *Table Talk*: here, Du Bois's publishing colophon is a personal *devise* that literally places him at the head of all the evangelical works that he published. Weiss, "La littérature de la Réforme française": "Grâce à cette devise, la vignette si expressive du titre représente la marque de *l'imprimeur*, c'est-à-dire de Simon Du Bois. Il se serait donc fait représenter lui-même dans l'attitude de l'oraison …" ("thanks to this *devise,* the evocative image accompanying the title is in fact the printer's mark: that of Simon Du Bois. He has represented himself in the position of prayer …"—37: 163). In this way, Du Bois explicitly affiliates himself with the evangelical perspective.

8. Weiss, "Les premières professions de foi des protestants français": "On trouve un dernier qui n'est autre que la traduction du petit catéchisme du réformateur saxon, imprimé et publié en France, peut-être à Alençon, par Simon Du Bois" ("There is a final [pamphlet] which is none other than the translation of the 'Small Catechism' by the Saxon reformer, printed and published in France, perhaps in Alençon, by Simon Du Bois"—60).

9. Weiss, "La littérature de la Réforme française": "Voici, en effet, la courte liste des volumes exécutés par cet imprimeur et pourtant, outre son nom, une date et une indication de lieu qui permettent de fixer sa résidence à diverses époques: 1525, 25 avril, Paris (le privilège est du 16 mars) pour Galliot du Pré, les *Chants royaulx* de Guillaume Cretin … *dédiés à Marguerite d'Angoulême* … 1525, du 6 au 19 octobre, Paris la dernière édition parue en France, *du N[ouveau] T[estament] de Lefèvre d'Etaples* …" ("Here is, in effect, the short list of titles printed by this publisher and bearing, in addition to his name, a date and a place indication enabling us to establish where he lived at different times: April 25, 1525 in Paris. The permission is dated March 16, for Galliot du Pré [to publish] Guillaume Cretin's *Chants royaulx* dedicated to Marguerite d'Angoulême … from October 6–19, 1525, in Paris, the last edition to be printed in France of Lefèvre d'Étaples's translation of the New Testament"— 36: 669; emphasis added).

10. Weiss, "La littérature de la Réforme française": "… 1531. Alençon. La première édition du célèbre *Miroir de l'âme pécheresee*, de Marguerite … 1533. Alençon. Le *Dialogue en forme de vision nocturne* … suivi du *Miroir*, etc., de la même princesse" ("1531, in Alençon, the first edition of the famous *Miroir* of the sinful soul by Marguerite; 1533, in Alençon, the *Dialogue,* in the form of nightly vision, followed by the *Miroir*, by this same princess"—36: 670).

11. Luther, *Table Talk* 452.

12. De LaGaranderie: "Si, dans le paysage des années 1515–35, Erasme est presque omniprésent, le devant de la scène, aux environs de

1520, revient à Luther. A travers les tracasseries, les censures, les persécutions, qui s'exercent contre les positions, plus nuancées, et plus incertaines, de l'évangélisme, c'est lui qui polarise et obsède les esprits" ("If, during the years 1515–1535, Erasmus nearly totally usurps center stage, the forefront of the scene around 1520 belongs to Luther. Through all the struggles, censorship, persecutions exercised against the more nuanced, as yet uncertain evangelicalism, it is Luther who polarizes and obsesses the contemporary mind"—27).

13. Kloek: "From certain details it is possible to deduce an unmistakable Reformation interpretation of the parable, which supplies a conclusive reason for the absence of a signature" (76).

14. Harbison: "In northern Europe, a principle of creative fragmentation and reconstruction was followed ... we are not meant to be able to [see] absolutely clearly the relation between the fragment we see and the world beyond the picture frame. Visual intrigue and a personal imaginative experience of the environment played [into the interpretation]" (38).

15. Harbison 114; emphasis added.

16. Hans Holbein, who espoused Lutheranism in 1528, used detail in similar ways and for similar purposes. Some art critics feel that Albrecht Dürer's program, and that of other Lutheran artists, to communicate Reformed doctrine through visual media was, in large measure, a failure. Harbison:

> such efforts to embody Luther's doctrine in art were doomed, since the spiritual leaders of the Reformation looked upon religious images with indifference ... or ... hostility, even though Luther himself seems to have been relatively tolerant of them. (533)

In many cases, Dürer's "passion prints" are deemed to have aimed at aesthetic impact rather than at any pious use, so as to avoid idolatrous emphasis on the graven image. In a similar approach, Dürer, a Lutheran, used his painting *The Last Supper* (1523) to illustrate Luther's mandate that communion was not a daily repetition of Christ's sacrifice in each mass—since that sacrifice had been efficacious once for all—but rather a commemoration. Dürer omitted a customary iconographic feature to convey his stance: Catholic convention displayed a sacrificial lamb on the plate, but Dürer's platter is pointedly empty. Gérard David, an evangelical active at the court of François Ier, painted his 1520 *Virgin and Child with Porridge* to display Mary as a secular woman, engaging in the ordinary activities of eating and feeding, so that she might furnish a model for human conduct: in this way, he avoided any problematic—because, for Reformers, potentially blasphemous—depiction of the divine.

17. Luther, *Table Talk* 56.

18. As long as they were written in Latin, religious texts could appear in print after being submitted for approval. In addition to Bibles, publishing religious texts in French was forbidden, a rule that Marguerite ignored in the *Marguerites de la Marguerite*.

19. Weiss, "Les premières professions de foi des protestants français": ["En ce qui concernait *Les Bibles latines* d'Estienne"]: "... ce qui doublait, triplait le prix de cette propagande indirecte, ce sont les annotations de plus en plus nombreuses et importantes, ajoutées en marge du texte pour les rendre plus intelligible et en serrer de plus près le sens original ... on verra [en 1545] que ces annotations ont fini par occuper presque autant de place que le texte lui-même" ("what doubled, even tripled the price of the clandestine propaganda were increasingly numerous and extensive annotations added in the margin of the text to make it more intelligible and to make the original meaning explicit ... by 1545, these annotations took up almost as much space as the text itself"—72).

20. Luther, *Table Talk* 221.

21. There are some exceptions to this rule, however, where Luther is concerned. See, for example, Luther, *Table Talk* 245.

22. Luther, *Table Talk* 138.

23. Concerning textual transmission and authenticity, it has been said that the transcription of *Table Talk* was attributable to "second-rate Boswells" who surrounded Luther at supper, such that a distinct, unified authorial "Luther" persona does not exist in *Table Talk* (issue raised by David Lotz, during a discussion at Union Theological Seminary, February 2001). However, whether or not he actually uttered every phrase ascribed to him is not at issue here. Key, rather, is the fact that a like-minded coterie forged a recognizable evangelical style, and that one of its hallmarks is this creative tension with the material world.

24. Luther, *Table Talk* 12.

25. Luther, *Table Talk* 24.

26. Luther, *Table Talk* 183.

27. Luther, *Table Talk* 22.

28. Charles Taylor 56.

29. Harbison: "Northern art is [characterized] by space, private and enclosed" (33).

30. Harbison: "In this sense it is legitimate to speak of the secularization of artistic expression in the later sixteenth century" (118).

31. Luther, *Table Talk* 71.

32. Luther, *Table Talk* 377.

33. Luther, *Table Talk* 46.

34. Luther, *Table Talk* 406.

35. Such features are also often characteristic of the still life.

36. Luther, *Table Talk* 351; emphasis added. This theme—and related themes—recur in the *Heptaméron*. See, for example, "Celluy qui est vray juge" ("in Him who was the true judge"—Hept. 4.60.277; Chilton 370) "nous n'avons que ung Sauveur" ("we have but one Saviour"—*Hept.*

4.33.249; Chilton 339). Any such image, however, while illustrative of doctrine, had to tread a fraught path between representation and evocation. Kibbey: "The second commandment, in forbidding images, forb[ade] not only bodily images (graven or molten or painted) but all spiritual images also, which are the imaginations and inventions of men. [But] whatever kind of image the commandment could prohibit, it could also sanction ... [There was] a concern to find a sanction for images that were verbal, poetic, or visionary, what we would call today literary or mental images rather than icons ... [Thus] iconoclasm [could also be] a verbal phenomenon ... With the exception of Luther ..., Reformation intellectuals proposed some kind of figurative interpretation of the sacrament's consecrating words ... point[ing] to the Reformers' insight into the figurative nature of religious language" (66–67). Artists worked out similar tensions.

37. Luther, *Table Talk* 292.

38. Luther, *Table Talk* 292.

39. Luther, *Table Talk* 418. This is akin to Marguerite's use of *compte,* meaning both story and accounting.

40. Luther, *Table Talk* 212.

41. Luther, *Table Talk* 80.

42. Luther, *Table Talk* 97.

43. Perhaps for this reason, the *Heptaméron* refers less and less frequently to material objects in the later books, as the message, rather than materiality, prevails. It is also appropriate that the *Heptaméron* remains unfinished, for, since a book is also a thing—however salvific a message it may convey—it must never purport to be autotelic, but rather must always look beyond itself for fulfillment.

44. While this anecdote appears to be an allegory, because of the transformation of one element into another to produce an entirely new substance, the story surpasses allegory in that components of the story's conclusion do not possess corresponding ciphers as they would in an allegorical grid of interpretation.

45. Luther, *Table Talk* 277.

46. Luther, *Table Talk* 160.

47. Rabelais refers to this in his Prologue to the *Quart livre*: "one of the sons of the prophets in Israel was splitting wood near the River Jordan—as is written in II Kings, 6—when the iron worked loose from his hatchet and fell into the river ..." (trans. Cohen 441).

48. Cotgrave: "coignee."

49. Rabelais: "his mark" (trans. Cohen 446).

50. See Luke 24.52; Gal. 5.22; Phil. 1.18 and 1.25–26, and many others.

51. Just so, frame narratives with a metaphysical perspective like that of the *Heptaméron* collect the diverse shards of human experience, putting together a mosaic of worldly objects that do not signify *in se* or even in relationship, but only by virtue of their inclusion in the frame.

52. See the components of Quaresmeprenant's description in Rabelais, *Quart livre* 644–45.

53. Taschen 8.

54. Taschen 25.

55. Taschen: Arcimboldo's "sumptuously ornamental paintings full of fruit and blossom, flower bunches and garlands, angels and little cherubs, as well as an abundance of scroll-shaped ornaments ... do not leave space for anything else" (12).

56. This is a customary evangelical preoccupation, as evidenced by Pierre Ramus's ordering schemas.

57. The phrase also recalls Catholic doctrine that the Pope is "God on earth" (*Deus in terris*).

58. See also *Hept.* 3.26, the story of a lover who disguises himself as a groom to be near his lady; and *Hept.* 7.69, where a serving girl costumes her master in a disguise that reveals to her mistress his designs on her, among others.

59. Marguerite de Navarre, *Le miroir de tres chrestienne Princesse Marguerite.*

60. Schama, *Rembrandt's Eyes*: We see a similar technique in the area of fine arts with Rembrandt who "could make the things of the world to come, yet manage, somehow, not to trespass impiously across the borders. He had created what the preachers said was impossible: Protestant icons" (479).

61. Castellani 30–31.

62. Rabelais, *Quart livre*: "Avoir les pieds en l'air, la teste en bas, estoit imitation du Créateur de l'univers, veu que les cheveulx sont en l'homme comme racines ..." ("To have one's feet in the air and one's head down, therefore, was to imitate the creator of the Universe, seeing that hair in men was like their roots, and their legs were like branches"—trans. Cohen 520).

63. Harbison 114.

64. See also Luke 22.31. This motif is found throughout the Gospel of Matthew, and in Mark as well.

65. Simon Schama makes this observation at several points in his analyses of various of Rembrandt's paintings in *Rembrandt's Eyes.*

66. Cotgrave: "chiquan."

67. This theme—and related themes—recur in the *Heptaméron.* See, for example, "Celluy qui est vray juge" ("in Him who isthe true judge"—*Hept.* 4.60.277; Chilton 370); "nous n'avons que ung Sauveur ("we have but one Saviour"—*Hept.* 4.33.249; Chilton 339).

68. Other contemporary artists, evangelical or Reformed, also favored this theme. Lucas Cranach (1472–1553), a Protestant, crafted a didactic engraving entitled *The Allegory of Law and Grace.*

69. Harbison 91.

Chapter Five
The Evangelical Narrative: Des Périers, Du Fail, and Yver

1. These evangelical authors also owed a debt to Philippe de Vigneules. However, his tales preceded theirs by a generation or more.

2. Des Périers's stories were composed in the 1530s, and no later than 1540. Marguerite shows the influence of her secretary and valet de chambre, Marot, and similarly shows the influence of her secretary, Des Périers. Disregarding a law requiring any blacklisted works to be destroyed, Marguerite kept all of Des Périers's works in her library.

3. Bonaventure Des Périers, *Les nouvelles récréations et joyeux devis.*

4. Des Périers: "Recommandez-vous à Dieu.—Recommandez-vous à luy, et vous y serez en huy" ("Commend yourself to God, and you will remain in Him"—*Les nouvelles récréations* 24).

5. Pierre Jourda, ed. *Conteurs français du XVI*[e] *siècle.*

6. Like Rabelais and Marguerite, too, Du Fail depicts the falling away from clerical vows and from God as a form of journey ("peregriner"), a misbegotten itinerary that marks physical space with the stigma of error and sin.

7. Noël Du Fail, *Les baliverneries d'Eutrapel.*

8. His sources are Marguerite de Navarre, Boccaccio, Rabelais, and Bandello.

9. Yver xlii.

Chapter Six
Earthly Treasures: Marguerite's *Mondain* Monstrances

1. Kibbey: Luther's "complete separation of words and things … denigrated the worldly object … The material object was unrecognized in the consecrating words that Luther accepted as definitive of reality in the mass. The bread [for instance] was so fully taken over by Christ's body that it ceased to be significant in the most fundamental sense" (75).

2. Palliser, qtd. in Paré: "That he was not a devout Catholic comes through … Was he secretly in sympathy with the Huguenots? The Haags, in their treatment of him in the celebrated France protestante … seek to demonstrate that this was the case" (23).

3. Palliser, qtd. in Paré 155–56.

4. Kibbey 82.

5. Schama, *Rembrandt's Eyes*: "the glossy rendering of material surfaces … was always a tool of his storytelling." Rembrandt's emphasis on things is aimed at demonstrating the impermanence and insignificance of these things: he "reveal[s] the material texture of metals, while paradoxically suggesting their insubstantiality. This was one of the commonplaces of the Protestant culture of the time" (265).

6. There was a class dimension to the way in which things of the world were regarded, as well. Evangelicals could take a more detached, critical look at things because, in many cases, they were part of the socio-economic elite. Better off materially, they had the luxury to do so. Later Reformers also often came from such upper strata, but tended to be more diffused throughout socio-conomic ranks.

7. Appadurai 38.

8. Appadurai 112.

9. Danielle Trudeau: "la réflexion sur le langage au xvie siècle se libère peu à peu de la théologie pour adopter la vision du monde profane dont la politique ... définit les ... 'valeurs' ... [de] l'accumulation" ("... meditation of 16th century language progressively detaches itself from theology to adopt a view of the secular world whose policies define 'values' [as] accumulation"—qtd. in Desan, *L'Imaginaire économique* 189).

10. See, for instance, *Hept.* 3.22, the story of Sister Marie Héroët and the discussion of "relicques dudict prieuré" (180).

11. The veneration accorded the "muletiere d'Amboise" in *nouvelle* #2 is a good example: "toutes les femmes de bien de la ville ne faillirent à faire leur debvoir de l'honorer autant qu'il estoit possible ... l'honneur que l'on faisoit à ce corps" ("All the women of the town did not fail to do their duty, and give her the greatest honor ... the respect that they showed for her body"—*Hept.* 1.2.21).

12. I owe the suggestion that the *Heptaméron* in fact offers the depiction of a transitional theological moment to François Rigolot, Princeton University, and his comments on a paper that I presented at the Modern Language Association Convention in San Francisco in 1998.

13. This is akin to Calvin's notion of the labyrinth or the maze of the world in which the self, without stability in Christ, wanders confusedly.

14. Baudrillard, *The System of Objects* 60.

15. Bermingham and Brewer 32.

16. Kloek 54–58.

17. Many Protestants share this artisanal aspect, as many were craftsmen, goldsmiths and watchmakers, and furniture makers. Guillaume Salluste Du Bartas stresses this "making" or fashioning quality when he refers to God always as a productive creator. Finney, *Seeing beyond the Word*, includes in his collection many examples of this Protestant involvement in the decorative arts and crafts.

18. This treatment differs from that analyzed by Paula Sommers in her study *Celestial Ladders*.

19. Desan, *L'Imaginaire économique* 12.

20. Brugerolles 20.

21. To take another example, in another vein, the Catholic Niccolo dell'Abbate's work at Fontainebleau includes a fresco of "Angels Bearing the Instruments of the Passion" (circa 1550). These implements represent events in Jesus' suffering, but they are monumental, rendered heroic, devoid of affective content or the stamp of personality.

22. Kloek 72.

23. Desan, *L'Imaginaire économique* 21.

24. Desan, *L'Imaginaire économique* 179–15.

25. Desan: "L'objet littéraire est bien le lieu et le support privilégié où l'on peut exposer des imaginaires" ("the literary object is actually the privileged place in, and framework on which, one can display imagined systems" (*L'Imaginaire économique* 8).

26. "*Wunderkammer*: a wonder-cabinet: a form of collection peculiar to the Renaissance, characterized primarily by its encyclopedic appetite for marvelous or strange objects and by an exceptionally brief historical career. The Wunderkammer was established in Vienna; for perhaps 100 years such collections flourished, but by the middle of the seventeenth century they were rapidly vanishing." Schnapper, in his study of collecting, *Le géant, la licorne et la tulipe,* maintains that these collectors' cabinets were begun in France, the first with François Ier around 1527, and Henri IV the next major collector (180). I speculate that the severe fractures of the Wars of Religion, followed by the epistemological primacy of rationalist discourse in the late sixteenth-century, were among the factors causing their disappearance in France.

27. Mullaney 68.

28. Schnapper, *Le géant* 220.

29. Schnapper, *Le géant* 231–52.

30. Kloek 40.

31. Janson 542; emphasis added.

32. "Printsheets" with examples of models for furniture and ornamental patterns proliferated in the sixteenth century.

33. Kloek 39: "From the late 15th century onwards, prints were made in Italy of decorative elements, ornaments, vessels and other applied art objects, in which the new vocabulary was applied in numerous variations."

34. Cf., e.g., *Hept.* 2.18.137.

35. The fact that the captain tried to woo the lady and wanted to commit marital infidelity is underscored by the phrasing of his letter, which repeats the sound */di/* in "diamant" and "dy" ("speak"/"tell"), equating the story of his wrongful wooing with the substance of the precious stone representing both his wedded state and his adulterous project: "Ce *di*amant ... O, *di*amant, *dy* ..." (*Hept.* 2.13.104).

36. "Elle se trouva fort empeschée du diamant; car elle n'avoit poinct accoustumé de se parer aux despens d'autres que son mary. Parquoy, elle, qui estoit de bon entendement, pensa de faire prouffiter cest anneau à la conscience de ce capitaine ... la bonne vieille veid ... l'anneau ... et ... baisant l'anneau ..." ("The diamond was an embarrassment. She was not in the habit of wearing jewelry obtained at the expense of any other than her husband. But being a lady of good sense, she decided to use the ring to the benefit of the husband's conscience … the [wife saw] … the wedding ring and … kissed it"—*Hept.* 2.13.104–15; Chilton 174).

37. We will explore the phenomenon of serial storytelling and the rhetoric of repetition in more detail in Chapter 7.

38. Baudrillard, *The System of Objects* 76.

39. Auslander iii.

40. Baudrillard, *The System of Objects* 4.

41. Shell: "In the grail tales the royal courts of the world … such as those of King Arthur … are centers of wastelands. They are sterile deserts" (*Money, Language and Thought* 27).

42. Baudrillard, *System of Objects* 17.

43. Auslander 99.

44. Auslander 98.

45. Campbell 109.

46. Luther, *Table Talk* 62.

47. Campbell 109.

48. Campbell: "The collections of Giovio, the Duke of Prussia, and many more, were continuing, elaborating and systematizing an ancient tradition of gathering together series of princes and famous men" (191).

49. Campbell 3.

50. Schama, *Rembrandt's Eyes* 333.

51. Campbell 134.

52. Schama details a revisionist Protestant technique on Rembrandt's part, as Rembrandt invoked conventional iconography paradoxically by foregrounding its absence; he collapsed the customary expected *object* (the glove) into intimate relationship (two subjectivities) in *The Shipbuilder Jan Rijksen and His Wife Griet Jans* (1633). Schama: The artist has "reserved, right at the heart of the painting, one of the formal, symbolic attributes of marriage, the *dextrarum iunctio* … But instead of it being euphemized in a pair of gloves, he has dissolved the emblem into a moment of imminent contact between husband and wife: the compass and the letter. It's a strike typical of his determination to honor the traditional conventions of marriage portraits while drastically altering their representation" (*Rembrandt's Eyes* 379).

53. On this, see Rabelais, *Pantagruel*, III (in *Œuvres*), where Grandgousier laments the loss of his wife, Badebec, calling her "mon petit con, ma savate, ma pantoufle." My thanks to Gérard Defaux for reminding me of this incident and similarity in treatment between Rabelais and Marguerite.

54. Other Protestants similarly reworked expected meanings of objects. Schama: Rembrandt "was very much more likely to point to the [sexual] allusion [of the slipper] by turning it upside down, using the misstep as a gesture of innocence, the fumbling foot as a reproof to the slavering gaze" (*Rembrandt's Eyes* 398).

55. The story of Madame de Roncex exemplifies such reification: Madame de Roncex sullies herself with excrement and is then publicly derided.

56. "Ledict Gallery luy monstroit cinq ymaiges de boys ... Il nous fault faire de telles ymaiges de cire que ceulx cy, et celles qui auront les bras pendans, ce seront ceulx que nous ferons mourir" ("Gallery was explaining: 'We've got to make dolls like these, but out of wax. The ones with their arms hanging down are the ones we're going to cause to die"—*Hept*. 1.1.16; Chilton 76).

57. "In medieval Europe, puppeteers were regularly attacked by the church for violating God's privilege. The principle of animism, of an object infused with meaning beyond its material self, becomes the principle of metaphor, and puppets are perfect metaphor" (McCracken 27).

58. Serlio relied on Alberti's system of perspective to visualize Vitruvius's descriptions of theater.

59. Janson 486.

60. Du Bois 149.

Chapter Seven
Costuming the Christiform Text; or, *L'habit ne fait pas le moine*

1. Briçonnet to Marguerite, qtd. in Defaux,"Evangelism," qtd. in Hollier 163; emphasis added.

2. It is possible, in fact, that they *prefigure*: it is nearly impossible to unravel whether text influences image, or image, text, in this period of creative cross-pollination.

3. Roberto Campo, *Ronsard's Contentious Sisters: the Paragone between Poetry and Painting in the Work of Pierre de Ronsard.*

4. Campo 242.

5. Campo 203.

6. Some critics, like Gérard Defaux, found this indebtedness to be exaggerated; Defaux convincingly opposed Abel Lefranc, who argued for a Neo-Platonic tenor to the *Heptaméron.*

7. Ficino, qtd. in Campo 203; emphasis added.

8. Swann: "the extravagant display of hospitality [was] construed as an assertion of nobility ... this code of elite generosity persisted well into the seventeenth-century" ("The Politics of Fairylore in Early Modern England" 457).

9. Du Bois 125.

10. Du Bois 128.

11. Du Bois 128.

12. For instance, in her materialist examination of varieties of depictions of subjectivity such as those found on miniature and ornamented precious objects, Fumerton: "aristocratic selfhood was rooted in its experience of the fragmentary, peripheral and ornamental" (qtd. in Swann, "The Politics of Fairylore in Early Modern England" 469).

13. "La désaffection du XVIe siècle par ces grands rassemblements … ne subsisteront que les pélerinages liés aux espérances de guérison et dotés de vertus curatives admises dans la vaste majorité de la société. La raison … réside … dans le désintérêt, voire une méfiance à l'égard des pratiques religieuses extérieures au cercle de la paroisse …" ("The disaffection during the sixteenth century for great crowds … will only persist in pilgrimages linked to the hope of cure and endowed with healing powers in which the majority of society believes. The reason [for this] is found in the lack of interest, even the distrust, manifested toward religious practices external to the parish"—Lobrichon, qtd. in Nora 4167).

14. Defaux, "De la Bonne Nouvelle aux nouvelles."

15. *Feutre* can also designate a filter, something to "distill, or straine things through." *Feutre*, thus, connotes an interpretive lens, one that admits some things while straining out others.

16. Trichet, *Le costume du clergé, ses origines et son évolution en France d'après les règlements de l'Eglise*, qtd. in Grau 36.

17. 4th Lateran Council, qtd. in Grau 36.

18. The cast of characters whose testimony Natalie Zemon Davis analyzes in *Fiction in the Archives* is often Protestant.

19. *Nouvelle* #23 will be discussed in Chapter 8.

20. St. Augustine also refers explicitly to needing to set aside "the garment of [his] flesh," but then earthly treasures, "vain trifles and … triviality," try to hold him back from Christ (Augustine 151).

21. "O ye wicked and accursed generation, no sign shall be given unto you …" (Matt. 16.4).

22. The mark placed on her from behind may recall the "mark of Cain," the special sign designating sinfulness that God placed on Cain after his murder of Abel in Genesis.

23. This is one of Marguerite's—and Luther's—favorite stage-settings for divulging truth, as we have seen in Chapter 2.

24. These constitute a figurative reversal of the pictures cast by firelight on Plato's cave, which he viewed as mere approximations of a beauty yet to be experienced.

25. This is actually a bit of a reversal, or a surprising twist on Scripture, since Scripture enjoins that the husband cherish his wife as Christ does the Church; the wife is never explicitly enjoined to model her behavior on that of Jesus. Oisille thereby indicts the husband's behavior in a subtle way.

26. Gaines and Herzog 184.

27. Gaines and Herzog 23.

28. Du Bois: "… met en cause la réalité des référents auxquels renvoie l'écriture de son modèle et propose d'aller plus loin que lui" ("questions the reality of the referents on which the writing is modeled, and proposes to surpass that"—*L'Imaginaire* 251).

Chapter Eight
Interior Decoration and External Trappings: Space for the Spirit

1. Auslander 121.

2. Auslander 15.

3. Auslander 218.

4. For instance, the monks' *retraict* is both the occasion for the unmasking of the pretensions of a worldly woman (Madame de Roncex), as well as for the literal revelation of the monks' crude and filthy nature.

5. The serial substitution of one lover for another reinforces the rhetorical strategy of layering already discussed in Chapter 6.

6. This is a space that Marguerite does not display frequently; it only appears rarely, as in the episode of Madame de Roncex, the woman who soils her skirt while defecating in the monks' pile of feces.

7. "luy … dist qu'il ne venoit que du retraict" (*Hept.* 4.37.267).

8. Auslander 18.

9. Auslander: "It is in the everyday world that politics and the polity, economics and the economy, aesthetics and beauty, are concretized, experienced, and perhaps transformed—in short, lived … The challenge, therefore, is to grasp the manifestations of the very large and abstract structures and transformations of the world within the small details of daily life" (3–4).

10. Marguerite deals ambivalently with objects, since they are contaminated by the materiality of the postlapsarian world: the *garderobbe* just discussed and the *tapisserie* both participate in, as well as disclose, misdeeds. However, in *nouvelle* #32, the woman's portrait, commissioned by the king who is impressed with her story as Bernaige has told it, and who wants the portrait as a reminder of it and executed *after* her pardon by her husband, is a fine arts furnishing with a restorative function. The king, secular source of authority, doubles as God, from whom, by confessing her sins in accordance with the instruction of the Pauline intertext, the woman receives absolution.

11. *Hept.* ed. M. François, p. 477n543. "Jean Perréal, dit de Paris, est le peintre fameux de la fin du XVe siècle dont le nom même était resté à peu près ignoré jusqu'aux travaux du conte Léon de Laborde. Célèbre dans la région de Lyon, il vint à la cour de Charles VIII où il reçut le titre de peintre ordinaire et de valet de chambre du roi. Louis XII et François Ier lui gardèrent successivement leur faveur; son contemporain, Jean Le Maire de Belges, n'hésite pas à le nommer un second Zeuxis ou Appelles. Nous n'avons malheureusement conservé aucune œuvre qui puisse être attribuée avec certitude à l'artiste."

12. Auslander: "the Sun King had his shining silver destroyed rather than [have it] fall into the hands of others" (53–54).

13. Alternatively, *bourse* may designate "vagina."

14. Among others, "vous," "mon," "me," and "vostre."

15. For example, the clothes chest housed in the Campin room of the Cloisters Museum in New York City possesses elongated, ogival ornamentation on its face that imitates aspects of church architecture.

16. Auslander 64.

17. The quote is de Thou's heading for *nouvelle* #55, not Marguerite's own phrasing, and my translation of it, as Chilton does not translate de Thou's headings.

18. Thysell 54–56.

19. As Chapter 3 on emblems has shown, the multiplicity of viewpoints expressed by the *devisants* nonetheless ultimately coalesces into a consistent message, just as evangelicals implicitly expected that reading Scripture would produce a unitary meaning rather than manifold individual interpretations. This unity of spirit as typical of evangelicals in community is one of the strongest points argued by Thysell. Thysell: "as the *devisants* listen to the Word as interpreted by the Spirit, their regeneration as a community becomes obvious" (58).

20. The *devisants* ask sarcastically, "si elle se soulcyoit tant de sa conscience, comme du prouffict de son mesnaige?" ("wasn't she just as concerned about [her husband's] conscience as she was about doing well for her family?"—*Hept.* 6.55.346; Chilton 449).

21. Clearly, Marguerite does not exemplify Max Weber's thesis about Calvinists and the discernible character of election through the extent of one's possessions.

22. Metys lived c. 1514. Another contemporary who contributed to the development of this genre was Martin van Reymerswaele.

23. Schama, *Rembrandt's Eyes* 447.

24. Schama, *Rembrandt's Eyes* 378.

25. Lucas van Leyden, possibly, and Jan Swart, who illustrated the 1528 Vosterman Antwerp Bible. Kloek: "In [his illustrations of] stories from the Old Testament the focus is on lawgiving and disobedience to God, while the accent falls on the contrast between those who obstinately cling to the old faith and those who are receptive to the good news and the Gospel … [this] evinces [his] careful reading of the Bible … [but] cannot serve as grounds for labeling Lucas a Protestant sympathizer" (17). However, his unveiling of events in a pictorial, narrative step-by-step way seems to affiliate him with the evangelical treatment we have been examining. Interestingly, traditional focal figures of Catholic iconography seem to recede in importance in works such as his *Last Judgement* (1527): "the Virgin and the Saints have been relegated to a hazy background" (19).

26. Making an accounting to the mistress facilitates moral redressing of the situation; the accounting is "bien comptant," which produces a state of "bien contant" ("satisfaction"). Such a narrative rectification of equilibrium is opposed, in *nouvelles* such as #70, to "mal contant": a poorly or incorrectly rendered account of one's actions or inner being. In *nouvelle* #70, a man who has bragged about a love affair has been verbally "mal comptant" and so is "mal contant" of his own tongue: "O ma langue, pugnye sois-tu comme celle du Mauvais Riche en enfer! O mon cueur, trop craintif de mort et de bannissement, deschiré soys-tu … mal contant de moy, de mon cueur et de ma langue" ("O my tongue, may you burn like Dives' tongue in Hell! O my heart, too afraid of death and banishment, may you ever more be torn apart … [I am] displeased … with … my heart and my tongue!"—*Hept.* 7.70.415; Chilton 529).

27. This treatment stresses even further the stain of sin that things contain. Before returning to his wife, the husband settles his *debte* to the servant girl in a monetary way, recalling consumerism or payment for prostitution. He dismisses her, and his wandering, in a worldly way ("après avoir argent à sa mestayere"; "after having given money to his mistress"—*Hept.* 4.38.271) but acknowledges a theological *debte* to Christ whose charity he recognizes in his wife: "il … s'en retourna à sa femme, à laquelle il confessa la debte; et que, sans le moien de ceste grande doulceur et bonté, il estoit impossible qu'il eust jamais laissé la vie qu'il menoit" ("he returned to his wife, to whom he confessed his debt, and that, without her great kindness and goodness, he would never have been able to quit the life he had been leading"—*Hept.* 4.38.271). The wife's christological role is evident in the life-changing conversion that it provokes, and enables, in her husband.

28. Telling a tale is described in terms of mercantile transaction: one produces a product, and also acquires products from others, as is the case with a woman "qui sçavoit bien dire ung compte et de bonne grace, et en rire aussy, quant on luy en disoit quelcun" ("who was well-known for her ability to tell a good story in an elegant style, as well as for her ability to laugh at a good story told by others"—*Hept.* 7.62.377; Chilton 485).

29. "Preach the Word at all times! Be ready in season and out of season. Convince, rebuke, exhort, with all longsuffering and teaching" (2 Tim. 4.2).

30. For instance, Luther talks about the need for the inspiration of the Holy Spirit in order to speak truly. Luther: "the human voice remains when I preach. Yet it is in truth the power of God" (*Table Talk* 12). Also, Luther: "First, if some passage is obscure I consider whether it treats of grace or law … and with which of these it agrees better … The second rule is that if the meaning is ambiguous I ask those who have a better knowledge of the language than I have whether the Hebrew words can bear this or that sense which seems to me especially fitting" (42–43).

31. Luther, "The Argument of St. Paul's *Epistle to the Galatians*" 103–04.

32. Considerable attention has been paid to post-Tridentine changes in preaching practice, and to the counter-Reformation response from the Catholic pulpit to inroads made by Protestant preaching. Larissa Taylor's

Soldiers of Christ: Preaching in Late Medieval and Renaissance France examines these alterations in detail.

33. We may contrast Marguerite's prototype for preaching, in which fairly nuanced, psychologically complex individuals thrash out their beliefs in dialogue with other interlocutors, all within the conscious framework of Scripture, with that found, for example, in the *Mistere de l'Institution de l'Ordre des Freres Prescheurs* (1504–12). This drama represents how the Dominican orders are established to be itinerant preachers. Here we find the persistent late medieval "types": the symbolic Everyman along with his requisite fragmentary aspects of charity, compassion, obstinacy, false belief, and other allegorical personifications of not-yet-integrated personality traits. (This assessment is not intended as a disparagement, but simply to demonstrate Marguerite's innovations in the sense of proto-Protestant exploration of the heart and soul of the *individual*—and *the sort of preaching* needed to reach such individuals.) De Reyff, ed. Trepperel: "'Qui parle?' interroge Hervé Martin au terme d'un relevé systématique de tous les grands thèmes conducteurs de la prédication des XIVe et XVe siècles. A travers cette formule, l'historien désigne non seulement l'univocité de la doctrine, mais encore l'uniformité des attitudes psychologiques et morales qui sous-tendent un discours où les inflexions singulières se font extrêmement rares" and concludes that such preaching remains oriented toward illustrating the doctrine of the church ("... sa forme dirige le spectateur vers les réalisations en prose qui lui sont constamment offertes à l'église ou sur la place publique" (qtd. in Trepperel 95) rather than at exemplifying Scripture *strictu sensu*. And, indeed, a didactic sermon concludes the play, launching into an attack on heresy ("De zizanie faulse, dampnable, / Il a semé parmy le grain. / Pour le jourd'huy, il est certain / Que zizanie se multiplie / En l'Esglise, par Heresie" (Trepperel 348) as destructive to the Church and requiring a conformity to doctrine of the sort against which evangelicals were shortly to react.

34. Thysell, *The Pleasure of Discernment: Marguerite de Navarre as Theologian.*

35. Randall, *Building Codes: The Calvinist Aesthetics of Early Modern Europe.*

36. The possibility that Marguerite is providing a prototypical preaching manual is also intriguing when viewed from the historical perspective of the development of homiletics and doctrine: later, seventeenth-century writers—among them Madame Guyon, the mystic, Quietist, and author of *Le moyen court*, or the "short way (or method)"—devised "methods" offering techniques for understanding Scripture and for encouraging the believer's relationship with Christ; John Wesley in the eighteenth century and latter-day Methodists are directly indebted to this practice. For more on these affiliations, see the extensive bibliographic note in Randall, "'Loosening the Stays:' Madame Guyon's Quietist Opposition to Absolutism" (29).

37. Examples include Erasmus's *Colloquies*; Béroalde de Verville's *Le Moyen de parvenir*; Martin Luther's *Table Talk*.

38. Defaux, "De la Bonne Nouvelle aux nouvelles" 23–43. John Lyons has written on religious questions in the *Heptaméron* in John Lyons, *Exemplum: The Rhetoric of Example in Early Modern France and Italy*.

39. For instance, she observes "Nomerfide et Ennasuite … commencerent à se reconforter avecq les exhortations du bon abbé … Et le matin ouyrent la messe bien devotement" ("Nomerfide and Ennasuite … began to take some consolation from their reunion. The next morning they heard the mass with great devotion"—*Hept*. prologue.4; Chilton 63).

40. She constructs a neat contrast through verbal play in the story of the female boatkeeper who defends herself from violation at the hands of two Cordeliers by taking each to a separate island in the river and leaving them there to say their prayers—which, of course, they never do. Marguerite calls them "ses deux bons peres aux desertz" ("the poor friars"—*Hept*. 1.5.36; Chilton 99), compelling the contrast between them and the sainted anchorites, or "Desert Fathers, of the early Christian Church."

41. This formulation foreshadows Michel de Montaigne's appeal for a "suffisant lecteur" some fifty years later. Just as Montaigne applies "suffisant" to his ideal reader, Marguerite also hopes for an experience in interpreting and reading as concerns her evangelical portrait of an effective preacher, whose views should always be structured on scriptural understanding.

42. Cotgrave, *A Dictionarie of the French and English Tongues*.

43. Marguerite may make such assurances in an attempt to circumvent the interdiction on fictional creation made by theologians such as Jean Calvin. See Coats, *Subverting the System*.

44. "You are the epistle written in our hearts, known and read by all men, clearly you are an epistle of Christ … written not with ink, but with the spirit of the living God" (2 Cor. 3.2–3).

45. "You have … *learned* Christ" (Eph. 4.20; emphasis added).

46. Eisenstein, *The Printing Press as Agent of Change*. See also the work of Henri Jean Martin and Roger Chartier.

47. "Gallery luy dist: 'Il fault mectre ces ymaiges soubs l'autel où ilz orront leur messe, avecq des parolles que je vous feray dire à l'heure" ("'we have to put these dolls underneath the altar,' Gallery went on, 'so that they can hear mass being said, and when we put them there we have to say certain words, which I'll tell you later'"—*Hept*. 1.1.16–17; Chilton 76). The intent is that the people whom these images represent, including Marguerite herself, will perish subsequently.

48. Roper, *Holy Household: Women and Morals in Reformation Augsburg*.

49. Among them, Agrippa d'Aubigné in *Les tragiques*, where antithesis serves to separate war-torn France into evil and good, black and white, apostates and believers.

50. This is preferred to a proliferation of platitudes or implicit permission to continue in one's sinful ways (such as penance seems to provide, since as long as one performs an act of contrition, absolution for future wrong-doing is always available).

51. Luther: "experience alone makes the best theologian" (*Table Talk* 7).

52. In many respects, Marguerite anticipates here the sort of "Puritan conversion narrative" that Patricia Caldwell analyzes in *The Puritan Conversion Narrative: The Beginnings of American Expression.* Puritan preachers placed special emphasis on the proper preparation of the heart of the hearer for the reception of the Holy Spirit, and developed an elaborate morphology of the conversion experience which Marguerite's several, carefully structured days of scriptural readings seem to prefigure, at least in rudimentary form.

53. Cotgrave, *A Dictionarie of the French and English Tongues.* The secondary meaning is cited through reference to a proverb ("qui pourchatz plus qu'il n'en").

54. Caldwell 58.

Conclusion:
From Self to Soul: Treasures of the Heart

1. Marguerite's evangelical contemporary, Rabelais, performs a similar textual treatment of multiple idioms and interpretations. In *Pantagruel*, Rabelais describes the jargon that the Escholier Limousin jabbers in his encounter with the uncomprehending and frustrated Pantagruel; it is a *galimatias* of scholastic Latin, fragments of German, Italian, French, *dialectes du pays,* and even some Hebrew. This unmoored logorrhea only resolves into sense when Pantagruel takes the Escholier by the throat, causing him to beg for *caritas. Caritas* generates the semantic lexicon of the Gospel, a language that speaks to Pantagruel's heart and dissolves the incomprehension between the two interlocutors. Stable *Verbum* corrals errant *verba.*

2. This is de Thou's summation, and my translation, as Chilton does not translate these headings.

3. This is perhaps a reference to the doctrine of election or predestination.

4. "Marguerite fait ici un jeu de mots avec la chambre des comptes de Paris" ("Marguerite is punning on the name for the 'chambre des comptes' in Paris"—*Hept.* 7.67.editor's note #840).

5. This is de Thou's encapsulation of the issue.

6. Hircan acknowledges that this is the case, observing: "encores n'est pas finée la tragédie qui a commencé par rire" ("the tragedy that began with laughter is not yet at its end!"—*Hept.* 8.72.427; Chilton 543).

7. Medieval texts used objects, too, but in a way markedly different from Marguerite's. The medieval use of objects can be seen in works such as the *Farce de Maistre Pathelin*, obviously in part a play that displays commodity culture. The *drap* coveted by Pathelin does constitute a textual motor for the drama, but in no way contributes to any sort of lifting-out of context or orienting beyond the material world such as we have seen in Marguerite's prose.

8. In late Medieval France, these were, primarily, Catholic.

9. This awareness individualized Luther and set him apart. While he never sought to leave the community of Catholics, the Church forsook him when the Pope banned him as a heretic.

10. In every case down through the ages, whether that of Marguerite Porete (whom Thysell mentions), Madame Guyon and the Quietists or the Jansenists later, the Catholic church has tried to quell such nonconformity and has viewed it as heretical. Why? In good measure, I believe, because such expressions are the theological manifestation of a psychological phenomenon: the development of the individual as separate from the collectivity. (Hence, the *devisants*' often divergent interpretations of the same event, and Marguerite's evangelical ease in allowing them to retain their differences.)

11. Thysell 125.

12. Defaux: "le biais des débats qui opposent les devisants les uns aux autres … tout aussi conflictuel et oppositionnel … elle construit pour mieux mettre en valeur tout la mobilité agonistique … et c'est au lecteur qu'elle laisse finalement l'ultime responsabilité de l'interprétation de cette richesse" ("De la Bonne Nouvelle" 39).

13. De Certeau, *The Mystic Fable* 20.

14. De Certeau, *The Mystic Fable* 20.

Bibliography

Appadurai, Arjun, ed. *The Social Life of Things*. Cambridge: Cambridge U, 1986.

Aubailly, Jean-Claude, et al. *Aspects du théâtre populaire en Europe au XVIe siècle*. Paris: Société des éditions du seizième siècle, 1989.

Augustine, Saint. *Confessions*. New York: Oxford UP, 1991.

Auslander, Leora. *Taste and Power: Furnishing Modern France*. Berkeley: U of California P, 1996.

Baetjet, Katherine. *European Paintings in the Metropolitan Museum of Art: A Summary Catalogue*. New York: The Museum, 1980.

Bakker, B. "Levenspelgrimage ofvrome wandeling? Claes Janszoon Visscher in Zijn serie 'Plaisante Plaetsen.'" *Oud Holland* 107 (1993): 97–115.

Baudrillard, Jean. *Le miroir de la production*. Paris: Plon, 1968.

———. *La société de la consommation*. Paris: Plon, 1970.

———. *The System of Objects*. Trans. James Benedict. London: Verso, 1996.

Baudrillart, Henri. *Histoire du luxe, privé et public depuis l'antiquité jusqu'à nos jours*. Vol. 4. Paris: Lahue, 1881.

Baumgartner, Frederic J. *France in the Sixteenth Century*. New York: St. Martin's, 1998.

Bauschatz, Cathleen. "The Problem of the Dedication of Rabelais's *Tiers livre* to Marguerite de Navarre." Unpublished ms.

Beck, Jonathan. *Théâtre et propagande aux débuts de la Réforme: Les pièces polémiques du Recueil La Vallée*. Geneva: Slatkine, 1986.

Berg, Maxine, and Helen Clifford. *Consumers and Luxury: Consumer Culture in Europe 1650–1850*. Manchester, UK: Manchester UP, 1999.

Bermingham, Ann, and John Brewer, eds. *The Consumption of Culture 1600–1800: Image, Object, Text*. London: Routledge, 1995.

Bertrand, Christine. *Le meuble et l'homme: Essai sur une philosophie du meuble*. Verviers: Vinche, 1946.

Beurdeley, A. "Les meubles d'art." *Revue des Arts Décoratifs* 3 (1882–83): 2–3.

de Bèze, Théodore. *Chrétiennes méditations*. Ed. Mario Richter. Geneva: Droz, 1964.

Blanc, Monique. *Moyen Age et Renaissance*. Musée des arts décoratifs. Paris: Edition de la Réunion des Musées Nationaux, 1998.

Boccaccio, Giovanni. *The Decameron*. Trans. Mark Musa and Peter Bondanella. New York: Penguin, 1982.

Bonnaffé, Edmond. *Inventaire des meubles de Catherine de Médicis en 1589*. Paris, 1874.

Bourdieu, Pierre. *Distinction: A Social Critique of the Judgement of Taste*. Trans. Richard Nice. Cambridge, MA: Harvard UP, 1984.

———. *Language and Symbolic Power*. Ed. John Thompson. Cambridge, MA: Harvard UP, 1991.

Bouwsma, William. *John Calvin: A Sixteenth-Century Portrait*. New York: Oxford UP, 1988.

Brantôme, Sieur de. *Les dames galantes*. Paris: Garnier Frères, 1960.

Braudel, Fernand. *The Structures of Everyday Life*. Trans. Sian Reynolds. London: Collins, 1981.

Brooks, Peter. *Body Work: Objects of Desire in Modern Narrative*. Cambridge, MA: Harvard UP, 1994.

Brugerolles, Emmanuelle. *The Renaissance in France: Drawings from the Ecole des Beaux-Arts, Paris*. Cambridge, MA: Harvard University Art Museum, 1995.

Bruyn, J. "Le paysage hollandais du XVIIe siècle comme métaphore religieuse." Paris: Service culturel, 1987. 67–88.

———. "Toward A Scriptural Reading of Seventeenth-Century Dutch Landscape Painting." Sutton 84–103.

Caldwell, Patricia. *The Puritan Conversion Narrative: The Beginnings of American Expression*. Cambridge: Cambridge UP, 1987.

Calvin, Jean. *La famine spirituelle*. Sermon inédit sur Esaïe 55, 1–2 (Eglise française de Londres, ms. viii, f.2, fo. 532ro–543vo). Ed. Max Engammare. Geneva: Droz, 2000.

———. *The Institutes of Christian Religion*. Ed. Tony Lane and Hilary Osborne. Grand Rapids, MI: Baker Book House, 1987.

Calvin, John. *Des scandales*. Ed. Olivier Fatio. Geneva: Droz, 1984.

Campbell, Lorne. *Renaissance Portraits: European Portrait Painting in the Fourteenth, Fifteenth and Sixteenth Centuries*. New Haven, CT: Yale UP, 1980.

Campo, Roberto. *Ronsard's Contentious Sisters: The Paragone between Poetry and Painting in the Works of Pierre de Ronsard*. North Carolina Studies in Romance Language and Literatures. Chapel Hill: U of North Carolina P, 1998.

Camporesi, Piero. *L'officine des sens: Une anthropologie baroque*. Paris: Hachette, 1989.

Cerati, Marie. *Marguerite de Navarre*. Paris: Sorbier, 1981.

de Certeau, Michel. *The Mystic Fable: Sixteenth and Seventeenth Centuries*. Chicago: U of Chicago P, 1992.

———. *The Practice of Everyday Life*. Trans. Steven F. Rendall. Berkeley: U of California P, 1984.

Chambers, Ross. *Room for Maneuver: Reading (the) Oppositional (in) Narrative*. Chicago: U of Chicago P, 1991.

Champeaux, Alfred de. *Le meuble*. Paris: Société française d'éditions d'art, 1885.

Chesney, Elizabeth. *The Countervoyage of Rabelais*. Durham, NC: Duke UP, 1982.

Chilton, Paul, trans. *The Heptaméron*. By Marguerite de Navarre. London: Penguin, 1984.

Coats, Catharine Randall. *(Em)bodying the Word: Textual Resurrections in the Martyrological Narratives of Foxe, Crespin, de Bèze and d'Aubigné*. New York: Lang, 1991.

———. *Subverting the System: D'Aubigné and Calvinism*. Kirksville, MO: Sixteenth Century Publishers, 1989.

———. See also Randall, Catharine.

Cotgrave, Randle. *A Dictionarie of the French and English Tongues*. London: Dent, 1611.

Cotrugli, Benedetto. *Traictés de la marchandise et du parfaict marchand*. Trans. I. Boyran. Didier, 1582.

Cottrell, Robert. *A Grammar of Silence: A Reading of Marguerite de Navarre's Poetry*. Washington, DC: Catholic U of America P, 1986.

Czikszentmihalyi, Mihaly, and Eugène Rochberg-Halton. *The Meaning of Things: Domestic Symbols and the Self*. Cambridge: Cambridge UP, 1981.

Davis, Natalie Zemon. *Fiction in the Archives: Pardon Tales and Their Tellers in Sixteenth-Century France*. Stanford, CA: Stanford UP, 1987.

Defaux, Gérard. "De la Bonne Nouvelle aux nouvelles: Remarques sur la structure de l'*Heptaméron*." *French Forum* 27 (Winter 2001): 23–43.

———. *L'écriture comme présence: Marot, Rabelais, Montaigne*. Paris: Champion, 1987.

Defaux, Gérard. "Evangelism." Hollier 162–66.

———. "Marguerite de Navarre et la guerre des sexes: L'*Heptaméron*, 1ere Journée." *French Forum* 24.2 (May 1999): 134–61.

Deloche, Bernard. *L'Art du meuble: Introduction à l'esthétique des arts mineurs*. Lyon: Hermès, 1980.

Desan, Philippe. *Les commerces de Montaigne: Le discours économique des "Essais."* Paris: Nizet, 1992.

———. *L'Imaginaire économique de la Renaissance*. Paris: Editions Inter-Universitaires, 1993.

Des Périers, Bonaventure. *Nouvelles récréations et joyeux devis* (1558). Jourda, *Conteurs français* 8–194.

———. *Les nouvelles récréations et joyeux devis*. Ed. Constantin Castera. Abbeville: Paillart, 1932.

Diefendorf, Barbara. *Beneath the Cross: Catholics and Huguenots in Sixteenth-Century Paris*. New York: Oxford UP, 1991.

Donaldson-Evans, Lance. "Baroque and Mannerism." *French Forum* 7.3 (1981): 210–23.

Douglas, Mary, and Baron Isherwood. *The World of Goods: Towards an Anthropology of Consumption*. London: Routledge, 1996.

Du Bois, Claude-Gilbert. *L'imaginaire de la Renaissance*. Paris: Presses Universitaires de France, 1985.

Du Fail, Noël. *Propos rustiques* (1547), *Les Baliverneries d'Eutrapel* (1548). Jourda, *Conteurs français* 601–53.

Eagleton, Terry. *The Ideology of the Aesthetic*. Oxford: Oxford UP, 1990.

Eisenstein, Elizabeth. *The Printing Press as an Agent of Change: Communications and Cultural Transformations in Early Modern Europe*. Cambridge: Cambridge UP, 1979.

Ennès, Pierre. *Céramique du moyen-âge et de la Renaissance* 91. Paris: Palais du Louvre, Editions de la Réunion des Musées Nationaux, 2000.

Falkenburg, Reindert. "Calvinism and the Emergence of Dutch Seventeenth-Century Landscape Art—A Critical Evaluation." Finney 343–68.

Farge, John. *Orthodoxy and Reform in Early Reformation France: The Faculty of Theology of Paris, 1500–1543*. Leiden: U of Leiden, Studies in Medieval and Renaissance Texts, 1985.

Febvre, Lucien. *Amour sacré, amour profane*. Paris: Gallimard, 1944.

Ferguson, Gary. *Mirroring Belief: Marguerite de Navarre's Devotional Poetry*. Edinburgh, UK: U of Edinburgh P, 1992.

———. "Towards a Protestant Theology of Justification: A *Sommaire* or Microcosm." *Bibliothèque d'Humanisme et Renaissance* 51 (1989): 601–08.

Ferry, Luc. *Homo aestheticus: The Invention of Taste in the Democratic Age*. Trans. Robert de Loaiza. Chicago: U of Chicago P, 1993.

Finney, Paul Corby, ed. *Seeing beyond the Word: Visual Arts and the Calvinist Tradition*. Grand Rapids, MI: Eerdmans, 1999.

Forty, Adrian. *Objects of Desire*. New York: Pantheon, 1986.

Fragonard, Marie-Madeleine. *La plume et l'épée: La littérature des guerres de religion à la Fronde*. Paris: Gallimard, 1989.

Freedberg, David. *The Power of Images: Studies in the History and Theory of Response*. Chicago: U Chicago P, 1989.

Fritsch, Julia. *Vitraux civiles et religieux du XVIe siècle* 141. Ecouen: Musée national de la Renaissance, 1999.

Fumerton, Patricia. *Cultural Artifacts: Renaissance Literature and the Practice of Social Ornament*. Chicago: U of Chicago P, 1991.

———, ed. *Renaissance Culture and the Everyday*. Philadelphia: U of Pennsylvania P, 1999.

———. "'Secret' Arts: Elizabethan Miniatures and Sonnets." Greenblatt 93–135.

Gaines, Jane, and Charlotte Herzog, eds. *Fabrications: Costume and the Female Body*. New York: Routledge, 1990.

Gombrich, E. H. "The Museum: Past, Present, and Future." *Critical Inquiry* 3 (1977): 110–35.

Goody, Esther, ed. *From Craft to Industry: The Ethnography of Proto-industrial Cloth Production*. Cambridge: Cambridge UP, 1982.

Goux, Jean-Joseph. *The Coiners of Language*. Trans. J. C. Gage. Norman: U of Oklahoma P, 1994.

Grau, François-Marie. *Histoire du costume*. Paris: Presses Universitaires de France, 1999.

de Grazia, Margaret, Peter Stallybrass, and Maureen Quilligan, eds. *Subject and Object in Renaissance France*. Cambridge: Cambridge UP, 1996.

Greenblatt, Stephen, ed. *Representing the English Renaissance*. Berkeley: U of California P, 1988.

Haag, E. *La France protestante*. Paris, 1846–59. Rpt. Geneva: Slatkine, 1966.

Harbison, Craig. *The Mirror of the Artist: Northern Renaissance Art in its Historical Context*. New York: Abrams, 1955.

Hart, Keith. "On Commoditization." Goody 39–52.

Hegel, G. W. F. *Aethetik.* New York: Modern Library, 1955.

Heinselman, Kurt. *The Economics of Imagination.* Amherst: U of Massachusetts P, 1980.

Heller, Henri. "Marguerite de Navarre and the Reformers of Meaux." *Bibliothèque d'Humanisme et Renaissance* 33 (1971): 271–301.

Hollier, Denis. *A New History of French Literature.* Cambridge, MA: Harvard UP, 1989.

Holst, Neils von. *Creators, Collectors and Connaisseurs: The Anatomy of Public Taste from Antiquity to the Present Day.* New York: Abrams, 1967.

Hughes, Diane Owen. "Representing the Family: Portraits and Purposes in Early Modern Italy." Rotberg and Rabb 25–34.

Impey, Plivier, and Arthur MacGregor, eds. *The Origin of Museums: The Cabinet of Curiosities in Sixteenth and Seventeenth Century Europe.* Oxford: Clarendon, 1986.

Janneau, Guillaume. *Les styles du meuble français.* Paris: Presses Universitaires de France, 1972.

Janson, H. W. *History of Art.* Vol. 2. 5th ed. New York: Abrams, 1997.

Jardine, Lisa. *Worldly Goods: A New History of the Renaissance.* New York: Doubleday, 1966.

Jeanneret, Michel. *Des mots et des mets: Banquets et propos de table à la Renaissance.* Paris: J. Corti, 1987.

Jones, Ann Rosalind, and Peter Stallybrass. *Renaissance Clothing and the Materials of Memory.* Cambridge: Cambridge UP, 2001.

Jourda, Pierre, ed. *Conteurs français du XVI*[e] *siècle.* Paris: Gallimard, 1965.

———. "La première nouvelle de l'*Heptaméron.*" *Mélanges Littéraires* 45–50. Paris: Gallimard, Nouvelle Revue Française, 1965.

Kandinsky, W. *Concerning the Spiritual in Art.* New York: Wittenborn, 1972.

Kibbey, Ann. *The Interpretation of Material Shapes in Puritanism: A Study of Rhetoric, Prejudice and Violence.* Cambridge: Cambridge UP, 1986.

de Klijn, Maarten. *De invloed van het calvinisme op de Noord-Nederlandse landschapschilderkunst 1570–1630.* Apeldoorn: Willem de Zwijgerstichting, 1982.

Kloek, W. Th. *Art before the Iconoclasm: Northern Netherlandish Art 1525–1580.* Amsterdam: Rijksmuseum, 1986.

Kroll, Richard. *The Material World: Literate Culture and the Restoration in the Early Eighteenth Century*. Baltimore: Johns Hopkins UP, 1991.

Ladurie, Emmanuel Le Roy. *Creating French Culture: Treasures from the Bibliothèque nationale de France*. New Haven: Yale UP, 1995.

La Garanderie, Marie-Madeleine de. *Christianisme et lettres profanes (1515–1535)*. Paris: Champion, 1976.

LeCoq, Anne-Marie. *François Ier imaginaire: Symbolique et politique à l'aube de la Renaissance française*. Paris: Macula, 1987.

LeFranc, Abel. *Les dernières poésies de Marguerite de Navarre*. Paris: A. Colin, 1896.

Legrand, Catherine. *Le paysage en Europe du XVIe au XVIIIe siècle. Actes du colloque organisé au musée du Louvre par le Service culturel du 25 au 27 janvier 1990*. Paris: Réunion des Musées nationaux, 1994.

Lewalski, Barbara Kiefer. *Writing Women in Jacobean England*. Cambridge, MA: Harvard UP, 1993.

Lurie, Alison. *The Language of Clothes*. New York: Random, 1981.

Luther, Martin. *Against the Jews*. Minneapolis: Luther Press, 1908–09.

———. "An Appeal to the Ruling Class of German Nobility as to the Amelioration of the State of Christendom." Spitz 1–33.

———. "The Argument of St. Paul's *Epistle to the Galatians*." *The Protestant Reformation*. Ed. Hans Hillerbrand. New York: Harper–Torchbook, 1968.

———. *Luther's Works. Table Talk*. 54. Trans. Theodore Tappert. Philadelphia: Fortress, 1967.

Lyons, John. *Exemplum: The Rhetoric of Example in Early Modern France and Italy*. Princeton: Princeton UP, 1989.

Lyons, John, and Mary McKinley. *Critical Tales: New Studies of the "Heptaméron" and Early Modern Culture*. Philadelphia: U of Pennsylvania P, 1993.

Marius, Richard. *Martin Luther: The Christian between God and Death*. Cambridge, MA; Harvard UP, 1999.

Martineau, Christine. *Le thème de la mort dans la poésie française de 1450 à 1550*. Paris: Champion, 1977.

Marot, Clément. *Œuvres lyriques*. [London]: University of London, Athlone Press, 1964.

Mathieu-Castellani, Gisèle. *La conversation conteuse: Les Nouvelles de Marguerite de Navarre*. Paris: Presses Universitaires de la France, 1992.

McCloskey, Donald. *If You're So Smart: The Narrative of Economic Expertise*. Chicago: U of Chicago P, 1990.

McCracken, Grant. *Culture and Consumption: New Approaches to the Symbolic Character of Consumer Goods and Activities*. Bloomington: Indiana UP, 1988.

McDannell, Colleen. *Material Christianity: Religion and Popular Culture in America*. New Haven: Yale UP, 1995.

McGowan, Margaret. *Ideal Forms in the Age of Ronsard*. Berkeley: U of California P, 1986.

McGrath, Alistair. *Reformation Thought*. 2nd ed. London: Blackwell, 1993.

McKeon, Michael. "Politics of Discourses and the Rise of the Aesthetic in Seventeenth Century England." Sharpe and Zwicker 35–52.

Michalski, Sergiusz. *The Reformation and the Visual Arts: The Protestant Image Question in Western and Eastern Europe*. London: Rouledge, 1993.

Miernowski, Jan. "Literature and Metaphysics." *Etudes Rabelaisiennes* 35 (1998): 131–51.

Miller, Daniel. *Material Culture and Mass Consumption*. Oxford: Oxford UP, 1987.

———, ed. *Material Culture: Why Some Things Matter*. Chicago: U of Chicago P, 1998.

Montenay, Georgette de. *Emblesmes ou Devises Chrestiennes*. Lyon: Marcorelle, 1571. Rpt. New York: Scolar, 1973.

Moore, W. G. *La réforme allemande et la littérature française*. Strasburg: La Faculté des Lettres, 1930.

Moss, A. "Rhetoric and the Evolution of Ideas and Styles in the Renaissance." *Renaissance Studies* 3.2 (1989): 99–105.

Mullaney, Stephen, "Strange Things." Orgel 113–28.

Mullin, Robert Bruce. *Miracles and the Modern Religious Imagination*. New Haven: Yale UP, 1996.

Navarre, Marguerite de. *L'Heptaméron*. Ed. Simone Reyff. Paris: Garnier-Flammarion, 1982.

———. *L'Heptaméron*. Ed. Michel François. Paris: Garnier, 1967.

———. *Les Marguerites de la Marguerite des Princesses*. Lyons: Jean de Tournes, 1547. Paris: Cabinet du Bibliophile, 1873.

———. *Le miroir de treschrestienne Princesse Marguerite de France, Royne de Navarre, Duchesse D'alençon & de Berry: auquel elle uoit & son nenat, & son tout*. Paris: Augereau, 1533.

Niebuhr, H. Richard. *Christ and Culture*. New York: Harper, 1951.

Nora, Pierre, ed. *Les lieux de mémoire*. Paris: Gallimard, 1997.

North, Michael. *Art and Commerce in the Dutch Golden Age*. New Haven: Yale UP, 1997.

Obelkevich, J., ed. "Popular Religion and Holy Shrines: Their Influence on the Origins of the German Reformation and Their Role in German Cultural Development." *Religion and the People*. Chapel Hill: U of North Carolina P, 1979.

O'Neill, John P., ed. *From Van Eyck to Bruegel: Early Netherlandish Painting in the Metropolitan Museum of Art*. New York: Metropolitan Museum of Art, 1998.

Orgel, Stephen. *Political Shakespeare*. New York: Garland, 1999.

Orth, Myra. "Radical Beauty: Marguerite de Navarre's Illuminated Protestant Catechism and Confession." *Sixteenth Century Journal* 24.2 (1993): 383–425.

Paine, Sheila. *Embroidered Textiles*. London: Thames & Hudson, 1990.

Palissy, Bernard. *Recepte véritable*. Ed. Keith Cameron. Paris: Textes Littéraires Français, 1988.

Paradin, Claude. *The Heroicall Devises*. Ed. John Doebler. Delmar, NY: Scholars' Facsimiles, 1984.

———. *Quadrins historiques de la Bible, revuz et augmentez d'un grand nombre de figures*. Lyons: Jean de Tournes, 1558.

Paré, Ambroise. *Des Monstres det des prodiges*. Paris: Club français du livre, 1964.

Perrot, Philippe. *Fashioning the Bourgeoisie: A History of Clothing in the Nineteenth Century*. Trans. R. Bienvenu. Princeton: Princeton UP, 1994.

Pinkus, Karen. *Picturing Silence: Emblem, Language, Counter-Reformation Materiality*. Ann Arbor: U of Michigan P, 1996.

Pradière, Alexandre. *French Furniture Makers*. Trans. Perran Wood. London: Routledge, 1989.

Praz, Mario. *Histoire de la décoration: Philosophie d'ameublement*. Paris: Thames & Hardson, 1994.

Rabelais, François. *Œuvres complètes*. Ed. Jacques Boulenger. Paris: Gallimard, 1955.

Randall, Catharine. *Building Codes: The Calvinist Aesthetics of Early Modern Europe*. Philadelphia: U of Pennsylvania P, 1999.

———. "'Loosening the Stays': Madame Guyon's Quietist Opposition to Absolutism" *Mystic Speech* 26.1 (Mar. 2000): 8–31.

———. See also Coats, Catharine Randall.

Reddy, William M. *The Rise of Market Culture: The Textile Trade and French Society, 1750–1990*. Cambridge: Cambridge UP, 1984.

Rheims, Maurice. *The Strange Life of Objects: Thirty-Five Centuries of Art Collecting and Collectors*. Trans. D. Pryce-Jones. New York: Atheneum, 1961.

Richey, Esther Gilman. *The Politics of Revelation in the English Renaissance*. Columbia, MO: U of Missouri P, 1998.

Roper, Lynda. *Holy Household: Women and Morals in Reformation Augsburg*. Oxford: Clarendon, 1989.

Rosasco, Betty. "A Sixteenth-Century Limoges Enamel *Tazza* Illustrating the Judgment of Moses." Finney 231–43.

Rotberg, Robert I., and Theodore Rabb, eds. *Art and History: Images and Their Meaning*. Cambridge: Cambridge UP, 1988.

Russell, Daniel. *The Emblem and Device in Renaissance France*. Lexington, KY: French Forum, 1985.

Salet, Francis. *La tapisserie française du moyen-âge à nos jours*. Paris: Vincent, 1946.

Salminen, Renja, ed. *L'Heptaméron*. Geneva: Droz, 1999.

Saunders, Alison. *The French Sixteenth-Century Emblem Book: A Decorative and Useful Genre*. Geneva: Droz, 1988.

Schama, Simon. *The Embarrassment of Riches: An Interpretation of Dutch Culture in the Golden Age*. New York: Knopf, 1987.

———. *Landscape and Memory*. New York: Random, 1995.

———. *Rembrandt's Eyes*. New York: Knopf, 1999.

Schnapper, Antoine. *Le géant, la licorne et la tulipe: Collections et collectionneurs dans la France du XVIIe*. Paris: Flammarion, 1988.

———. "The King of France as Collector in the XVIIe Century." *Journal of Interdisciplinary History* 17 (Summer 1986): 189–95.

Sharpe, Kevin, and Stephen Zwicker, eds. *Politics of Discourse: The Literature and History of Seventeenth Century England*. Berkeley: U of California P, 1987.

Sharpling, Gerard. *Role of the Image in the Prose Writings of Erasmus, Rabelais, Marguerite de Navarre and Montaigne*. Studies in French Literature 62. Lewiston, NY: Mellon, 2003.

Shell, Marc. *Money, Language and Thought*. Berkeley: U of California P, 1982.

———. *The Economy of Literature*. Baltimore: Johns Hopkins UP, 1978.

Shuger, Debora Kuller. *The Renaissance Bible: Scholarship, Sacrifice and Subjectivity*. Berkeley: U of California P, 1994.

Sommers, Paula. *Celestial Ladders: Readings in Marguerite de Navarre's Poetry of Spiritual Ascent*. Geneva: Droz, 1989.

Spitz, Lewis, ed. *The Protestant Reformation*. Englewood Cliffs, NJ: Prentice, 1966.

Stone, Donald. *From Tales to Truths: Essays on French Fiction in the Sixteenth Century*. Frankfurt-am-Main: Klostermann, 1973.

Sutton, P. C. *Masters of Seventeenth Century Dutch Landscape Painting*. Boston: Museum of Fine Arts, 1987.

Swann, Marjorie. *Curiosities and Texts: The Future of Collecting in Early Modern England*. Philadelphia: U of Pennsylvania P, 2001.

———. "The Politics of Fairylore in Early Modern England." *Renaissance Quarterly* 53 (2000): 449–73.

Tanis, James. "Netherlandish Reformed Traditions in the Graphic Arts 1550–1630." Finney 369–97.

Taschen, Benedikt. *Arcimboldo*. [N.p.], Germ.: Benedikt Taschen, 1994.

Taylor, Charles. *Sources of the Self: The Making of Modern Identity*. Cambridge, MA: Harvard UP, 1989.

Taylor, Larissa. *Soldiers of Christ: Preaching in Late Medieval and Renaissance France*. New York: Oxford UP, 1992.

Tervarent, Guy de. *Attributs et symboles dans l'art profane, 1450–1600: Dictionnaire d'un langage perdu*. Geneva: Droz, 1958.

Thirion, Jacques. "Bernard Salomon et le décor des meubles civils français à sujets bibliques et allégoriques." *Centre des Recherches d'histoire et de philologie de la IVe section de l'Ecole pratique des hautes études, VII, histoire et civilisation du livre, 1. Cinq études lyonnaises*. Paris: Ecole pratique, 1966.

Thysell, Carol. *The Pleasure of Discernment: Marguerite de Navarre as Theologian*. Oxford: Oxford UP, 2000.

Trepperel, Jehan. *Mistère de l'Institution de l'Ordre des Freres Prescheurs (1504–1512)*. Ed. Simone de Reyff, Guy Bedouelle, and Marie-Claire Gérard-Zai. Geneva: Droz, 1997.

Trichet, F. "Le costume du clergé, ses origines et son évolution en France d'après les règlements de l'Eglise." Grau 23–136.

Trudeau, Danielle. "Langue et monnaie au XVIe siècle." *Stanford French Review* 7.1 (1983): 37–55.

Veldman, Ilja. "Protestantism and the Arts: Sixteenth and Seventeenth-Century Netherlands." Finney 397–421.

Waldis, Burkhard. *Der Verlorene Sohn* (1527). München, Germ.: Kaiser, 1929.

Wandel, Lee Palmer. "Envisioning God: Image and Liturgy in Reformation Zurich. *Sixteenth Century Journal* 24 (1993): 21–40.

———. *Voracious Idols and Violent Hands: Iconoclasm in Reformation Zurich, Strasbourg and Basel.* Cambridge: Cambridge UP, 1995.

Waswo, R. *Language and Meaning in the Renaissance.* Princeton: Princeton UP, 1987.

Watts, Tessa. *Cheap Prints and Popular Piety, 1550–1640.* Cambridge: Cambridge UP, 1991.

Weiss, N. "La littérature de la Réforme française. Notes sur les traités de Luther traduits en français et imprimés en France entre 1525 et 1534." *Bibliothèque de la Société Historique du Protestantisme Français* 36 (1887): 664–71; 37 (1888): 155–63, 432–39, 500–03.

———. "Les premières professions de foi des protestants français 1532–1547." *Bibliothèque de la Société Historique du Protestantisme Français* 43 (1894): 57–79.

Westermann, Mariët. *A Worldly Art: The Dutch Republic, 1585–1718.* New York: Abrams, 1996.

Willis, Susan. *A Primer for Daily Life.* New York: Routledge, 1991.

Yver, Jacques. *Le printemps.* Jourda, *Conteurs français* 1132–1275.

Index

Abbate, Niccolo dell', 320n21
Abecedario (Mariette), 54
Acts of the Apostles, 282–83
ad fontes, 23
Aertsen, Pieter, 107, 186
Aesope, 53, 112, 121, 313n4
agape feast, 113
Alberti, Leon Battista, 323n58
Albret, Henri d', 294n29
Alciati, Andreas, 74
Alençon, 112, 314n8
allegory, 9, 10, 28, 50, 114, 119, 122, 150, 164, 294n33, 317n44
Amadour, 40–42, 87, 92, 93, 95, 304n28, 309n31, 310n37
Amadunt, 127
Amboyse, 96
Anabaptists, 174
anamorphosis, 56, 106, 311n58
Andouilles, 113
Anthonisz, Cornelis, 114
anti-clericalism, 4, 66, 152
antithesis, 268
Antwerp, 99
aphorism, 112, 222, 223, 224, 284
Apocalypse, apocalyptic, 3, 53, 121, 142, 143, 144, 147, 215, 276, 284, 285
Apocrypha, 310n45
Arcimboldo, Giuseppe, 125, 126, 318n55
ars nuova, 78, 105
arts, fine and decorative, 3, 47, 54, 57, 59, 65, 69, 74, 77, 114, 125, 152, 165, 169, 173, 186, 187, 190, 205, 229, 235, 247, 250, 291n2, 309n12
Astillon, 220, 221, 233
Aubigné, Agrippa d', 329n49
Augustine, Saint, 13, 67, 293n20, 324n20
Auslander, Leora, 237
axehead, 111, 123, 124, 317n48

Badebec, 322n53
Bandello, Matteo, 319n8
banquet, 113, 160, 163, 169, 203, 260
Bartas, Guillaume Salluste Du, 311n49, 320n17
Baudrillard, Jean, 187, 188, 189
bed (bed-linens, sheets, *linceuls*, *draps*), 62, 63, 66, 74–75, 89, 110, 150, 158, 189, 227, 231, 234, 238, 243, 244, 256, 257
Bérain, Jean, 100
Bernaige, 29, 30, 31, 32, 33, 34, 35, 301n28, 302n38, 325n10
Berquin, Louis de, 112
Bèze, Théodore de (Beza), 50, 302n39, 311n62
biens, 18, 21, 64, 82, 106, 132, 133, 137, 139, 159, 163, 206, 238, 242, 244, 245, 246, 250, 279
bienfaictz, 21
bishop's miter, 10
blason, 133
Blessed Sacrament of the Holy and True Body of Christ, The (Luther), 47
Boccaccio, Giovanni, 291n7, 303n6, 319n8
Boel, Pieter, 9, 10, 65
Bonnivet, 200, 201, 202
book, 4, 6, 11, 58, 76, 82, 106, 109, 110, 188, 189, 227, 285
Borel, Pierre, 186
Bos, Cornelius de, 101
Bouchet, Guillaume, 164
Bourdeilles, Pierre de. *See* Brantôme, Sieur de

Bourdichon, Jean, 183, 184
Branteghem, Willem van, 78
Brantôme, Sieur de (Pierre de Bourdeilles), 59, 62, 63, 191, 304n14
Brenz, Johannes, 6
Briçonnet, Guillaume, 195, 292n10, 294n28, 298n6
bridge, 14, 85, 115, 273, 274, 277, 278, 286
Brittany, 156
Bucer, Martin, 28
Budé, Guillaume, 293n17

Caldwell, Patricia, 330n52
Calvin, Jean; Calvinism, Calvinist, 1, 3, 11, 25, 77, 91, 109, 114, 119, 128, 157, 162, 174, 247, 261, 291n2, 292n11, 293n18, 293n20, 308n4, 308n11, 312n69, 313n3, 320n13, 326n21
Campo, Roberto, 291n2
candelabrum, 186, 197
candle, 44, 45, 52, 103, 192
cape, cloak, 58, 66, 68
caritas, 32, 237, 252, 330n1
Castiglione, Baldassare, 294n28
Catherine, Saint, 183
Catholic, Catholicism, Catholic theology, 2, 3, 4, 10, 23, 24, 26, 50, 84, 86, 90, 91, 103, 114, 119, 160, 174, 178, 183, 190, 192, 197, 199, 204, 258, 259, 272, 292n11
Cent nouvelles nouvelles, Les, 232
Cerceau, Jacques Androuet du, 97, 98, 310n46
Cercle de Meaux, 1, 23, 298n6
Certeau, Michel de, 290
chalice, 30, 31, 84, 111, 189
Chambre des comptes, 287
Charles VIII, 325n11
Château de Lude, 54
chest, *coffre*, 189, 219, 221, 231, 232, 233, 234, 235, 325n10
chiaroscuro, 42, 99
Chiquanous, 113, 142, 143, 144
Chrestiennes méditations (Théodore de Bèze), 302n39
Christ and Culture (H. Richard Niebuhr), 3
Christus, Petrus, 6, 8
ciborium, 97
Cleve, Joos van, 80, 81, 84, 85, 86, 87, 88, 91
Cloisters Museum, 326n15
collector's cabinet. *See* curiosity cabinet
Commandment, Second, 308n4
communion in both kinds ("species"), 30, 84, 90, 190
companionate marriage, 51, 90, 143, 240, 293n22
"compositional inversion," 142, 146
Condé, Louis de, 304n14
conduplicatio, 187
confessional, 26, 27, 28, 29, 32, 33, 34, 35, 36, 37, 40, 103, 154
Coninxloo, Gillis van, 91
consubstantiation, 90, 174
conte, compte, 137, 138, 139, 150, 163, 183, 184, 185, 225, 252, 254, 255, 269, 306n40, 317n39
Cotgrave, Randle, 109, 141, 144, 173, 200, 261, 303n4, 303n7, 329n42, 330n53
Couillatris, 123, 124
Courtey, Pierre, 54, 308n3
Cranach, Lucas, 318n68
crown, 64, 65, 223
crucifix, 58, 114, 226
curiosity cabinet, 4, 11, 12, 69, 70, 91, 175, 185, 188, 285, 292n14, 295n39, 295n42, 296n46, 321n26

curtains (*rideaux*), 37, 38, 42, 50, 70, 132, 189, 200, 201, 202, 300n25, 301n26

Dagoucin, 179, 285
dames galantes, Les (Brantôme), 62, 191
dames illustres, Les (Brantôme), 191
Dante, 311n49
David, Gérard, 87, 91, 96, 315n16
David (king and prophet), 117, 257
Davis, Natalie Zemon, 324n18
Décrétales, 133, 134, 135
Defaux, Gérard, 199, 260, 291n2, 292n9, 292n13, 301n30, 322n53, 323n1, 329n38, 331n12
Delaune, Etienne, 54, 97, 98, 100
Desan, Philippe, 177, 184, 312n69, 320n189
Descordance, 127
Des Périers, Bonaventure, 148, 149, 150, 151, 152, 153, 154, 155, 156, 290, 291n8, 319n2Ch5, 319n3Ch5, 319n4Ch5
devis, *devises*, 49, 52, 54, 57, 75, 165, 179, 303n4
devisants, 14, 24, 26, 27, 35, 37, 39, 46, 49, 50, 61, 62, 66, 67, 70, 71, 72, 73, 74, 92, 96, 98, 100, 101, 102, 103, 105, 108, 113, 115, 116, 117, 126, 128, 136, 148, 160, 164, 167, 171, 182, 199, 202, 206, 207, 217, 218, 226, 229, 250, 257, 263, 264, 267, 271, 274, 281, 283, 286, 287, 291n2
dextrarum iunctio, 192, 322n52
Dijon, 98
Divine Providence, 25
dolls, *poupées*, 183, 193, 194, 235, 264, 279, 323n56

double-entry bookkeeping, 138, 184
draps. See bed
Du Bois, Claude-Gilbert, 198
Du Fail, Noël, 148, 156, 159, 160, 161, 163, 164, 290, 292n8, 319n7
du Mesnil, 14–16
Durassier, 220, 221, 233
Dürer, Albrecht, 55, 56, 59, 77, 90, 105, 305n34

ecclesiology, 25
Eisenstein, Elizabeth, 329n46
Election, 53, 162
Elijah, 57
Elisha (prophet), 123
emblems, 10, 44, 47, 48, 49, 50, 51, 52, 53, 54, 55, 57, 58, 59, 61, 64, 65, 68, 69, 74, 75, 76, 146, 165, 192. 215, 234, 303n4, 303n9
Emblesmes ou devises Chrestiennes (Montenay), 52
Enchiridion, or Manual of the Christian Soldier (Erasmus), 77
England, 294n26
Ennasuite, 218
enumeratio, 58
Ephesians (Eph.), Letter to the, 67
Erasmus, Desiderius, 77, 113, 298n4, 329n37
eschatology, 149, 286
Estienne, Henri, 75, 316n19
Estienne, Robert, 116
Eucharist, 27, 67, 90, 97, 113, 117, 160, 170, 174, 190, 203, 215, 260, 264, 274, 283
evangelical,1, 23–31, 34, 37, 38, 39, 43, 46, 48, 49, 50, 52–54, 58, 59, 64, 66, 75, 77–80, 84, 87, 91, 97, 99, 108, 111–16, 121–23, 126, 129, 130, 137, 139, 146, 148,

evangelical (continued), 149, 152–57, 159, 160, 164, 167, 173, 174, 176, 178, 183, 188, 192, 193, 197–200, 202, 204, 206, 208, 209, 214–17, 221, 223, 228, 230, 233, 239, 246, 248, 251, 253, 258, 259, 261, 264, 271–73, 275, 277, 280–82, 288–95, 297–99, 302–07, 310, 312, 329–31
exemplum, 21, 71, 282, 297n59
Eyck, Jan van, 104, 105, 294n29, 302n35, 312n65

fable, 112, 121, 123, 310n40, 313n4
Faculty of Theology (Paris), 113
faith, 4, 139, 277, 292n12
Farce de Maistre Pathelin, 330n7
felix culpa, 21
Ferguson, Gary, 292n9
Ficino, Marsilio, 113, 197, 294n28
Fiorentino, Rosso, 54, 97, 98, 99, 100, 101, 197
Flanders, 96, 105
Floride, 40–42, 87, 92, 93, 95, 302n40, 305n28, 310n37
Fontainebleau, 54, 65, 77, 97, 197, 309n14
France, 29, 34
Franciscans, *cordelier*, 66, 227, 261, 267, 271
François Ier, King, "le Roy," 1, 4, 12, 33, 34, 35, 36, 45, 65, 80, 87, 88, 97, 112, 176, 189, 197, 203, 220, 221, 231, 236, 242, 253, 256, 287, 292n14, 307n1, 309n18, 315n16, 321n26, 325n11
friar, monk, prior, abbot, 66, 67, 158, 159, 200, 222, 223, 226, 259, 263, 267, 289
Fumerton, Patricia, 291n2

Gabriel, Angel, 86, 302n36
Galatians (Gal.), Letter to the, 13
Gallery (magician), 264, 323n56
Gargantua, 126
Gaster, Messer, 140
Gaverol, François, 186
Geburon, 202, 269
Geneva, marginalia Bibles published at, 116
Geneva Bible, 54, 141
genre painting and painters, 4, 5, 6, 10, 12, 39, 86, 91, 118, 120, 146, 183, 302n36, 309n18
Germany, 29, 34, 54
gloves, *gantz,* 11, 58, 59, 60, 61, 62, 63, 64, 76, 143, 184, 191, 192, 195, 222, 294n26, 305n29, 305n34, 322n52
Golden Legend (Jacobus Voragine), 23, 83, 183
grace, *gratia*, 4, 21, 26, 31, 32, 79, 117, 252
  prevenient grace, 30
Grandgousier, 322n53
grotesques, 98, 101, 186, 310n46
Guyon, Madame, 328n36

Harbison, Carig, 142
Heemskreck, Maarten van, 184
Hegel, G. W. F., 308n7, 309n18
Heller, Henri, 292n9, 292n10, 292n12
Hemessen, Caterina van, 105
Henri IV, 321n26
Héroët, Marie, 289, 320n10
Hircan, 73, 199, 261–62, 269
historiation, 49, 179, 181
Holbein, Hans, 294n29
Holy Spirit, 39, 67, 115, 139, 190, 222, 263, 265, 274, 279, 280, 284
Homenaz, 132, 133, 134
homiletics, 23–24, 47–48, 74, 152, 153, 155, 158, 161, 215, 255, 259, 261, 262,

265, 269, 270, 272, 273, 297n59
homo artifex, 188
Hondius, Hendrik, 91
Huguenots, 52, 100, 116, 164, 175, 311n54, 319n2Ch6
humanist, 23, 125

Icones, les vrais pourtraicts des hommes illustres (Théodore de Bèze), 50
iconoclasm, 5
Initiatoire instruction en la Religion chrestienne pour les enffans, 6
Institution de la Religion Chrestienne (Calvin), 91

Jambicque, 218–20
James (Jas.), Book of, 198
Jan, Frère, 127
Jansenism, 331n10
Jeanneret, Michel, 299n13
Jesuits, 303n2
  Ignatius (of Loyola), 304n27
  Père Sucquet, 303n9
  Quarles 303n2
jewelry, 6, 9, 11, 58, 59, 61, 64, 106, 150, 188, 201
John, Gospel of, 80, 274, 280, 287
Joseph (husband of Mary), 80, 81, 107
joye, 21, 71, 72, 124, 129, 148, 167, 215, 306n45
Judgment, The Last, 9, 80, 205, 252
justification, 29, 53, 291n4, 292n11

keys, 132
Kings (2), Book of, 123, 317n47
Kulmbach, Hans Suess von, 6–7

landscape, 79, 84, 88, 91, 92, 93, 94, 95, 96, 184
La Rochelle, 164
Lateran Council, 204
law, legalism, 31, 32, 35, 55, 89, 121, 122, 144, 246, 274
lectio divina, 288
Lefèvre d' Étaples, Jacques, 112, 113, 291n4, 294n28, 298n6
Lefranc, Abel, 323n6
letter, 19, 58, 63, 110, 188, 189, 208, 214, 215, 288
Leyden, Lucas van, 39, 115, 326n25
Limbourg *frères*, 6
Limousin, Escholier, 330n1
linceuls. See bed
Lives of the Saints, 23
locus amœnus, 189
Longarine, 196, 281
Lotz, David, 316n23
Louis XIV, 237, 326n12
Lyon, Corneille de, 305n29
Lyons, John, 21, 301n29, 329n38
Luke, Gospel of, 80, 121, 129, 231, 318n64
Luther, Martin; Lutheran, Lutheranism, 1, 2, 3, 5, 6, 13, 23, 25, 26, 27, 28, 29, 30, 31, 32, 38, 45, 47, 48, 50, 53, 54, 77, 80, 84, 86, 90, 105, 107, 112, 113, 114, 115, 116, 117, 118, 119, 120, 121, 122, 123, 124, 125, 129, 130, 136, 139, 140, 157, 159, 160, 161, 162, 174, 175, 176, 183, 184, 190, 215, 258, 261, 274, 289

Madame de Roncex. *See* Roncex, Madame de
Malachi (Mal.), Book of, 147, 181
marginalia Bibles, 116
Mariette, P.-J., 54
Marin, Louis, 136
Mark, Gospel of, 318n64

Marot, Clément, 299n12
Martha (sister of Mary), 107
Mary (sister of Martha), 107
Mary (Virgin), 80–81, 86, 87, 88, 107, 302n36
Mary's alabaster box, 293n23,
masks and disguises, 76, 106, 135, 136, 140, 191, 200, 201, 211, 212, 219, 229
Master LC, The, 94
Master of the Female Half-Lengths, The, 93, 94
Mathieu-Castellani, Gisèle, 141
Matthew (Matt.), Gospel of, 1, 3, 121, 130, 142, 144, 277, 280, 299n12, 318n64, 324n21
McKinley, Mary, 291n2
metaphor, 23, 89, 93, 171, 182, 204, 277, 286, 294n33
Methodism, 328n36
metonymy, 182, 238
Metys, Quentin, 253, 326n22
millstone, 121–22
Miroir de l'âme pécheresse (Marguerite de Navarre), 30, 137–38, 314n10
mirror, 8, 9, 11, 30, 37, 38, 43, 44, 45, 49, 52, 54, 58, 75, 76, 102, 103, 104, 106, 179, 190, 218, 289, 294n32, 304n13, 311n58
monde à l'envers, 141
monstre, monstrance, 68, 132, 173, 174, 176
Montaigne, Michel de, 184, 296n49, 297n50, 329n41
Montenay, Georgette de, 52, 53
Montpellier, 134
Moore, W. G., 28, 292n9
Moors, 41
motto (*inscriptio*), 64, 66, 69
mystery plays, 38

Naples, 96
Neo-Platonism, 113, 197, 323n6
Netherlandish, 39, 91, 114, 118, 253, 305n29, 309n18
Nicodemism, 157, 259
Niebuhr, H. Richard, 3
Nole, Coljin de, 99
nouvelle #1, 14, 15, 16, 17, 192
nouvelle #2, 50
nouvelle #3, 64
nouvelle #4, 43, 45, 52, 103, 192
nouvelle #8, 51
nouvelle #9, 224
nouvelle #10, 41, 42, 92, 96, 135, 304n27, 304n28, 309n31, 310n38
nouvelle #11, 234
nouvelle #12, 82–83, 268
nouvelle #13, 18, 19, 20, 21, 22, 96, 187, 322n36
nouvelle #14, 200, 201, 202, 205
nouvelle #15, 58
nouvelle #16, 202–03, 264, 269
nouvelle #18, 135
nouvelle #19, 82, 279, 281
nouvelle #20, 39, 96
nouvelle #21, 80, 82, 89, 90, 242, 300n20
nouvelle #22, 204, 205, 206, 207, 208, 209, 267, 268
nouvelle #23, 66, 209, 227, 267
nouvelle #24, 135, 178–79, 215, 225
nouvelle #26, 177, 210, 211, 212, 213, 214, 269, 318n58
nouvelle #27, 185
nouvelle #28, 264
nouvelle #30, 72
nouvelle #31, 35
nouvelle #32, 29, 30, 31, 32, 33, 34, 35, 36, 127, 236, 301n26, 301n27, 301n31
nouvelle #33, 66, 67, 68, 312n66
nouvelle #34, 73, 196
nouvelle #35, 73–74, 214, 215, 216, 217, 218, 270
nouvelle #36, 69, 180, 270, 273, 279

nouvelle #37, 179, 180, 233, 234, 235, 237
nouvelle #38, 109, 236, 237, 239, 245
nouvelle #40, 96, 239, 240, 241, 242, 243
nouvelle #41, 107
nouvelle #43, 106, 218, 219, 220
nouvelle #44, 262, 271, 272, 273
nouvelle #45, 236
nouvelle #47, 243, 244, 245, 246
nouvelle #48, 244
nouvelle #49, 138, 218, 220, 221, 222, 231, 232–33
nouvelle #50, 253
nouvelle #52, 179
nouvelle #53, 180–81
nouvelle #54, 227, 228
nouvelle #55, 247, 248, 250, 251, 252, 253
nouvelle #56, 222, 224, 225
nouvelle #57, 59, 60, 61, 62, 64, 69, 272
nouvelle #59, 253, 254, 255
nouvelle #61, 272
nouvelle #62, 106, 256, 257
nouvelle #63, 69, 283, 285
nouvelle #65, 225, 226, 227
nouvelle #66, 282
nouvelle #67, 271, 273, 282, 283, 286
nouvelle #69, 145, 146, 318n58
nouvelle #70, 177
nouvelle #72, 285
Numbers, Book of, 121
Nyort (Niort), 96, 164

Oisille, 34, 35, 53, 62, 70, 72, 73, 75, 101, 108, 109, 136, 165, 168, 194, 196, 200, 209, 221, 224, 226, 228, 252, 261, 262, 264, 265, 267, 269, 272, 273, 281, 287, 301n31, 324n25
original sin, 157

Palissy, Bernard, 296n45, 305n38, 310n46
Panigon, King Sainct, 113
Pantagruel, 132–33, 134, 136, 138–39
pantagruélisme, 129, 138
Panurge, 128, 133, 136
Papimanes, 132, 133, 134, 205
parable, 9, 45, 53, 71, 99, 112, 120, 121, 130, 131, 144, 176, 231, 302n41
Paradin, Claude, 52, 54, 55, 57, 64, 75, 79, 304n15, 306n40, 307n3
Paré, Ambroise, 175
Paris, 96, 113, 116, 287, 305n29
Paris, Jean de (Jean Perréal), 236, 325n11
Paris, University of, 4
Parlamente, 21, 38, 61, 196, 269, 272, 281, 286
parolles gelées, 136
passementerie, 109
passetemps, 72, 73, 92, 101, 108, 109, 110, 125, 136, 167, 210
patenostre, 199
paterfamilias, patriarch, 10, 80, 81, 117, 118, 160, 266
Patinir, Joachim, 91, 93, 94, 95
pattern book, 74, 182
Paul, Saint, 3, 13, 25–26, 29, 30, 34, 53, 67, 70, 72, 82, 112, 117, 144, 167, 168, 209, 215, 228, 243, 249, 251, 252, 256, 274, 278, 282, 286, 287, 293n20, 300n21, 300n22, 300n24, 327n31
Peace of Saint-Germain, 164
Pentecost, 168, 260, 274, 280, 281, 287
Périgord, 96
Peter (1; Pet.), Letter of, 36
Peter, Saint, 272
Pharisees, 32

"plain style." *See stylus rudus*
plates, vessels, 69, 74, 111, 125, 151, 169, 181, 189, 238
Plato, 113
Poissy, Colloque de, 169
Poitou, Poitiers, 127, 164, 166
Poling, Wilhelmina, 184
Politiques, Les, 164
Pope, 27, 28, 132, 134, 135, 205, 318n57
  Pope Clement V, 134
Porete, Marguerite, 331n10
portrait, 36, 45, 49, 52, 54, 56, 76, 79, 102, 103, 104, 105, 106, 126, 132, 144, 183, 184, 190, 191, 205, 304n14, 309n13
pourchatz, 137, 253
predestination, 128, 308n11
priest, 73, 103, 136, 149, 152, 153, 154, 155, 156, 158, 159, 160, 161, 170, 203, 204, 215, 216, 218, 222, 223, 225, 226, 264
"priesthood of all believers," 38, 50, 78, 84
prints, printmaking, 115
Protestant, 5, 11, 25, 48, 50, 51, 56, 75, 78, 81, 91, 94, 97, 98, 100, 102, 118, 120, 138, 142, 146, 156, 160, 161, 162, 164, 182, 183, 184, 186, 192, 194, 240, 259, 265, 268, 293n23
protrahere, 36
profit (*profict, proufict, proufit*), 108, 129, 130, 131, 137, 138, 150–57, 159, 163, 183, 185, 225, 252, 254, 255, 269, 306n40, 317n39
proverbs, 108, 112, 158, 159, 181, 204, 284, 294n26
Proverbs (Prov.), Book of, 108
Psalms (Ps.), 84, 117, 137

Quaresmeprenant, 125, 127, 318n52
Quart livre (Rabelais), 111, 113, 123, 125, 126, 128, 129, 130, 131, 132, 133, 134, 135, 136, 137, 138, 139, 140, 141, 142, 143, 144, 306n45, 313n4, 317n47
Quietism, 328n36, 331n10

Rabelais, François, 53, 54, 92, 111, 112, 121, 123, 125, 126, 127, 128, 129, 130, 132, 134, 135, 136, 139, 140, 141, 142, 144, 148, 149, 152, 156, 160, 163, 169, 184, 205, 290, 294n28, 295n34, 304n12, 306n45, 310n34, 310n35, 313n4, 317n47, 318n52, 318n62, 319n6, 319n8, 330n1
Ramus, Pierre, 11, 318n56
rebus, 66, 68
Recouvrance, Antoine de, 98
Recueil Montmer, 45
Reformation, Reformer, 6, 25, 28, 30, 52, 54, 80, 93, 96, 98, 105, 107, 118, 136, 184, 206, 208, 214, 266, 274, 282, 291n6, 313n5. *See also* Reformed
Reformed, 2, 3, 5, 9, 10, 11, 29, 43, 78, 79, 84, 90, 91, 92, 103, 108, 114, 115, 116, 120, 142, 146, 156, 178, 197, 275, 318
relic, 6, 10, 34, 59, 61, 119, 127, 158, 174, 178, 183, 237, 320n10
Reymerswaele, Martin van, 326n22
Rigolot, François, 320n12
ring, 19, 20, 21, 51, 58, 60, 74, 82, 184, 187, 191
robe, clothing, 4, 6, 10, 58, 64, 66, 67, 74, 82, 106, 110, 134, 143, 144, 145, 146, 147, 150, 151, 177, 179, 180, 188, 191, 197, 200, 201, 207, 208, 211, 212,

213, 219, 220, 221, 222, 224, 225, 229, 254
Rolandine, 87, 89, 189, 242, 300n20
Romans (Rom.), Letter to the, 29, 119, 258, 282, 300n24
Roncex, Madame de, 261, 300n22, 323n55, 325n4
Ronsard, Pierre de, 197
Roussel, Gérard, 113, 292n10, 298n6
Russell, Daniel, 49, 304n13
Ruysdael, Salomon van, 91

Saffredent, 71, 224
Saintonge, 127, 164
Saladin, Sultan of Babylon, 64
Salomon, Bernard, 54, 79, 307n3
Sambin, Hugues, 98
sarks, 13, 82, 293n20
scale, 9, 252, 253
scepter, 65
Schnapper, Antoine, 12, 292n14, 321n26
Serlio, Sebastiano, 193–94, 323n58
Shuger, Debora, 102
simile, 58, 125, 201, 202, 204, 294n33
Simontault, 196, 198, 243, 282
skandalon, 24
skull, 30, 31, 106, 127, 301n31
slippers, sabots, shoes, 132, 187, 191, 192, 200, 214, 216, 322n54
sola fidei, 79
sola gratia, 79
sola scriptura, 29, 152, 251, 271
Solier, Jules-Raymond de, 186
Sommers, Paula, 310n36
spectacles, 80, 81
Stallybrass, Peter, 291n2
statuary, 6, 114, 165, 174
still life, *nature morte*, 65, 79, 105, 106, 107, 186, 302n37
Stoics, 139
strapwork, 97, 98, 99, 100, 101, 102, 181
Strasbourg, 6, 28, 114
stylus rudus, "plain style," 24, 29, 57, 120, 149, 154, 157, 167, 258
surplus, 162
Susannah and the elders, 181
Swart, Jan, 326n25
sword, 6, 58, 64, 75, 106, 181, 222
symbol, 10, 20, 31, 50, 107, 109, 183, 184, 188, 215, 297n51

table linens, 69, 74, 111, 151, 169, 181, 189, 306n41
Table Talk (Luther), 27, 113, 116, 117, 136, 157, 258, 313n4, 314n7, 316n23, 329n37
tapestries, 69, 74, 106, 110, 139, 231, 236, 238, 300n26, 306n49, 308n3, 311n50, 325n10
Taylor, Charles, 5, 84, 111, 312n2
Taylor, Larissa, 23, 327n32
Teatrum mundi, 2
Testament, New, 26, 32, 34, 54, 115, 130, 271, 280
Testament, Old, 31, 54, 98, 280, 310n45
Théâtre profane (Marguerite de Navarre), 28
Thélème, Abbey of, 136
Thysell, Carol, 9, 289
Timothy (Tim.), Letter(s) to, 72, 73, 176, 240, 327n29
Tobias (and the Angel), 310n45
Toledo, Spain, 96
Toulouse, 144
Tournes, Jean de, 54, 307n3
Transubstantiation, 90, 117, 174
Treatise to the Christian Nobility (Luther), 27
trompe l'œil, 39, 40, 81, 87, 89, 103, 104, 125, 190
Tyndall, William, 291n2

unicorn, 139, 306n49

Valnebon, 221
van de Velde, Esaias, 91
vanitas, vanity, 52, 61, 105, 106, 107, 254, 294n32, 304n13
Vaugelas, Claude de, 296n49
Verville, Béroalde de, 113, 184, 329n37
vestments, 65, 67, 132, 181, 215, 216, 224
Victors, Jan, 91
Vigneules, Philippe de, 319n1Ch5
Visscher, Claes Jansz the Elder, 91
Vitruvius, 323n58
Voragine, Jacobus, 83, 183
Vries, Hans Vredeman de, 99

Wars of Religion, 148, 155, 164, 166, 167, 321n26
Weber, Max, 326n21
Wesley, John, 328n36
Weyden, Rogier van der, 302n36
window (*fenestre*), 11, 37, 39, 40, 41, 42, 50, 51, 70, 81, 82, 86, 87, 88, 90, 132, 181, 208, 228, 240
wordplay (*équivoque*), 65, 66, 67, 68, 83, 123, 202, 203, 306n40
works-righteousness, 247, 251
Wunderkammer. See curiosity cabinet
Würtemberg, 6

Yver, Jacques, 148, 164, 165, 166, 168, 169, 171, 290, 319n9

Zwingli, Ulrich, 174

About the Author

Catharine Randall, Fordham University, is the author of five books and some fifty articles and book chapters. A book manuscript about the Huguenots and Camisards in the seventeenth and eighteenth centuries entitled *From a Far Country* is currently under review, and her latest project is an updated edition of a selection of the Jesuit *Relations* entitled *Going in by Their Door* for Fordham University Press. Her professional career has been oriented around exploring the constraints that varieties of Protestantism imposed on writers of particular confessions (such as Calvinism or Lutheranism) as well as the permissions for artistic expression that—somewhat surprisingly—may be discerned in those theological systems.